SCENTS OF CHINA

In this vivid and highly original reading of recent Chinese history, Xuelei Huang documents the eclectic array of smells that permeated Chinese life from the High Qing through to the Mao period. Utilizing interdisciplinary methodology and critically engaging with scholarship in the expanding fields of sensory and smell studies, she shows how this period of tumultuous change in China was experienced through the body and the senses. Drawing on unexplored archival materials, readers are introduced to the 'smellscapes' of China from the eighteenth century to the mid-twentieth, via perfumes, food, body odours, public-health projects, consumerism and cosmetics, travel literature, fiction, and political language. This pioneering and evocative study takes the reader on a sensory journey through modern Chinese history, examining the ways in which the experience of scent and modernity have intertwined.

Xuelei Huang is Senior Lecturer in Chinese Studies at the University of Edinburgh.

SCENTS OF CHINA

A Modern History of Smell

Xuelei Huang

University of Edinburgh

Shaftesbury Road, Cambridge CB2 8EA, United Kingdom

One Liberty Plaza, 20th Floor, New York, NY 10006, USA

477 Williamstown Road, Port Melbourne, VIC 3207, Australia

314–321, 3rd Floor, Plot 3, Splendor Forum, Jasola District Centre,
New Delhi – 110025, India

103 Penang Road, #05-06/07, Visioncrest Commercial, Singapore 238467

Cambridge University Press is part of Cambridge University Press & Assessment,
a department of the University of Cambridge.

We share the University's mission to contribute to society through the pursuit of
education, learning and research at the highest international levels of excellence.

www.cambridge.org
Information on this title: www.cambridge.org/9781009207041

DOI: 10.1017/9781009207065

First published 2023

A catalogue record for this publication is available from the British Library.

A cataloging-in-Publication data record for this book is available from the Library of Congress.

ISBN 978-1-009-20704-1 Hardback

Contents

List of Figures   *page* vii
List of Tables   ix
List of Charts   xi
Acknowledgements   xiii
A Note on the Text   xvii

Introduction: The Cesspool and the Rose Garden 1

PART ONE: A SNIFF OF CHINA

1 Aromas of the Red Chamber 31

2 China Stinks 63

PART TWO: SMELLSCAPES IN FLUX

3 Deodorizing China 101

4 Re-perfuming China 143

PART THREE: A WHIFF OF ALTERITY

5 The Bouquet of *Eros* 189

6 The Politics of Smell 219

Epilogue: The Smell of Winter White Cabbage 245

CONTENTS

Bibliography   255

Index   291

Figures

I.1 'Fragrance 香' in the oracle bone script 6

I.2 'Sniff/stink 臭' in the oracle bone script 6

1.1 A set of three incense accoutrements, eighteenth century 36

1.2 An assemblage of objects to celebrate the Chinese New Year, *c.* 1800 . . . 37

2.1 'A-Shing and A-Yow at the Chinese Collection' 75

2.2 A dried-fish shop in Hong Kong, 1946–1947 77

2.3 'Opium Smokers' 80

2.4 'Da ai weisheng' (An Impediment to Hygiene) 95

3.1 The growth of Shanghai, 1846–1914 108

3.2 Map of the walled city of Shanghai, 1871 121

3.3 Slum districts in Shanghai before 1949 131

3.4 Zhaojia Creek's past and present 140

4.1 Burroughs Wellcome & Co. 1888 calendar poster for China 154

4.2 Lundborg perfume advertisement, 1894 155

4.3 Burroughs Wellcome & Co. 1911 calendar poster for China 157

4.4 Two Girls calendar poster, 1932 165

4.5 Palmolive soap advertisement 173

4.6 Palmolive soap bar, 2021 173

4.7 'Yuanfenghuo' (Sealed Goods) 177

4.8 'Qu shu si miao' (Four Summer Delights) .179

4.9 4711 eau de cologne advertisement 181

4.10 Xiangya advertisement 182

4.11 The cover of *Dongfang zazhi* 182

5.1 'Weixin de xiujue' (Idealist Olfaction) 199

6.1 A screenshot of *Sentinels* 237

Tables

I.1 Selected symbolic correlations in the Five Elements System 20

4.1 Distribution of imported perfumery and cosmetics in China, 1927 160

Charts

4.1 Foreign imports of soap, perfumery, and essential oil, 1891–1942 147

4.2 Perfumery and cosmetics imports from abroad, 1927 159

4.3 Essential-oil imports, 1925–1940 174

4.4 Major essential-oil importing countries, 1934. 174

Acknowledgements

The idea of writing a book about smell germinated in the scents of a Taiwanese summer. A coincidental encounter with Alain Corbin's *The Foul and the Fragrant* lured me into a decade-long journey in search of lost smells. It was a privilege to start this project at Academia Sinica: its remarkable libraries allowed me to explore the feasibility of such a bold (if not whimsical) idea by delving into a vast collection of physical and digital resources; conversations with its learned scholars brought timely encouragement, stimulating questions, and a steady supply of source materials from their packed bookshelves. I am especially indebted to Chang Che-chia, Chang Li, Chang Ning, Lei Hsiang-lin, Lien Ling-ling, Lin May-li, Sun Huei-min, Wu Jen-shu, Yu Chien-ming, and Yu Miin-ling for their help.

A refreshing whiff of autumn greeted me when I landed in France to continue my olfactory adventure. My deep gratitude goes to the Nantes Institute for Advanced Studies for the fellowship awarded to me and for the exceedingly welcoming, inspiring, and supportive environment. The weekly seminars, guest lectures, film club events, and conversations in our offices overlooking the Loire opened my eyes (and nostrils) to an intellectual garden of forking paths. I benefited tremendously from feedback and book/source recommendations from my fellow fellows: Perry Anderson, Joseph Bergin, Tatiana Bulgakova, Emmanuel Droit, Barbara Duden, Roberto Fragale, Parvis Ghassem-Fachandi, Danouta Liberski-Bagnoud, Vidya Rao, Suresh Sharma, and Wang Chaohua.

Vienna did smell of *fin de siècle* splendour when I was climbing up to the top floor of a grand building on Reichsratsstraße. The International Research Center for Cultural Studies (IFK) located in this building was the next stop of my smell research journey. I am grateful for the grant, for the equally stimulating intellectual atmosphere, and for the inspirations, critiques, and suggestions I received from Peter Höyng, Helmut Lethen, Jutta Wimmler, and Felix Wemheuer.

With an Alexander von Humboldt research fellowship, I not only became a privileged lifelong Humboldtian, but also returned to my alma mater, the University of Heidelberg. The old sinology library had a distinctive mixture of odours hanging in the air; just by inhaling it my nerves were calmed. While there I consulted a collection of travel writings, and with the funding provided by the Humboldt Stiftung my research assistant Zhao Cheng combed through the collection and extracted all smell-related content. Cheng's excellent work is greatly appreciated. In Heidelberg I had (still have) the wonderful support and guidance of Barbara Mittler, and I shared memorable times with Sun Liying, Wu I-wei, Ronald Po, and other friends. I owe a special debt of gratitude to the late Prof. Rudolf Wagner, whose learning, wit, and generosity set a remarkable example of how to be a scholar. In his last email to me (sent ten weeks before his passing in 2019), he shared a *Shenbao* article about Beijing's stinking streets in 1879, which I used in Chapter 2, in memory of his teaching.

Both experience and science tell us that our nose tends to stay muted to familiar things. It is true when it comes to my olfactory perception of Edinburgh, where I have spent most time during this smell research journey. While this charming city may smell of whisky or Scottish history to other noses, for me it smells of my everyday, my home away from home. I am fortunate to work in a congenial environment along with my great colleagues: Natascha Gentz, Joachim Gentz, Daniel Hammond, Youngmi Kim, Duo Luan, Mark McLeister, Aaron Moore, Christopher Rosenmeier, Holly Stephens, Julian Ward, Sophia Woodman, and others. My special thanks go to Joachim and Julian, who, in keeping their noses to the ground, supplied many olfactory sources they sniffed out. Support from librarian Shenxiao Tong and research office administrators Janet Black and Laura Tomlinson is deeply appreciated. My students Chen Silin, Dominic Hall, Liu Yixin, Pan Chienwei, Piotr Strzalkowski, and Zhao Yiran generously shared research materials with me and the Chinese Cultural Studies Reading Group offered constant intellectual stimulation.

My smell research journey also included many places where I presented my work and immersed myself in diverse smellscapes: Aberdeen, Beijing, Glasgow, Hong Kong, Hsinchu, Leeds, Leicester, London, Oxford, San Diego, Shanghai, St. Andrews, Taipei, Tokyo, and so on. I thank Isabella Jackson, Norman Stockman, Zhang Lihua, Wang Feng, Wu Shengqing, Guan Kean-fung, Stephen McDowall, Toby Lincoln, Andrea Janku, Margaret Hillenbrand, Zhang Chuntian, Mario I Aguilar, Cheng Wen-huei, and Iris Borowy for their kind invitations and hospitality, and I enjoyed discussions and appreciated comments and criticisms offered on these occasions.

The final phase of the project was a strange 'odourless' time when the world was hit by the COVID-19 pandemic. Whilst communications were confined to the inodorous Zoom screen, I profited from some immensely thought-provoking exchanges with fellow smell scholars. I wish to thank William Tullett for introducing me to a burgeoning network of historians, literary scholars, librarians, perfumers, art historians, and curators with a common passion for smell. My manuscript was reshaped by the insights I gained from our conversation for the AHR History Lab, an online smell studies workshop, and finally an in-person workshop in Amsterdam completed with a smell tour through the odoriferous canals and historic buildings. A historian's nose was finally in action!

I also want to acknowledge the generous funding from the Gerda Henkel Stiftung, the LLC research fund from the University of Edinburgh, the International Center for Studies of Chinese Civilization at Fudan University, and the Institute of Chinese Studies at the Chinese University of Hong Kong, as well as the following friends and colleagues who shared research materials, read my drafts, and offered help and support of many kinds: David Cheng Chang, Chen Jianhua, Chen Yunlian, Ka-Kin Cheuk, Lena Henningsen, Rachel Hsu, Huang Jin-zhu, Kien Ket Lim, Liu Wentsui, Lu Hanchao, Cristiana Messina, Paul Pickowicz, Christopher Rea, David Der-wei Wang, Wang Jialin, Wang Yan, Wangjiang Jiazhi, Xiao Zhiwei, and Yang Chia-hsien. Paola

Zamperini read an early draft of Chapter 1, and her insightful comments are most appreciated.

I am indebted to my editor, Lucy Rhymer, for her enthusiastic support for this unusual subject matter, and for her admirable efficiency and professionalism. I am also thankful for Emily Plater's expert guidance with preparing the manuscript. The final draft benefited greatly from perceptive comments offered by the anonymous readers, especially a ten-page report that was rigorous, insightful, and encouraging beyond comparison – to which the final shape of my book owes a great deal. All mistakes and flaws, of course, are my own.

Words are inadequate to express my gratitude to my parents and my sister's family in Shanghai: thank you for the sweetest aroma that is called home and forgive me for being so far away. Finally, this book is for M.D. – my smell journey has been joyfully enriched by his loving companionship, his pungent sense of humour, his peppery 'prickles' offered when reading and editing my drafts, and, last but not least, the rich aromas of the Yorkshire countryside, including cow muck, wild garlic, Farmer's Blonde, and everything that smells of real life I have enjoyed with him.

A Note on the Text

Chinese characters are provided for most Chinese names, terms, and titles in the main text when they first appear. Traditional characters (*fanti*) are used throughout unless the original source is published in simplified characters (*jianti*).

The following abbreviations are used in the notes:

ATRC Annual trade reports of the Chinese Maritime Customs, in *Zhongguo jiu haiguan shiliao* bianji weiyuanhui, ed., *Zhongguo jiu haiguan shiliao* (Archival Materials of the Chinese Maritime Customs), 1859–1948.

CCPMD The Contemporary Chinese Political Movements Database (Zhongguo dangdai zhengzhi yundongshi shujuku), at http://ccrd.usc.cuhk.edu.hk/Default.aspx.

DTRC Decennial trade reports of the Chinese Maritime Customs, in *Zhongguo jiu haiguan shiliao*.

HLM Cao Xueqin and Gao E, *Hongloumeng* (*Dream of the Red Chamber*).

MSMC Shanghai shi dang'an guan, ed., *Gongbuju dongshihui huiyilu* (Minutes of the Shanghai Municipal Council).

MXJ Mao Zedong, *Mao Zedong xuanji* (Selected Works of Mao Zedong).

NCH *North-China Herald*

RMRB *Renmin ribao* (*People's Daily*)

SB *Shenbao* (*Shanghai Daily*)

SMA Shanghai Municipal Archive (Shanghai dang'an guan)

SS Cao Xueqin, *The Story of the Stone*, translated by David Hawkes.

SWM Mao Zedong, *Selected Works of Mao Tse-tung*.

Introduction

The Cesspool and the Rose Garden

The past we bring to encounters is condensed in smell.

Anna Tsing[1]

I N 1906, THE CANADIAN MISSIONARY COUPLE Andrew and Margaret Thomson arrived in China to spread the word of God. During the ensuing thirty-six years, they built churches, hospitals, schools, and gardens in their mission field in north Henan. 'To bring some beauty to the bare, brown soil', they planted roses around a stinking town cesspool, into which drained all of the town's sewage, waste, and even the bodies of unwanted babies. The bushes thrived, the roses were 'gorgeous and abundant', and all survived the great changes and wars that came thereafter, still blooming 'in the New China'.[2] The cesspool rose garden gave off a peculiar mix of odours, one that encapsulates the thrust of this book on the foul, the fragrant, and the whole gamut of aromas in between.

Specifically, this book undertakes an eccentric history of smell in modern China, an all-pervading yet uncharted realm that intimately interacted with other terrains of social life. A scrutiny of such interactions, as I will show, sheds light on how sociopolitical forces operate at the sensorial and corporeal levels, and how the sense of smell mediates the ways in which historical changes are lived. Bringing the sensate into historical and historiographical consciousness is to tap into a new territory, a territory of embodied forms of knowledge, affect, and

---

[1] Tsing, *The Mushroom at the End of the World*, 50.

[2] Thomson, *A Daring Confidence*, 8–9, 123. The quoted phrases are from Robert McClure's preface.

transcorporeal practice. This book is conceived as a revisit to China's recent history – from the High Qing to the Mao era – through the nose, mapping the underexplored territory of bio-social dynamics. And yet, just as smells do not respect man-made boundaries, the book is not a history of Chinese scents per se; it is more about encounters through scents: chemicals meet neurons, bodies meet spaces, Self meets Other, East meets West, and so on.

The cesspool rose garden has some insights to offer on the matter of encounter. First, their incongruous coexistence is indicative of a global connectivity of the sensorium and olfactory sensibility. I came across Murray Thomson's family memoir in the Parisian bookstore Shakespeare and Company by the Seine. Along the same river, on 14 February 1790, the medical scientist Jean-Noël Hallé took a long walk to catalogue the variety of odours on the riverbanks. His meticulous record provided the first flash of inspiration to Alain Corbin for his *The Foul and the Fragrant: Odor and the French Social Imagination*, the pathbreaking book that forges a master narrative of Western olfactory modernity.[3] To a degree, as Corbin contends, Hallé's unusual survey signalled an olfactory revolution that was underway, characterized by heightened collective olfactory vigilance; deodorization of both environments and personal bodies; and redefined norms of olfactory pleasure, sensuality, and social order. He relates divergent modes of perception to social structures, charting this revolution of the nose in relation to sensualist philosophy, advances in chemistry and medical theory, bourgeois individualism, and public-health reforms, all essential ingredients of the Enlightenment–modernity compound. Concurrent with the interlocked enterprises of colonialism and industrial capitalism, projects of olfactory modernity mushroomed around the globe in localized ways.[4] A resonance to this currency, the Thomsons' choice to plant Irish roses

---

[3] Corbin, *The Foul and the Fragrant*, 1–4. To be sure, neither 'the West' nor 'modernity' should be essentialized and reified. Nevertheless, Corbin's study teases out some largely shared practices and sensibilities that can be aptly placed under the term 'olfactory modernity'. For a reflection on this matter, see Tullett, *Smell in Eighteenth-Century England*, 207–9.

[4] Kiechle, *Smell Detectives*; Rotter, *Empires of the Senses*, Chapter 5; Ramos, *History of the Air and Other Smells in Mexico City*, Chapter 2 and *passim*.

around the Chinese cesspool is highly symbolic, veritably an odoriferous metaphor for the 'civilizing mission' of the West.[5] One layer of my inquiry is to track such encounters – of smells, people, sensibilities, and ideologies – and their implications for the Chinese sensorium.

Yet the motley odour mix in the cesspool rose garden begs more questions. Could the sweet scent of the Irish roses offset the effluvia from the indigenous cesspool? Or did the latter overpower the effect of the former? No side could claim definitive victory, physically and figuratively; fragrant, foul, or neither, only each individual nose can tell. Odours, after all, are 'the most obstreperous, irregular, defiantly ungovernable of all impressions', as Zygmunt Bauman puts it.[6] Unwelcomed 'in the shiny temple of perfect order modernity set out to erect', smell's unruly personality disturbs order and challenges uniformity.[7] In this sense, Bauman considers that smell shares some key attributes with what he terms 'the stranger'.[8] Defined as a member of 'the family of *undecidables*' against the cosy antagonism of friends and enemies, strangers are all *neither/nor*, bringing 'the outside into the inside' and poisoning 'the comfort of order with suspicion of chaos'.[9] The neither-fragrant-nor-foul exhalation of the cesspool rose garden personifies Bauman's sociological stranger. I take *the stranger* as a working metaphor to capture the ambivalence and indeterminacy of the olfactory.[10] The tidy binary of foul and fragrant is often mobilized to construct discourses of race, gender, class, or simply the generic Other, but the true nature of smell is at odds with such dualistic programming. Just as the Thomson roses

---

[5] Andrew Thomson noted in his 1934 annual report, 'We have a good rose garden, the stock of which came from North Ireland, from one of the best known firms in the world.' See Thomson, *A Daring Confidence*, 122.

[6] Bauman, 'The Sweet Scent of Decomposition', 24.

[7] Ibid., 25. Bauman suggests the usefulness of smell for a postmodern critique through his reading of Jean Baudrillard.

[8] Ibid., 24.

[9] Bauman, *Modernity and Ambivalence*, 55–6 (emphasis original). Bauman is indebted to Georg Simmel and Jacques Derrida in developing the notion of the stranger.

[10] Haiyan Lee investigates the figure of the stranger in contemporary Chinese society. See Lee, *The Stranger and the Chinese Moral Imagination*. Whereas she focuses on actual strangers (foreigners, peasant migrants, unattached women, animals, and so on) and the problem of stranger sociality in China's modernization, I use the stranger concept metaphorically, emphasizing the ontological indeterminacy of the figure.

thrived on the 'constant moisture and fertilizer' provided by the sewage from the cesspool,[11] foul and fragrant are relational and symbiotic. Their encounters yield what Anna Tsing calls 'contaminated diversity', a common condition for survival, human and nonhuman.[12] However, neither strangers nor contamination have a position in the programme of olfactory modernity; they are in fact the archenemy. A deeper layer of my inquiry is to observe the encounters of 'human agents' with odours as strangers – the battles, negotiations, and hidden aporia involved.

Taken together, this book locates the scents of China within a globalizing regime of olfactory modernity, and critiques the insidious ways in which the sociopolitical was mapped onto the body. I revisit several chapters of recent Chinese history, chapters that comprised what may be aptly called an olfactory revolution. By invoking the highly charged trope 'revolution', I do not aim to write a teleological history of olfactory modernity that spread from the West to China. On the contrary, I consider revolutions as a prime site where ideas of progress and contingent happenings of contamination entangle. By envisaging an olfactory revolution in modern China, I not only underscore the vast changes in smellscapes and perception, but also draw attention to the tensions between revolutionary engineering and contaminated diversity that played out in physical and psychical spaces. Four specific episodes will be examined: environmental deodorization, the capitalist commodity culture of perfume, literary representations of sexual odour, and stenches in Communist propaganda. While the first two are staple components of (Western) olfactory modernity, the latter two are 'strange tales' reeking of alterity. These themes were imbricated with modern China's varied revolutions: the multiple political revolutions from 1911 to 1976, the literary revolution of the May Fourth era, and a widespread consumer revolution from the late Qing to the Republican era. So what is smell? To what degree does it match the profile of the sociological stranger? And why is this putatively lower sense able to engage the social?

---

[11] Thomson, *A Daring Confidence*, 9.
[12] Tsing, *The Mushroom at the End of the World*, 27–34.

WHAT IS SMELL? WHO IS THE STRANGER?

The sense of smell is first and foremost a survival skill in relation to food and defence, as the ancient Chinese oracle bone script (*jiaguwen* 甲骨文) tells us. In this Shang dynasty (*c.* 1600–1046 BC) writing system, the pictographic symbol for fragrance 香 (*xiang*) is wheat or rice on top of an earthenware pot, and the tantalizing smell is embodied by the dots as if wafting into the air (Figure I.1).[13] The association of *xiang* with crops or grains is also underlined in the earliest Chinese dictionary, *Shuowen jiezi* 說文解字 (Explaining Graphs and Analysing Characters) (*c.* AD 100).[14] The symbol for smell or stink 臭 (*xiu* or *chou*) depicts a nose on the top and a dog on the bottom, referencing the dog's extraordinary olfactory sensitivity that aids hunters to detect prey (Figure I.2).[15]

Modern science backs up the ancient Chinese comprehension of olfaction's animalistic heritage. Known as a chemical sense, smell is the most ancient of the senses, evolving alongside the adoption of a terrestrial, air-breathing lifestyle by vertebrates about 300 million years ago. It is a primal sense that affords most organisms the species-survival abilities 'to detect food, predators, and mates', and it is 'the central sensory modality by which most organisms communicate with their environment', as the 2004 Nobel Prize in physiology co-laureate Richard Axel explains.[16] Linda Buck's Nobel lecture highlights the olfactory system's 'exquisite sensitivity and discriminatory power'.[17] Through the sense of smell, humans and other mammals can normally perceive between 10,000 and 100,000 chemicals, but recent research suggests that the number is as high as a trillion.[18] All of these 'odorants' are small, volatile molecules, initially detected by olfactory sensory neurons located in the nasal cavity. These neurons transmit signals to the olfactory bulb of the brain, which then relays those signals to the olfactory cortex. From there, olfactory

---

[13] Xu, *Zhongguo gudai shehui*, 188–9, 200.   [14] Xu, *Shuowen jiezi*, vol. 8, 4450.

[15] Xu, *Zhongguo gudai shehui*, 68–9, 73. Xu, *Shuowen jiezi*, vol. 11, 6327.

[16] Axel, 'Scents and Sensibility', 235. Also see Stoddart, *The Scented Ape*, 12–48; Henshaw, *A Tour of the Senses*, 109–17.

[17] Buck, 'Unraveling the Sense of Smell', 267. Unless otherwise noted, the following account is my summary of Buck's longer explanation with more technical details in her Nobel lecture (267–9).

[18] Bushdid et al., 'Humans Can Discriminate More Than 1 Trillion Olfactory Stimuli'.

Figure I.1 'Fragrance 香' in the oracle bone script. Courtesy of the Xiaoxuetang Wenzixue Database, at https://xiaoxue.iis.sinica.edu.tw. Redrawn by Huang Xuehong.

Figure I.2 'Sniff/stink 臭' in the oracle bone script. Courtesy of the Xiaoxuetang Wenzixue Database, at https://xiaoxue.iis.sinica.edu.tw. Redrawn by Huang Xuehong.

information is sent to other brain areas involved in odour discrimination and the mediating of the emotional and physiological effects of odours.

The olfactory pathway is the most direct of any sensory system, but its simplicity is deceptive.[19] Notably, the olfactory system challenges the visuocentric model of perception that underscores 'the stable representation of objects' (303). Olfaction does not fit this 'correspondence model' in two interlinked ways (304). First, the sense of smell deals with a more fluid, unpredictable chemical environment. Molecules are 'promiscuous', to borrow Ann-Sophie Barwich's word (266); they can occur in unrelated objects and environments. A butyric and valeric acid mixture can smell vomity or cheesy because of their shared molecular structure (264–6). In other words, there is no intrinsic and definitive bond between the chemical identity and the conceptual identity of a given smell.[20] Smells (odorants) are volatile and polysemic by design. Second, the olfactory cortex in our brain, the vital coding device, functions rather like an Enigma machine (a German cipher device), 'scrambling' information in an apparently disorderly manner (244–5). In tracing the transmission of olfactory signals, scientists have discovered that, at the cortical level, information is distributed widely and irregularly, in contrast to the much more orderly patterns of signal projections in vision. Richard Axel explains, 'A given odor will activate a different representation in different brains ... and in the two sides of your own brain!' (quoted at 245). This implies that these representations may have no intrinsic value and 'no inherent meaning to the organism' (quoted at 248).

The messy, individualized, impromptu neural patterns of the olfactory brain sound counterintuitive, but this randomness is functional, reflecting 'how the olfactory system facilitates striking behavioral flexibility in response to a stimulus that affords different meanings in various environmental combinations' (249). Chaos is a condition for learning and tuning. So the odour mix of the cesspool rose garden ought to smell

[19] Barwich, *Smellosophy*, 202–3. Page references from the same source are given parenthetically in these two paragraphs.

[20] For a fantastic guide to the myriad volatile molecules we call smells, see McGee, *Nose Dive*. I thank Christopher Rea for drawing my attention to the book.

different to individual noses (olfactory cortices), and smells by nature are indeterminate strangers. Yet this biological feature does not render smell entirely without rules. Meanings can be imposed via 'higher brain connections' (248), connections to other parts of the brain that handle cognition, emotion, memory, and many other tasks of living. When olfactory signals meet experiential data in the neural network, the private language of smell is translated into a language comprehensible to a certain shared community.[21] It is the territory that this book maps. A pioneering foray into the social facet of the sensate was made by Georg Simmel in 1907.

'Soziologie der Sinne' (Sociology of the Senses) is part of Simmel's intellectual quest for a cultural sociology of modernity. The short essay aims to 'pursue the meanings that mutual sensory perception and influencing have for the social life of human beings, their coexistence, cooperation and opposition'.[22] Through an analysis of sight, hearing, and smell, he argues that '*every* sense delivers contributions characteristic of its *individual* nature to the construction of *sociated* existence' (110, emphasis mine). Whilst acknowledging the 'secondary importance' of the lower senses, he stresses that 'the peculiar vagueness and undevelopment' of olfactory impressions may have led to an erroneous neglect of smell's vital sociological roles (117). One of the roles is built on smell's 'instinctive antipathies and sympathies', which have 'significant consequences for the sociological relationship' among different races and classes. The prejudiced reception of the 'Negro' and Germanic peoples' 'often vague aversion' to Jews, owing to the assumed body odour of both groups, are such cases in point (118). As culture becomes more refined, its emphasis upon liking and disliking rises. Simmel believes that heightened sensibility in the modern era generally brings more suffering and repulsion, and the sense of smell functions even more as 'the dissociating sense' (119). Despite its fragmentary character, the essay represents an early endeavour to theorize the sensorial–social

---

[21] Uri Almagor proposed the concept of 'private language' for understanding smell. See Almagor, 'Odors and Private Language'.

[22] Simmel, 'Sociology of the Senses', 110. Further page references are given parenthetically in the text.

connectivity – the mutual bearing of 'the delicate, invisible threads that are spun from one person to another' and 'the web of society' (120). Another of his important insights is that the fulcrum of the social language of smell is the affective dyad of liking and disliking. Quite contrary to the ambiguous character of the olfactory cortex, society and culture desire to ascribe clear-cut meanings to olfaction. Training and learning, via 'higher brain connections' that process varied experiences, have accompanied the whole journey of becoming human.

The social language of smell has a limited dualism-oriented vocabulary, but its application has been far and wide, across diverse human cultures and religions, and moral, political, and quotidian spheres. The Sanskrit term *gandha* means both 'aromatic' and 'pertaining to the Buddha'.[23] Jesus is sweet-smelling, as the New Testament tells us: 'For we are unto God a sweet savour of Christ, in them that are saved, and in them that perish.'[24] Fragrance indicates sagacious governance and the emperor's virtue, as the ancient Chinese thinker claims: 'Perfect government is like piercing fragrance, and influences the spiritual Intelligences. It is not the millet which has the piercing fragrance; it is bright virtue (至治馨香，感于神明。黍稷非馨，明德惟馨爾).'[25] Stench, in contrast, is deployed to stigmatize the Other, be it gender, class, race, or ethnicity. A misogynistic remark in an English-speaking context goes: 'she smells likes a whore';[26] while 'stinking whore' (*chou biaozi* 臭婊子) is a common expletive in Chinese, too. The real difficulty for a self-claimed Communist of bourgeois upbringing to consider a working man his equal could be summarized, as George Orwell puts it, in the four 'frightful words': '*The lower classes smell.*'[27] In the Han-centric Chinese mentality, the rancid smell of mutton (*xingshan* 腥膻) is an olfactory metonym for Mongols and Tatars, the 'barbarians' (*yi* 夷).[28] This mapping in broad strokes exemplifies the cultural translation of smell, imposing meanings on the private language for multiple ends.

---

[23] Milburn, 'Aromas, Scents, and Spices', 463.

[24] Jütte, *A History of the Senses*, 94. The original text is New Testament, 2 Corinthians 2:15.

[25] *Shangshu*, 'Zhoushu/Junchen'; Legge, *The Chinese Classics*, vol. 3, 539.

[26] Largey and Watson, 'The Sociology of Odors', 31.

[27] Orwell, *The Road to Wigan Pier*, 119 (emphasis original).

[28] Santangelo, 'The Culture of Smells', 51.

What is smell, then? Pulling together the threads, I venture to postulate four 'grammatical' principles underlying the interlaced private and social language of smell. They will guide me in navigating the vast, amorphous universe of scents investigated in this book. First, let me reiterate, odour perception is *ambiguous* and *individualized*, determined by the molecular promiscuity of odorants and the neural patterns of the olfactory brain. Therefore it is difficult to name a scent for it is polysemic, resisting abstraction. The 'irrationality' of odour induced an 'osmophobic (smell-fearing) tradition' in the civilizing, enlightening world of modern Europe. From Kant, to Freud, to Elias, many thinkers have addressed the smell problem and contributed to its devaluation.[29] Yet the very same attribute opens up possibilities towards a postmodern, non-anthropocentric rethinking of smell and its slippery positioning in social structures and human as well as nonhuman lives.[30]

In opposition to its fuzzy, nebulous quality, the sense of smell commands a powerful *discriminating* capacity. It is a result of the active neural connectivity that has tuned the olfactory to meet survival demands. The most potent of all is perhaps the link to emotions: what guides the nose to judge is essentially about liking or disliking. Or, to borrow George Orwell again, smell is 'an impassable barrier' – 'For no feeling of like or dislike is quite so fundamental as a physical feeling.'[31] This grammatical rule bridges the private and the social sectors of a nose's jurisdiction, and accounts for its animated engagement with judgement, pure or defiled, sacred or profane, moral or immoral, and so on.

However, the nose does not have a uniform and consistent set of rules to dictate its judgement. Instead, it is remarkably *flexible*, or *plastic*, knowing how to read chemical information contingent on context, experience, memory, and learning. This ability harks back to the non-linear dynamics of the 'open, chaotic' olfactory system.[32] Flexible coding is fantastic, 'so that you can have a percept of something that you've never smelled before', as a scientist explains in plain language.[33]

---

[29] Many scholars have discussed this issue, especially Kant's and Freud's views on smell. See Hsu, *The Smell of Risk*, 15–16; Tullett, *Smell in Eighteenth-Century England*, 2–3.

[30] For example, Bauman, 'The Sweet Scent of Decomposition'; Tsing, *The Mushroom at the End of the World*, 45–52.

[31] Orwell, *The Road to Wigan Pier*, 119.   [32] Barwich, *Smellosophy*, 238.   [33] Ibid., 245.

Olfactory neurons are natural learners, learning from encounters, adapting to changes, and embracing contaminated diversity.[34] This biological feature, however, also enables diverse forms of power to mobilize or even manipulate olfaction to internalize new norms, stereotypes, or discrimination. This book in part tells such stories.

Last but not least, the encounter of the private and the social is conditioned on smell's airborne, *penetrating* nature and its *communicative* roles. Transferred through breathing, smell is a proximity sense,[35] and inherently 'trans-corporeal',[36] mediating between bodies and environments, interpersonal interactions, humans, nonhumans and arguably the supernatural. The spatially immersive and connective properties have made the sense of smell a fruitful avenue to interrogate material entanglements in the burgeoning field of ecocriticism.[37]

Taken together, it is clear that the sensory faculty of smell is incoherent, oscillating between assertive and erratic, persistent and volatile, impromptu and calculative, elusive and ubiquitous. In short, smell is *ambivalence* par excellence, bringing us back to the concept of the stranger. Why is this working metaphor pertinent to a Chinese history of smell? What can it lend to our inquiry? These questions merit further contemplation. Zygmunt Bauman, among others, is an adamant critic of modernity's gardening ambitions towards annihilating ambivalence. Ambivalence, as he defines, 'the possibility of assigning an object or an event to more than one category', is a 'language-specific disorder', though it is a normal feature of linguistic practice.[38] The main symptom of this disorder is a cognitive discomfort or anxiety caused by the feeling of indecision and loss of control. One way to abate this sense of unease is through classification, which inevitably relies on inclusion and exclusion, essentially 'an act of violence perpetrated upon the world' demanding

---

[34] Smell's learning ability through neural plasticity is the central argument of Wilson and Stevenson, *Learning to Smell*. For a summary of this argument, see 175–6.

[35] Howes and Lalonde, 'The History of Sensibilities', 130.

[36] Transcorporeality is a key concept in Hsuan Hsu's book. It is defined by Stacy Alaimo as 'the material interconnections of human corporeality with the more-than-human world'. See Hsu, *The Smell of Risk*, 10.

[37] Hsu, *The Smell of Risk*, 20–1.

[38] Bauman, *Modernity and Ambivalence*, 1. Further page references are given parenthetically.

'the support of a certain amount of coercion' (2). Such operations, however, can never be neatly accomplished, historically and theoretically. The side product is ambivalence, which in turn calls for yet more classifying effort. Therefore the struggle against ambivalence is, as Bauman sees it, 'both self-destructive and self-propelling', and modern times are an era 'of particularly bitter and relentless war against ambivalence' (3).

The task of order (or, more precisely, of *order as a task*) is 'the archetype of all other tasks' that modernity set itself (4).[39] Drawing on the classical Hobbesian conception of a natural world in flux vis-à-vis the human creation of order to restrain it, Bauman goes on to claim that 'the *alternative* of order and chaos' is the crux of modern consciousness and existence. By underlining 'alternative', he posits,

> The other of order is not another order: chaos is its only alternative. The other of order is the miasma of the indeterminate and unpredictable. The other is the uncertainty, that source and archetype of all fear. The tropes of 'the other of order' are: undefinability, incoherence, incongruity, incompatibility, illogicality, irrationality, ambiguity, confusion, undecidability, ambivalence. (7, emphasis original)

It is upon this premise that he puts forward the notion of the stranger as positioned outside the friend/foe dichotomy, and applies it to his analysis of the Holocaust and modernity's other maladies.[40]

The Chinese programmes of modernization have reserved little room for strangers either. The family of *undecidables* is at odds with the

---

[39] There is no agreement on the definition and dating of modernity. Bauman makes it clear that he calls modernity in this book 'a historical period that began in Western Europe with a series of profound social-structural and intellectual transformations of the seventeenth century and achieved its maturity: (1) as a cultural project – with the growth of Enlightenment; (2) as a socially accomplished form of life – with the growth of industrial (capitalist, and later also communist) society' (Bauman, *Modernity and Ambivalence*, 4). This definition is relevant to this study not because I uncritically take modern Chinese history as part of the progressionist teleology of (Western) modernity, but because I'd like to track the problems of the Chinese pursuit of 'modernity' intricately connected to the master narrative. For a concise overview of the modern and of modernity in Chinese literary and cultural studies, see Jones, *Developmental Fairy Tales*, 14.

[40] Bauman, *Modernity and the Holocaust*.

discourse of development, 'a governing faith in modern Chinese life and letters', as Andrew Jones aptly puts it.[41] Emerging out of 'the fraught nineteenth-century encounter between the seemingly inexorable dominance of a new imperialist world order and local aspirations for national self-determination, wealth, and power', the spectre of developmentalism has haunted the 'triumphalist narrative of socialist modernity', the post-Mao discourse of a de facto capitalist marketization, and the Xi-era 'China Dream' rhetoric alike.[42] Holding hands with the siblings of Civilization (*wenming* 文明), Progress (*jinbu* 進步), Modernity (*xiandai* 現代), and Revolution (*geming* 革命), the logic of development has marched forward with determination and resolution, and rationalized various acts of violence incurred on humans, nonhumans, and environments in its name. The slippery strangers do not have a role in these 'developmental fairy tales', yet they have indeed always been there, undefeatable by the 'self-destructive and self-propelling' struggle against ambivalence.

Smells are such strangers. As both the suppressed and the invincible, they lend us a 'handle' to grasp the pervasive narrative of progress and its often concealed problems. Despite their subjugation by power in manifold forms, odours 'ridicule pretence of mastery, make solemnity laughable, embarrass and put to shame', and they are 'treacherous', 'really and truly embarrassing, as the nagging reminder of failure'.[43] Revisiting modern Chinese history through the nose, as this study will show, captures elements that the eyes and ears may be unable to detect: the ludicrous ironies, the indeterminacy of modern individuals, the alterity of progress, and illogical logics. Furthermore, our olfactory brain's philosophy of chaos confutes the Darwinist plot of survival: a sustainable approach to survival is not about relentless struggles, but about a flexibility to learn, to adapt, and to live with contaminated diversity. For everyone, every community, 'carries a history of contamination; purity is not an option'.[44] Isn't it a message already encrypted in the odours of the cesspool rose garden?

---

[41] Jones, *Developmental Fairy Tales*, 3.   [42] Ibid., 4.

[43] Bauman, 'The Sweet Scent of Decomposition', 25.

[44] Tsing, *The Mushroom at the End of the World*, 27.

THE SENSORY TURN

It is claimed that a 'sensory turn' has occurred in the humanities and social sciences over the past few decades.[45] Led by anthropology and history, starting in the early 1980s, the sensory turn has spread to geography, sociology, literary studies, and philosophy.[46] The momentum that sensory scholarship has gained is further illustrated by the publication of two large series on the senses towards the end of the 2010s. Edited by one of its leading scholars, the anthropologist David Howes, a four-volume comprehensive collection under the title 'Senses and Sensation: Critical and Primary Sources' was published in 2018, including 101 essays in the humanities, the social sciences, the arts and design, biology, psychology, and the neurosciences.[47] In 2014, a six-volume series on a cultural history of the senses throughout Western history from antiquity to the present was published under the general editorship of Constance Classen.[48] While the sense of smell certainly figures on this map of sensuous scholarship, generally speaking it remains relatively underexplored.

The publication in 1982 (in an English version in 1986) of Alain Corbin's *Le miasme et la jonquille* was a watershed moment which spawned the growth of smell-related research in the ensuing decades. A few general histories of olfaction have emerged from the late 1980s onwards.[49] Since the new millennium, a more specialized olfactory historiography has blossomed, mapping smell's sociocultural life in classical antiquity, in early Christianity across the Mediterranean region, in pre-modern South Asian religion and culture, in early modern France, and in eighteenth-century England, as well as olfactory racism in the Atlantic world.[50] Scholars have also investigated the two major subfields of olfactory studies: environmental history and the history of perfume, with work

---

[45] See, for example, Howes and Classen, *Ways of Sensing*, 11.

[46] For by far the most comprehensive survey of sensory studies across disciplines, with a bibliography, see Howes, 'The Expanding Field of Sensory Studies'.

[47] Howes, *Senses and Sensation*.   [48] Classen, *A Cultural History of the Senses*.

[49] Le Guérer, *Scent*; Classen, Howes, and Synnott, *Aroma*; Reinarz, *Past Scents*.

[50] Bradley, *Smell and the Ancient Senses*; Harvey, *Scenting Salvation*; McHugh, *Sandalwood and Carrion*; Muchembled, *Smells*; Tullett, *Smell in Eighteenth-Century England*; Kettler, *The Smell of Slavery*.

illuminating the Great Stink of nineteenth-century Paris; deodorization in nineteenth-century America; and perfume cultures in early modern England, modern Japan, and red Moscow.[51] Scent in literature is another area of concerted scholarly attention, which has yielded studies that focus on olfactory representations in Greek and Latin literature, Shakespeare's work, Victorian fiction, nineteenth- and twentieth-century European literature, post-Enlightenment Italian novels, and modern American literature and art.[52] The publications of *The Smell Culture Reader* in 2006 and *Smell and History: A Reader* in 2019 have signalled a surging academic interest in olfaction.[53] In addition to the book-length studies and anthologies, there also exists a wealth of journal articles and chapters in edited volumes.[54] Apart from academic publishing, the launch of the EU-funded *Odeuropa* project in 2020 marked a new milestone in smell studies. Aiming to 'recognize, safeguard, present, and promote olfactory heritage', this ambitious project applies AI techniques to identifying olfactory references in digital image and text collections spanning four centuries of modern European history, and creates digital and multisensory resources as its research outcome.[55] Partially connected to *Odeuropa* is a 'Conversation' article published in the *American Historical Review* in 2022, in which ten scholars from multiple disciplines engage in a stimulating discussion that reflects the latest thoughts on smell, heritage, and history.[56]

[51] Barnes, *The Great Stink of Paris and the Nineteenth-Century Struggle against Filth and Germs*; Kiechle, *Smell Detectives*; Dugan, *The Ephemeral History of Perfume*; Tu, 'Japan's Empire of Scents'; Schlögel, *The Scent of Empires*.

[52] Lateiner, 'Olfactoring Ancient Fictions'; Harris, 'The smell of *Macbeth*'; Carlisle, *Common Scents*; Maxwell, *Scents and Sensibility*; Rindisbacher, *The Smell of Books*; Hsu, *The Smell of Risk*.

[53] Drobnick, *The Smell Culture Reader*; Smith, *Smell and History*.

[54] For journal articles, see Jenner, 'Civilization and Deodorization?'; Chiang, 'The Nose Knows'; Plamper, 'Sounds of February, Smells of October'. For chapters, see Classen, *Worlds of Sense*, Chapter 1, 'The Odour of the Rose', and Chapter 4, 'The Odour of the Other'; Smith, *Sensing the Past*, Chapter 3, 'Smelling'; Jütte, *A History of the Senses*, Chapter 13, 'Scenting'; Ackerman, *A Natural History of the Senses*, Part 1, 'Smell'. For literature review essays on olfactory scholarship, see Jenner, 'Follow Your Nose?'; Low, 'Theorising Sensory Cultures in Asia'.

[55] See https://odeuropa.eu/mission (accessed 5 December 2021).

[56] Tullett et al., 'Smell, History, and Heritage'.

China, by and large, has remained uncharted territory on this expanding olfactory map. Few, if any, China-related essays feature in the aforementioned major collections. Chinese studies has yet to witness a sensory turn either.[57] Most smell-related studies focus on material culture of aromatics and incense in premodern China, the majority of which are published in Chinese.[58] There is no book-length study of the social and cultural history of smell in modern China in either English or Chinese academia. My book thus hopes to fill a lacuna not only by weaving together a history of Chinese scents, but also by provoking thinking about understanding history outside the familiar ocularcentric, intellect-oriented purview.

To rescue the senses from the regime of the intellect and to rescue the lower senses from visual dominance are the salient agendas underlying the sensory turn. As David Howes writes, the sensory turn was in part 'a reaction against the incorporeality of conventional academic writing' as well as 'a challenge to what has been called the hegemony of vision in Western culture'.[59] The two interlinked missions hinge upon the influential theory of a 'great divide' posed by Marshall McLuhan and Walter Ong in the 1960s. They maintain that following Gutenberg's printing revolution and the influence of the Renaissance and the Enlightenment, vision (by extension truth, reason, and rationality) became pre-eminent in Western thinking and the lower senses (as well as emotions and intuition) were sidelined.[60] The putative olfactory decline of the West is part and parcel of this master narrative.[61]

---

[57] There are some exceptions: Geaney, *On the Epistemology of the Senses in Early Chinese Thought*; De Pee et al., *Senses of the City*; Møller-Olsen, *Sensing the Sinophone*; Dong, *Gantong shenshou*; Wu and Huang, *Sensing China*; Chau, 'The Sensorial Production of the Social', among others.

[58] For the few English-language journal articles, see Milburn, 'Aromas, Scents, and Spices'; Lu and Lo, 'Scent and Synaesthesia'. For Chinese-language studies, see Fu, *Zhongguo xiang wenhua*; Wu, 'Xiangliao yu Tangdai shehui shenghuo'; Huang, 'Xiangliao yu Ming dai shehui shenghuo'. Wu's and Huang's dissertations both include a literature review of Chinese-language publications on aromatics (at 2–5 and 3–5 respectively).

[59] Howes, *Sensual Relations*, xii.

[60] For a summary of the theory, see Smith, *Sensing the Past*, 8–11; for a brief rethinking, see Smith, *A Sensory History Manifesto*, 68–9.

[61] For a summary of the olfactory decline, see Howes, 'Olfaction and Transition', 144–6. This claim has been reasserted in most smell-related studies.

It is not the objective of this study to address whether there were parallel trends in China or to offer an example of Chinese specificity. Postulating a Chinese sensorial hierarchy will demand research outside the scope of this study, but my foray into eighteenth-century Chinese smellscapes (in Chapter 1) suggests a cosmic order of sensory relations widely divergent from the vision of the 'great divide'. When China was embroiled in nineteenth-century colonial globality, a new mass visual culture started to thrive in the fertile soil of print capitalism and societal changes, as documented by voluminous literature on visuality in late Qing and Republican China.[62] My study converses with this scholarship and draws on the rich archive yielded by this print culture. But it is my contention that the five senses were, and are, not in competitive relations; instead, they *collaborate* with one another, mediating the encounters of the body and the material world. The visual turn in modern China aside, the sense of smell has actively engaged in meaning-making and world-making in the maelstrom of change. It is not so much an olfactory decline in modern history as an anosmic tendency in historiography. In this sense, I echo the call to rescue the lower senses from visual and intellectual hegemony, yet I underscore that it is more important to explore new avenues opened up by the overlooked sensory channels than just to reproduce old ontologies and epistemologies with new materials.

The initial phase of the sensory turn was characterized by the theory of 'cultural construction'. Dissatisfied with the dominantly scientific approach to the senses, Constance Classen, David Howes, and Anthony Synnott, for instance, declare, 'Smell is not simply a biological and psychological phenomenon, though. Smell is *cultural*, hence a social and historical phenomenon.'[63] The timely intervention instituted the senses in the humanities and this cultural approach has shaped the field of sensory studies. Yet the concerted investment in culture's dominion

---

[62] There has occurred a 'visual turn' in Chinese studies. See Pang, 'The Pictorial Turn'; Pang, *The Distorting Mirror*; Henriot and Yeh, *History in Images*; Crespi, *Manhua Modernity*; Judge, *Republican Lens*; Gu, *Chinese Ways of Seeing and Open-Air Painting*; Schaefer, *Shadow Modernism*; Wu, *Photo Poetics*.

[63] Classen, Howes, and Synnott, *Aroma*, 3 (emphasis original). For more studies, see Classen, *Worlds of Sense*; Howes, *Sensual Relations*, among others.

over the sensorium may have obliterated something else. Mark Jenner offers a line of critique, arguing that 'sensing is not only shaped by cultural categories, but also is and was part of an individual's active engagement with, and participation in, the world'. He proposes a phe-nomenological approach which 'unites perception and practice, the mental and the physical'.[64] I would like to propose a further shift from the preoccupation with 'how culture tunes the neurons' (to borrow Howes's phrase),[65] while directing attention to a critical rethinking of their encounters and their consequences. Whilst cultures do indisputably tune neurons, neurons – in encountering a myriad of sensorial stimuli, in navigating through an open, chaotic system of the brain – often remind us how futile, even harmful, such cultural tuning can be.[66] Staying attentive to the contingencies and incoherence resulting from the neuro-cultural rendezvous, I emphasize the entangled biological and sociated existence of lives, human and nonhuman. This entanglement renders any engineered human projects (such as modernity) impossible to be rid of ambivalence, making 'the modern human conceit' a laughing stock.[67]

Any historical inquiry into smell is confronted with a conundrum: volatile odour molecules are not archivable in the same way as visual and acoustic sources.[68] The historian of olfaction thereby has to rely on their historical agents' noses, or, precisely, textual and visual records of odours perceived through their noses. Fortunately, quite contrary to the modern olfactory-decline claim, there was a legion of acute sniffers in modern China who diligently documented a virtually boundless repertoire of scents. The travellers, officials, traders, novelists, publicists, journalists, scholars, and propagandists not only chronicled China's changing phys-ical smellscapes, but also conveyed experiences, emotions, desires, and imaginations through smelling. Informed by these odorous vestiges, this study blends conventional historical sources and ahistorical material.

---

[64] Jenner, 'Tasting Lichfield, Touching China', 670.   [65] Howes, *Empire of the Senses*, 7.
[66] Twenty-first-century mental-health problems in relation to digital media culture are a case in point.
[67] Tsing, *The Mushroom at the End of the World*, 19.
[68] For a discussion on the recent development in archiving smells, see Tullett et al., 'Smell, History, and Heritage', 271–2, 273–5.

Since the discipline of history has long overcome the obsession with the 'objective' Truth, the latter can safely join the former in the search for the past, the past we bring to encounters that is condensed in smell, as the epigraph to this Introduction beautifully phrases. As smells by nature cross borders, tracing their trajectories inevitably entails an interdisciplinary approach, criss-crossing environmental history, material culture, literary analysis, and political history. Before laying out the chapter structure, I provide a sketch of some smell-related notions derived from early Chinese texts that have patterned Chinese thought. Serving as foundational knowledge for this book aside, the survey probes how smell is configured into a generally dualistic moral language in the formative era of Chinese thought. To be sure, the cursory account is unable to capture the richness of Chinese olfactory culture and its own course of change prior to the modern era, a topic that warrants separate studies in their own right.

BETWEEN *XIN* 馨 (FLORAL–FRAGRANT) AND *XING* 腥 (FISHY–RANK)

Apart from the aforementioned oracle bone characters for fragrance and smell/stink, ancient Chinese script possesses a large olfactory vocabulary, including approximately thirty characters to describe different types of fragrance and a dozen for stench.[69] Little is known when and why the majority faded out of the living language. The variegated assembly of smells is condensed and conceptualized under a system of 'five scents' (*wuxiu* 五臭) that came to maturity during the Han dynasty (drawing on earlier material).[70] The five olfactory qualities – *shan* 羶 or *sao* 臊 (goatish, gamy), *xun* 薰 or *jiao* 焦 (burning, smoky), *xiang* 香 (fragrant), *xing* 腥 (rank, fishy), and *fu* 腐 or *xiu* 朽 (rotten) – symbolically correspond to the Five Elements (*wuxing* 五行) of wood, fire, earth, metal, and water – a theory at the heart of ancient Chinese natural philosophy (Table I.1). The Five Elements, in ever-flowing cyclical motion, represent a Chinese interpretation of the cosmic order,

[69] Yan, 'Qianyan', 2. Milburn, 'Aromas, Scents, and Spices', 453.
[70] Milburn, 'Aromas, Scents, and Spices', 450–3.

Table I.1 Selected symbolic correlations in the Five Elements System

Elements *xing* 行	Seasons *shi* 時	Cardinal points *fang* 方	Tastes *wei* 味	Smells *xiu* 嗅
WOOD	spring	east	sour	goatish
FIRE	summer	south	bitter	burning
EARTH		centre	sweet	fragrant
METAL	autumn	west	acrid	rank
WATER	winter	north	salt	rotten

Source: Needham and Ronan, *The Shorter Science and Civilisation in China*, 154, Table 9

according to which the variety of scents is classified.[71] But why does the goatish odour *shan* correspond to the spring season, the sour flavour, and the East? The key texts on the *wuxing* philosophy elucidate the logic, which does not seem entirely 'logical' to a modern reader.[72] Notably, the theory of 'five scents' is not a Manichean system; conversely, it emphasizes perpetual flow and transformation, and no intrinsic hedonic value seems to be attached to each smell. It invites a vision that the five olfactory attributes do not represent five smells per se; each rather indicates an orientation or a range that accommodates the infinity of odour variations and fuses with its adjacent ranges, just as spring sprouts from winter and flowers into summer. This modality perhaps comes closer to the messy coding approach of our olfactory neurons unveiled by modern science.

However, early Chinese thought is also testimony to the emergence of a social language of smell, a language building on the dichotomy of foul and fragrant. As Jane Geaney points out, early Chinese texts often discuss sense discrimination in relation to desire and aversion.[73] As the Confucian classic *Daxue* 大學 (*The Great Learning*) teaches, if one wishes to 'make the thoughts sincere (誠其意)', one should allow no self-

---

[71] Needham and Ronan, *The Shorter Science and Civilisation in China*, vol. 1, 151–61.

[72] *Liji*, 'Yueling'; Ban Gu, *Baihu tongde lun*, vol. 3 'Wuxing'; *Huangdi neijing*, Chapter 4, 'Jingui zhenyan lun'. For a study of some of these texts, see Milburn, 'Aromas, Scents, and Spices', 450–4.

[73] Geaney, *On the Epistemology of the Senses in Early Chinese Thought*, 34. For other studies of the senses in early Chinese thought, see Enzinger, *Ausdruck und Eindruck*; Gong, 'Senses and Cognition in Early Chinese Thought'. However, none of them discuss the metaphorical meanings of smell at length.

deception, 'as when we hate a bad smell, and as when we love what is beautiful (如惡惡臭，如好好色).'[74] Confucian scholar Xunzi 荀子 states, 'The nose distinguishes perfumes and fragrances, rancid and fetid odors … it is part of the nature that man is born possessing (鼻辨芬芳腥臊 … 是又人之所常生而有也).'[75] The Daoist classic *Zhuangzi* 莊子 contains a famed passage:

> The ten thousand things are really one. We look on some as beautiful because they are rare or unearthly; we look on others as ugly because they are foul and rotten. But the foul and rotten may turn into the rare and unearthly, and the rare and unearthly may turn into the foul and rotten.
>
> 故萬物一也，是其所美者為神奇，其所惡者為臭腐；臭腐復化為神奇，神奇復化為臭腐.[76]

Although it highlights the binary of *shenqi* (rare and unearthly) and *choufu* (foul and rotten), what the Daoist text conveys through the miasmic metaphor is the indeterminate, mutable nature of things. Yet the predominant trend in early Chinese thinking is to frame an unambiguous social language of smell.

Smell informs human relations: words exchanged between two gentlemen in harmony are redolent of the fragrance of the orchid (二人同心，其利斷金。同心之言，其臭如蘭).[77] Civilization is marked by delightful aromas, as Han Fei's 韓非 parable hints: at the time when people are still eating 'bloody and foul-smelling' (腥臊惡臭) raw food, a sage appears; he uses a drill to start a fire and instantly transforms the bloody and rank smell (鑽燧取火以化腥臊).[78] Moral principles are elucidated in olfactory terms. How should one understand *li* 禮 (ritual principles), the vital Confucian conception that represents 'the highest sense of morality, duty, and social order'?[79] Xunzi instructs us, 'rituals are what nurtures (禮者養也)', just as 'the fragrances of peppercorns and orchids, aromas

[74] *Liji*, 'Daxue'. English translation in Legge, *The Chinese Classics,* vol. 1, 366.
[75] *Xunzi*, 'Rongru'; Xunzi and Knoblock, *Xunzi*, vol. 1, 191.
[76] *Zhuangzi*, Waipian (Outer Chapters), 'Zhibei you'; Zhuangzi and Watson, *The Complete Works of Chuang Tzu*, 236.
[77] *Yi Jing*, 'Xici shang'.   [78] *Han Feizi*, 'Wudu'. Han Fei and Watson, *Han Fei Tzu*, 96.
[79] Knoblock, *Xunzi*, vol. 1, 49.

and bouquets, are what nurture the nose (椒蘭芬苾，所以養鼻也).'[80] Aromas are endowed with an elevated sense of meaning here. The point is further illustrated in a Han dynasty Confucian text, in a saying purportedly by Confucius himself:

> Staying close to a moral person is like entering a room filled with the fragrances of orchids and angelica. If you cannot smell the aromas after a while, it means you have become part of it. Staying close to an evil person is like entering a fish market. If you cannot smell the stinking odour after a while, it means you have become part of it.
>
> 與善人居，如入蘭芷之室，久而不聞其香，則與之化矣；與惡人居，如入鮑魚之肆，久而不聞其臭，亦與之化矣.[81]

The moral smell breezes further into political spheres, as demonstrated by the *Shangshu* 尚書 (*Book of Documents*, 772–476 BC), a foundational text of Chinese political philosophy.[82] A chapter records the teachings from the King of Zhou on the matter of excessive drinking and moral corruption. He takes the last king of the Shang dynasty as an example: he had abandoned himself to drinking, lewdness, and dissipation, and even the imminent extinction of the dynasty gave him no concern:

> ... he wrought not that any sacrifices of fragrant virtue might ascend to Heaven. The rank odour of the people's resentments, and the drunkenness of his herd of creatures, went loudly up on high, so that Heaven sent down ruin on Yin, and showed no love for it – because of such excesses.
>
> 弗惟德馨香祀，登聞于天；誕惟民怨，庶群自酒，腥聞在上。故天降喪于殷，罔愛于殷，惟逸.[83]

His failing governance, and the demise of the dynasty as a consequence, are embodied in the lack of fragrant virtue and the rank odour of the people's resentments. In another chapter, in a discussion of the perils of cruel punishment, the author writes, 'God surveyed the people,

---

[80] *Xunzi*, 'Li lun'; Knoblock, *Xunzi*, vol. 3, 55.   [81] Liu, *Shuoyuan*, 'Zayan'.
[82] Nylan, *The Five 'Confucian' Classics*, 120–67.
[83] *Shangshu*, 'Zhoushu/Jiugao'; Legge, *The Chinese Classics*, vol. 3, 409.

and there was no fragrance of virtue arising from them, but the rank odour of their (cruel) punishments (上帝監民，罔有馨香德，刑發聞惟腥).'[84] These passages all centre on the dichotomy between *xin* (fragrant) and *xing* (rank), evoking polarized emotions towards virtue and cruelty in governance. The same rhetoric appears in *Guoyu* 國語, a Warring States collection (475–221 BC): whenever a state is about to rise, the virtue of its ruler 'suffices to manifest its fragrant scent [observable for the spirits] (其德足以昭其馨香)'; conversely, whenever a state is about to vanish, its ruler is greedy and covetous, and 'its governance bears a rancid stench and fragrant scent does not rise [to reach the spirits] (其政腥臊，馨香不登)'.[85] While the key Confucian concept of virtue/*de* is usually associated with the sense of hearing,[86] *de* is in fact embodied, transmitted, and enhanced by aroma as well.

Alongside intellectual thinking about smell, a material culture of fragrance evolved in early China.[87] As the first line of the influential osmological text *Tianxiang zhuan* 天香傳 (On Heavenly Perfumes) (Ding Wei 丁謂, *c.* 1022–1025) states, 'the application of aromatics can be traced back to ancient times, used to worship gods and to purify air (香之為用從上古矣，所以奉神明，所以達蠲潔).'[88] Archaeological and textual evidence suggests that a perfume culture was already developing in the pre-Qin period, with a wide array of local aromatic plants and spices being used on religious and everyday occasions. However, a 'perfume revolution' took place during the reign of Emperor Wu of Han (Han wudi 漢武帝, 156–87 BC) thanks to his extensive campaigns of conquest and the opening up of the Silk Road, which introduced exotic aromatics from abroad. The contours of perfume culture further shifted under the influence of Buddhism, which arrived in China at the end of the Eastern Han dynasty (AD 25–220). Cultural contact with the highly

---

[84] *Shangshu*, 'Zhoushu/lüxing'; Legge, *The Chinese Classics*, vol. 3, 592.

[85] *Guoyu*, 'Zhouyu shang'. Jörn Grundmann kindly permitted me to use his English translation of these phrases in his unpublished article: 'From Ritual Efficacy to Moral Commitment: Investigations into a Major Turn in Early Chinese Intellectual History'.

[86] Geaney, *On the Epistemology of the Senses in Early Chinese Thought*, 23–7.

[87] Fu, *Zhongguo xiangwenhua*, 3–7; Needham, *Science and Civilisation in China*, vol. 5, part II, 128–47.

[88] Ding, *Tianxiang zhuan*, 233.

developed incense tradition from India had a long-lasting impact on the Chinese use of incense in the coming centuries.[89] A refined aromatic culture evolved thereafter. During the Tang dynasty (618–907), for example, fragrances pervaded multiple sites of private and social life, applied to perfume individual bodies, to please deities and lovers alike, to attract the auspicious, and to conduct state business in the proper frame of mind. Little distinction was made between incense, aromatics, perfumes, drugs, flavourings, colouring matters, and spices.[90] A case study of late imperial perfume culture will be presented in Chapter 1.

CHAPTER OUTLINE

The book consists of three parts. Part One (Chapters 1 and 2) takes 'A Sniff of China', considering how China smelled in her splendid eighteenth century and what propelled a modern olfactory revolution. Part Two (Chapters 3 and 4) tracks the 'Smellscapes in Flux', specifically the opposing processes at the centre of the olfactory revolution: deodorizing and re-perfuming. Part Three (Chapters 5 and 6) traces 'A Whiff of Alterity', a counterhistory of Western olfactory modernity. The unruly, unpredictable, and animalistic side of odour perception overrode the grand design of deodorized environs and perfumed bodies, producing an odoriferous alchemy of alterity at some particular moments of modern China.

Imagine that one summer day in the garden of a Qing aristocratic family, the young master Baoyu is playing guess-fingers with an opera singer known as Parfumée, with one elbow resting on a pouffe stuffed with rose and peony petals. After a crab banquet, the maids bring mung-bean flour scented with herbs and flowers for removing the odour of crab. Readers of *Hongloumeng* 紅樓夢 (*Dream of the Red Chamber*, by Cao Xueqin 曹雪芹) are dazzled by the sophistication of a perfume culture that permeates the fabric of everyday life. Chapter 1 explores the material culture of perfume and the spiritual, philosophical, and social

---

[89] For a detailed discussion of these issues, see Milburn, 'Aromas, Scents, and Spices', 441–8, 454–64. Also see Chen, 'Han Jin zhiji shuru Zhongguo de xiangliao'.
[90] Needham, *Science and Civilisation in China*, vol. 5, part II, 133–4.

subtexts of smell through a reading of the canonical novel. I ask how culture tunes neurons, cognitively and aesthetically, in keeping a particular order of things (time, space, gender, class, sexuality, and morality); and how odours disturb the order and evince the inevitability of contamination that lies at the heart of the parable. Unwittingly Cao Xueqin seems to have forecast the onset of a modern olfactory revolution premised on the arguable impurity of China.

The first stirrings of a Chinese olfactory revolution arose at a time of growing encounters between European nerves and oriental odorants in the nineteenth century. To most European travellers, China stank. Suffocating odours from manure buckets, vile fumes of opium, indescribable stenches from filthy streets and stagnant ditches, and the disagreeable reek from perspiring 'coolies' suffuse the pages of their writing. Drawing on a large corpus of English-language travel literature, Chapter 2 probes how China was implicated in the global history of olfactory modernity through a discourse of contamination, giving rise to new olfactory order and sensibility. I inquire into smell's role as the stranger in forging the 'China stinks' rhetoric, a mechanism that was not grounded upon a supposedly orientalist structure of feeling, but came into being through sensorial and psychical encounters. The private sensorium and the macroscopic sociopolitical changes were entangled.

Chapter 3 undertakes a comparative study of three deodorization projects, conducted respectively by Western colonial administrations from the 1850s to the 1890s, by reform-minded Chinese gentry of the late Qing and early Republic, and by the Communists in the 1950s, with a focus on the trope of stagnant water. Despite their disparate, if not antithetic, motives and rhetoric, these projects forged a continuous Chinese olfactory revolution through a common commitment to the progressive ideology of deodorization. I scrutinize how the threads of olfactory modernity tied in with a series of spatializing projects inherent to the 'developmental fairy tales' of modern China, and how these undertakings brought about an uneven redistribution of sense-scapes alongside capital and symbolic capital. I argue that the outcome of battling against contamination was not purity, but a stratified reorganization of purified and contaminated spaces.

Alongside the grand scheme of deodorization, the arrival of a variety of mass-manufactured scents instigated an olfactory revolution in everyday life, feeding new sensory data into Chinese bodies and neurons. Drawing on trade statistics, advertisements, and corporate archives, Chapter 4 restores the materiality of a changing smellscape, redolent of Parisian perfumes, English scented soap bars, domestically produced jasmine moisturizers, and state-of-the-art synthetic scents that invaded and contaminated the sensorium. The thrust of this inquiry is the question of how industrial capitalism tuned neurons to accept the strangers of new scents as friends, and how the body was re-educated to internalize a new set of olfactory codes, values, and aesthetics.

The link between aroma and *eros* is a time-honoured theme across cultures, and yet in the 1920s Chinese literary repertoire of *amour*, what mesmerize the modernizing men and women are not 'cultured' scents of perfume, but 'biological' odours of libido. Chapter 5 investigates the phenomenon of olfactophilia emerging in Chinese fiction during the Literary Revolution of the 1920s. Considered 'perverted' in late nineteenth-century Europe, olfactophilia was symptomatic of the discourse of emancipation in May Fourth China. The Chinese modernists discovered in the primitive sense of smell the true essence of being human, a gesture of defiance against Confucian culture. Embedded in their pursuits was the aporia of modernity, a parable about the porous boundary between purity and contamination.

The Communist revolution from the 1950s to the 1970s unleashed more olfactory anomalies. In the lexicon of Mao-era politics, class enemies are 'dog shit' and labour camps are 'cowsheds'. A method to castigate landowners and capitalists is to 'stinken' (*douchou* 鬥臭) them, and the bourgeois 'fragrant breeze' has to be perceived as stinking air. Chapter 6 measures the mighty symbolic power commanded by the olfactory in the moral–political regime of Maoist China, and ponders its jarring relationship with the teleology of olfactory modernity. Adopting the keywords approach initiated by Raymond Williams, I analyse a number of smell-related keywords that pervade Mao Zedong's writings, party documents, and official media. Bridging the biological and the social, this olfactory glossary maps the emotional states of paranoia, rudeness, ruthlessness, and love–hate, all necessary ingredients of the Communist revolution. Overall, Mao's olfactory revolution was yet another round of retuning the neurons, and yet smell never fails to laugh at the absurdity of human acts. The generally poorly understood mass of historical smells, physical and figurative, have in fact wafted into the present, the everyday, and the unconscious in today's China.

PART ONE

A SNIFF OF CHINA

1

Aromas of the Red Chamber

How could you possibly know what it was ... since this perfume is not to be found anywhere in your mortal world? It is made from the essences of rare plants found on famous mountains and other places of great natural beauty, culled when they are new-grown and blended with gums from the pearl-laden trees that grow in the jewelled groves of paradise. It is called "*Belles Se Fanent*".

此香塵世中既無，爾何能知。此係諸名山勝境初生異卉之精，合各種寶林珠樹之油所製，名為「群芳髓」。

Cao Xueqin, *Dream of the Red Chamber*[1]

JEAN-BAPTISTE GRENOUILLE, the keen-scented protagonist in Patrick Süskind's bestselling novel *Perfume*, discerns a whiff of 'exceptionally delicate and fine scent' in the air of eighteenth-century Paris. It makes his heart ache. Following the guidance of his perspicacious nose, he traces this stream of scent, often masked by thousands of other city odours, for half a mile until he finds the source of it: a teenage girl. Her sweat smells 'as fresh as the sea breeze', her hair 'as sweet as nut oil', her genitals 'as fragrant as the bouquet of water lilies', her skin 'as apricot blossoms'. All the aromatic atoms are blended in harmony, yielding one scent that is 'the higher principle, the pattern by which the others must be ordered'. Grenouille concludes, 'It was pure beauty.'[2] An analogous moment of olfactory enchantment occurs to Jia Baoyu, the sensorially sagacious protagonist in the eighteenth-century Chinese novel *Dream of the Red Chamber* (hereafter *Red Chamber*). In his prescient dream that foretells the destinies of the young women in his family,

---

[1] *HLM* 5, 56; *SS*, vol. 1, 137–8.   [2] Süskind, *Perfume*, 38–42.

Baoyu detects 'a faint, subtle scent, the source of which he was quite unable to identify'.[3] This wondrous fragrance, 'made from the essences of rare plants', 'culled when they are new-grown and blended with gums from the pearl-laden trees',[4] is likewise an allegory of transcendent purity.

Why did the two diametrically different authors both project their ideals of purity through an unnameable scent? Whereas the real eighteenth-century France saw the germination of a modern olfactory revolution, how was the Chinese universe of odours operating at the time when the Qing empire was at the height of its glory, yet to be 'contaminated' by European modernity (to a large degree)? Some answers may be found in the fictitious microcosm of High Qing society under the magical pen of Cao Xueqin (1715?–1763). Acclaimed as 'the most popular book in the whole of Chinese literature', 'the greatest of all Chinese novels', *Red Chamber* is a 120-chapter saga of the gradual decline of the aristocratic Jia clan, with a focus on the romantic relationships between Jia Baoyu (the young heir of the family line) and his two cousins (Lin Daiyu and Xue Baochai).[5] Renowned for its unrivalled meticulousness and aesthetic profundity, the novel has been under scrutiny for over two centuries. The scholarship on the subject even carries its own title, *Hongxue* 紅學 ('Red study' or 'Redology').[6] The elusive matter of aroma, however, has yet to breeze into scholars' nostrils.

[3] *HLM* 5, 56; *SS* I, vol. 1, 137. The dream sequence in Chapter 5 is widely accepted as a condensed allegory for the whole novel. For its importance, see Hsia, *The Classic Chinese Novel*, 262–3.

[4] *HLM* 5, 56; *SS*, vol. 1, 137–8.

[5] The two quotations are from Hawkes, 'Introduction', *SS*, vol. 1, 15; Hsia, *The Classic Chinese Novel*, 245. For a comprehensive introduction to the novel and its history in English, see Hawkes, 'Introduction', 15–46. The Chinese version I use is Cao Xueqin and Gao E, *Hongloumeng* (Beijing: Renmin wenxue chubanshe, 2000). This version is based on Chengyi ben 程乙本, edited by Yu Pingbo 俞平伯 and annotated by Qi Gong 啟功. Hereafter it is referenced as *HLM*, followed by chapter number and page numbers. The English version I use is Cao Xueqin, *The Story of the Stone*, translated by David Hawkes, 5 vols. (London: Penguin Books, 1973). It is referenced as *SS*, followed by volume number and page numbers. I consistently adopt Pinyin to romanize names (e.g. Baoyu, not Bao-yu).

[6] For an overview of *Hongxue*, see Edwards, *Men and Women in Qing China*, 10–32. For a selected bibliography of English-language writings on *Red Chamber*, see an appendix in Smith, *The Qing Dynasty and Traditional Chinese Culture*, 424–8.

In fact, aromas are not only symbolically meaningful in the novel, as Baoyu's dream shows. Physical spaces of the Jia family are replete with the scents of incense, flowers, and cosmetics, pervading religious rituals, ceremonies, literati pastimes, romantic courtships, and quotidian activities, such as eating and sleeping. Fragrant emblems abound in chapter titles, character names, and venues in the family's magnificent Prospect Garden (Daguan yuan 大觀園). A chapter title can evoke a scent-rich ambience: 'A Blissful Night, Earnestly a Flower Murmurs Her Inner Feelings; A Tranquil Day, Dreamlike the Jade Exudes a Lingering Aroma' (情切切良宵花解語，意綿綿静日玉生香, Chapter 19, my translation). Baoyu is cared for by an army of young maids, such as Aroma (Xiren 袭人), Musk (Sheyue 麝月), and Sandal (Tanyun 檀云); calling their names alone conjures up sensorial joyfulness. Poetry games take place in the Drenched Blossoms Pavilion (Qinfang ting 沁芳亭), the Rice Scent Village (Daoxiang cui 稻香村), and the Fragrant Lotus Pavilion (Ouxiang xie 藕香榭), where physical and evocative perfumes blend. The bounty of aromatic imageries makes reading a multisensory journey – it is no exaggeration to call *Red Chamber* a book of aromas.

Cao's masterly handling of olfactory details archives the intangible heritage of perfume culture in late imperial China. Despite his own disavowal of 'realism', it is a general consensus that the novel can be conceived as 'a kind of summation of the many elements of mid-Qing elite life'.[7] Being a descendant of an influential Chinese bannerman–bondservant favoured by Emperor Kangxi 康熙 (r. 1661–1722), Cao Xueqin undoubtedly commanded an intimate knowledge of the High Qing elite culture, society, and politics.[8] The Manchu conquest in 1644 did not fundamentally disrupt important socio-economic and cultural trends that had started in the Ming dynasty: commercialization, urbanization, improved access to education, the rise of the mercantile and gentry–merchant classes, and the boom of print culture and popular entertainments. After a period of consolidation of power, the Qing

---

[7] Spence, *The Search for Modern China*, 107.

[8] Jonathan Spence provides a perceptive summary of the ways in which *Red Chamber* sheds light on family structure, politics, economics, religion, aesthetics, and sexuality in the mid-Qing. See ibid., 106–10.

empire reached the pinnacle of prosperity in the eighteenth century. Its military prowess helped the fortification of borders, creating the largest empire in Chinese history. Foreign and domestic trade stimulated economic growth, strengthening the secular trends in consumer culture, urban expansion, and physical and social mobility. Building on the Ming achievements in scholarship and the arts, the Qing literati culture flowered in multiple directions. Reports from a limited number of European missionaries and traders suggest an undeniable sense of admiration for 'Chinese sophistication and splendor'.[9] Scents suffused the fabric of society, performing manifold tasks in keeping a particular order of things, as Cao's novel informs us. Yet beneath the veneer lies a parable of purity and contamination, as my olfactory reading will unveil.

This chapter explores the material culture of perfume and the spiritual, philosophical, and social subtexts of smell through the fictional world of *Red Chamber*, supplemented by historical sources.[10] I argue that Cao's engagement with the sense of smell is twofold. On the one hand, he illustrates how culture tunes neurons cognitively and aesthetically: smell acts as an embodied form of knowledge to conceptualize time, space, gender, class, sexuality, and morality; aromas also elevate the everyday into an aesthetic way of living. On the other hand, he indicates the futility of all this sophistication, all this painstakingly choreographed order of things. In other words, he weaves an allegory about contamination as an inevitable human condition through smell the stranger. Unwittingly he forecasts the onset of the modern olfactory revolution premised on the arguable impurity of China.

---

[9] This sketchy overview is mainly based on Naquin and Rawski, *Chinese Society in the Eighteenth Century*. The quotation is at x.

[10] I only focus on the first eighty chapters, which were authentically written by Cao Xueqin. Cao died before he was able to complete the novel. The authorship for the last forty chapters has been controversial, but Gao E's version is the most widely accepted one. My close reading of the entire 120 chapters, with a focus on the smell-related accounts, revealed that Gao E's knowledge in details of perfume culture was not comparable to Cao's since the last forty chapters only include brief and generic references to aromatics usage. This is why I decided to only focus on the first eighty chapters for this chapter. For debates on the authorship of the last forty chapters, see Wu, *On* The Red Chamber Dream, 267–85.

34

SCENTING THE RED CHAMBER

One way in which culture tunes neurons, as daily practices of the Jia house suggest, is by scenting your living spaces and bodies. The dominant method to perfume their numerous halls, drawing rooms, studies, and boudoirs, and the men and women themselves, is through the application of incense. At the outset of the novel, Lin Daiyu, newly bereft of her mother, is invited by her maternal grandmother, Grandmother Jia, to live with her in the capital. The sumptuousness of the Jia house unfolds before Daiyu's eyes as soon as she enters the family compound. Later, in the drawing room of Lady Wang, her aunt, she notices a pair of low plum-blossom-shaped tables: on the left is 'a small, square, four-legged *ding*, together with a bronze ladle, metal chopsticks, and an incense container'; and on the right a vase produced by the prestigious Ru kiln (Ruyao 汝窯), with a spray of freshly cut flowers in it.[11] The 'three incense accoutrements' (*lu ping sanshi* 爐瓶三事) – the incense burner, container, and a vessel where a bronze ladle and chopsticks are placed – are an essential tabletop display in any type of room in a well-to-do household in Ming and Qing China (Figure 1.1; also see Figure 1.2).[12] Later, at one of Grandmother Jia's home banquets, at the side of each dining table stands a smaller ornamental table, on which are arranged a vase with fresh seasonal flowers and an exquisite three-piece incense set.[13] The floral scent and the burning Hundred Blend incense (a gift from the Imperial Palace) create an elegant ambience in tune with a fine range of cuisine to the delight of both olfactory and gustatory senses. An incense set is in place even for an informal open-air drinking party in the Prospect Garden.[14]

Incense in the shape of a lozenge is often burned with charcoal in a larger brazier or a smaller hand-warmer to heat and perfume space simultaneously. Shi Xiangyun, Baoyu's cousin, eloquently links the two in a game of verse linking: 'Now coals perfumed with musk in precious

---

[11] *HLM* 3, 31; *SS*, vol. 1, 96.

[12] Meng, *Huatang xiangshi*, 151. For a discussion of the incense table see Hay, *Sensuous Surfaces*, 328. For an introduction to incense accoutrements (*xiangpin qi* 香品器), see Chen, *Xinzuan xiangpu*, 200.

[13] *HLM* 53, 575; *SS*, vol. 2, 577.   [14] *HLM* 40, 430; *SS*, vol. 2, 297.

Figure 1.1 A set of three incense accoutrements, eighteenth century, Heavenly Fragrance and Agarwood (Tianxiang qienan 天香茄楠) exhibition, Palace Museum, Taiwan, December 2018. Author's photograph.

braziers burn' (*shemei rong baoding* 麝煤融寶鼎).[15] When Baoyu pays an unexpected visit to Aroma in her parents' house, fearful that the disagreeable smell of the commoner's house would offend her young master's olfactory nerves, Aroma hastily takes a couple of 'plum-blossom-shaped perfume lozenges' (*meihua xiangbing* 梅花香餅) from a little purse and pops them onto the burning charcoal of her hand-warmer, and stuffs it into the front of Baoyu's gown.[16]

This seemingly trivial detail not only implies the class dimension of olfaction, but also showcases an accessory indispensable to Chinese perfume culture, namely the little purse or sachet (*hebao* 荷包) worn by Aroma. Baoyu, too, often wears a *hebao* sachet for carrying powdered incense. One day when he needs some incense to conduct a personal memorial ceremony for a deceased friend in a deserted place, he is delighted to find 'a pinch or two of powdered agalloch' in the bottom of his sachet.[17] Perfume sachets have a long-established tradition in

[15] *HLM* 50, 533; *SS*, vol. 2, 489 (modified).   [16] *HLM* 19, 195; *SS*, vol. 1, 380 (modified).
[17] *HLM* 43, 462; *SS*, vol. 2, 356.

Figure 1.2 An assemblage of objects to celebrate the Chinese New Year (including these aromatic items – plum blossoms in the vase, the 'Buddha's hands' in the porcelain dish, and a set of three incense accoutrements on the wooden stand). Hanging scroll, ink and colour on silk, 89.6 × 58.7 cm, Qing dynasty, c. 1800. Courtesy of Freer Gallery of Art, Smithsonian Institution, Washington, DC (gift of Charles Lang Freer, F1916.541).

Chinese culture and spice bags were found in a Mawangdui 馬王堆 tomb of the Western Han dynasty (206 BC–AD 8).[18] Maintaining pleasant body odour is also a rule of good conduct stipulated in the Confucian classic *Liji* 禮記 (*Book of Rites*), which instructs that young children should wear perfume sachets (*rongxiu* 容臭).[19] *Red Chamber* demonstrates the Qing inheritance of this line of Han Chinese perfume tradition.

Alongside incense, scented trinkets and ornaments are another source of fragrance wafting in the air of the red chambers. On his return from a trip to Suzhou, Xue Baochai's brother Xue Pan brings back a box of gifts sourced from the sophisticated lower Yangtze region: a variety of fancy stationery and an assortment of aromatic novelties (perfumed sachets, prayer beads, fans, face powder, rouge, and so on).[20] These items are indicative of a thriving consumer culture that aided the nationwide diffusion of perfume fashions and sensibilities in the High Qing era. The Imperial Palace was a trend-setter of fashion as well, and aromatic beaded bracelets appeared to be in vogue at the time, often gifted to privileged households like the Jias, as documented in *Red Chamber* multiple times.[21] Despite her distaste for heavy perfumes, Xue Baochai wears a string of musk-scented rosewood beads (*hongshe xiangzhu* 红麝香珠) gifted by the Imperial Consort, an understated display of status that only the most sagacious nose can discern.[22]

While incense and aromatics infuse the red chambers with an air of opulence, natural floral and herbal scents impart elegance and seasonal rhythm to the smellscapes. The *Ruyao* vase in Lady Wang's drawing room is always displayed with freshly cut flowers for both visual and olfactory delectation, and making trinkets with flowers is a favourite pastime for

---

[18] Lu and Lo, 'Scent and Synaesthesia', 41–2.

[19] *Liji*, 'Neize'. For a discussion of the sachet culture, see Yan, 'Gudai xiangnang de xingzhi jiqi wenhua yiyi'.

[20] *HLM* 67, 736; *SS*, vol. 3, 311.

[21] Examples include the gifts from the Imperial Concubine Jia Yuanchun 賈元春 (*HLM* 71, 779; *SS*, vol. 3, 395) and 'five wristlets of aromatic beads' given as presents to the Jia girls from someone known as Imperial Concubine Nan'an 南安太妃 (*HLM* 71, 781; *SS*, vol. 3, 398).

[22] *HLM* 28, 306; *SS*, vol. 2, 66.

the young ladies of the family. After a dinner party in the Prospect Garden, beneath a flowering tree sits Jia Yingchun (Baoyu's cousin), 'stringing jasmine blossoms into a flower-chain with a needle and thread'.[23] These chains may be made into a bracelet, hair ornament, or flower balls for hanging in a framed bed.[24] Dried flowers are never out of vogue, as showcased by Baoyu, who plays guess-fingers with Parfumée with one elbow resting on a 'newly-made turquoise-coloured pouffe stuffed with rose and peony petals'.[25] This fashion dates back to the Han dynasty, evidenced by the discovery of a spice pillow stuffed with *peilan* 佩蘭 (*Eupatorium fortunei*) in the aforementioned Mawangdui tomb.[26] Citrons, particularly a finger-shaped type known as 'Buddha's hands' (*foshou* 佛手), are a treasured decorative display that pleases both the nose and the eye (Figure 1.2).[27] In the boudoir of Jia Tanchun there is 'a large Northern Song porcelain dish heaped with those ornamental citrus fruits'.[28]

The most luxurious floral product in *Red Chamber* is perhaps two bottles of flower essences given to Baoyu by Lady Wang when he is sick. Since the initial introduction of rosewater to China from the Arab world during the Wudai period (907–960), China gradually mastered the technology of distillation and by Qing times had developed approximately thirty home-grown flowers and herbs suitable for extracting essences.[29] Lady Wang's two bottles, the Essence of Osmanthus and the Essence of Rose, are derived from the Palace. She carefully instructs Aroma to 'mix a teaspoonful of essence in a cupful of water' to ensure a delicious flavour.[30] Flavouring rice, tea, and wine with flower essences is a refined culinary tradition. Drinking 'special mimosa-flavoured samshoo' is culturally acceptable for the most genteel ladies such as Lin Daiyu.[31] A fondness for rice perfumed with essences of jasmine, osmanthus, and

---

[23] *HLM* 38, 405; *SS*, vol. 2, 248.   [24] Meng, *Huatang xiangshi*, 187.

[25] *HLM* 63, 688; *SS*, vol. 3, 221.   [26] Lu and Lo, 'Scent and Synaesthesia', 42.

[27] Meng, *Huatang xiangshi*, 161–3.   [28] *HLM* 40, 427; *SS*, vol. 2, 292.

[29] Chen, *Xinzuan xiangpu*, 94; Meng, *Huatang xiangshi*, 116–17.

[30] *HLM* 34, 359–60; *SS*, vol. 2, 161–2.

[31] *HLM* 38, 406; *SS*, vol. 2, 248. Jasmine wine is commonly drunk by women in *Jin ping mei* (*The Plum in the Golden Vase*). See Meng, *Huatang xiangshi*, 116.

citron (*xiangyuan* 香櫞) marks taste of the literati class, according to the Ming scholar Li Yu 李漁 (1611–1680).[32]

Finally, cosmetics and toiletries perfume the bodies of the women and men living in the red chambers. Traditionally falling under four classifications – powder (*fen* 粉), umber-black dye for the eyebrow (*dai* 黛), rouge (*zhi* 脂), and perfume (*xiang* 香) – beauty items were readily available in perfume shops prevalent in the commercializing Qing cities and towns, and certain brands, such as Guilin xuan 桂林軒 and Xiangxue tang 香雪堂 enjoyed a nationwide reputation.[33] Yet the elite had a penchant for home-crafted perfumery. Facilitated by the flourishing print culture, recipe books were in wide circulation, instructing the reader to make ointments, powders, and toilet water for hair, face, and body with natural ingredients.[34] This tradition is illustrated by a casual remark Baoyu makes to Daiyu before going to school in the morning: 'Wait till I get back . . . and I will give you a hand with that rouge.'[35] Baoyu exhibits his erudition in the arts of perfume when he offers powder and rouge to Patience (Ping'er), a senior maid, whose makeup has been spoiled by tears. He tells her that the powder is crafted by 'crushing the seeds of garden-jalap and mixing them with perfume', and that the rouge is made by 'squeezing the juice from the best quality safflower, carefully extracting all the impurities, mixing it with rose-water, and then further purifying it by distillation'.[36] Following Baoyu's guidance, Patience's complexion acquires a radiant freshness, glowing in 'the most delectable perfume'. Finally, Baoyu cuts the twin blossoms from an autumn-flowering orchid and sticks them in Patience's hair. The organic powder, rouge, and orchid transform the teary young woman into a fragrant beauty.

A plethora of perfuming and deodorizing techniques are also in place in maintaining personal hygiene. Baoyu's morning routine starts with washing his face with a bar of scented soap and rubbing salt all round his teeth vigorously with a finger and rinsing his mouth out with water.[37] An

---

[32] Li, *Xianqing ouji*, 'Yinzhuan bu', 243.

[33] Shanghai shi baihuo gongsi et al., *Shanghai jindai baihuo shangye shi*, 82.

[34] Tu and Che, *Huazhuang pin ji xiangliao zhizao fa*, 3.   [35] *HLM* 9, 98; *SS*, vol. 1, 205.

[36] *HLM* 44, 471–2; *SS*, vol. 2, 376.   [37] *HLM* 21, 216; *SS*, vol. 1, 416.

ointment crafted with honey, powder, and perfume (known as *ouzi* 漚子) functions as hand lotion,[38] and a combination of oil of flowers (*hualuyou* 花露油), hen's eggs, and scented soap is the Qing version of shampoo.[39] After a crab banquet, the maids bring 'mung-bean flour scented with chrysanthemum leaves and osmanthus flowers for cleaning the fingers and removing the smell of crab'.[40] When nineteenth-century Western travellers frowned upon Chinese people's lack of personal hygiene, and when Western merchants sought to sell their industrially manufactured soap and cosmetics via preaching modern concepts of sanitation, they clearly had not read *Red Chamber*. As Cao demonstrates, China did not lack advanced techniques and sensibilities to tune neurons to appreciate bodily cleanliness before the modern olfactory revolution. Aromas of the red chambers, however, are not only a matter for the nose; rather, they engage more profoundly with ordering space and time.

PERFUMING TIME AND SPACE

In the Ming dynasty classic *Xiang sheng* 香乘 (Book of Perfume), the author Zhou Jiazhou 周嘉冑 (1582–1661) maintains that perfume empowers one 'to communicate with Heaven and divinities, to worship ancestors, Confucian sages, the Buddha and bodhisattvas, to prey to Daoist spirits for the sake of reaching immortality, to dispel miasma and contamination, to ward off evil spirits, and to heal illness'.[41] In short, by virtue of its capacity in transcorporeal mediation, perfume helps maintain order across human and supernatural worlds. Cao Xueqin employs aromas to create a microcosm of ideal cosmic order, an order that will ultimately be 'contaminated'. This section surveys the techniques of defining, demarcating, and experiencing different spaces and times with scent. These techniques are testimony to how culture tunes neurons cognitively and aesthetically.

The first spatial type is *space of reverence*. Throughout human history, across cultures, incense is principally found in religious and ritual spaces because of the shared notion akin to Zhou Jiazhou's: good smells can

---

[38] *HLM* 54, 582; *SS*, vol. 3, 26–7.   [39] *HLM* 58, 635; *SS*, vol. 3, 128.
[40] *HLM* 38, 403; *SS*, vol. 2, 243.   [41] Zhou, *Xiang sheng*, 350, my translation.

'cleanse, purify, heal, ward off, or initiate communion with the Almighty' and bad smells 'contaminate, pollute and endanger'.[42] In China, the practice of burning aromatic wood and herbs in rituals dates back to around 6000 BC, and domestically grown aromatic flora constituted the main source of perfume (pepper, cinnamon, ginger, and so on), as extensively documented in ancient texts.[43] During the Han dynasty, a variety of foreign spices and aromatics became available thanks to the expanding Chinese empire; the development of the Silk Road connecting China to Central Asia, the Middle East, and Europe; and the growing maritime trade with South East and South Asia. Thereafter, exotic aromatic substances – agalloch (*chenxiang* 沉香), sandalwood (*tanxiang* 檀香), sweetgum (*fengxiang* 楓香), oriental sweetgum (*suhexiang* 蘇合香), cloves (*dingxiang/jishexiang* 丁香/雞舌香), frankincense (*ruxiang* 乳香), and myrrh (*moyao* 沒藥) – figured centrally in Daoist, Buddhist, and popular religious spaces.[44]

The red chambers teem with these fragrances, employed most significantly to demarcate diverse spaces of reverence. The Qing period witnessed a particularly varied religious life, engaging with 'shamanic, Daoist, Chinese Buddhist, Tibetan Buddhist, and popular religious traditions' adopted by the Manchus syncretically.[45] Buddhism in particular received substantial imperial patronage and held appeal to people from all walks of life.[46] In *Red Chamber*, the Prospect Garden hosts a Buddhist convent where the young nun Adamantina (Miaoyu) resides. During her magnificent home visitation (*xingqin* 省親), the Imperial Concubine Jia Yuanchun, Baoyu's elder sister, tours the garden built purposely for this occasion, and when she comes to the little convent nestled under a hill, she washes her hands before entering the shrine 'to offer incense and pray before the image of the Buddha'.[47] This simple ritual of purification

---

[42] Reinarz, *Past Scents*, 25.

[43] Huang, 'Xiangliao yu Ming dai shehui shenghuo', 7–9. For a list of commonly used Chinese domestic spices and aromatic materials, see Lu and Lo, 'Scent and Synaesthesia', 43.

[44] For a concise history of the import of foreign aromatics, see Chen, *Xinzuan xiangpu*, 11. Also see Fu, *Zhongguo xiang wenhua*, 23–7; Milburn, 'Aromas, Scents, and Spices', 458–62.

[45] Smith, *The Qing Dynasty and Traditional Chinese Culture*, 238.   [46] Ibid., 251–9.

[47] *HLM* 18, 192; *SS*, vol. 1, 372.

(cleansing, deodorizing, and perfuming) defines and preserves the space of the sacred. Later in the novel, when Baoyu is invited to the convent, he takes a bath and burns incense to purify himself before his visit.[48]

Space of reverence is not only reserved for divinities but also for ancestors, as ancestor worship is essential in Chinese culture. An elaborate ancestral veneration ceremony held on the eve of the Lunar New Year sums up the olfactory configuration of a solemn space of worship. At the centre of the Jia clan's ancestral temple, high above 'the smoking incense and flickering candles of the altar', hang the portraits of the ancestors against a background of brilliantly decorated screens.[49] Incense serves to purify the air and to transform the site into a sacred space. Making offerings to ancestors is the crux of the ceremony. Following lavish offerings of drink, food, and silk comes the climax, namely the offering of incense. Grandmother Jia, the highest living authority of the entire clan, clasps 'a little bundle of burning joss-sticks with both her hands' and kneels, and the entire congregation of men and women kneel down in perfect time with her.[50] Whereas drink, food, and clothing are material essentials for deceased ancestors, believed to be living in another world, the superiority of incense indicates the vital role of aroma as a messenger between living beings and the deceased. This custom is akin to the practice of offering fragrant objects as sacrifices in other religious traditions.[51]

As a cleansing agent and a messenger, incense can also be used to create a special space of reverence at the personal level, for which Baoyu has an elaborate theory. Seeing an opera actress burning 'spirit money' in memory of her deceased lover, Baoyu offers his advice to the actress's friend:

> Tell her never, never to use that paper stuff again ... All she needs to do when feast-days come round is to light a little incense in a burner. Provided that it's done with reverence, that's all that's needed for conveying one's feelings to the dead. It's the sincerity with which we make

---

[48] *HLM* 63, 696; *SS*, vol. 3, 236. [49] *HLM* 53, 573, *SS*, vol. 2, 569.
[50] *HLM* 53, 573, *SS*, vol. 2, 571. [51] Reinarz, *Past Scents*, 27–30.

the offering, not the offering itself that counts. You see that burner on the table over there? Whenever I want to remember someone dear to me – it doesn't necessarily have to be on a feast-day or any particular day, by the way – I light some incense in it and put out a cup of fresh tea or water, or sometimes some flowers or fruit if I have any. You can even use 'unclean foods' – as long as they're devoutly offered: that's the important thing.[52]

Baoyu's message emphasizes the versatile role of incense, making it applicable to religious and non-religious spaces alike. A prime example of constructing such an olfactory space is Jia Yuanchun's splendid family visitation permitted by the Emperor himself, an event that exhibits the wealth and status of the Jias at their peak. A few days prior to the visit, cleaners sent by the Metropolitan Police and the Board of Works have been busy sweeping the surrounding streets.[53] The arrival of the Imperial Concubine is heralded not only by the faint sound of music and the pyrotechnic sight of embroidered banners, fans, and umbrellas, but also by the fine aromas of special 'palace incense' burning in gold-inlaid censers carried by eunuchs. Her travelling kit includes scented beads, an embroidered handkerchief, and other items.[54] All these measures guarantee a sanctified space that shields her from contamination, as her physical body carries symbolic meaning in connection to the Emperor, the Son of Heaven.

In addition, lavish employment of valuable incense imbues the cere-monial space with an aura of utmost opulence: while gleaming gold, silverwork, sparkling jewels, and gems present a visual spectacle, the 'Hundred Blend incense' (*baihe zhi xiang* 百合之香) smouldering in brazen censers and the 'everlasting flowers' (*changchun zhi rui* 長春之蕊) blossoming in china vases constitute an olfactory feast.[55] Being ushered into the garden, Yuanchun is dazzled by a multisensory impres-sion of the space basking in 'curling drifts of incense smoke and gleaming colours'.[56] The principal reception hall is heavily perfumed with 'a fragrant scatter' that has been dropped on the flagstones and 'musk and borneol' (*shenao* 麝腦) burning in tripods, evoking the classic

[52] *HLM* 58, 638–9; *SS*, vol. 3, 133.   [53] *HLM* 18, 183; *SS*, vol. 1, 354.
[54] *HLM* 18, 184; *SS*, vol. 1, 356.   [55] *HLM* 18, 183; *SS*, vol. 1, 354.
[56] *HLM* 18, 184; *SS*, vol. 1, 357.

image of 'cassia halls and orchid chambers' (*guidian langong* 桂殿蘭宮) inhabited by imperial consorts.[57]

The specific incense types Cao selected reflect two principal rationales behind creating this ritual space: purification and status. The Hundred Blend incense (a blend of various aromatics) is famed for its ability to 'dispel filth and pollution' (*pohui* 破穢).[58] While the earliest record of this incense can be found in the biography of Emperor Wu of Han, it later became a popular incense type, featured in poems by Du Fu 杜甫 and Bai Juyi 白居易 in the Tang dynasty (618–907).[59] Musk and borneol are amongst the most treasured aromatic substances; the distant relative Jia Yun once even bribes the powerful Wang Xifeng with them in order to obtain a lucrative job in the Jia house.[60] Originally extracted from the musk deer native to western China, musk is probably the most sought-after fragrant animal product in the history of both East and West.[61] Borneol (or Borneo camphor), known in Chinese as dragon's brain (*longnao* 龍腦, or *bingpian* 冰片), is a valuable South Asian and Arabian aromatic substance deriving from tree resins, once worth its weight in gold.[62] Imported from Persia and Arabia to China in the Sui (581–618) and Tang dynasties, it was allegedly used to scent the roads on which emperors walked in the Tang period.[63] These two most precious aromatics act to transform the central symbolic site of the ceremony into a space that matches Yuanchun's noble status.

Beyond the space of reverence, aromas are involved in the configuration of a *space of culture*. A gentleman's study is incomplete without incense. The Chinese literati class is marked by a mastery of not only Confucian classics but also the arts of poetry, calligraphy, painting, and music, as well as the cultivation of an elegant lifestyle built on such 'superfluous things' as garden art, tea culture, and a taste for antiques.[64] The art of incense is one of the 'superfluous things' a man of letters

[57] *HLM* 18, 186; *SS*, vol. 1, 359. For legends and fables about perfumed chambers built for imperial concubines, see Meng, *Huatang xiangshi*, 21–31.
[58] Chen, *Xinzuan xiangpu*, 136.   [59] Fu, *Zhongguo xiang wenhua*, 71–2.
[60] *HLM* 24, 252; *SS*, vol. 1, 477.   [61] Reinarz, *Past Scents*, 128.
[62] Ibid., 62–3. For a history of the aromatic, see Donkin, *Dragon's Brain Perfume*.
[63] Chen, *Xinzuan xiangpu*, 14–19; Fu, *Zhongguo xiang wenhua*, 70.   [64] Wen, *Zhangwuzhi*.

should excel at, and theories on this art started to proliferate during the Song dynasty (960–1279), when a few specialized books on perfume emerged.[65] In the preface to Chen Jing's *New Book on Perfume*, compiled in the late Southern Song, the author writes, 'In a scholar's study, where a *qin* [a musical instrument] is laid in front of the window and books are filled in the bookshelves, without this volume how could he practice the art of incense?'[66]

The ideal image of a space of culture appears in passing in a comment by Baoyu's father, Jia Zheng, who, despite being only a court official, aspires to be seen as a refined lettered man. On his first tour of inspection of the Prospect Garden, at a 'cool, five-frame gallery with a low, roofed verandah running round it', he remarks, 'Anyone who sat sipping tea and playing the *qin* to himself on this verandah would have no need to burn incense if he wanted sweet smells for his inspiration.'[67] Although it is not an exclusively male privilege (since women from elite families at that time also relished activities of learning, as richly documented in *Red Chamber*),[68] the space of culture is predominantly reserved for male literati. For this reason, depictions of this spatial type are sparse in *Red Chamber*, a book of defiance against 'mainstream' Confucian culture at its heart. Instead, Cao devotes much of his enthusiasm to other domains of life, including *space of intimacy*.

One staple accessory indispensable to spaces of intimacy is the aforementioned perfume sachet (*hebao*). In addition to its neutral functions, *hebao* has a romantic, even erotic, connotation in line with smell's primordial role in attracting mates. It features in an apparently trivial scene in the long history of innocent squabbles between Baoyu and Daiyu. Assuming that Baoyu's young servants have taken her crafted *hebao* purse for Baoyu, Daiyu begins to cut up an unfinished embroidered perfume sachet she is making for him at his own request. When Baoyu tears open his collar, she sees that the little purse has all along been hanging round

---

[65] For example, *Xiangpu* 香譜 (Book on Perfume) compiled by Hong Chu 洪芻, *Tianxiang zhuan* 天香傳 (On Heavenly Perfumes) by Ding Wei 丁謂, *Xinzuan xiangpu* (New Book on Perfume) by Chen Jing. See Lu and Lo, 'Scent and Synaesthesia', 41; Yan, 'Qianyan', 4–5.

[66] Chen, *Xinzuan xiangpu*, 1. [67] *HLM* 17, 177; *SS*, vol. 1, 340.

[68] Mann, *Precious Record*, 76–120.

his neck and there is no risk of it being taken from him.[69] The perfume sachet, crafted by Daiyu's own hands and hanging close to Baoyu's heart, signifies a tender space of intimacy shared only by the two of them.

The *hebao* is often a subtle (or otherwise) cue of sexual intimacy as well. In the later part of the novel, an erotic-themed embroidered sachet sheds light on the aromatic–erotic association and an underlying message about contamination. Behind an artificial mountain in the Prospect Garden, Simple (Sha dajie), a half-witted fourteen-year-old maid, finds 'a beautifully embroidered purse', on one side of which is an image of 'a pair of naked human figures locked together in an embrace'.[70] The design of the erotic *hebao* ingeniously resonates with the seductive nature of perfume, rendering the visual, olfactory, and tactile dimensions of sexuality a harmonious unity. Interestingly, modern perfume advertising uses a similar tactic by deploying visual sensuality to perform olfactory seduction. This erotic purse found in the private space of the Jia girls causes a panic among the matriarchs of the family, leading to a search of the Garden for the owner, who is found to be the maid Chess (Siqi). Her secret lover has sent a love letter, along with a string of scented beads and two risqué 'spring-picture' perfume sachets.[71] The implied space of sexual intimacy, replete with aromas, is certainly a space of transgression and defilement, disrupting the order of things within the inner chambers. Therefore this episode is often interpreted as a portent of the doom of the Jia clan.

Another type of olfactory–amatory item evocative of sensual imagination is the cummerbund (*hanjin* 汗巾) and the chest cover (*dudou* 肚兜, or breast wrap). At a banquet Baoyu meets a famous opera actor (a female impersonator) named Jiang Yuhan and is beguiled by his 'winsome looks and gentleness of manner'. Their mutual affection is expressed by exchanging gifts: while Baoyu gives the actor a jade pendant from his fan, Jiang reciprocates by offering 'an unusual thing' as 'a token of my [his] warm feelings' – the crimson cummerbund with which he fastens his trousers. Jiang explains, 'It comes from the tribute sent by the queen of the Madder Islands. It's for wearing in summer. It makes

[69] *HLM* 17, 181; *SS*, vol. 1, 348–9.   [70] *HLM* 73, 805; *SS*, vol. 3, 443.
[71] *HLM* 74, 824; *SS*, vol. 3, 477.

you smell nice and it doesn't show perspiration stains.'[72] Baoyu receives this gift with delight and takes off his own sash to give to Jiang. This episode implies a space of homosexual intimacy, hinted by the cummerbund's tactile nature and its olfactory function to 'make you smell nice'.[73] The chest cover (*dudou*) has an analogous role in a heterosexual sphere. It was allegedly a vogue among courtesans of the Qing time to wear a type of musk-scented *dudou*, exuding an alluring fragrance as soon as they were undressed (*zhajie luojin, bianwen xiangze* 乍解羅襟，便聞香澤).[74]

In sum, aromas not only suffuse the red chambers but also mediate the perception of different types of space, as an embodied form of knowledge. The same applies to another dimension of the cosmos; that is, time. First, incense is literally a device to mark *quotidian time*. In the poetry club set up by the young women and Baoyu, the timing tool for their poetry competitions is a particular kind of incense known as Sweet Dreams (*mengtian xiang* 夢甜香), about three inches long and very thick so that it burns down fairly rapidly.[75] The incense clock (*gengxiang* 更香) figures as poetic imagery in a lantern riddle composed by Daiyu:

With me, at dawn you need no watchman's cry 曉籌不用雞人報，
At night no maid to bring a fresh supply 五夜無煩侍女添。
My head burns through the night and through the day 焦首朝朝還暮暮，
And year by year my heart consumes away 煎心日日復年年。 [76]

The riddle not only references this innovative incense timing technique, but also conveys a profound sense of experiencing time as a bodily and sensory construct.[77] Ultimately, sensorial perception unfolds in time, and in many cultures scents engage with the signification of *cosmic time*. As discussed before, in ancient Chinese natural philosophy, within the

---

[72] *HLM* 28, 302; *SS*, vol. 2, 61–2.

[73] For a discussion of Baoyu's bisexuality, see Edwards, *Men and Women in Qing China*, 37–49.

[74] Zhuquan jushi, *Xu Banqiao zaji*, vol. 1, 55. Quoted in Wu, *Youyou fangxiang*, 274.

[75] *HLM* 37, 392; *SS*, vol. 2, 222.   [76] *HLM* 22, 233; *SS*, vol. 1, 449.

[77] I was inspired by my student Zhao Yiran for this reading. See her PhD dissertation 'Time in the Literary Constructions of Self, Love, and Fate in *Honglou meng*'. For an introduction to a type of incense made in a specific shape and used as clock (known as *yinxiang* 印香, *zhuanxiang* 篆香 or *xiangzhuan* 香篆), see Chen, *Xinzuan xiangpu*, 167–70.

overarching Five Elements (*wuxing*) cosmic system, the osmological cycle of five scents accords with the seasonal cycle: spring is associated with the gamy smell *shan*, summer with the burning smell *jiao*, autumn with the rank or fishy smell *xing*, winter with rot *xiu*, and the fragrant scent *xiang* is associated with the centre (see Table I.1). Although they are not strictly in accordance with this theory, aromatic practices in the red chambers evince a keen sensitivity towards the cosmic rhythm of time.

In August one year, Daiyu instructs her maids to move a table to the outside room, put the dragon incense burner on it, and fetch some melons, caltrops, and lotus roots for a personal offering according to the guidance in the *Book of Rites*: 'in each season of the year ... offer things seasonable (春秋薦其時食).'[78] On the night of the Mid-Autumn Festival, when lamps are lit, incense is burnt, and offerings of seasonal fruit and mooncakes are set out on dishes, Grandmother Jia washes her hands, lights some sticks of incense, kneels on the carpet, bows down, and offers up the incense.[79] Seasonal floral scents are another medium to shape the aesthetic experience of cosmic time. Mastering the art of flower cultivation and display, in harmony with the seasonal cycle, is a symbol of refinement, as elaborated in Ming scholar Wen Zhenheng's 文震亨 (1585–1645) renowned manual of taste.[80] Amongst the forty floral types featured in Wen's treatise, osmanthus flowers (*guihua* 桂花) are highly appreciated in Chinese culture, and there is no dearth of their overpowering sweet scents drifting in the autumn air of the red chambers. Baoyu one time picks a few first sprays of the year and arranges them in a pair of exquisite vases as thoughtful gifts to his grandmother and mother. Grandmother Jia is 'so delighted you just can't imagine'.[81] The signature scent of osmanthus could even sustain the modern olfactory revolution, and continued to perfume modern bodies as a classic ingredient in mass-manufactured cosmetics, as we will encounter in Chapter 4.

The two sections have delineated how aromas in *Red Chamber* pervade the sublime, the quotidian, and the intimate dimensions of life

---

[78] *HLM* 64, 704–5; *SS*, vol. 3, 252–3.   [79] *HLM* 75, 837; *SS*, vol. 3, 500.

[80] Wen, *Zhangwuzhi*, vol. 2, 9–23.

[81] *HLM* 37, 395; *SS*, vol. 2, 227. Hawkes translates 桂花 as 'cassia', which is inaccurate.

throughout time and space. The dazzling variety of aromatics and their multiple usages demonstrate the cognitive and aesthetic tuning of the olfactory nervous system for keeping a particular order of things. The novel also offers a glimpse of the arts of perfume in late imperial China, a highly *cultured* field of taste vigorously engaging with the biological system of olfaction. This culture brings into sharp relief the curious mix of chemical scents, sexual odours, and scatological metaphors that would take the stage in the Chinese olfactory revolution. Yet Cao's gift is manifested not only in his connoisseurship of perfume art, but also in deep messages he encodes in scents, messages in relation to beauty and decay, and the adulteration of order.

L'ESSENCE DE FLEURS: AN ALLEGORY

L'essence de fleurs (*qun fang sui* 群芳髓), a 'faint, subtle scent', can be conceived as the olfactory icon of the novel, condensing within it the allegory of purity/contamination that lies at the heart of *Red Chamber*.[82] It assails Baoyu's nostrils in his dream as he enters a room on the Land of Illusion (Taixu huanjing 太虚幻境). Immersed in this sublime perfume, Baoyu listens to a cycle of twelve prophetic songs, responding to the fates of the twelve young women in the novel, as introduced earlier.[83] While the perfume of transcendence under Patrick Süskind's pen is a blend of the virgin girl's fragrant emanations likened to floral scents (water lilies, apricot blossoms, and so on), Cao Xueqing's aromatic icon is made from the essences of freshly grown rare plants. Just as Grenouille finds in the extraordinary perfume the higher principle, Baoyu inhales from *l'essence de fleurs* a distillation of utmost feminine beauty. He famously declares, 'Girls are made of water and boys are made of mud. When I am with girls I feel fresh and clean, but when I am with boys I feel stupid and nasty.'[84] Female purity is one of the major symbols of *Red Chamber*, an

---

[82] David Hawkes translated *qun fang sui* as *belles se fanent* (the fading beauty). Though it matches its allegorical meaning, I prefer to translate it literally. Since the Chinese term literally means 'the essence of blossoms', I translate it as *l'essence de fleurs*, following Hawkes's cue on his choice of French for an exotic air.

[83] *HLM* 5, 50–60; *SS*, vol. 1, 127–48.   [84] *HLM* 2, 19; *SS*, vol. 1, 76.

instrument Cao deploys to critique patriarchal Confucian culture.[85] And yet Cao's 'feminist' stance is manifested not through essentializing the fairer sex, but through individualizing his female characters. Smell is one of his literary devices, as each important female protagonist is endowed with a unique aroma that embodies her distinctive being, in connection to her disposition and destiny. Resonating Grenouille's mega-perfume made up of the particular scents of maidens, we may envision *l'essence de fleurs* as a metaphorical blend of the distinct fragrances of the Jia young women.

Neither Süskind nor Cao, however, aims to romanticize either of their marvellous master scents. In order to create a *great* perfume to fulfil his dream of tyranny, Grenouille embarks on a menacing journey to collect 'ingredients' from a dozen maidens he will have to murder. Richard Gray perceptively points out, 'In this parable of the nose demon who destroys living creatures to capture and control their "spirits" or "absolute essences," Süskind dramatizes the consequences of enlightened reason's destructive dialectic.'[86] The ambivalence of olfaction makes smell a potent medium to expose the contrasting narratives of 'refined discernment and bestial sensuality'.[87] Encoded in *l'essence de fleurs* is likewise a paradox. The otherworldly scent encapsulates the evanescence of beauty, fading away as the Jia women's tragic destinies unfold. Notably, it is this enigmatic aroma that accompanies Baoyu's initiation into sexual life in the amorous ending of his dream. The transcendent and the carnal, the virginal purity and its 'defilement', coalesce in the fleeting waft, pointing to the novel's Buddhist undertone that centres on the conception of impermanence of all material and sentient beings. Taken together, I argue that *l'essence de fleurs* serves as a key metaphor, and an examination of its 'ingredients' is vital to comprehend Cao's understanding of humanity.

To construe *Red Chamber* merely as a love story is too reductive; however, there is no denying that, as Anthony C. Yu puts it, 'this story of the fragile and transient nature of love' is one that 'succeeds in the

---

[85] Edwards, *Men and Women in Qing China*, 51.

[86] Gray, 'The Dialectic of "Enscentment"', 238.

[87] Mark Bradley's phrase, in Tullett et al., 'Smell, History, and Heritage', 302.

most permanent engagement of our sympathy'.[88] The centrepiece of the love tragedy lies in the triangular relationship between Jia Baoyu and his two cousins, Lin Daiyu and Xue Baochai. Leaving her home town in Yangzhou after her mother's death, Daiyu lives in the Jia household at the insistence of Grandmother Jia. Her intellectual brilliance and literary talent are unsurpassable, as is her beauty, but she is renowned for her oversensitivity and neurotic temperament. Moreover, she suffers chronic illnesses, making her physically delicate and emotionally vulnerable. Being Grandmother Jia's favourite granddaughter, she enjoys special privileges otherwise only reserved for Baoyu. Sharing each other's company regularly, Daiyu and Baoyu develop 'an understanding so intense' that it is almost as if they have grown into 'a single person'.[89] Unfortunately, their profound romantic affinity fails to consummate into a marriage as Baoyu is arranged to marry Baochai, and Daiyu dies of a broken heart.

Baochai's mother Aunt Xue and Baoyu's mother Lady Wang are siblings. Widowed at a young age, Aunt Xue brings her two children to the capital, where they have a family business, and Lady Wang invites them to stay in the Jia mansion. Despite Baochai and Daiyu both being aesthetically beautiful, their personalities are polar opposites. Baochai possesses 'a generous, accommodating disposition which greatly endeared her to subordinates',[90] and she is reputed for her common sense and rationality. Although she is intellectually gifted, she subscribes to orthodox Confucian moral teachings, considering only 'spinning and sewing' as the proper occupation for a young woman.[91] While Daiyu never presses Baoyu to seek success in his career, Baochai encourages him to pursue fame and repute as Confucian teachings instruct.[92] All these traits make Baochai a more suitable wife and daughter-in-law in the illustrious Jia clan.

The sense of smell is employed to render tangible the disparate disposition, intellectual and emotional make-up, and moral outlook between the two women. Daiyu's characteristic aroma is first introduced

---

[88] Yu, *Rereading the Stone*, 225.   [89] *HLM* 5, 48; *SS*, vol. 1, 124.
[90] *HLM* 4, 44; 5, 48; *SS*, vol. 1, 118, 124.   [91] *HLM* 42, 450; *SS*, vol. 2, 334.
[92] *HLM* 36, 377; *SS*, vol. 2, 195.

in Chapter 19 when Baoyu pays her a midday visit while she is resting on the couch.[93] Lying down beside her, Baoyu is soon preoccupied with 'an ethereal fragrance' (*youxiang* 幽香) emanating from her sleeve – a fragrance that 'intoxicated the senses and caused one to feel rather limp'.[94] A discerning connoisseur of the perfume art, Baoyu fathoms this to be 'a very unusual scent. Not the kind you would get from a scent-cake or a perfume-ball or sachet'.[95] Its real source, as the influential marginal comment by Red Inkstone (Zhiyanzhai 脂硯齋) suggests, is none other than Daiyu's own body.[96] This reading corresponds to the Chinese notion of *tianxiang* 天香 (heavenly fragrance), belonging uniquely to women with otherworldly beauty.[97] I contend that the ethereal fragrance *youxiang* is an olfactory symbol of Daiyu. It is hardly coincidental that Cao Xueqin depicts Baoyu's first sniff of *l'essence de fleurs* with the same word, *youxiang*. Equivalent to 'faint, subtle, delicate', *you* 幽 also denotes 'deep, profound, and elegant'. Therefore *youxiang* elicits an ethereal perfume with delicacy, richness, and profound elegance, once again reminiscent of the magic scent in the novel *Perfume*. Even the somatic responses of those who inhale it are intriguingly akin: Baoyu feels 'intoxicated and limp', and Jean-Baptiste Grenouille is 'almost sick with excitement'.[98]

A whiff of *youxiang* features in another crucial episode, one that witnesses the blossoming romantic love between Baoyu and Daiyu. During an unplanned visit to Daiyu's apartment, Baoyu captures 'a faint sweetness in the air' (*yilü youxiang* 一縷幽香), drifting out through the green gauze of the casement. He hears Daiyu emitting a long and languorous sigh as she recites, 'Each day in a drowsy waking dream of love.'[99] This sentence, from the Yuan dynasty play *Xixiang ji* 西廂記 (*Romance of the Western Chamber*), articulates Cui Yingying's longing for

[93] The chapter title already highlights fragrance: 'A blissful night, earnestly a flower murmurs her inner feelings; A tranquil day, dreamlike the jade exudes a lingering aroma (情切切良宵花解語，意綿綿靜日玉生香).'

[94] *HLM* 19, 203; *SS*, vol. 1, 394. Hawkes translated *youxiang* as 'a delicate fragrance'; I think 'ethereal' is more accurate according to my analysis of this unique scent.

[95] Ibid.   [96] Cao Xueqin and Zhiyanzhai, *Zhiyanzhai piping ben Hongloumeng*, 191.

[97] Li, *Xianqing ouji*, 'Shengrong bu', 123. I thank Paola Zamperini for drawing my attention to this source. Also see Santangelo, 'From *Huchou* to *Tianxiang*', 46–7.

[98] Süskind, *Perfume*, 39.   [99] *HLM* 26, 274–5; *SS*, vol. 1, 516.

her lover Zhang Sheng, echoing Daiyu's own unspeakable feeling for Baoyu. The 'faint sweetness'/*youxiang*, the source of which is unidentifiable,[100] reinforces its olfactory association with Daiyu and the profound attachment between her and Baoyu. Bestowing the most exquisite aroma onto both Daiyu and *l'essence de fleurs* betrays Cao Xueqin's 'partiality' for Daiyu. She is the quintessence of the purity of femininity, and her tragic destiny points to the philosophy underlying the novel – the Buddhist sense of emptiness (*kong* 空) and the illusionary nature of worldly possessions and existence. The private language of scent is transformed into a memorable literary trope.

While Daiyu is reputed for her 'delicate charm', Baochai's 'rose-fresh beauty' is endearing in a different way.[101] Her snow-white arms make Baoyu ponder: 'If that arm were growing on Cousin Lin's body, I might hope one day to touch it.'[102] As Louise Edwards compellingly argues, Baochai and Daiyu represent the binaries of strength versus weakness, practical versus frivolous, rational versus emotional, masculine versus feminine, and *yang* versus *yin*.[103] Baochai's hallmark aroma is aligned with the Chinese cosmic order of *yin/yang*: a 'refreshing and delicious fragrance' (*liang sensen tian sisi* 涼森森甜絲絲) from the medicine to cure her weird illness diagnosed by a monk as 'a congenital tendency to overheatedness' (*redu* 熱毒).[104] Known as Cold Fragrance Pill (Lengxiang wan 冷香丸), the unusual prescription requires 'twelve ounces of stamens of the spring-flowering white tree-peony, twelve ounces of stamens of the summer-flowering white water-lily, twelve ounces of stamens of the autumn-flowering white lotus, and twelve ounces of stamens of the winter-flowering white plum', mixed with powder as well as 'twelve drams of rain water . . . on the Rain Days in the second month . . . twelve drams of dew on the day White Dew in the ninth

---

[100] Hawkes's translation is 'a faint sweetness in the air, traceable to a thin curl of incense smoke which drifted out through the green gauze of the casement', but Cao's original text only indicates '*yilü youxiang* 一縷幽香', without any mention of the source of the fragrance. See ibid.

[101] *HLM* 5, 59; *SS*, vol. 1, 145.   [102] *HLM* 28, 306; *SS*, vol. 2, 66.

[103] Edwards, *Men and Women in Qing China*, 47.

[104] *HLM* 8, 89; 7, 74; *SS*, vol. 1, 190–1, 168.

month, twelve drams of frost at Frost Fall in the tenth, and twelve drams of snow at Lesser Snow in the last month of the year'.[105]

Named after its cooling scent, behind the Cold Fragrance Pill is an intricate philosophy of harmony. The white colour of the flowers and the four kinds of water required in the prescription strengthen the cold/*yin* quality of the medicine, a counterbalance to Baochai's congenital tendency to overheatedness. The cold fragrance also conveys an allegorical message: it balances Baochai's *yang* attributes of worldly ambition and rationality. In other words, in Cao Xueqin's deep thought only Daiyu's pure femininity deserves the ethereal *youxiang* shared with *l'essence de fleurs*, whilst Baochai's beauty is flawed by the contamination of male values prescribed by Confucian dogmatism. Baoyu's reaction to Baochai's admonitions supports this argument: 'Why should a pure, sweet girl like you want to go imitating that ghastly crew of thievish, place-hunting *career worms*, bothering her head about 'fame' and 'reputation' and all that sort of rubbish?'[106] Seen in this light, the enigmatic Cold Fragrance Pill allegorizes the *yang* side of Baochai's persona.

Through smells, Cao crafts not only the chief female protagonists but also two less principal characters: Qin Keqing and Adamantina. They are also polar opposites to a degree: Qin 'a motif of sexual immoderation' and the nun Adamantina a paragon of sexual abstinence.[107] Qin Keqing is the wife of Jia Rong, the young heir of another branch of the Jia clan, the Ning house. She is assumed to have committed suicide as a result of the discovery of her incestuous relationship with her father-in-law. The extant text of the novel does not make it evident because, as is widely accepted, Cao Xueqin took the advice of an elder and amended the text. However, Red Inkstone's marginal comments and the portents of Qin's fate in Baoyu's dream all hint at her 'lustful death'.[108] Moreover, it is in Qin Keqing's bedroom that Baoyu has the prophetic dream which ends with his first sexual experience with Qin herself. Therefore Qin's image as a sexual transgressor is firmly established, and her sensuous charm is embodied by a particular scent.

[105] *HLM* 7, 74; *SS*, vol. 1, 168–9. [106] *HLM* 36, 377; *SS*, vol. 2, 195 (emphasis original).
[107] Edwards, *Men and Women in Qing China*, 85. [108] Ibid.

In the middle of a party in the Ning mansion, Baoyu feels tired and is taken by Qin Keqing to her boudoir for an afternoon nap. As Baoyu enters, 'a subtle whiff of the most delicious perfume' (*xixi de tianxiang* 細細的甜香) assails his olfactory cleft, producing 'a sweet stickiness inside his drooping eyelids and causing all the joints in his body to dissolve'.[109] Whilst no sexual connotation is embedded in Daiyu's ethereal *youxiang* and Baochai's refreshing *lengxiang*, this sweet fragrance *tianxiang* undoubtedly embodies 'assertive, unfettered sensualism', as sweetness and sensual indulgence are often interlinked.[110] In tune with this sensuous olfactory imagery is Qin's lavish room decor, rich with objects associated with women in Chinese legend and history (in)famous for 'disrupting social order through transgressive sexual charms'.[111] For example, a pair of calligraphic scrolls read, 'The coldness of spring has imprisoned the soft buds in a wintry dream; the fragrance of wine has intoxicated the beholder with imagined flower-scents (嫩寒鎖夢因春冷，芳氣籠人是酒香).'[112] This couplet, evoking a multisensory scene filled with wine fragrance, floral scents, dreams, and intoxication, is commented on by Red Inkstone as 'exceedingly sensuous, exceedingly amorous' (*yanji, yinji* 艷極，淫極).[113] The titillating sweet aroma *tianxiang* personifies the sensual being of Qin Keqing and allegorizes contamination by lust.

Adamantina is the opposite. The uncompromising nun, arrogant and fastidious, is obsessed with maintaining her sexual and spiritual purity.[114] Despite no reference to any scent directly attached to her, one particular aroma discloses her peculiar being through Baoyu's nose. Heading to a poetry gathering on a snowy morning, Baoyu's senses are suddenly 'ravished by a delicate chilly fragrance' (*hanxiang* 寒香) wafting from 'the dozen or so trees of winter-flowering red plum growing inside the walls of Green Bower Hermitage' inhabited by Adamantina.[115] Later, when Baoyu loses the poetry competition and needs to settle the

---

[109] *HLM* 5, 49; *SS*, vol. 1, 126.   [110] The quotation is from Yu, *Rereading the Stone*, 199.
[111] Edwards, *Men and Women in Qing China*, 85.   [112] *HLM* 5, 49–50; *SS*, vol. 1, 126.
[113] Cao Xueqin and Zhiyanzhai, *Zhiyanzhai piping ben Hongloumeng*, 48.
[114] Edwards, *Men and Women in Qing China*, 65.
[115] *HLM* 49, 528; *SS*, vol. 2, 482 (modified).

incurred debt, Adamantina grants him a branch of plum blossoms.[116] The chilly fragrance, *hanxiang*, is Adamantina incarnate. She is more than 'cold'; her 'overly pure' character, setting her at odds with the rest of the world,[117] is accurately personified as the *chilly* fragrance of red plum blossoms flowering in snow, a long-standing emblem of pride and dignity (*aogu* 傲骨) in Chinese culture. This olfactory imagery has an echo in the prophetic song dedicated to Adamantina in Baoyu's dream:

> Nauseous to you the world's rank diet 你道是啖肉食腥羶
> Vulgar its fashion's gaudy dress 視綺羅俗厭
> But the world envies the superior 卻不知太高人愈妒
> And hates a too precious daintiness 過潔世同嫌[118]

The stark contrast between the chilly fragrance and the rank diet implies in olfactory terms Adamantina's disgraceful end as a prostitute, an ultimate defeat by defilement.[119] The affective potency of smell is enlisted to signify the extremes of unadulterated and polluted.

Cao Xueqin dedicates the otherworldly perfume *youxiang* to Lin Daiyu, the sophisticated fragrance *lengxiang* to Xue Baochai, the sensuous scent *tianxiang* to Qin Keqing, and the spiritual *hanxiang* to Adamantina, revelatory of their disparate temperamental, sexual, moral, and spiritual inclinations. In comparison to the techniques and discourses of olfactory modernity that often homogenize and commodify women with manufactured scents, Cao's non-objectifying approach to crafting female characters is truly progressive. Apart from the four chief characters, aromas in association with other less complex characters are equally convincing. For example, on New Year's Eve, the reception hall of Grandmother Jia's apartment is loaded with 'delicious odours of pine and cedar incense and Hundred Blend aromatic'.[120] Since the Hundred

---

[116] *HLM* 50, 537; *SS*, vol. 2, 497.

[117] For example, Li Wan 李紈, Baoyu's widowed sister-in-law, once comments, 'I find Adamantina such a difficult person that I prefer not to have anything to do with her.' See *HLM* 50, 536; *SS*, vol. 2, 495.

[118] *HLM* 5, 58; *SS*, vol. 1, 142.

[119] For an insightful analysis of Adamantina, see Edwards, *Men and Women in Qing China*, 56, 64–6.

[120] *HLM* 53, 574; *SS*, vol. 2, 573.

Blend incense dispels pollution and the woody aromas of pine and cedar symbolize honour, nobility, and longevity,[121] this mix impeccably suits Grandmother Jia's status and the particular space. The aromatic fruit 'Buddha's hands' that scents Tanchun's apartment likewise matches her character. Compared to sweet incense and floral fragrance, refreshing citric scents are less feminine, thus a more apt olfactory symbol of Tanchun, famed for her managerial knack and masculine tendency.[122] Empress Dowager Cixi (1835–1908) was reportedly particularly fond of fresh fruit and citrus (including Buddha's hands) for perfuming her chambers, an olfactory image that matches her power and authority.[123]

The fascinating smellscapes of the red chambers and the rich dynamics of perfuming and smelling attest to Cao Xueqin's literary virtuosity and connoisseurship in the high culture of late imperial China. All the aromas discussed hitherto are confined within the walls of the Jia mansions. What about odours of the world inhabited by common people? What can they tell about the social dimension of smell as well as the parable of purity/contamination? Whilst the main focus of the story is unquestionably the elite life inside the Jia compound, Cao sporadically touches upon ordinary people's life outside the domain of the Jias.

ODOURS OUTSIDE THE RED CHAMBER

Grannie Liu (Liu laolao), from a humble household with a remote family connection to the Jias, is perhaps one of the most beloved characters in *Red Chamber*. In the hope of gaining some benefits, she pays a visit to this distant relation; her rustic manners and simple country talk bring immeasurable amusement to Grandmother Jia and everyone in the house. Cao's animated narrative of her two visits gives the reader vicarious pleasure in savouring the luxury living of the Jia house from an outsider's perspective. Allegorically, the outsider represents a force that has the potential to trouble established order. Needless to say, the issue of class is also brought to the fore. Smell is a powerful register of all these matters. Grannie Liu's first impression of the Jia house is an olfactory

[121] Fu, *Zhongguo xiang wenhua*, 10–11. [122] *HLM* 40, 427; *SS*, vol. 2, 292.
[123] Carl, *With the Empress Dowager*, 36; Jin, *Gongnü tan wang lu*, 55.

one. As she and her grandson enter the main reception hall of Wang Xifeng's apartment, 'a strange, delicious fragrance' reaches forward and embraces them, 'producing in Grannie Liu the momentary sensation that she had been transported bodily to one of the celestial paradises'.[124] The sensation compellingly illustrates smell's transcorporeality, mediating between bodies and environments, humans and the supernatural. Yet her illusion of crossing the border into paradise is in reality a crossing between class boundaries. Outside the walls of the upscale residential compounds such as the Jias', eighteenth-century Beijing reeked of poorly drained sewers, unpaved roads with heaps of horse manure, the pungent smell of night soil, and numerous other stenches.[125] Having been living in such an olfactory environment her entire life, Grannie Liu's neurons are unaccustomed to the heavily perfumed atmosphere of the Jia house.

How, then, does Grannie Liu smell to those living in the red chambers? On her second visit, as soon as she sets foot in Grandmother Jia's apartment, the chief maid Faithful (Yuanyang) orders 'some of the older domestics to conduct her to a bath' and to change her into clean clothes from the maid's own wardrobe.[126] A practical precaution to avoid afflicting Grandmother Jia's nose aside, Faithful's ritual of deodorization can be construed as a subconscious act of defending the order within the Jia house. In another well-known episode featuring an amusing banquet, the tipsy Grannie Liu is lost in the Prospect Garden after her privy visit and strays into Baoyu's apartment, ending up asleep on his bed. As Aroma enters the bedroom, 'a heavy stink, compounded of farts and wine-fumes', horrifies her. Hurriedly, she throws 'three or four whole handfuls of Hundred Blend aromatic onto the incense burner'.[127] Smell clearly is the most obstreperous interloper on the one hand, and the most unabashed arbiter of class distinction on the other. Notably, these instances show that culture has tuned the neurons of Faithful and Aroma, the housemaids who are of a lower class. We are reminded of Baoyu's unexpected visit to the house of Aroma's parents: for fear of the lower-class smell's contaminating potential, she immediately hands a perfumed hand-warmer to Baoyu. This begs the question: how does the

[124] *HLM* 6, 68; *SS*, vol. 1, 157–8.   [125] See Chiu, 'Fengchen, jierang yu qiwei', 181–225.
[126] *HLM* 39, 416; *SS*, vol. 2, 269.   [127] *HLM* 41, 443; *SS*, vol. 2, 321.

outside world smell to those cultured noses when they occasionally venture out?

As is the case with most elite families in late imperial China, women and young men in the Jia house have little contact with the real world; attending religious events is one of the few exceptions. Imperial Concubine Jia Yuanchun once orders a three-day Pro Viventibus, a Daoist purification ceremony, to be conducted by the Daoists of the Lunar Queen temple with plays performed as part of the offering. The whole Jia family goes to the temple that day. The abbot of the temple wants to take the rare opportunity to show Baoyu's magic jade to his monks and students. Instead of inviting Baoyu out to the courtyard, he offers to place the jade in a tray and take it himself because, as he explains to Grandmother Jia, 'with so many of them [monks] here today and the weather so hot, the smell is sure to be somewhat overpowering. Our young friend here is certainly not used to it. We shouldn't want him to be overcome by the – ah – effluvia, should we?'[128] Baoyu does overcome effluvia as a gallant act on another occasion. At the funeral of Jia Jing (Baoyu's uncle), when the monks are going round the coffin, Baoyu stands in front of the women of the family, and everyone comments how ill-mannered he is. Later he explains, 'I noticed how dirty some of those monks were and I was afraid that the smell of them might distress you.'[129] Underlying this act is Baoyu's quixotic desire to safeguard purity and beauty from contamination. The malodours symbolize the inevitable defilement of the wondrous *l'essence de fleurs*, the collective aroma of pure femininity.

As the story progresses, the destiny of the downfall of the Jia clan looms large. A whiff of lower-class odour foreshadows the decline. This symbolic whiff occurs in the house of Skybright's (Qingwen's) cousin after Lady Wang has banished the favourite maid of Baoyu from the Jia house due to a false accusation of licentiousness. Baoyu pays a secret visit to Skybright, who is gravely ill. Lying on a rush mat, she is desperate for a cup of tea. Baoyu finds a teacup on the table, with its 'greasy, rancid

---

[128] *HLM* 29, 312; *SS*, vol. 2, 78.

[129] *HLM* 66, 728; *SS*, vol. 3, 294. For more references to the stench of monks, see *HLM* 80, 898; *SS*, vol. 3, 608–9.

odour' (*youshan zhi qi* 油膻之氣) reaching his nostrils even before he has picked it up.[130] Having washed and rinsed it twice, and sniffed it, he half fills it with tea. In his protest earlier, Baoyu has made a comment: 'Sending her [Skybright] to that place now is like taking a potted orchid that has just started putting out its first tender spears of growth and setting it down in a pigsty.'[131] The delicate perfume of the orchid is in stark contrast to the greasy, rancid odour of the 'pigsty'. The clean essence of feminine beauty is contaminated and this is a portent of the tragic collapse of the Jia clan, as well as of the cultivated order. People in the red chambers, as genteel and refined as they are, will have to face the outside world, including its smells.

CODA

Red Chamber weaves a microcosm of the perfume culture that patterned late imperial Chinese society. The story can virtually be read as a training manual for the nose: how meanings are imparted to particular times, spaces, genders, and classes, and how olfactory knowledge and aesthetics are mutually informed. This body of knowledge challenges the conventional sensory hierarchy, especially the modern Western ocularcentric thinking. In the eighteenth-century Chinese life-world, the olfactory coordinates with the visual, acoustic, tactile, and gustatory spheres, comprising an inseparable whole. The wholeness of sensory experience operates not only cognitively but also aesthetically. In this sense, Cao Xueqin would surely disagree with Kant on the following judgement:

> Which organic sense is the most ungrateful and also seems the most dispensable? The sense of smell. It does not pay to cultivate it or to refine it at all in order to enjoy; for there are more disgusting objects than pleasant ones (especially in crowded places), and even when we come across something fragrant, the pleasure coming from the sense of smell is fleeting and transient.[132]

---

[130] *HLM* 77, 863; *SS*, vol. 3, 544.   [131] *HLM* 77, 860; *SS*, vol. 3, 540.
[132] Kant, *Anthropology from a Pragmatic Point of View*, 50–1.

For Cao Xueqin, it does pay to cultivate and to refine the sense of smell, and the evanescence of aromas is part of the aesthetic experience of beauty and its fading, of purity and contamination that frame the lives of sentient beings.

The dream of the red chamber vanishes as the Jia family collapses in the tide of imperial politics. So did the aromatic realm of the eighteenth century, since the nineteenth century brought to China a foreign novelty that is called (Western) modernity. While Baoyu takes great pleasure in helping make 'organic' rouges, a century later he would have found a French brand with a stylish wrapper more appealing. Yet the most startling contradiction to Baoyu's olfactory perception of his world would have been the realization, had he read foreign travel books of the ensuing century, that China stinks.

2

China Stinks

Over the walls came the usual street noises of a crowded Chinese city ... The air was oppressive with sickening odours, for in China, as a visitor once wisely remarked, 'There are seventy-five smells one can identify and twenty-five unknown ones.' It would take walls several leagues high to keep these odours from penetrating.

Jean Cochran, *Foreign Magic*[1]

To the cultured, privileged noses of the Western travellers of the long nineteenth century, accustomed as they were to their perfumed parlours, the stench of China was an olfactory shock. This overall sentiment, exemplified by the epigraph, throws into sharp relief the laudatory comments by earlier generations of travellers. Sixteenth-century Spanish missionaries, for example, exclaimed in admiration that the Chinese, both in their streets and in their houses, were marvellously clean.[2] The stark contrast might have less to do with physical change in smellscapes than it does with shifts in olfactory sensibility, in relation to the changing position of China vis-à-vis the West. As Alain Corbin suggests, 'it would be futile to analyze social tensions and conflicts without accounting for the different kinds of sensibilities that decisively influence them. Abhorrence of smells produces its own form of social power.'[3] This chapter inspects how China was implicated in the global history of olfactory modernity through a discourse of

---

[1] Cochran, *Foreign Magic*, 111.

[2] Mendoza, *The History of the Great and Mighty Kingdom of China*, vol. 1, 27; quoted in Mackerras, *Western Images of China*, 25.

[3] Corbin, *The Foul and the Fragrant*, 5.

contamination, giving rise to a new olfactory order and sensibility. In doing so, it evaluates the role of the body in the all-too-familiar history of China's century of humiliation, still a powerful narrative that underpins the Xi-era political discourse of national rejuvenation. Via a close reading of Western travel literature about China in the nineteenth century and the first half of the twentieth, this chapter seeks to understand the mechanisms through which the private sensorium and the macroscopic contours of history were entangled.

Travel writing, as a popular genre and an ideological instrument, occupied a special position in the European colonial enterprise.[4] The period under scrutiny was its heyday. As Lynne Withey remarks, 'at times it has seemed as if everyone who left home in the nineteenth century wrote a book about it.'[5] With enhanced accessibility, nineteenth-century China attracted an incessant stream of travellers (missionaries, officials, businessmen, scientists, journalists, and adventurers); collectively they produced a vast archive of narratives and images.[6] The appetite of the domestic readership for this mysterious land made China a sought-after theme for publishers, and the influence of these books was 'probably much greater than sinologues would like to acknowledge'.[7] While statistics on the exact size of this literature are unavailable, I have consulted approximately 100 titles mostly written in English.[8]

---

[4] For a classic study of this subject, see Pratt, *Imperial Eye*.

[5] Withey, *Grand Tours and Cook's Tours*, xi.

[6] Recent publications include Dupée, *British Travel Writers in China*; Clifford, 'A Truthful Impression of the Country'; Kuehn and Kerr, *A Century of Travels in China*; Chang, *British Travel Writing from China, 1798–1901*. Chinese smells in Japanese travel writing deserve careful attention in a separate study. For relevant literature, see Fogel, *The Literature of Travel in the Japanese Rediscovery of China, 1862–1945*; Chang, 'Health and Hygiene in Late Qing China as Seen through the Eyes of Japanese Travelers'.

[7] Cameron, *Barbarians and Mandarins*, 364; quoted in Dupée, *British Travel Writers in China*, 41. For a brief account of the thriving Victorian literary production on China, see Forman, *China and the Victorian Imagination*, 8.

[8] Within the limited scope of this chapter, I only focus on English-language publications. I use 'Western' travellers/authors as an umbrella term for the sake of convenience, though the majority of the authors discussed here are British (with a few French, German, American, and Australian). A small portion of my material is not strictly travel literature, but popular books about China.

It is certainly not my goal to chronicle a social history of Chinese stench by accepting these travel accounts as 'truthful'. They undoubtedly belong to, in Edward Said's words, 'a system of knowledge about the Orient, an accepted grid for filtering through the Orient into Western consciousness'.[9] In other words, this type of writing unmistakably conveys the tenor of high imperialism and colonialism as well as a package of associated sentiments, an overall sense of self-righteousness in undertaking the self-styled civilizing mission. I do not disagree with this overarching narrative, yet I emphasize that there did not exist a pre-defined orientalist structure of feeling at disposal for experiencing China; instead it was an unfolding process of physical and psychical encounters with the Orient that bred new sensibilities of racializing olfactory modernity.[10]

The methodological significance of smell – by extension, visceral sensations – warrants special attention as it indicates how neurons and molecules actively participated in meaning-making. There might be an assertive 'imperial eye' empowered by the rational mind to make 'informed' judgment on the Other, but when it comes to the 'imperial nose' there was a large zone of ambivalence. Chinese malodours under the Victorian travellers' noses were the strangers incarnate. They were uninvited, intrusive, at odds with the ocularcentric order of rationality, and yet they were not simply the enemy because they were intimately familiar, prevalent in the travellers' own past and present, as well as their own bodies. Therefore, as I will demonstrate, it was the travellers' coping strategy to invent a discourse of contamination to transform the uneasy stranger into a definitive Other. By exercising what may be termed 'power somatic',[11] they desired to redefine olfactory criteria, remould olfactory sensibilities, and bring them into the consciousness of both

[9] Said, *Orientalism*, 6.
[10] Hence this study joins some scholarly efforts to reposition orientalism not only by extending it to China, but also by highlighting China's role as a civilizational Other. See Hayot, *The Hypothetical Mandarin*, 8–11; Forman, *China and the Victorian Imagination*, 6–7.
[11] Said argues that orientalism is produced and exists in an uneven exchange with various kinds of power, including what he calls power political, power intellectual, power cultural, and power moral. See Said, *Orientalism*, 12. 'Power somatic' is defined along the same lines.

their home audience and the Chinese. This project of retraining the neurons transpired to be powerful in terms of fuelling the humiliation narrative in the long arc of modern Chinese history. Alongside the intellectual, political, and military dimensions, I emphasize that the bodily and the sensate played a unique role in this history.

This chapter aims to illuminate these dynamics, guided by the following questions: what were the specific Chinese odours that rattled the travellers' nerves and in what ways did they represent the stranger to modernity? What were the particular strategies of producing the contamination rhetoric? How did the underlying mechanisms work and how did the 'China stinks' discourse permeate the Chinese *imaginaire* of modernity, paving the way for the olfactory revolution?

'SICKENING MIASMA OF POISONOUS CHINESE STENCH'

Given the paucity of olfactory vocabulary, when Constance Gordon-Cumming (1837–1924), a keen-scented Scottish writer and painter, came up with the intensely evocative phrase 'sickening miasma of poisonous Chinese stench',[12] the reader can sense a high dose of anxiety and abhorrence. Echoing Melanie Kiechle's premise that 'moments when people felt obligated to translate their olfactory experience into words deserve careful attention',[13] I likewise feel an urge to document the rich odoriferous lexicon and tropes that saturate the books under scrutiny. Upon close inspection, a few types of stench recur most frequently, which stand for the quintessential strangers to modern Western sensibilities.[14]

REEKING ENVIRONS

Most Victorian travellers toured the four regions where the treaty ports were located: north China, the lower Yangtze delta, the middle and

---

[12] Gordon-Cumming, *Wanderings in China*, 247.   [13] Kiechle, *Smell Detectives*, 8.

[14] There is no denying that the travel literature also features delightful aromas of nature, gardens, tea, and other things Chinese, but overall stench dominates their perception of China. Nicholas Clifford's research on British and American travel writing in China (from 1880 to 1949) coincides with my observation. See Clifford, *'A Truthful Impression of the Country'*, 46–50.

upper Yangtze river, and the south coast. To them China did not smell fundamentally different from region to region, and the particularly offensive atmospheric odours stemmed from ill-paved streets and malfunctioning sewers, two paramount targets in modern sanitation campaigns.

The imagery of an archetypal Chinese city, teeming with narrow, winding streets and ripe with all-pervasive malodours, recurs time and again in the travel literature of the time. The old town of Yantai (Chefoo) in 1901 was a 'reeking mess': the 'narrow and crooked streets' thronged with people, donkeys, and mules; the pestilential ditches; and 'indescribable' filth.[15] Demarcated from the foreign settlements only by a moat, the walled city of Shanghai of the 1880s, where 'ancient China sleeps on', was criss-crossed by narrow streets, 'poorly lighted, ill-drained and ill-scavenged', 'with evil smells and sights innumerable'.[16] Guangzhou (Canton) presented to its foreign observers around 1900 a 'labyrinth of some 600 evil-smelling, dimly lighted, stone-flagged streets, packed with a seething mass of humanity'.[17] Beside generic portraits, some authors ventured to explain the 'technology' of stench. British merchant Archibald Little (1838–1908) detailed the topography of Beijing's 'evil-smelling' streets:

the roadways are nothing but the natural soil dug out from the sides and heaped up in the centre with the added garbage. This central causeway, with its surface of hill and dale, is bounded by two lines of stagnant foul-smelling swamp which intervenes between it and the narrow side walks that run under the eaves of the gaudily decorated shops or alongside the endless walks of the residential parks and temple grounds which occupy so much of the city's space.[18]

---

[15] Brown, *New Forces in Old China*, 49. The author was an influential American clergyman and missionary.
[16] Moule, *New China and Old*, 90. The author was an English missionary who lived in Shanghai from 1882 to 1894.
[17] Wright and Cartwright, *Twentieth Century Impressions of Hong Kong, Shanghai and Other Treaty Ports of China*, 784.
[18] Little, *Gleanings from Fifty Years in China*, 82. His wife mentioned 'the evil-smelling streets of Peking' in her book: Little, *Round about My Peking Garden*, 40.

Different street-paving techniques in Guangzhou, around 1892, seem to have had the same capacity to produce stench. According to the English missionary T. M. Morris, the streets were paved with 'transverse slabs of stone, not closely joined, and beneath flows or stagnates the drain'. This design kept the pavement comparatively clean, while allowing 'the disgusting odours which rise from the festering filth beneath to assail the nose of every passer-by'.[19]

In addition to the streets, sewers and rivers drew equally abundant attention. Clarke Abel (1780–1826), the chief medical officer on Lord Amherst's embassy to China in 1816–1817, noted in his journal an arche-typical fetid river in Tongzhou, one that was charged with 'all kinds of effluvia produced by the uncleanly habits of a large population living on the water, and the decomposing vegetable and animal matter ejected from the boats'.[20] Countless rivers, ditches, and ponds of its kind (the cesspool in the Introduction being one of them) were to take to the stage in the travel writings. While 'stagnant and foul-smelling canals' formed part of an impressionist portrait of Tianjin,[21] English missionary William Cornaby's (1861–1921) olfactory sketch of Hankou featured 'dark pond waters' doing their best 'to break the record for unwholesome stench'.[22] Concerns with public health buttressed by medical theory often accom-panied plain depictions, imbuing their texts with an air of authority, as exemplified by James Ball (1847–1919):

> The simple drainage systems in vogue in Chinese cities are periodically flushed by nature ... But their work is stultified to a large extent by the crass ignorance of all sanitary matters by the Chinese and by their utter indifference to the offensive odours which give warning of the dangers to life and health around them ... so when a period of draught [sic] ensues, the inhabitants naturally suffer from their neglect of the filth which surrounds them and the effluvia therefrom, whose subtle essence perme-ates the whole atmosphere which they breathe. Given such conditions,

[19] Morris, *A Winter in North China*, 200.
[20] Abel, *Narrative of a Journey in the Interior of China*, 128.
[21] Bodde, *Peking Diary, a Year of Revolution*, 250.
[22] Cornaby, *Rambles in Central China*, 46.

the plague, if once introduced, runs a wild riot in its congenial surroundings ...[23]

Their particular sensitivities towards cityscape, street paving, and sewerage derived from nineteenth-century discourses and practices of hygienic modernity in the West. A correlation between stench, poor sanitation, and disease was a prevailing belief. Grand city renovation projects were gradually transforming European metropolises from over-crowded medieval towns into well-paved, drained, and deodorized modern cities. The construction of underground drainage systems miti-gated the stench from open sewers (I shall return to this topic in more detail in Chapter 3). Malodour, therefore, was turned into 'the sinister Other of everything modernity stood for: of order, predictability, control and self-control'.[24]

However, I argue, Chinese stenches in these odorous dramas were not only the Other, but also a part of the Self. On the one hand, as the American sociology professor Edward Ross (1866–1951) put it, 'China is the European Middle Ages made visible.'[25] The temporal dimension of atmospheric malodour must have been embedded in the travellers' unconscious, since they could not disavow their own miasmic medieval history. On the other hand, they could not deny the fact that few, if any, of the odours were exclusively Chinese. Industrializing Europe of the nineteenth century stank, too. In Britain a sanitary crisis was striking its cities and towns in the first half of the century. Graphic depictions of appalling squalor and reek abound in such influential texts as Edwin Chadwick's *Report on the Sanitary Condition of the Labouring Population of Great Britain* (1843) and Friedrich Engels's *The Condition of the Working-Class in England in 1844*. In a 'most horrible spot' in Manchester's working-class district, as Engels writes, the atmosphere was poisoned by the effluvia from 'masses of refuse, offal and sickening filth' and 'the smoke of a dozen tall factory chimneys'. He laments that 'this race [who lives there] must really have reached the lowest stage of humanity'.[26]

---

[23] Ball, *Things Chinese*, 525. The author was a linguist and scholar, born into an American Scottish family in Canton.

[24] Bauman, 'The Sweet Scent of Decomposition', 25.   [25] Ross, *The Changing Chinese*, 3.

[26] Engels, *The Condition of the Working-Class in England in 1844*, 60.

Victorian London was notorious for its foulness originating from the River Thames and numerous 'filthy objects, horse and cattle dung ... refuse from hospitals ... fishmongers' and fishmarket washings and offal; slaughterhouse offal ... refuse from chemical works, gas works, dye works ... dead rats, dead dogs and cats, and sad to say, dead babies'.[27] The climax was the Great Stink of 1858, when unprecedented amounts of foul stench accumulated on the banks of the Thames in the hottest months of the year.[28]

An obvious explanation for the travellers' act of othering Chinese stenches is what Mary Pratt calls 'sheerest hypocrisy', a quality she detects in the capitalist vanguard's nineteenth-century travel writing about South America. As she argues, 'neglect became the touchstone of a negative aesthetic that legitimated European interventionism'.[29] A more nuanced facet, I posit, is concerned with the psychological mechanism of being unable to disavow their own heritage and 'ownership' of malodour; the corrective measure was thus to declare that China stinks. A subtle hint of this mental formation is betrayed by the affinity of language used in the China travelogues and the Victorian sanitary literature. In this sense, smell is the true stranger, a member of 'the family of *undecidables*' that disregards the intellectually demarcated boundary between Self and Other.

UNWASHED PEOPLE

Introducing Chinese theatre to his Western readership, James Ball spelled out not only its artistic features, but also the multisensory theatre-going experience. Amidst 'the indescribable effect of the Chinese music' and 'the heat of the crowded building', 'the disagreeable odour from the perspiring and unwashed masses' rose to the nose, causing an inevitable headache – 'the Westerner's reward for the patient sitting out of a Chinese play'.[30] The body odour of the Chinese is another olfactory stereotype recurring in the travelogues. Bathing habits, diet, clothing, and a lack of hygiene products were arguably the root causes.

[27] Picard, *Victorian London*, 5.   [28] Halliday, *The Great Stink of London*.
[29] Pratt, *Imperial Eyes*, 145–50. The two quotations are from 148, 146.
[30] Ball, *Things Chinese*, 705.

The attendants of two officials who met the Amherst embassy, according to Clarke Abel, 'threw off a most disagreeable odour, arising in some measure from their use of garlic and asafoetida, but more from their want of cleanliness'.[31] This portrait sheds light on an initial olfactory image-making of Chinese people in the nineteenth-century Western discourse. At the heart is the highly charged issue of cleanliness, intimately interlocked with bodily configuration of modernity and the civilizing process, as Norbert Elias famously delineates.[32] Equipped with this sensibility, Abel remarked that baths were used as a remedy in China, rather than as a means of cleanliness.[33] Seven decades later, in the 1880s, the English missionary Edwin Dukes still regarded it as a thoroughly 'Oriental' predisposition that washing was not 'one of the necessary duties of life'.[34]

A related matter concerns the alleged lack of hygiene products in China, whilst industrial capitalism was manufacturing and selling such items eagerly to the global market. Speaking of the Chinese ignorance of soap, American missionary Arthur Smith (1845–1932) remarked satirically that the motto 'cheaper than dirt' could never be made intelligible even if the soap dealer put it in the window of a Chinese house; conversely, the Chinese regarded foreigners as 'soap-wasters'.[35] The British artist Thomas Liddell (1860–1925) sighed with relief on finishing his work in Shanghai's native city in 1907, being freed from the 'very bad' smells and the 'most loathsome creatures' assembling around him each day. Before starting for the native city, he sprinkled himself 'plentifully with Keating's Powder', a product of the chemical industry of Victorian Britain.[36] Without the 'civilized' habit of bathing and 'advanced' hygiene items, the Chinese population smelled horrendous to the travellers, who were tormented by a 'foul-mouthed coolie',[37] the 'donkey-boys' who 'were abominably dirty' and 'reeked of garlic',[38] the Chinese interpreters who

---

[31] Abel, *Narrative of a Journey in the Interior of China*, 70.   [32] Elias, *The Civilizing Process*.

[33] Abel, *Narrative of a Journey in the Interior of China*, 160.

[34] Dukes, *Everyday Life in China*, 3.   [35] Smith, *Chinese Characteristics*, 24.

[36] Liddell, *China, Its Marvel and Mystery*, 45. An 1887 advertisement for Keating's Insect Powder is available in the Evanion Collection at the British Library (Evan.6885).

[37] Cornaby, *A String of Chinese Peach-Stones*, 56.

[38] Birch, *Travels in North and Central China*, 37.

brought 'bad odour' to their employers,[39] and the 'decrepit and decaying beggars' who rendered the country 'foul and loathsome and terrible'.[40]

To what extent are these sensational depictions true to life? China actually has a sophisticated bathing tradition dating back to ancient times.[41] One is reminded of Qu Yuan's 屈原 (343–278 BC) elegant poem: 'Bathe in orchid broth, purify yourself with fragrances, and richly adorn your coloured clothes with ginger petals (浴蘭湯兮沐芳，華採衣兮若英).'[42] Fragrant beauties and the dazzling variety of hygiene items in *Red Chamber* also disprove the faithfulness of the above picture. It is fair to say that the body odours documented by the Victorian travellers were more class-specific than racially determined. Zhang Deyi 張德彝 (1847–1918), a member of the Qing diplomatic missions to Europe, made an apt comment. On his 1871 mission to France, when witnessing that 'lower-class people' (*xiadeng ren* 下等人) did not wash, he remarked, 'The foreigners who ridiculed the uncleanliness of the Chinese never reflected deeply on the situation of their own countries, did they?'[43]

Apart from hypocrisy, a similar tension between Self and Other was involved. The well-educated travellers were undoubtedly conscious of the European history of bodily emanations as a 'joyous matter' that permeated poetry, fables, and fine arts in early modern times.[44] Moreover, medieval Europeans considered water a threat, and only in the late eighteenth century was bathing slowly established amongst the elite.[45] More ironically, despite the self-styled high standards of hygiene, Caucasians did not smell agreeable to the Chinese nose at the time, a deep-rooted stereotype documented even in the same corpus of travel writing.[46] T. M. Morris noted, 'strange to say, the Chinese declare that

---

[39] Little, *Gleanings from Fifty Years in China*, 290.   [40] Moule, *New China and Old*, 124.

[41] Zhang, 'Muyu yu weisheng'.

[42] Qu Yuan, *Chuci*, 'Jiuge/Yunzhongjun'. This is Michael Schimmelpfennig's translation (based on his reading of Wang Yi's commentary). I'm grateful for his kind permission.

[43] Zhang, 'Suishi Faguo ji', 421.

[44] Muchembled, *Smells*, Chapter 3. Muchembled's focus is on sixteenth-century France, which, as he claims (at 34), showed no signs of anal or sexual repression.

[45] Vigarello, *Concepts of Cleanliness*, 7–20.

[46] Reinders, *Borrowed Gods and Foreign Bodies*, 170–1. A detailed account by a contemporary can be found in Crow, *400 Million Customers*, 137–48. Also see Soothill, *A Passport to China*, 64.

one reason for their dislike of us is that they do not like the smell of us –
we smell like sheep'.[47] This olfactory cliché also appeared in an
1896 travel book: a Chinese washerwoman was said to have given up
her well-paid job at a foreigner's house because 'the clothes smelt so
strongly of mutton'.[48] A Chinese gentleman's opinion was more
forthright:

> You cannot civilize these foreign devils. They are beyond redemption.
> They will live for weeks and months without touching a mouthful of rice,
> but they eat the flesh of bullocks and sheep in enormous quantities. That
> is why they smell so badly; they smell like sheep themselves. Every day they
> take a bath to rid themselves of their disagreeable odours, but they do not
> succeed. Nor do they eat their meat cooked in small pieces. It is carried
> into the room in large chunks, often half raw, and they cut and slash and
> tear it apart. They eat with knives and prongs. It makes a civilized being
> perfectly nervous.[49]

Despite their anecdotal nature, these accounts show that the travel
writers were conscious of how they smelled under the Chinese nose. In
other words, they were not unaware of the aporia when it came to the
private matter of body odour, and yet ambivalence was deeply unsettling.
One tactic was to transform the stranger into a racialized other, even an
object. The *Times* correspondent George Cooke (1814–1865) offered an
example to illustrate the racial discourse of cleanliness. As he found the
odour of some Chinese soldiers in 1850s Shanghai 'not fragrant', he
commented, 'If one of these ragged ruffians would come to London and
submit to be washed, Mrs. Leo Hunter would ask lords and ladies to meet
him, and present him to her guests as "a mandarin from China".'[50]

The desire to wash, deodorize, and display them was a desire to
objectify them and to claim the subjectivity of the self. The late nineteenth century did witness a trend of displaying African people in World
Fairs.[51] Indeed, two Chinese youngsters were 'exhibited' in 1845 at a

---

[47] Morris, *A Winter in North China*, 47.
[48] Armstrong, *In a Mule Litter to the Tomb of Confucius*, 6.
[49] It is a letter from the gentleman quoted by Arthur Brown. See Brown, *New Forces in Old China*, 88.
[50] Cooke, *China*, 214 (emphasis mine). [51] Qureshi, *Peoples on Parade*.

London gallery of Chinese art. Known as A-shing and A-yow, they were born in Canton and were brought to Liverpool by a captain, who had intended to educate them in England for the benefit of himself trading with the Chinese. Arranged by Mr Langdon, the Lessee of the Chinese Collection, their presence in the art gallery was announced as 'a very interesting arrival'.[52] From the image in the *Illustrated London News* (Figure 2.1), we can assume that they had been 'washed' before being displayed. By washing away the avowedly putrid body odour, they were converted from the ambivalent stranger to an unambiguous Other for the pleasure of the rational, distanced sight. As a transcorporeal, proximity sense, olfaction is too intimate and hence too treacherous for the modern (Western) self. This biological mechanism can be seen as the foundation of sensorial racism, running throughout many chapters of colonial history, most notably the history of slavery.[53]

PECULIAR-SMELLING FOOD

'An irresistible topic for travel writers', food generated abundant attention from Victorian travellers, and their accounts can be read, in Jeffery Dupée's words, 'as culinary exotica, as hygienic horror story, as mystery meal, as monotonous gruel'.[54] Whereas Clarke Abel characterized the smell arising from numerous cook-shops on a Tongzhou street as 'peculiar odours',[55] Edwin Dukes depicted food sold at street eating stalls in Xiamen as 'odds and ends of edibles that are nameless to us ... tasting queer and smelling worse'.[56] Dupée thus coins the term 'culinary melodrama', arguing that each author seemed 'trapped within a literary process of his own making'.[57] If compared with the cosmopolitan mentality of twenty-first-century round-the-world travellers, eager to embrace 'mobility, tolerance and openness to difference',[58] Victorian travellers' gustatory disposition was symptomatic of an impulse to discriminate. The culinary regime

[52] 'Chinese Youths', *Illustrated London News* 7, no. 184 (8 November 1845), 289–90.
[53] Kettler, *The Smell of Slavery*.
[54] Dupée, *British Travel Writers in China*, 259. For another study on the subject, see Forman, 'Eating out East'.
[55] Abel, *Narrative of a Journey in the Interior of China*, 96.
[56] Dukes, *Everyday Life in China*, 27.   [57] Dupée, *British Travel Writers in China*, 262.
[58] Molz, 'Cosmopolitan Bodies', 5.

Figure 2.1 'A-Shing and A-Yow at the Chinese Collection', *Illustrated London News* 7, no. 184 (8 November 1845), 289.

turned out to be yet another battlefield for Self, Other, and the stranger. Amongst a vast variety of 'peculiar' Chinese foodstuffs, dried fish and garlic stand out as the most sensational of culinary melodramas.

With a distinctive smell detestable to the average foreign palate, dried fish can be safely positioned as an Other. The British surgeon Frederick

Treves (1853–1923) compared dried-fish shops in Guangzhou to 'depots for discarded museum specimens' and the stench arising from them was 'beyond words'.[59] An influential travel handbook introduced the fishing port of Ningbo with a warning of 'the pervasive odor of drying cuttle-fish' wafting in 'nearly every breeze that blows over the town' each spring.[60] French writer Abel Bonnard (1883–1968), travelling in Macau, discerned the 'acrid smell of dried fish' along the quay where fishermen lived.[61] German photographer Hedda Morrison (1908–1991) captured the visual details of fish-drying and salting fields and seafood shops in Hong Kong, eliciting an unnameable heavy pungent smell in the viewer's nostrils (Figure 2.2).[62]

This conclusive Other, therefore, was often subjected to discipline and control. In her study of a dried-fish-related dispute in California, Connie Y. Chiang demonstrates the symbolic power of the particular odour in connection with the negative stereotyping of the Chinese. Beginning in the 1890s, white residents and tourists in Monterey condemned Chinese fishermen for the 'unpleasant smells' emitted from their squid-drying fields and ultimately forced the Chinese out. Intertwined with existing discourses of racial difference (i.e. the Chinese being inherently repugnant), subjectively perceived offensive smells became the legitimate accused in the institutionalized execution of power.[63]

Compared to dried fish, garlic is a less definitive Other than an undecidable stranger. Despite its prominent negative image in English history, regularly taken as a sign of poverty and rusticity, garlic is a complex character. As Mark Jenner's study shows, it symbolized simple and authentic society in the sixteenth and early seventeenth centuries, and its French associations made it attractive to sections of eighteenth-century polite society. It was believed to have therapeutic functions, and it was being cultivated and used throughout the early modern period.[64]

[59] Treves, *The Other Side of the Lantern*, 275; quoted in Dupée, *British Travel Writers in China*, 262.
[60] Crow, *The Travelers' Handbook for China (Including Hong Kong)*, 140.
[61] Bonnard, *In China, 1920–1921*, 311.   [62] Stokes and Morrison, *Hong Kong as It Was*.
[63] Chiang, 'Monterey-by-the-Smell', 185.
[64] Jenner, 'Civilization and Deodorization?', 138–43.

Figure 2.2 A dried-fish shop in Hong Kong, 1946–1947. Photograph by Hedda Morrison, 28 × 36 cm. Courtesy of Harvard-Yenching Library, the Hedda Morrison photograph collection.

Yet when it came to Chinese garlic, Western travellers often exhibited the symptom of alliumphobia. The Irish nurse Emily Daly's three children were fond of Chinese dumplings, but after their gourmet dumpling meal, she 'did not want to see or smell them, as the odour of garlic did not appeal to me'.[65] In addition to vegetable oil, Scottish adventurer Isabella Bird-Bishop's (1831–1904) chief objection to Chinese food was 'the prevalent flavour of garlic': it was seldom possible to be 'out of their odour' as onions, garlic, leeks, scallions, and chives were consumed

[65] Daly, *An Irishwoman in China*, 90.

enthusiastically by rich and poor in Sichuan.[66] And yet, ironically, Scotland (Wales and Ireland as well) was frequently associated with garlic eating in English satires to denigrate other national groups.[67] In fact, to these travel writers the reek of garlic was neither Self nor Other, but the stranger. It marked social, national, and racial distinctions which fluid in the matrix of global mobility. To abate the unease of being caught in ambivalence, they aligned themselves with 'an image of sensibility, and therefore higher social status', through 'displays of nervous refinement'.[68] Garlicky scent of Chinese origin was thus transformed into the Other.

Apart from putrid fish and garlic, the culinary melodramas were replete with larger-than-life characters. William C. Hunter (1812–1891), an American merchant, noted the 'overpowering' smell of a Chinese snack: 'a compound of sour buffalo milk, baked in the sun, under whose influence it is allowed to remain until it becomes filled with insects, yet, the greener and more lively it is, with the more relish is it eaten'.[69] An equally strange dish was featured in an 1871 article in the Shanghai-based illustrated newspaper *Puck*: a compound of 'treacle, Chinese fat, lamp oil, ditch water, chopped garlic, and flour' exuding a 'strange smell' found in a cook-house with 'lots of noise and sundry conflicting aromas'.[70] Present-day scientists may consider these portrayals a symptom of 'food neophobia' (anxiety over trying new food). As the psychologist Robert Frank contends, 'neophobia is a matter of attitude, not chemistry'.[71]

Neophobic attitudes can be observed in Chinese travel literature of the same period. Drawing on Chinese olfactory and gustatory lexicon,[72] Zhang Deyi's occidentalist culinary melodramas are equally sensational. Meals served in the British-run cruise liner (beef and mutton in large

[66] Bird-Bishop, *The Yangtze Valley and Beyond*, vol. 2, 23–4.
[67] Jenner, 'Civilization and Deodorization?', 139.
[68] Tullett, *Smells in Eighteenth-Century England*, 194.   [69] Hunter, *Bits of Old China*, 39.
[70] Dyce, *Personal Reminiscences of Thirty Years' Residence in the Model Settlement Shanghai, 1870–1900*, 229.
[71] Quoted in Fox, 'The Nose Knows', 22.
[72] For a discussion of the Chinese perception of Western food, see Swislocki, *Culinary Nostalgia*, 114–15.

chunks, roasted chicken and duck, and fish and prawn) did not please his palate, as they were 'rank' (*xing* 腥), spicy, or sour, causing him to 'vomit upon smelling them' (*yi xiu ji tu* 一嗅即吐).[73] The food he consumed in San Francisco was 'rank and rancid' (*xingsao* 腥臊) and a mutton dish served in London was 'sour and gamy' (*suanshan* 酸膻).[74] The flavour of a French soup was 'rank and spicy' (*ji xing qie la* 既腥且 辣), and fried soybeans cooked in the Chinese method tasted 'salty and rank' (*xian xing* 鹹腥) owing to 'the use of butter'.[75]

As Roland Barthes writes, the notion of food is 'a system of communication, a body of image, a protocol of usages, situations, and behavior'.[76] Simply put, it signifies; behind a particular foodstuff hides a 'veritable collective imagination'.[77] By mutual othering, both the Western and Chinese travellers were striving for their own identity, their own definition of sensibility and order.

THE SICKLY SWEET FUMES

The nineteenth century saw the ascendancy of 'evil-smelling' opium as a sensorial symbol of China, replacing the delicate taste of tea, and the visual and tactile indulgence of silk and porcelain. The epoch-making Opium Wars (1839–1842, 1856–1860) and their consequences transformed the drug into a fraught imagery, a metonym of China's sickness, moral degeneration, and shame. Under the Victorian traveller's gaze, through their nostrils, opium had to be projected as an unequivocal Other. Through a passage, at the 'native end' of a steamer sailing on the mid-Yangtze river, 'our nostrils are assured that the *baneful* drug is in full use'. Greeting the missionary writer's senses was a typical scene of opium-smoking (as illustrated by a woodcut picture, Figure 2.3): 'Half the passengers in the dimly-lit and crowded 'tween-deck space are reclining beside their little lamps inhaling the fumes of the vaporised dark brown *abomination*, which, you know, looks and feels like rather pliable gutta-percha.'[78]

---

[73] Zhang, 'Hanghai shuqi', 450.   [74] Zhang, 'Ou Mei huanyou ji', 643, 722.
[75] Zhang, 'Suishi Faguo ji', 447, 429.
[76] Barthes, 'Toward a Psychosociology of Contemporary Food Consumption', 50.
[77] Ibid., 49.   [78] Cornaby, *Rambles in Central China*, 81 (emphasis mine).

Figure 2.3 'Opium Smokers', an illustration in Cornaby, *Rambles in Central China*, 81.

The olfactory faculty seemed to be the most unforbearing of the senses with the immorality of opium, probably because of its judgemental personality and the immediacy of odours. Edwin Dukes remarked on the inescapability of opium in Chinese inns, 'a great nuisance ... for the smell of the fumes is very *vile* and *sickening*.'[79] Speaking of hiring chair-bearers, he wrote, 'one is obliged to look at them – and shall I say, smell them? – to calculate whether they *shek-in* (eat smoke)'.[80] Engaging the five senses as a moral judge, Alicia Little found a 'weird, wicked' kind of music going on all night long, 'quite in character with the general look of the place and the *sweet sickly* opium smell' hanging in the air of the small town in Sichuan.[81] The next morning, as they escaped from 'the filth of the town', they were in the 'prosperous-looking, healthy poppy-fields again':

---

[79] Dukes, *Everyday Life in China*, 164 (emphasis mine).   [80] Ibid., 165.
[81] Little, *Intimate China*, 70 (emphasis mine).

Most were white, a delicate, fair, frail blossom; others were white, with fringed petals edged with pink; others altogether pink, or mauve, or scarlet, or scarlet-and-black, or, perhaps best of all, crimson, which, when looked up at on a bank standing out against the brilliantly blue sky, made our eyes quite ache with colour-pleasure.[82]

Vis-à-vis the heavenly beauty that enchanted the eyes, the evil scent registered by the nose evoked a sensation that may aptly be called 'the uncanny'. A canonical Freudian concept, the uncanny (*umheimlich*, unhomely) is 'that species of the frightening that goes back to what was once well known and had long been familiar'.[83] Vital to the 'unhomely' frightening effect is the 'homely' element that 'has been repressed and now returns'.[84] Freud invokes smell to illuminate how the uncanny effect arises when one is faced with 'the reality of something that we have until now considered imaginary'. It is a story about a young couple who move into a flat in which there is a table with crocodiles carved in the wood. Towards evening, the flat is regularly pervaded by 'an unbearable and highly characteristic smell', producing an 'extraordinarily uncanny' effect because the palpable olfactory sensation (among others) renders *real* the imaginary fantasy about the ghostly crocodiles.[85] The pervasive odour of opium was uncanny to the travellers in a similar vein. Being haunted by its 'evil' smell everywhere in China rendered real their imagination of the fraught icon. More importantly, they were unable to disavow their own 'homely' association with this addictive drug. In short, the scent of opium was not an unambiguous enemy; it was a stranger, the ambivalent figure that disturbs the boundary.

It has been an overfamiliar story how opium figured centrally in redressing the trade imbalance between China and Britain, eventually leading to Britain's gunboat diplomacy which wrecked the Qing empire bit by bit. From Lord Macartney's 1793 comment on 'the opium of Bengal' as a promising commodity for the future of Sino-British trade, to the milestone of 1834 when the end of the East India Company's exclusive trading rights in China sparked soaring opium smuggling conducted by private British traders, to the eventual legalization of opium imports after

---

[82] Ibid., 70–1.   [83] Freud, 'The Uncanny', 124.   [84] Ibid., 148.   [85] Ibid., 150–1.

the Second Opium War, Britain's role in China's opium epidemic is undisputable.[86] The authors of the travel literature were often first-hand witnesses to this 'sin' because many of them had to ride on opium-freighting ships to go to China.[87] When George Cooke arrived in Shanghai by boat in 1857, he was greeted in a receiving ship anchored in the mouth of the Yangtze. Previously a floating garrison, this ship named *Emily Jane* was not likely to test her guns any more 'for the mandarin junks are no longer her enemies'; instead 'she is a very *wicked* Emily Jane, for she is crammed with opium, and the odour of the drug is strong in her spacious cabins'.[88] Being a 'total-abstinence-from-opium advocate', Cooke's animosity was nonetheless calmed, as he wrote half-jokingly, by 'some well-cooled sauterne [*sic*], a joint of capital Shanghai mutton, and a successfully concocted rice pudding'.[89] Yet not every Englishman's moral sense could so readily yield to sensual delectation, and there was no shortage of critique from church leaders in England, some of whom even called the opium trade a 'national sin'.[90] Opium induced the strongest anxiety and moral quandary among the missionaries working in China:

> You don't know how this horrible vice meets us day by day, how it points the sarcasm and insults levelled at the foreigner, and how it dishonours the name of Christ in disgracing the Christianity we profess as our national faith.[91]

Therefore, under their noses the fumes of opium ought to smell baneful, vile, sickly, wicked, and abominable. I argue that it was neither opium's inherent olfactory quality nor the common association of moral failings with stench that generated the moralized discourse imposed upon opium in China. Rather, it was out of the defence mechanism to battle against the disturbing sensation of the uncanny that made opium reek of the devil. In fact, in its heyday, when opium was a symbol of taste relished by the privileged classes in China, it smelled fragrant:

> Sharpen wood into a hollow pipe,
> Give it a copper head and tail,

---

[86] Zheng, *The Social Life of Opium in China*, 53, 92–3, 105–8.   [87] Ibid., 106.
[88] Cooke, *China*, 94 (emphasis mine).   [89] Ibid., 94–5.
[90] Zheng, *The Social Life of Opium in China*, 94–5.   [91] Dukes, *Everyday Life in China*, 164.

Stuff the eye with bamboo shavings,
Watch the cloud ascend from nostril.
Inhale and exhale, *fragrance* rises,
Ambience deepens and thickens
When it is stagnant, it is really as if
Mountains and clouds emerge in distant sea.[92]

Written by the future Emperor Daoguang 道光 (1782–1850) at the dawn of the nineteenth century, the sensuality of opium in this poem was the polar opposite of the stigmatized imagery it acquired in the years to come. No demonized odour was attributed to it in the official account of the 1793 Macartney embassy, either. As its author observed, Manchu officials 'employed part of their intervals of leisure in smoking tobacco mixed with odorous substances, and sometimes a little opium'.[93]

It is evident that opium is not intrinsically evil-smelling. Behind the ostensibly personal perception of opium's scent lay a convoluted web of sociopolitical, moral, and psychical operations. The same holds true for the collective olfactory imagination of Chinese cities, people, and food, all of which 'reek with meaning'.[94] Paramount to the meaning-making impulses of our travel writers was a desire to alleviate the gnawing sensations of the uncanny, the strange, and the ambivalent stirred up by encountering China, including her smells. The next two sections survey an array of techniques designed by the travellers, consciously or otherwise, to create a dichotomy between Self and Other in order to forestall contamination by the Other. Power somatic derived from representation and rationalization.

MODES OF REPRESENTATION

The Foucauldian alliance of power and knowledge has been well established. Given there was no means of capturing actual smells, the

---

[92] Zheng, *The Social Life of Opium in China*, 57, emphasis added. Zheng's book chronicles the trajectory of opium's changing status, from a luxurious aphrodisiac in the mid-Ming court, to a tasteful indulgence appreciated by scholars and officials in the mid-Qing, to common people's addictive drug in the nineteenth century.

[93] Staunton, *Authentic Account of an Embassy*, vol. 2, 70. Quoted in Zheng, *The Social Life of Opium in China*, 53.

[94] Stoller, *The Taste of Ethnographic Things*, 25.

vehicle in which the travellers produced olfactory knowledge was through the power of the pen. Various modes of representation can be identified in their texts that collectively forged the 'China stinks' master narrative. A salient expressive mode is *hyperbole*. A Shakespearean phrase, 'the rankest compound of villainous smell that ever offended nostril', quoted by William Cornaby to depict the air of Hankou,[95] sums up the travellers' dexterity with the art of exaggeration. A vital device in the English rhetorical tradition, hyperbole deals not simply with the description of experience, but with the understanding and evaluation of it; that is, 'the subjective importance to oneself'.[96] Thus hyperbole has an affective component and a persuasive or even manipulative aspect, influencing the audience's opinions via the emotions aroused.[97] Through hyperbole the travel writers sensationalized their perception of Chinese malodour, amplified its 'subjective importance' to themselves, and thus provided the reader with vicarious sensory thrills. Amongst the profuse hyperbolic expressions, many of which are previously cited, one particular trope duplicates itself within this corpus of literature time and again.

On an expedition to the east coast of China in 1860, British Army officer Charles Gordon (1821–1899) was walking down the 'narrow, tortuous streets' of Guangzhou when he noticed that the odours were 'different in nature from all other stenches we had ever previously perceived' and '*all different* from each other, and from all others'. Simply put, the odours were 'purely and thoroughly Chinese'.[98] A related hyperbolic rhetoric appears in Edwin Dukes's 1885 writing: 'How the poor live is a question that puzzles philanthropists at home, but how the Chinaman manages to survive the fetid smells that meet his olfactories at *every* turn in town and village, is a question that the traveller asks himself *each* hour of the day.'[99] By performing the art of hyperbole, both authors amplified the spatial and temporal ubiquity of Chinese malodours, their multifariousness and uniqueness. The British railway engineer John Grant Birch (1847–1900) deployed the same expressive

---

[95] Cornaby, *A String of Chinese Peach-Stones*, 338.   [96] Claridge, *Hyperbole in English*, 1.
[97] Ibid., Chapter 7.
[98] Gordon, *China from a Medical Point of View in 1860 and 1861*, 70 (emphasis mine).
[99] Dukes, *Everyday Life in China*, 128 (emphasis mine).

mode: walking along the street approaching Chengdu in 1899, he was 'oppressed by an all-pervading stink with which at *every* few steps a *various* odour was united'.[100] In short, we may return to the epigraph to this chapter: in China, 'there are seventy-five smells one can identify and twenty-five unknown ones'.[101]

Paradoxically, the 'thoroughly Chinese' stenches were not entirely unique. India's odours were equally extraordinary under British travel writers' hyperbolic pen. 'Even before they landed, a whiff of India was borne out to them on the breeze', according to Margaret MacMillan. It was 'un-nameable . . . a queer intangible drift never experienced before'. 'When you lose your way in Gurgaon district you find your way by your nose', advised a British civil servant in India.[102] The grammar of hyperbole was applicable transnationally, hand in hand with the ideology of the empire.

The second representational technique of othering is *satire*. French poet and novelist Abel Bonnard seems to have been a master of this art: a sardonic tone often garnishes his striking narratives, and thus his subjective feelings are blended seamlessly into fleeting olfactory experiences. On those hot dusty Beijing streets, 'poisoned with evil smells', as he narrated, tuberose flowers exuding 'the scent of the moonlight' were being sold in every 'nauseously smelly little shop'. Given that 'the very same men who inhale this perfume with the delight of connoisseurs, will breath [*sic*] in the noisome exhalations', he asked, 'Are they capable of shutting off the power of their senses at will? Or do they by a sort of perversion derive some strange enjoyment from a fetid odour?'[103] Subtly, China was caricatured, and objectified, by the comic portrait of the strange olfactory imagery – the sweet tuberose perfume drifting in the stinking air (reminiscent of the cesspool rose garden motif).

The same expressive mode was applied in another episode of Bonnard's olfactory adventure. Travelling in Fuzhou 涪州 (Fou-tcheou) around 1920, his eyes were plagued by the sight of the greenish

---

[100] Birch, *Travels in North and Central China*, 216 (emphasis mine).
[101] Cochran, *Foreign Magic*, 111.   [102] Quoted in Rotter, *Empires of the Senses*, 162, 179.
[103] Bonnard, *In China, 1920–1921*, 52.

complexion of opium eaters and a blind man's face seared by leprosy, but the cacophony of odours was most imposing:

> The overflow from these drains spreads itself almost with an air of pomp into sheets of filth, breaks out into bubbles and mixes its disgusting eddies to such an extent that when I passed a stable from which there came a strong smell of horse manure it struck me as such a pleasant, wholesome smell by contrast that I stood still an instant to breathe it in as a corrective. But I had to return to the suffocating stench, and noticing the ease and indifference with which the wan occupants of the street absorbed it, I had a nightmare sensation of being the only one of my species in a weird town built at the bottom of a swamp.[104]

The hyperbolic, satirical remark on the smell of horse manure as a pleasant corrective was surely highly entertaining for his home readership, an affective quality pivotal in the art of differentiation. By laughing at *you* (the object), *I* become the subject.

However derisive these narratives are, Bonnard's evocative portraits of the slices of the Chinese smellscape almost give off a *poetic* vibe, the third mode of representation thriving in the travel literature. The poetic mode was a by-product of the cult of the Chinese exotic in Europe. As Jonathan Spence analyses, this currency resulted from 'the awareness of Chinese sensuality', initially tied to new aesthetics (as seen in the eighteenth-century fad of chinoiserie), but moving out in the nineteenth century to embrace 'something harsher and ranker, something unknowable, dangerous, and intoxicating, composed of scent and sweat, of waves of heat and festering night air'.[105] Perceiving the Chinese stench in a poetic vein echoed the orientalist appreciation of, in Edward Said's words, 'barbarous splendour', 'unimaginable antiquity', and 'inhuman beauty'.[106] Bonnard himself offered a comment along these lines. The sensory universe surrounding him – the sight, sound, and smell – was a metaphor of China: on the one hand, 'it is the Orient without sunshine, deaf, dumb and extinguished'; on the other, 'amidst this barbaric disregard of hygiene there still exists the extreme refinements of a very ancient civilisation'.[107] Other travellers documented a similar sentiment.

---

[104] Ibid., 193–4. [105] Spence, *The Chan's Great Continent*, 146.
[106] Said, *Orientalism*, 167–8. [107] Bonnard, *In China, 1920–1921*, 194.

Paul Claudel (1868–1955), a French poet and diplomat, concocted a poetics of Chinese odour with metaphors. 'I walk in a black gravy', he wrote, and 'along the ditch whose crumbling border I follow, the odor is so strong that it is like an explosive. There is the smell of oil, garlic, filth, ashes, opium, and offal'.[108] In an opium den, full of blue smoke, 'one breathes an odor of burning chestnuts. It is a heavy perfume, powerful, stagnant, strong as the beat of a gong'.[109] His mellow, murmuring voice conveys a picture of 'the city of other days, when, free of modern influences, men swarmed in an artless disorder', or, in sum, 'the fascination of all the past'.[110] Equally enthralled by the oriental charm, Bertrand Russell expressed a similar quandary towards China's backwardness, exoticism, and excitement.[111] The Greek philosopher Nikos Kazantzakis (1883–1957) claimed that the goal of his journey to China was not 'to understand' but 'to saturate my five senses'. In accordance with the ancient Greek notion that 'the soul is the simultaneous exercise of all the senses', to him China was 'a new meadow where my five senses can graze'.[112] By aestheticizing Oriental sensuality, the Orient was turned into an Other.

Apparently opposite to the poetic mode is an *ethnographic* approach to chronicling Chinese smells. Adopted by the European explorers (especially the naturalists and anthropologists) from the outset of the colonial enterprise, ethnography evolved into a 'scientific' discipline of understanding foreign lands.[113] Many travel writers embraced the probing ethnographic spirit to record the minute stimuli that fell upon their five senses in China. Edwin Dukes's sketch of the typical hurly-burly of Chinese streets, in 1880s Xiamen, reads,

> The vast throngs of people, the din of daily toil, the yelling of street-hawkers, the ceaseless shouts of burden-bearers – 'Look out; stand aside!' – the stuffy and choking smells, varied at every few steps, but never for the better; an occasional procession with drums and fifes; the huge and

---

[108] Claudel, *The East I Know*, 17.   [109] Ibid., 15–16.   [110] Ibid., 16.

[111] See Huang, 'Deodorizing China', 1093, 1119–20.

[112] Kazantzakis, *Japan, China*, 180. Quoted in Dupée, *British Travel Writers in China*, 65.

[113] See Pratt, *Imperial Eyes*, Chapter 2; Konishi, 'Discovering the Savage Senses'.

unwholesome pigs and the mangy dogs that are clearing the streets of rubbish; the firing of crackers, the burning of incense, the smoke of cooking-stoves, – these are the things that assail the senses as one threads one's way through the intricacies of a Chinese city.[114]

George Cooke documented the comparably boisterous sense-scape of a food market in 1850s Xiamen:

> It is a *congeries* of huts with open fronts. Upon the floor is heaped and exposed for sale every indescribable edible in the Chinese dietary. Some, hissing hot, are for immediate consumption; lumps of roast pork, stews curiously compounded of gelatinous matter, a small square piece of meat, and vegetables of different kinds, cut into long regular strips. Some coldly taint the air, and call for fire and quick consumption, such as fresh fish, caught perhaps in the bay a few hours before, but now rapidly decomposing. Livid joints of beef hang upon bamboo poles, despite the precepts of Fo [the Buddha]; and within reach of their odour is a mountain of Chinese confectionery – bean cakes, looking like cakes of honey soap; dark treacly substances, which quiver as they are divided into small portions; and a light compound which looks like that pleasant mixture of honey and almonds wherein the Turks are so cunning.[115]

Only by quoting the lengthy depictions in full can one grasp the sense of inquisitiveness and meticulousness. Placing China under the ethnographic microscope, a dividing line between the observer and the observed was drawn. Moreover, under the veneer of matter-of-factness lies a subtext of judgement. Dukes's own sentence betrays his subjective feelings towards bustling Chinese life: 'It is like a troubled dream rather than stern fact.'[116] Cooke's judgement comes across as more subtly wrought, as he concludes the passage about the market: 'but I saw nothing which ministered to the elegance of life, except a warehouseful of artificial flowers'.[117] Alluding to the synonym for kitsch (artificial flowers), his stealth sarcasm is unmistakable. In short, the ethnographic mode of representation granted the often anecdotal accounts a scientific

---

[114] Dukes, *Everyday Life in China*, 36. [115] Cooke, *China*, 87 (emphasis original).
[116] Dukes, *Everyday Life in China*, 36. [117] Cooke, *China*, 88.

quality, a much-needed instrument to distance the subject from its object. It is manifest that power somatic was embedded in the hyperbolic, satirical, poetic, and ethnographic representations of Chinese odours. Alongside the weaponry of rhetoric, the psychical apparatus of rationalization was equally critical.

TACTICS OF RATIONALIZATION

Being intuitive and judgemental, smell can be a gifted rhetorician to incite emotions, but it may not be a convincing preacher if reason is demanded by the audience. Endeavours to rationalize why China stinks became pivotal to dispel the perennial vexation invoked by uncanny odours. An overarching discourse at disposal was the universalizing, civilizing programme of modernity. Travelling in the Himalayas in the hot season of the 1870s, American missionary Jeanette Hauser's sentiments sum this up: 'those dirty, ragged coolies, so foul smelling for lack of bathing', made it necessary 'for a *civilized nose* to keep to the windward of them'.[118] When encountering China, however, this belief system of European superiority was challenged by the Chinese frame of *hua/yi* (Han Chinese/barbarian) antithesis, and the concept of civilization figured equally centrally in this ingrained Chinese mentality, a fact that the travellers were acutely aware of.[119] Therefore, more carefully devised tactics of rationalization were imperative to legitimize the 'China stinks' discourse.

The first tactic is a simple one, centring on *difference*. Clarke Abel spearheaded the collective impulse to differentiate. At a public bath in Nanjing, despite its name as 'The Bath of Fragrant Waters', he recoiled from the bathwater 'saturated with dirt' and the steam arising from it: 'however fragrant to the senses of the Chinese, [it] was to mine really intolerable'.[120] This narrative can be read in the light of Mary Douglas's theory on purity and contamination. As she argues, 'dirt is essentially disorder. There is no such thing as absolute dirt: it exists in the eye of the

---

[118] Hauser, *The Orient and Its People*, 79 (emphasis mine).

[119] Forman, *China and the Victorian Imagination*, 6–7, 14; Liu, *The Clash of Empires*, 31–69.

[120] Abel, *Narrative of a Journey in the Interior of China*, 159.

beholder'.[121] Hence 'it is only by exaggerating the difference between within and without, above and below, male and female, with and against, that a semblance of order is created'.[122] Through the psychological mechanism of differentiation, the stranger is transfigured into the Other. Within this frame, one can comprehend the psychical activities behind some ludicrous anecdotes. Travelling in central Sichuan, John G. Birch noted in his journal 'an appalling smell' in a 'wretched hamlet', one that was 'apparently not disliked by the Chinese'. However, when walking through the air 'perfumed with the honey-sweet scent of the yellow rape in flower', he was delightedly breathing in the pleasant aroma, whilst his Chinese escort said, 'Yes, it is a very bad smell.'[123]

A more sophisticated tactic evolved from the pseudoscientific assertion that the Chinese race has inherently *blunt olfactory nerves*. Writing on putrid fish that 'sent forth a stench quite intolerable to European organs', Abel cited the French sinologist Joseph de Guignes (1721–1800): 'The Chinese are utterly insensible to bad smells.'[124] This theory soon went viral, spreading on the pages of the travel literature:

> ... the Chinese seem destitute of all sense of smell, they live contentedly in the midst of odours which to an Englishman are almost unbearably disgusting.[125]

> Chinamen were created without the sense of smell.[126]

> ... the whole Chinese nation are apparently altogether devoid of the sense of smell![127]

> ... the sensory nervous system of a Chinaman is either blunted or of arrested development.[128]

Published in 1880s and 1890s Britain, all these opinions are redolent of polygenetic racism, a belief that human races emerged from multiple

[121] Douglas, *Purity and Danger*, 2.   [122] Ibid., 5.
[123] Birch, *Travels in North and Central China*, 313.
[124] Abel, *Narrative of a Journey in the Interior of China*, 231–2.
[125] Morris, *A Winter in North China*, 47.
[126] Gordon-Cumming, *Wanderings in China*, 32–3.   [127] Ibid., 320.
[128] Morrison, *An Australian in China*, 104.

origins, based on which racial hierarchy can be justified. A popular form of racial thinking throughout the seventeenth and eighteenth centuries, this belief peaked in the nineteenth century within languages of scientific racism.[129] Under the banner, African bodies are inherently pungent, and Chinese nerves are biologically blunt.

This rationalizing tactic stemmed from a discursive network that brought the sensorium and broader sociopolitical discourses together. One relevant discourse is the stereotype of Chinese cruelty in Western imaginations. Originating from mid-sixteenth-century Portuguese travel accounts, this stereotype was reproduced in a vast array of genres (including photographs, paintings, textual accounts of Chinese punishments and executions, and so on). In doing so, as Eric Hayot argues, the West has affirmed 'the phatic and ceaselessly necessary production of its unique difference'.[130] The long nineteenth century was the climax of such representations; in fact, George Morrison's comment, quoted above, on the blunted 'sensory nervous system of a Chinaman' was preceded by a discussion of the cruelty of Chinese punishment.[131] Callousness and insensitive nerves are two sides of the same coin. By aligning the olfactory discourse with a more established belief, the travellers reasserted their fundamental biological/racial difference from the Chinese.

Recurring references to the nerves point to another discourse with which the olfactory narratives were interlinked.[132] Interestingly, the Australian adventurer George Morrison was a University of Edinburgh graduate in medicine, which may explain his use of neurological terminology. The rise of nerve theory in eighteenth-century Britain was not only a shift in medical discourse, but also had a sweeping influence on 'an associated culture of sensibility'. Sensitive feelings now encompassed both the senses and the emotions, becoming a significant marker of social status.[133] Concomitant with nerve theory was the philosophy of

---

[129] Kettler, *The Smell of Slavery*, 84.   [130] Hayot, *The Hypothetical Mandarin*, 36.

[131] Morrison, *An Australian in China*, 103–4.

[132] See Ball, *Things Chinese*, 22; Dingle, *Across China on Foot*, 90. The English journalist Dingle wrote, 'the dung-heap charms the sight of this agricultural people, without in the slightest wounding their olfactory nerves'.

[133] Tullett, *Smell in Eighteenth-Century England*, 4. For nineteenth-century developments, see Salisbury and Shail, *Neurology and Modernity*.

sensualism, stressing the source of knowledge deriving empirically from sense perceptions. Identified by Alain Corbin as the philosophical foundation of olfactory modernity, John Locke's sensualist thinking was reinforced through sensory education, instrumental in forging a particular bourgeois sensibility. In the olfactory domain, tolerance of smell suddenly came to define class: the lower one's tolerance the higher one's status.[134] These broader developments in modern European history patterned our travellers' thinking and perception. Engaging with this repository of knowledge, they rationalized their interpretation of pervasive Chinese stench as a result of the defective Chinese nervous system. Thereby ambivalence was dispelled, and the territory of the Self guarded.

Alongside the tactics of differentiation and pseudoscientific racism, the final – and most destructive – technique of rationalization is *disgust*. 'The most embodied and visceral of emotions', as William Miller puts it, disgust is 'one of our most aggressive culture-creating passions'.[135] A psychological defence mechanism conducive to the operation of moral hierarchy, disgust effectively transforms the stranger into the enemy in one's own psyche. No doubt this feeling is the fulcrum of the 'China stinks' discourse. American General James H. Wilson's (1837–1925) remark (on Shanghai's native city) is a familiar one: 'It is all inconceivably squalid and offensive to foreign eyes and nostrils, and fills the foreign soul with a sentiment of *unutterable disgust*.'[136] Following a lengthy depiction of 'promiscuous and insupportable filth' in a Chinese inn, Edwin Dingle paused and wrote in a separate one-sentence paragraph, 'I remember, however, that I am in China, and must not be *disgusted*.'[137]

The transition of disgust from an emotion to a tool of the rational mind can be traced back to Immanuel Kant. Interestingly, the clichéd 'spoiled, stinking fish' features in his work as an example of the eating habits of Asian people, based on which he posits that the consumption of

---

[134] Corbin, *The Foul and the Fragrant*, 5–6; Jütte, *A History of the Senses*, 159–62, 170–2; Howes and Lalonde, 'The History of Sensibilities', 131.

[135] Miller, *The Anatomy of Disgust*, xii.

[136] Wilson, *China*, 20–2; quoted in Clifford, '*A Truthful Impression of the Country*', 60 (emphasis mine).

[137] Dingle, *Across China on Foot*, 90 (emphasis mine).

'disgusting dishes' is no longer contingent on starvation, but on ethno-graphic vantage.[138] This distinction relativizes the concepts of disgust and enjoyment, and yet it is precisely such relativism that allows a space to build disgust's cultural content. Kant's thinking on filth, disgust, and civilization is further expounded:

> Filth is an object of vision; but it cannot directly excite visual aversion, rather drawing our imagination to smell and taste ... we also find that disgust at filth is only present in cultivated nations; the uncultivated nation has no qualms about filth. Cleanliness demonstrates the greatest human cultivation [*Bildung*], since it is the least natural human quality, causing much exertion and hardship.[139]

Cultivating disgust thus figures among the highest educational goals in Kant's *Education* (*Pädagogik*). As Winfried Menninghaus summarizes, 'Disgust allows him, above all, to establish through education, and to maintain, decisive moral order-demarcations ... The "nature of disgust" is consequently to civilize.' Thereby Kant erects 'a politics and morals of disgust' long before Freud and Elias.[140] Moreover, engaging the eighteenth-century tide of olfactory sagacity, Kant regards olfactory disgust as the true basis and innermost form of impurity-linked dis-gust.[141] The moral terrain of disgust was also extended, becoming integral to the 'socio-aesthetics' of eighteenth-century England, as 'ways of sensing that performed the role of marking social and cultural boundaries, especially in the olfactory arenas provided by polite soci-ability'.[142] Performance of disgust hence engaged with an ensemble of psychological, moral, and aesthetic meanings, all of which helped the travellers to rationalize their perception of Chinese malodours. These performative acts would leave a lasting impact on the Chinese social life of smell.

---

[138] Kant, 'Physische Geographie', 379, 384; quoted in Menninghaus, *Disgust*, 108.

[139] Kant, 'Reflexionen zur Anthropologie', 104; quoted in Menninghaus, *Disgust*, 108.

[140] Menninghaus, *Disgust*, 109.

[141] Apart from the above quote, his similar opinion is also found in Kant, *Anthropology from a Pragmatic Point of View*, 50.

[142] Tullett, *Smell in Eighteenth-Century England*, 4.

CODA: CHINA (RE)ACTS

If we consider Jia Baoyu's discerning nose and the refined smellscapes under Cao Xueqin's pen, the 'China stinks' discourse is far from the truth biologically and historically; it was a product of selective perceptions filtered through certain psychosocial mechanisms. But the dynamic workings of the stranger/enemy symbiosis were effective in rewiring Chinese sensibilities for a simple, yet powerful, reason: nobody likes to be disgusted by others. The strong emotions of shame, humiliation, and sense of failure arose amongst the Chinese, underpinning the rise of Chinese nationalism. Stench produced a robust form of power, the power somatic, and inducted China into globally intertwined spheres of olfactory modernity. It is beyond the scope of this chapter to chart a genealogy of Chinese (re)actions;[143] a cursory mapping will illuminate how the Chinese neurons were tuned by the rhetoric of contamination.

An early agent that mediated between the Western and Chinese spheres of knowledge and opinion was the Chinese-language press run by foreigners, such as the influential *Shenbao* 申報 in Shanghai. The 1870s and 1880s saw a proliferating coverage of Chinese malodour and poor sanitation in print media. For example, an 1872 article in *Shenbao* portrays the contrasting profiles of Shanghai's foreign settlement and the native city, the latter of which was characterized by a 'fetid smell and muddy roads'.[144] An 1879 essay in the same newspaper lists a litany of problems of Beijing's streets that gave rise to fearful dust and smell, an account that bears a striking resemblance to Archibald Little's depiction cited above.[145] Chinese intellectuals started to display a growing sensibility about ill-paved, foul-smelling streets during the period. For example, the scholar and industrialist Zheng Guanying 鄭觀應 (1842–1922) almost duplicated the polarized imageries of Shanghai, the native city being 'fetid and filthy' and the foreign settlement 'well-paved and tidy'. He commented, 'How can you blame the foreigners for their scorn and

[143] Research that has touched upon this topic include Hu, '"Bu weisheng" de huaren xingxiang'; Xu, 'Policing Civility on the Streets'.
[144] 'Zujie jiedao qingjie shuo', *SB*, 20 July 1872, 1.
[145] 'Lun Jingshi jiedao', *SB*, 30 September 1879, 1. Little, *Gleanings from Fifty Years in China*, 82. I thank Rudolf Wagner for sending me the *Shenbao* source.

Figure 2.4 'Da ai weisheng' (An Impediment to Hygiene), *Renjing huabao* 13, 1907.

contempt (何怪乎外人轻侮也)?'[146] Most notably, during the eventually abortive Hundred Days' reform in 1898, the Guangxu Emperor issued a decree about 'paving streets and cleaning ditches and canals' in Beijing. He resorted to the same arsenal of language to describe Beijing's squalor and filth as well as the detrimental effect on public health, stressing that 'foreigners had seen [our city] as a pigsty (洋人目之為豬圈)'.[147]

The Chinese discourse of overcoming stench continued in the twentieth century. Visual means joined the public clamour, as illustrated by the cartoon in a late Qing pictorial, warning of the peril of sanitary ignorance by referring to the modern concept of *weisheng* (hygiene) (Figure 2.4). Personal cleanliness also entered the consciousness of Chinese elites. As the scholar Sun Baoxuan 孫寶瑄 (1874–1924) noted

[146] Zheng, 'Xiulu', 663. Quoted in Hu, '"Bu weisheng" de huaren xingxiang', 2–3.
[147] Su, *Qingting Wuxu chaobian ji*, 19. I'd like to thank Song Xue 宋雪 for sharing this material with me.

in his diaries of 1906, Western gentlemen pay close attention to personal hygiene, whereas Chinese 'eccentric men of letters' (*mingshi* 名士) are proud of their 'unkempt appearance' (*qiushou goumian* 囚首垢面). Yet, as he asserted, maintaining personal cleanliness is a matter of respect for others, a quality integral to public virtue.[148] This argument, in line with Western bourgeois values, reveals the conscious construction of a new ideal of the physical body, differing from the stereotypes of dishevelled Daoist scholar and Jia Baoyu-type connoisseur of perfume. As time went by, more vocal advocates emerged in the increasingly radical social milieu on the eve of the May Fourth era. In 1916, the eminent educator Cai Yuanpei 蔡元培 (1868–1940) delivered a passionate speech in his home town, Shaoxing, on how to remove stench from stinking cesspools, dung tubs, and burial grounds for the benefit of hygiene and national strengthening.[149] Chen Duxiu 陳獨秀 (1879–1942), a founding father of the Chinese Communist Party (the CCP), promulgated in the iconic journal *Xin qingnian* 新青年 (*New Youth*) his view on the humiliating label 'filthy nation' attached to China by Westerners.[150] Fast-forwarding to 1935, during the Nationalist government's New Life movement aimed at disciplining Chinese bodies and behaviours, the charged issue of drying fish emerged on a list of things prohibited in Nanjing.[151] If these fragments of voices, narratives, and actions should be described in olfactory terms, I would say that they smell uncanny, a strange tinge of neither entirely homely nor entirely unhomely scent. Emulating the grammar of the 'China stinks' discourse for an opposite cause, these familiar/*heimlich* tropes, somehow, smell *unheimlich*. Such is the polysemy of the language of scents.

This chapter has delineated the ways in which the discourse of contamination was forged in Western perceptions about China through smelling her environments, people, food, and opium. For the travellers, the airborne Chinese odours were inescapable, but their discriminating olfactory nerves were ceaselessly making judgement during their

[148] Sun, *Wangshanlu riji*, vol. 2, 862–3. Quoted in Hu, '"Bu weisheng" de huaren xingxiang', 25–6.
[149] Cai, 'Zai Shaoxing gejie dahui yanshuo ci', 479–82.
[150] Chen, 'Wo zhi aiguo zhuyi', 4.
[151] Shoudu Xinshenghuo yundong cujinhui, ed., *Shoudu Xinshenghuo yundong gaikuang*, 29.

molecular encounters. Their moral judgements, however, often reflected their own psychological need to battle the ambiguity of meanings in smells, rather than the foul or fragrant quality of smells per se. In other words, defining the foul and the fragrant empowered them to define the Self. Contaminated diversity was not programmed in the ideology of modernity. For the plastic olfactory brains (of all the parties involved), it was a learning process, during which certain perceptions and discourses were moulded and affirmed. The stories told in this chapter pose a challenge to the sweeping claim concerning the post-Enlightenment decline of olfaction in the West. In fact, smell was a robust actor in encountering the East and in constructing racial discourses underlying the colonial enterprise worldwide. The happenings in the sensorium were not just a storm in a teacup; their implications would be felt in the forthcoming Chinese olfactory revolution.

PART TWO

SMELLSCAPES IN FLUX

3

Deodorizing China

Poor Tom, that eats the swimming frog, the toad, the tadpole, the wall-newt and the water; that in the fury of his heart, when the foul fiend rages, eats cow-dung for sallets, swallows the old rat and the ditch-dog, drinks the green mantle of the standing pool ...

William Shakespeare, *King Lear*[1]

SHAKESPEARE CREATES in *King Lear* a classic stagnant pool as a synecdoche of the grotesque and the insane. When Poor Tom eats the creatures in the pool and drinks the water covered by a cloak of algae scum, we are repulsed. The trope of stagnant water – as well as the excessive stench of putrefaction – is a constant theme in the world of contamination, the cesspool rose garden that starts this book being one example. The preoccupation with water is 'one of the subdivisions of the religion of progress',[2] and eliminating its noxious vapours a prime mission of olfactory modernity. And yet, as William Miller puts it, 'the gooey mud, the scummy pond are life soup, fecundity itself'.[3] What disgusts is, para-doxically, 'the capacity for life'.[4] It is the decay that engenders life in the Shakespearean pond, the Chinese cesspool, and innumerable ditches, sewers, moats, creeks, and swamps that will take the stage in this chapter. The rank odour of filthy water may be more anodyne than assumed, not categorically a foe, but a stranger. It was the gardening ambition of modernity that was determined to turn the stranger into an enemy.

---

[1] Shakespeare, *King Lear*, Act 3, scene iv, ll 123–7.
[2] Goubert, *The Conquest of Water*, 1. The quoted phrase is from the introduction written by Emmanuel Le Roy Ladurie.
[3] Miller, *An Anatomy of Disgust*, 40–1.   [4] Ibid., 40.

This chapter traces the Chinese war against malodour in its modern olfactory revolution. It delineates the ways in which environmental deodorization – as imported ideology and practice, generally speaking – was embedded in the Chinese pursuit of 'hygienic modernity'.[5] At the same time, it probes the conditions and consequences of such initiatives, often involving asymmetrical power relations that the discourse of progressive deodorization tended to smooth over. Hsuan Hsu argues that deodorization has been 'a partial and differential project of air conditioning', simultaneously producing 'atmospheric disparities'.[6] Echoing his call to reframe the cultural suppression of smell through 'the concept of differential deodorization', this chapter strives to unravel the diverse techniques deployed to reorganize inhabited spaces and inhaled atmospheres in China's bumpy path of modernization. Overall, I argue that deodorizing China was essentially a series of spatializing projects inherent to the 'developmental fairy tales' of modern China, narratives that obliterated the uneven redistribution of sense-scapes alongside capital and symbolic capital. The outcome of battling against contamination was not purity, but a stratified reorganization of purified and contaminated spaces.

Deodorizing China occurred in myriad realms; a comprehensive study is not feasible within one chapter. I therefore narrow the scope down to three anchors. First, I primarily focus on miasmic water for its allegorical and practical powers in the engineering of modern life. Traditionally a 'dominant force' that was 'generally feared', water became a foremost subject for conquest in nineteenth-century Europe, transfigured by science and technology into 'an industrial and commercial product'.[7] Concurrently, eradicating stagnant water figured prominently in modern sanitary campaigns worldwide. Yet in Chinese imperial bureaucracy and ecosystems, water was positioned differently. Vital to farming and transport, control of water was at the centre of China's later premodern economic history.[8] Water thereby

---

[5] The famous term was coined in Rogaski, *Hygienic Modernity*.
[6] Hsu, *The Smell of Risk*, 14.   [7] Goubert, *The Conquest of Water*, 21, 25.
[8] Elvin, *The Retreat of the Elephants*, 115.

was a contentious site that harboured clashes and negotiations in the Chinese olfactory revolution.

Second, I compare three projects undertaken by Western colonial administrations from the 1850s to the 1890s, reform-minded Chinese gentry of the late Qing and the early Republic, and the Communists in the 1950s. Despite their disparate, if not antithetic, motives and rhetoric, the three shared common beliefs and forged a continuous Chinese olfactory revolution for over a century. All testify to the interpenetration of ideology and sensorium, body and power. Taking this *longue durée* approach, I demonstrate a trajectory of how the imbricated cityscape and smellscape were differentially reordered.

Third, the three projects all took place in Shanghai, the spearhead of Chinese modernity in many well-documented ways.[9] As one of the first treaty ports thriving within a global colonial capitalist economy, Shanghai also pioneered the Chinese olfactory revolution as the Europeans imported new sensibilities, institutions, and technologies. Within its own Confucian tradition (fused with a nascent nationalist impulse), Shanghai's native city exemplifies an early initiative of olfactory modernity outside the West. As arguably an epitome of vice and corruption (inflicted by imperialism), Shanghai under Communist rule displayed fascinating new dynamics in revolutionizing its smellscapes. A thick description of the long pedigree of olfactory modernity in this one city, I believe, suggests broader patterns of the social life of smell in modern China. Before zooming in on the three case studies, I provide an outline of stench and stagnant water in Chinese medical tradition and modernizing Europe.

DEODORIZATION AND THE TROPE OF STAGNANT WATER

Atmospheric deodorization is not a preoccupation unique to Western olfactory modernity. Pestilential vapours (*liqi* 戾氣, or *huiqi* 穢氣) are identified as the key pathogenic agent that causes epidemic diseases, according to traditional Chinese medical theory, especially the Warm

---

[9] For a concise overview of the competing interpretations of Shanghai's modern history, see Johnson, *Shanghai*, 8–17.

Factor School (*Wenbing pai* 溫病派) dating back to the Ming dynasty.[10] During a cholera outbreak in 1860s Shanghai, Wang Shixiong 王士雄 (1808–1868), a renowned physician of this school, observed, 'densely packed houses gave off putrid emanations, the city moat contained innumerable filth, the turbid water was reeking', and all in all 'obnoxious effluvia' (*chou du* 臭毒) was the root cause of the epidemic. Accordingly, he advised locals to dredge and cleanse the rivers, to dig wells purified by alum and realgar, and to purify and deodorize drinking water with dried calamus roots and lakawood (*jiangxiang* 降香).[11] Wang's diagnosis bears a resemblance to miasma theory that was governing medical discourse of the same age in Europe.[12] Holding a similar view regarding miasma's pernicious effects on health, the Europeans, however, diverged from the Chinese in sensibilities and action, as Ruth Rogaski argues. Whereas Qing medical thinkers often planned 'preventions for individuals' (as Wang Shixiong did), the Europeans combated miasmas through 'sanitary engineering'.[13] The latter was the backbone of the olfactory revolution.

As previously introduced, the modern olfactory revolution germinated in eighteenth-century France, resulting from the confluence of sensualist philosophy, changing bourgeois sensibilities, and scientific advances in chemistry and medicine. Within this context arose a distinct phobia about pungent odours, and water occupied a specific position in this miasmic mindset: rivers of stench, marshes, swamps, and even the smallest puddle remained a focus of public anxiety.[14] A contemporary report featured a real-life version of the Shakespearean pool in *King Lear*:

> When water from ponds or swamps was evaporated over a low flame, several worms, several insects, and other animals were deposited, along with a great deal of yellowish, earthy materials ... [This water was]

---

[10] Rogaski, *Hygienic Modernity*, 58. Also see Ming scholar Xie Zhaozhe's 謝肇淛 commentary, quoted in Chiu, 'Mingdai Beijing de gouqu shurui jiqi xiangguan wenti', 62.

[11] Yu, 'Qingdai Jiangnan de weisheng guannian yu xingwei', 19. Tianjin's Warm Factor physicians held similar views. See Rogaski, *Hygienic Modernity*, 60.

[12] Cipolla, *Miasmas and Disease*.   [13] Rogaski, *Hygienic Modernity*, 82.

[14] Corbin, *The Foul and the Fragrant*, 32–3.

overloaded with substances that were foreign to it, emanations, vapors, exhalations from earth, mines, ooze, plants, fish, decomposed insects, and other substances with which the air is always to a greater or lesser degree infected.[15]

Modernity resolutely defined the grotesque figure of stench as an enemy, and the French hygienists' weaponry comprised a form of sanitary policy now known as public health. Replacing the old ad hoc tactics to tackle each epidemic, the new strategy aimed to coherently implement such vital deodorizing measures as draining, paving, and ventilation.[16] At the end of the eighteenth century, as Alain Corbin observes, the increased degree of cleanliness dramatically lowered the thresholds of olfactory tolerance among the masses, 'who made a direct connection between odors and death'.[17]

The nineteenth century witnessed Britain's rise as a pivotal player in sanitary engineering. The landmark was the publication of Edwin Chadwick's *Report on the Sanitary Condition of the Labouring Population of Great Britain* in 1842, a 'foundational text of modern public health'.[18] Its central medical tenet was also miasma theory; Chadwick made clear at the outset that 'atmospheric impurity' was the main cause of the ravage of epidemic, endemic, and contagious diseases.[19] The imperative of deodorization derived from a rapid process of 'odorization' – a corollary of the Industrial Revolution which had brought about a growing urban working-class population living in squalor.[20] Chadwick's triumph was marked by the ultimate passage of the Public Health Act in 1848, a decisive moment not only because 'for the first time the British Government charged itself with a measure of responsibility for safeguarding the health of the population',[21] but also because it crystallized an institutionalized form of sanitary engineering that would reign over

---

[15] Ibid., 33. Originally in M. F.-B. Ramel, *De l'influence des marais et des étangs sur la santé de l'homme* (first published in 1784 in the *Journal de médecine*).

[16] Corbin, *The Foul and the Fragrant*, 89–100.

[17] Ibid., 58. Also see Vigarello, *Concepts of Cleanliness*, 142–55.

[18] Hamlin, *Public Health and Social Justice in the Age of Chadwick*, 85.

[19] Chadwick, *Report on the Sanitary Condition of the Labouring Population of Gt. Britain*, 79.

[20] See M. W. Flinn's 'Introduction', in ibid., 3–18.   [21] Ibid., 1.

the modern sensorium. Stagnant water was a major concern, as one clause states that the local board of health is responsible for draining, cleansing, covering, or filling up 'all ponds, pools, open ditches, sewers, drains'.[22]

Alongside the legislative and institutional initiatives, technology played a cardinal role, with the underground sewerage system the most life-changing invention in the history of olfactory modernity. The late 1840s saw the British invention of a new form of piping that enables the flushing away of waste by a high-speed water supply.[23] The merit of water-sluiced sewers was magnified by the arrival of the epoch-making germ theory around the 1860s, which identifies bacteria, instead of miasmic odours, as the root of many diseases. Yet hygienists still saw filthy water as a prime hazard as it facilitates the transmission of germs. They were convinced that by confining waste and filth underground in sewers and flushing them away, disease transmission could be brought under control.[24] Thus began a 'Victorian revolution in urban sewerage systems' that swept the West from the mid-nineteenth century on.[25] Since then, the engineered underground worlds of Victorian London and Haussmann's Paris have remained modern mythology. By the dawn of the twentieth century, most large cities in the West had been equipped with extensive drainage systems beneath the cityscape.[26] At the same time, sewerage construction and management became a new branch of knowledge, popularized by burgeoning print capitalism.[27]

A more far-reaching consequence of this underground revolution, as David Inglis argues, was its generation of 'modern sensory dispositions, which revile both the smell *and* sight of human faeces'. Far from being a 'neutral' technology of waste disposal for the sake of 'public health', modern sewerage should be regarded as 'symbolic entities that met other needs' which had been developing amongst West European elites since

---

[22] 'The Public Health Act, 1848', Clause LVIII, in Glen, *The Law Relating to the Public Health and Local Government in Relation to Sanitary and Other Matters*, 264.

[23] Inglis, 'Sewers and Sensibilities', 120.   [24] Ibid., 120–1.   [25] Ibid., 106.

[26] Ibid., 108.

[27] Sanitary handbooks were circulating widely, see Boulnois, *The Municipal and Sanitary Engineer's Handbook*; Cain, *Sanitary Engineering*.

the early modern period.[28] At the temporal level, mains drainage symbolizes the rational control – and repression – of an archaic, odoriferous past by bourgeois civilization. Spatially and socially, it often incurs an uneven redistribution of sense-scapes across different social strata. As historians have asserted, Haussmann's reconfiguration of Paris could be interpreted as a 'social dichotomy of purification', implying the expulsion of the poor and the inflated value of disinfected bourgeois space.[29] Deodorization is not a linear progression towards public health and atmospheric salubrity in a generic sense; it rather entails hierarchical operations of power and a differential division of order/disorder. These dynamics will also play out in the Chinese stories of deodorization in their own sociopolitical contexts. So, in the mid-nineteenth century when the legions of British officers and merchants arrived in Shanghai, bringing with them an arsenal of concepts about modern smellscapes, what would they do about the numerous Shakespearean ponds and indigenous ditches offensive to their nasal sensitivities?

COLONIAL DEODORIZATION

To Chinese eyes (and noses), the area where Shanghai's foreign settlements and all the splendours of an urban culture were to arise was typical of the bucolic charm of Jiangnan (the lower Yangtze delta): cotton and rice fields, uncultivated fields of reeds, winding footpaths, and waterways patterned the landscape.[30] Yet the foreigners perceived it differently. Among many other things, Shanghai's water, in multiple forms, was constantly considered a nuisance. Located virtually at sea level, Shanghai lies at the juncture of Suzhou Creek on the left bank of the larger Huangpu river, which flows northward to merge with the Yangtze (Figure 3.1).[31] The foreign settlements were situated on land leased to them by the Chinese. The British Settlement, established in 1845 and

---

[28] Inglis, 'Sewers and Sensibilities', 106 (emphasis original). A similar argument can be found in Pike, 'Sewage Treatments', 52.
[29] Corbin, *The Foul and the Fragrance*, 134–5. For more discussion on the argument, see ibid., 268, footnote 21.
[30] Lu, *Beyong the Neon Lights*, 26.   [31] MacPherson, *A Wilderness of Marshes*, 16.

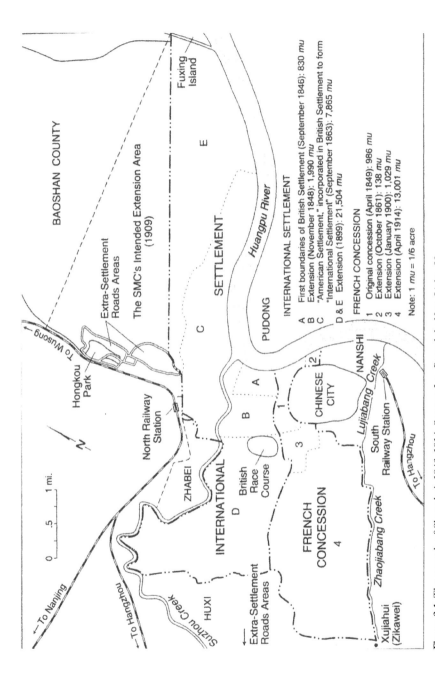

Figure 3.1 The growth of Shanghai, 1846–1914. Source: Lu, *Beyond the Neon Lights*, 30.

INTERNATIONAL SETTLEMENT

A First boundaries of British Settlement (September 1846): 830 *mu*
B Extension (November 1848): 1,990 *mu*
C "American Settlement," incorporated in British Settlement to form "International Settlement" (September 1863): 7,865 *mu*
D & E Extension (1899): 21,504 *mu*

FRENCH CONCESSION

1 Original concession (April 1849): 986 *mu*
2 Extension (October 1861): 138 *mu*
3 Extension (January 1900): 1,029 *mu*
4 Extension (April 1914): 13,001 *mu*

Note: 1 *mu* = 1/6 acre

located north of the walled Chinese city, was deemed a 'wasteland' dotted with 'cemeteries, natural marshes, and rice fields, i.e. artificial marshes', never short of miasmas.[32] An American Settlement was created in 1848 north of the British Settlement across Suzhou Creek in Hongkou 虹口; it was amalgamated with the British one in 1863 to become the International Settlement. This land was 'malodorous' and 'malarious' because of its marshy grounds dosed with liquid night soil.[33] The French Concession, formed in 1849, was bounded by the Chinese city to the east, separated by a ditch. The natural boundary between the British and French communities was Yangjing Creek (Yangjingbang 洋涇浜), a major canal connected to the moat that surrounded the city wall and the numerous irrigation ditches that cut through suburban villages. Both Yangjing Creek and the moat proved to be trouble spots, medically and politically, for many years.[34]

Not surprisingly, Father Gotteland, a French Jesuit, hyperbolically described Shanghai as 'the tomb of Europeans'.[35] A more 'scientific' analysis was supplied by French physician Alexandre Duburquois: intermittent fever was caused by 'the effluvia of decomposing vegetable matter in stagnant water, marshes, or paddies' in hot and humid environments, and dysentery was attributed to 'emanations from decomposed animal matter'.[36] Firmly in line with the miasmic mindset, the early Shanghailanders waged a war with the oppressive stenches and omnipresent water. This section scrutinizes the ways in which they regulated, administered, and engineered the Shanghai smellscapes.[37]

---

[32] Galle, *Shang-hai au point de vue médical: Contributions à la climatologie médicale*, 13; quoted in MacPherson, *A Wilderness of Marshes*, 16.

[33] Jamieson, 'Dr Alexander Jamieson's Report on the Health of Shanghai for the Half-Year Ended 30th September, 1871', 33.

[34] For an overview of the development of Shanghai's foreign settlements, see Lu, *Beyond the Neon Lights*, 28–9.

[35] Gotteland, '30e lettre, le R. P. Gotteland'; quoted in MacPherson, *A Wilderness of Marshes*, 21.

[36] Duburquois, *Notes sur les maladies des européens en Chine et au Japon*, 39; quoted in MacPherson, *A Wilderness of Marshes*, 34.

[37] Within the limited space, I will mainly focus on the British/International Settlement.

A concern over malodour was on their minds from the outset. In the first edition of the 'Shanghai Land Regulations' (1845, hereafter SLR), equivalent to 'a basic municipal code, and a constitution of sorts' for the governance of the British Settlement,[38] there is a brief reference in Article 18 to the prohibition of 'the heaping up of filth, running out of gutters on the roads' in order to 'afford lasting peace and comfort to the mercantile community'.[39] The revised editions (in 1854 and 1869) contain more public-health measures. Of forty-two articles comprising the by-laws in the 1869 edition, nine concern the management of sewers and drains, and another nine the cleansing of streets, stagnant pools, waste, and excrement.[40] These articles closely resemble the 1848 British Public Health Act (hereafter PHA), which contains twelve clauses (XLIII–LIV) on sewers, drains, privies, and water closets, and eleven (LV–LXV) on cleaning and managing streets, ditches, drains, slaughterhouses and other 'noxious or offensive business'.[41] Deodorization is a common goal of both laws, and building drains and removing polluted water are key strategies.

For example, Article 27 of the by-laws attached to the 1869 SLR states that 'no person shall suffer any offensive waste or stagnant water' and 'a penalty or fine not exceeding ten dollars' will be given to people who fail to remove such nuisances within forty-eight hours of receiving the council's notice. A further penalty not exceeding two dollars will be incurred for every day during which such a nuisance continues. The same penalty also applies to every person 'who allows the contents of any privy or cesspool to overflow or soak therefrom' and 'who keeps any pig or pigs within any dwelling house'.[42] The PHA of 1848 contains a similar clause, which stipulates that 'whosoever keeps any swine or pigstye in any dwelling-house ... or suffers any waste or stagnant water ... for twenty-four hours after written notice to him from the Local Board of Health to remove the same, and whosoever allows the contents of any watercloset, privy, or cesspool to overflow or soak therefrom', shall be liable to

---

[38] MacPherson, *A Wilderness of Marshes*, 5.

[39] 'Shanghai Land Regulations (29 Nov. 1845)', *NCH*, 17 January 1852, 99.

[40] SLR (1869), in *Land Regulations and By-laws for the Foreign Settlement of Shanghai* (1907), ii. All subsequent references to SLR refer to this edition.

[41] PHA, 257–67.   [42] SLR, 16–17.

'a penalty not exceeding forty shillings, and to a further penalty of five shillings for every day during which the offence is continued'.[43]

The two statutes also comprise analogous strategies for the construction and management of drains and sewers. For example, both grant the local board of health (in Britain) and the municipal council (in Shanghai) full power to control and manage public sewers and drains;[44] to enlarge, alter, repair, and improve them;[45] and to regulate the building of new houses in order to comply with new rules concerning drainage.[46] Some measures are specifically targeted at fetid smells. For example, the SLR (Article 6) states that all sewers and drains shall be provided with 'proper traps or other coverings or means of ventilation, so as to prevent stench', whereas the PHA (Article 46) stipulates that the local board of health shall 'cause the sewers vested in them by this Act to be constructed, covered, and kept so as not to be a nuisance or injurious to health, and to be properly cleared, cleansed, and emptied'.

Behind the dry technicality of the texts was precisely what Ruth Rogaski calls a new package of 'sensibilities and action' that distinguished the British public-health perspective from the Chinese frame of individual healing. Through the practice of colonial mimicry in legislation, a globally connected sensorium was in the making. The new sensibilities and action were also manifested in administration. Matters related to public health were under the charge of the Shanghai Municipal Council (hereafter SMC), the governing body of the Settlement set up in 1854.[47] In 1871, the SMC created the post of health officer, and in 1898 the Public Health Department was established, which marked a new era of public-health management in the Settlement.[48] Superficially, this system was different from the British

[43] PHA, Article 59, 264–5. More similarities can be identified: for example, SLR, Article 30, and PHA, Article 60, both on houses to be purified and drain, privy or cesspool to be amended; SLR, Article 31, and PHA, Articles 62–4, both on the regulation of slaughterhouses, and other offensive business.

[44] PHA, Article 63, 257; SLR, Article 1, 11.   [45] PHA, Article 65, 258; SLR, Article 3, 11.

[46] PHA, Article 69, 259–60; SLR, Article 8, 12.

[47] For overviews of the development of public-health administration in the Settlement, see Peng, *Gonggong weisheng yu Shanghai dushi wenming*, 41–2; Jackson, *Shaping Modern Shanghai*, Chapter 4, 164–202.

[48] MacPherson, *A Wilderness of Marshes*, 132.

one, which consisted of the General Board of Health and the local boards of health that superintended sanitary administration by incorporating the work of medical professionals and hygienists.[49] In reality, as the colonial officer Alexander Jamieson pointed out, the SMC could be 'considered as the Board of Health',[50] and the Shanghai system shared the salient features of institutionalization, professionalization, and the deployment of the specialized roles of medical officers, inspectors, and surveyors, hitherto unknown roles in China.

The united forces of legislation and administration turned Chinese stench into an enemy within a rationally designed infrastructure. When it came to the day-to-day governance of odour that is by nature the stranger – 'the most obstreperous, irregular, defiantly ungovernable of all impressions'[51] – could the foreigners tame the Chinese smellscapes according to their blueprint? The publication of the twenty-eight-volume minutes of the SMC meetings (1854–1943) allows us a glimpse into the intricacy of handling odours on Chinese soil.[52] As I have discussed elsewhere, the first three decades of the British administration witnessed a persistent preoccupation with filling up ponds and draining stagnant water, though most cases remained small in scale.[53] From the early 1880s onwards the number and scale of cases began to surge. We should emphasize here that the intensified efforts of deodorization were an immediate corollary of environmental 'odorization', an aspect often obscured by the 'China stinks' discourse, or by what Ruth Rogaski terms 'an indelible rhetoric of Chinese deficiency' centred on hygiene.[54]

The sanitary exigencies reflected a paradox of the Western model of urban and industrial growth, as was true worldwide in the nineteenth century.[55] Shanghai's stellar performance as a major treaty port entailed drastic topographical change. The half square kilometre of land leased

---

[49] Hamlin, *Public Health and Social Justice in the Age of Chadwick*, 275–301.

[50] Jamieson, 'Memo. on the Sanitary Condition of the Yang-King-Pang and Hongque Settlements at Shanghai', *NCH*, 22 March 1870, 210. But we also need to bear in mind that the SMC lacked 'a full colonial government's capacity to effect change through legislation'. See Jackson, *Shaping Modern Shanghai*, 175.

[51] Bauman, 'The Sweet Scent of Decomposition', 24.   [52] MSMC.

[53] Huang, 'Deodorizing China', 1105–7.   [54] Rogaski, *Hygienic Modernity*, 168.

[55] Kiechle, *Smell Detective*, Chapter 1.

to the British had morphed into a densely populated urban district of 14.5 square kilometres by 1899 (see Figure 3.1). While the area of the British/International Settlement grew twenty-ninefold, its population ballooned by over 1,600 times within the half-century.[56] Since the end of segregation between the Chinese and the foreigners in 1855, about 97 per cent of the population were Chinese, the majority of whom were migrants from every corner of China.[57] Apart from a small proportion of elites, most rural migrants came to Shanghai for factory work, as the last few decades of the century witnessed the beginnings of industrialization, with naval repair yards, silk mills, and cotton mills mushrooming in the city.[58] The earliest factories, especially Western-run shipyards, were located in Hongkou (and later Yangshupu) along the north-east banks of the Huangpu river (marked C and E in Figure 3.1).[59] These were the two districts where most cases of filthy ponds were reported.[60] For example, the SMC meeting on 1 June 1885 discussed a letter sent by the missionary Young John Allen (1836–1907, aka Lin Lezhi 林樂知), who complained about 'the frightful state of the ponds at the head of the Chapoo road' in Hongkou, where his newly founded Anglo-Chinese College was located.[61] The subsequent years saw a continuous rise of such cases; some key dynamics of colonial deodorization can be teased out.

During the three-year period from 1890 to 1892, the SMC tackled about thirty-five cases regarding putrid water.[62] At the council meeting of 19 February 1890, a member reported that several stagnant ponds on

---

[56] In 1850 there were only 210 foreign residents in the British Settlement, while in 1900 its population stood at 352,050. See Lu, *Beyond the Neon Lights*, 32, *Shanghai tongzhi* bianzuan weiyuanhui, ed., *Shanghai tongzhi*, vol. 3, Chapter 1.1.

[57] Lu, *Beyond the Neon Lights*, 42–3.

[58] Bergère, *Shanghai*, 58–62. A larger-scale industrial growth would start after 1895 when the Treaty of Shimonoseki permitted direct foreign investment, and Shanghai grew to be China's largest industrial centre in the early twentieth century.

[59] Lu, *Beyond the Neon Lights*, 44–5.

[60] In MSMC 8, reports about stinky ponds in Hongkou can be found at 502, 616, 622, 637, 667, 682. For a pond in Yangpu, 693.

[61] MSMC 8, English version 263, Chinese version 622, 1 June 1885. Hereafter the page numbers of the original English version and the Chinese version, both printed in this volume, are presented in that order, separated by a slash.

[62] This period is covered in MSMC 10. I select it for a case study.

Yang-tsze-poo (Yangshupu) Road near a silk filature had been emitting 'an offensive smell' and become a 'public nuisance'.[63] In May, the inspector of nuisances informed that work had been under way to have them filled in,[64] which, however, triggered local Chinese residents' protest. They petitioned the district magistrate (*zhixian* 知縣), demanding that the SMC stop their work because filling in the ponds would interfere with water supply in the neighbourhood. This concern was at odds with the overarching agenda of the British sanitary officials and professionals. A surveyor reasoned that filling the ponds would allow 'the road being widened, then drain pipes will be laid', and a Dr Burge confirmed that polluted water there had long been 'a nuisance in hot weather', detrimental to public health.[65]

This case sums up the tensions underlying colonial deodorization. All started with 'odorization' caused by the silk filature, one of the earliest types of industry in Shanghai fuelled by the European fascination with Chinese silk.[66] In fact, behind the innocent molecules of foul smells existed a larger sociopolitical system of capitalist expansion. The measures taken by the British administration typify the 'sensibilities and action' guided by modern knowledge of sanitary engineering. Yet a different set of biological and social logics reigned in the local Chinese community. Malodour was outweighed by the importance of water, the essence of life in the Jiangnan region, indispensable for cooking, drinking, washing, irrigation, travel, and transport of goods. Besides these opposing sensibilities and practical concerns, economic inequity was another crucial player in the power game of deodorization.

In March 1892, Hongkou resident Mr Osborne Middleton and thirteen foreigners complained to the SMC about 'the filthy and dangerous state of the ponds' in a Chinese village, as they were mostly fed by surface drainage, into which the villagers threw all their refuse, giving forth an

---

[63] MSMC 10, 27/655, 19 February 1890.   [64] MSMC 10, 71/669, 6 May 1890.

[65] MSMC 10, 190/706, 11 November 1890.

[66] More examples of industrial pollution and stench can be found. For example, a dye pond (associated with a cotton mill) near Boone Road in Hongkou emitted 'a peculiar sickening smell' and caused many cases of illness. See MSMC 10, 405/775, 10 November 1891; MSMC 10, 427/782, 15 December 1891.

exhalation 'unbearable in warm weather, causing a great deal of sickness'.[67] This classic narrative – compounded of filth, miasma, the Chinese inattention to hygiene, and public health – brought an equally typical reaction from the council. An inspector investigated the matter and discovered that the principle pond under review was connected with a main drain, a large portion of which had been recently cleansed by the council. Yet half of it belonged to several Chinese residents, who had declined to fill it in for several reasons. Apart from their needs for water for irrigation, some homes were built on piles on the banks of the ditch, with 'swamps of dirty, stagnant and offensive water' underneath. While two of the owners agreed to fill in the swamp, the third was too poor to fund the work.[68] The sheer reality of poverty and wishful thinking about 'public' health were irreconcilable. Instances of incompatibility can be found in a more severe clash provoked by a larger-scale project in 1891.

This project was designed to fill in eight reeking ponds in Hongkou and build a culvert between two others at a cost of 1,063 silver taels.[69] The SMC's rationales were as usual: filth and stench had caused 'numerous deaths from Cholera' in Hongkou.[70] When a contractor went to survey the area, he met with a great deal of opposition from local villagers. Under the leadership of Xiang Detai (Hang Te-Tai), they sent a petition to the magistrate, stating that apart from the creek's function of meeting their daily needs, filling in it would 'interfere with the Feng Shui of the ancestral graves of the Hang (Xiang) family, which dates back to the Ming dynasty'.[71] Moreover, they were afraid of 'the road being taken by the Council when the ponds are filled in'.[72] The magistrate and his superior, the circuit intendant (*daotai* 道台), pressed the British consul general with a warning of further disturbance, but the SMC

---

[67] MSMC 10, 481–2/800, 15 March 1892. For the original letter, see Shanghai Municipal Council, *Report for the Year Ended 31st December 1892 and Budget for the Year Ending 31st December 1893*, 78.

[68] MSMC 10, 481–2/800, 15 March 1892.

[69] MSMC 10, 349/757, 11 August 1891. One tael was equivalent to 37.8 grams at the time. See ATRC 1892.

[70] MSMC 10, 381/767, 29 September 1891.

[71] MSMC 10, 380–1/767, 29 September 1891.

[72] MSMC 10, 363/761, 1 September 1891.

resolved to conduct the work and would dispatch the police to 'put down any attempt to forcibly stop the work'.[73]

At the heart of this collision were two Chinese concerns that overrode the purported importance of deodorization and sanitation. One was *fengshui*, the renowned concept deeply rooted in traditional Chinese beliefs in the harmonic concord of human life and environments. The *fengshui* of ancestral tombs is of particular significance for safeguarding the prosperity of the living. Western insensitivity to this matter caused ceaseless strife in urban planning and construction during the time. The most influential case was probably the Ningbo Cemetery Riots (the Siming gongsuo 四明公所 incident) in 1874 and 1898, triggered by the French plan to clear a Chinese cemetery.[74] Xiang Detai and his fellow villagers' protest occurred in this context. Being such a high-profile actor in Sino-European clashes, *fengshui* might have been manipulated as a Chinese strategy of political resistance against foreign demands, but in this particular case it does seem convincing that the 'trivial' problem of odour could not compete with their firmly ingrained *fengshui* thinking. The second Chinese concern was the charged issue of territorial expansion through road building by Western powers, and this microscopic dispute mirrored the larger political landscape of imperialist aggression and Chinese nationalism. From the villagers' point of view, the ownership of the noxious ponds mattered far more than a deodorized land belonging to the foreigners.

These stories demonstrate the implausibility of building an odourless utopia of modernity. Airborne, transcorporeal odours cannot be contained by artificial boundaries; the interstices are their permanent home, as are water and much organic matter. Contamination is inevitable and purity unattainable. The Shanghailanders' diligent battle against miasmas is modernity's punctilious fight in miniature against strangers – the undefinable, unpredictable creatures that constantly challenge categorization. What happened on the miasmic soil of Hongkou shows that

---

[73] For the details of the negotiation process, see correspondences discussed at the SMC meetings on 11 August, 1 September, 29 September, and 13 October 1891 (MSMC 10, 390–1/770).

[74] Belsky, 'Bones of Contention'; Henriot, *Scythe and the City*; Yuan, 'Gongbuju yu Shanghai luzheng', 192–5.

the more effort they put into deodorizing, the more resistance and chaos they occasioned; the more intricate the sanitary plans they devised, the more noxious fumes arose from modernity's other terrains of business. And yet their impulse to govern the ungovernable persisted. By disregarding the locals' practical and spiritual needs, sensibilities, and affordabilities, their project was a differential deodorization, a stratified reorganization of urban spaces and atmospheres. The stories in Hongkou and Yangpu were only a prelude. While water-related disputes continued to emerge in the following years,[75] the number gradually decreased from the late 1890s on. The 1890s saw the peak of road construction in Hongkou, and by 1899 an extensive road network was in place.[76] In the new century the SMC gave more attention to improving Shanghai's main waterways (Yangjing Creek, Defence Creek, and Huangpu River).[77] But this does not mean that the goal of deodorization was accomplished; it only means that miasmas were displaced to two locations, the peripheries of the city, inhabited by the poor, and the underground world beneath the foreign settlements.

The subject of sewerage construction occupied a sizable portion of time at SMC meetings.[78] As early as April 1855, the new municipality distributed a notice to landowners about 'the location of drains in the different properties in the settlement' in order to make 'a plan of the lines of sewage for general convenience'.[79] The council's annual report of 1859 pointed out, 'A complete and uniform system of drainage is a growing want; many of the roads are at present altogether without drains.'[80] This was in the midst of the Taiping Rebellion (1850–1864), when numerous refugees flocked from neighbouring regions to Shanghai's foreign concessions, causing serious overcrowding and the termination of the initial segregation of Chinese and

---

[75] MSMC 11 (1893–1894) and 12 (1895–1896) still include a considerable number of cases concerning filling in ponds and ditches.

[76] Yuan, 'Gongbuju yu Shanghai luzheng', 183–4. Also see Sun, *Shanghai jindai chengshi gonggong guanli zhidu yu kongjian jianshe*, 115–26.

[77] For example, MSMC 15 (1902–1904) includes a great deal of discussion about filling in Yangjing Creek.

[78] To take MSMC 1 (1854–1863) as an example, discussions of this issue can be found at 594, 595, 606, 614, 615, 617, 622, 625, 630, 633, 635, 638, 644, 647, 667, 677, 685, 700.

[79] MSMC 1, 53/581, 2 April 1855.   [80] *NCH*, 25 February 1860, 31.

foreign residence.[81] The year 1859 was also when the construction of London's modern sewage system commenced.[82]

The SMC's Defence Committee submitted a detailed report in 1861, stressing the urgency of seeking relief from 'the intolerable evils resulting from the damming up of all the water outlets of the central quarter of the Settlement'.[83] Since it was impossible to build a proper system immediately (because the Taiping army cut off supplies of bricks), the committee proposed a tentative plan: digging three main open tidal ditches, into which open ditches and ponds could drain; the ditches should be covered with planking in order to avoid noxious exhalation. These measures, the committee believed, would 'unquestionably clear that part of the town of the stagnant waters now poisoning the air'. The report also included the design of a comprehensive drainage system for the future: 'barrel drains of an oval shape 3 feet by 5 feet' should be laid five feet under the ground to replace the ditches, and medium drains measuring 1.5 by 2.5 feet buried two feet under the ground along smaller streets. The drains should be cleansed by forcing clean water through them. Designed by Colonel Moody, this scheme should be carried out to 'great perfection' with 'the services of an engineer'.

The decision makers of the SMC did not wait too long to officially launch the ambitious project. Starting in spring 1862, fundraising (of 132,000 taels) was sought through advertising, and assistance from the admiral was requested 'in the use of a Gun Boat' to protect the boats transporting bricks to Shanghai.[84] Construction commenced in summer of the same year. Council meetings in subsequent years devoted a large amount of time to discussing minute technical details, ranging from manholes and tide gates,[85] to the method of draining stagnant ponds into a new drain,[86] to the consultation of a London-based civil engineer.[87] Needless to say, building the system was costly. In the 1863–1864 financial year, the expenditure on sewerage (35,290 taels) was roughly equivalent to the total cost of constructing roads, buildings, bridges,

---

[81] Lu, *Beyond the Neon Lights*, 36.   [82] Halliday, *The Great Stink of London*, 90.

[83] 'Report upon Drainage and Water Supply', *NCH*, 5 April 1862, supplement, n.p. All the quotations in this paragraph are from this source.

[84] MSMC 1, 256/635, 7 April 1862.   [85] MSMC 1, 644, 21 July 1862.

[86] MSMC 1, 647, 10 September 1862.   [87] MSMC 1, 695, 4 November 1863.

jetties, and all repairs (32,599 taels).[88] An underground network was steadily growing, with large main drains running north to south through the principal streets to Suzhou and Yangjing Creeks, and small drains in the streets running east and west connecting to the main drains.[89] The beginning of 1871 marked the completion of the main project with a 'fully satisfactory' result: the drains were 'effective', having 'retained little or no deposit' after several years of trial.[90]

This work exemplifies the coalition of different forces behind colonial deodorization. Economic and military power as well as the bureaucratic system of sanitary engineering ensured the disciplined progress of the project, as demonstrated by the ways in which funds were raised, the transport of materials was guaranteed, and the construction work was planned and carried out. Knowledge and technology guaranteed that stagnant water was made tidal and filth and stench were confined within the drainpipes. Key materials were sourced from the motherland, such as the legendary Doulton's drainpipes.[91] The best-known brand for industrial ceramics, the Doulton factory in England pioneered the manufacture of oval-shaped earthenware pipes, instrumental in Chadwick's sanitary reform.[92] From brick sewers to ceramic pipes and box drains (a small rectangular-shaped drainage structure),[93] Shanghai's subterranean network kept pace with global technological innovations. From 1891 onwards, the new material cement was used in drainage construction, and the SMC even owned a factory that produced cement drainpipes, which generated a revenue of 12,000 taels in

---

[88] See 'Municipal Council Finance' in Shanghai Municipal Council, 'Municipal Report for the Year Ending 31st March 1864', n.p.

[89] For the layout of this drainage system, see 'The Municipal Report, 1870–71', *NCH*, 5 May 1871, 317. For the locations of the sewers, see 'Municipal Report for the Year 1862', 59; 'Municipal Report for the Half Year Ending 30th September, 1863', 2; 'Municipal Report for the Year Ending 31st March, 1864', 32, and so on.

[90] 'The Municipal Report, 1870–71'.

[91] The council authorized its Works Committee to place an order for these drainpipes. See MSMC 7, 81/608, 3 August 1877.

[92] Inglis, 'Sewers and Sensibilities', 120; Eyles, *Royal Doulton, 1815–1965*.

[93] Brick sewers were constructed in the 1860s, and earthenware pipes and box drains were more popular in the 1870s. For references to box drains, see MSMC 7, 661, 13 January 1879; Shanghai Municipal Council, *Report for the Year Ended 31st December 1879 and Budget for the Year Ending 31st December 1880*, 103.

1895.[94] That year, a total length of 17,280 feet (5.267 kilometres) of 'egg-shaped cement concrete sewer tubes and pipe drains' were laid in the Settlement.[95] No wonder there were much fewer complaints about fetid ponds in the twentieth century, as most of them within the enclave of the Settlement had been conquered. Roads were paved, drainpipes were laid underneath, and the topography of Jiangnan metamorphosed. But miasmas did not vanish; they were gathering densely outside the zone of olfactory modernity, waiting to confront other sociopolitical agents.

DEODORIZING THE WALLED CITY

In the immediate neighbourhood of the foreign settlements stood 'a filthy native city contaminating both air and water, and forming a nest wherein contagious diseases are generated and whence they are disseminated', as the medical officer, Alexander Jamieson, lamented.[96] No politically demarcated border can prohibit the flow of air, water, and microbes, a perennial conundrum in the modern history of deodorization. The engineered atmosphere of the foreign districts was in a symbiotic relationship with that of the territory under Chinese jurisdiction. For a fuller comprehension of the vicissitudes of Shanghai smellscapes, Jamieson's assertion needs to be tested against a longer trajectory of environmental change. Contrary to the popular fishing-village myth, Shanghai was a major centre of cotton production and a bustling commercial port city in late imperial times.[97] By the time of the arrival of the British, Shanghai proper was a round city surrounded by a wall and a moat, a little under two kilometres in diameter (Figure 3.2). A sprawling urban area extended outside the walls, especially to the east, connecting to the port.[98] Intersected within the streets and alleys was a maze of small canals feeding into a larger nexus of waterways in Jiangnan. This spatial

---

[94] Yuan, 'Gongbuju yu Shanghai luzheng', 185; MSMC 12, 332/545, 30 June 1896.
[95] Shanghai Municipal Council, *Report for the Year Ended 31st December 1895 and Budget for the Year Ending 31st December 1896*, 178.
[96] Jamieson, 'Memo. on the Sanitary Condition', 208.   [97] Johnson, *Shanghai*, 9.
[98] Ibid., 7, 96–116.

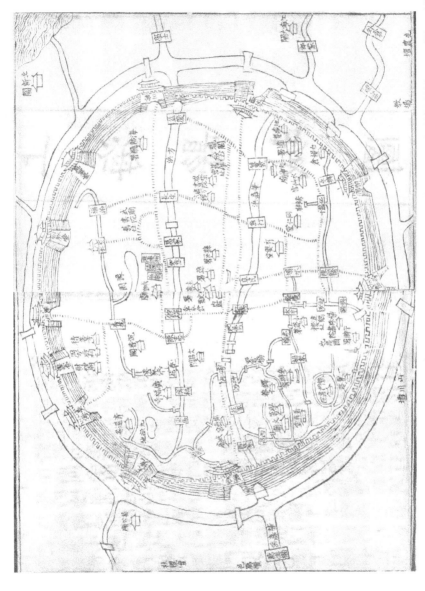

Figure 3.2 Map of the walled city of Shanghai, 1871. Source: *Shanghai xianzhi* (Shanghai gazetteer), 1871 (10th year of Tongzhi).

pattern was vital to 'a flourishing waterborne commerce' in this region dating back to the Southern Song, if not earlier.[99]

Sanitary conditions and atmospheric qualities garnered scant attention in local gazetteers and Confucian scholars' lyrical form of writing. Through a late Ming poem, we can almost inhale the breath of the city, its serenity and vigour: 'Mist and clouds wind and coil together with the smoke from cooking fires above the streams and flat lands'.[100] But little vestige is left of the actual lived environment of the populous city, home to an estimated 200,000 residents and sojourners in the early nineteenth century.[101] Official records about water are predominantly concerned with dredging and conservancy work in the service of transport and irrigation; hygienic considerations are scarcely visible in written form.[102] According to a widely accepted explanation, waste disposal in premodern East Asia relied upon a balanced rural–urban ecosystem, an ever-flowing cycle of exchange between agricultural products and human excrement (to fertilize soil). Therefore urban waste was less a public-health affair than a commodity within an intricate economy of night-soil collection and sale. This organic system of 'nutrient cycles' ensured relatively healthier, cleaner, and better-smelling urban environs, as compared to European medieval cities.[103] Unrecyclable refuse was dumped into rivers and the majority was washed away by tidal currents. Once the water channels had silted up, the government or local gentry would organize dredging work.[104] Despite a lack of public-health provision, these ecosystems by and large maintained

[99] Elvin, 'Market Towns and Waterways', 441.

[100] Quoted and translated in Johnson, *Shanghai*, 82; originally from *Kangxi Shanghai xianzhi, juan* 1.

[101] Johnson, *Shanghai*, 120–1. According to Mark Elvin, Shanghai reached a density of more than 1,000 people per square mile shortly after 1800. See Elvin, 'Market Towns and Waterways', 444. It is a high percentage of urbanization for any premodern society.

[102] Yu, 'Qingdai Jiangnan', 14–15. Yu gave some examples showing that exceptions did exist, but overall sanitary improvements were only implied, not explicitly stated.

[103] Yu, 'The Treatment of Night Soil and Waste in Modern China', 51–6; Marks, *China: An Environmental History*, 181–3.

[104] Yu, 'The Treatment of Night Soil and Waste in Modern China', 57. For a study of dredging work in Beijing during the Ming dynasty, see Chiu, 'Mingdai Beijing de gouqu shurui jiqi xiangguan wenti'.

'a social and ecological equilibrium' in premodern China, as Yu Xingzhong asserts.[105]

This equilibrium was changing, however. Without sufficient pre-1843 data, it is hard to gauge precisely the extent to which sanitary degradation accelerated in Shanghai after its opening as a treaty port. What remains visible is a plethora of Western records (such as Jamieson's report) and a spurt of internal 'China stinks' discourse, emerging in the modern press of the 1870s. As discussed in Chapter 2, the voices from Chinese elites centred on the contrasting images of the dual city, the native parts seething with piles of rubbish, repugnant canals, and filthy streets, while the foreign districts were the paragon of order and hygiene. Smell was a register of their desperation. Some perceived the matter through the lens of Chinese miasma theory, interpreting local residents' 'acute ailment' (*jisha zhi zheng* 急痧之症) a result of inhaling 'noxious vapours' (*huiqi* 穢氣) and 'miasmic fumes' (*zhangqi* 瘴氣).[106] Yet the dominant frame of interpretation was aligned with the rhetoric of 'Chinese deficiency' – deficiency in terms of the Chinese ways of governance, civic attitudes, and sanitary habits.[107] Their discontent was often compounded by moral–psychological distress, as we can sense from the writing of the reputable gentleman Li Pingshu 李平書: 'Whenever I talk about Shanghai after its opening to foreign trade, I feel ashamed and sad (吾一言通商以後之上海而為之愧爲之悲).'[108] These moral sentiments, however, eclipsed the more fundamental cause of the city's worsening breath; that is, its shifting ecosystems.

The immediate, and self-evident, odorizing engine was the city's drastic economic restructuring and demographic pressure. Pre-treaty-port Shanghai was primarily an agriculture-based economy operating in sync with the aforementioned ecosystems, even though commercial activities had been expanding since Kangxi lifted the prohibition on sea traffic in 1684.[109] The exponential growth of trade and commerce after

---

[105] Yu, 'Qingdai Jiangnan', 18.
[106] 'Lun Chengnei ruihe huiqi niang sha shi', *SB*, 13 June 1873, 2.
[107] Xiong, 'Shanghai zujie yu Shanghai shehui sixiang bianqian', 126–31; Yuan, 'Gongbuju yu Shanghai luzheng', 199.
[108] Xiong, 'Shanghai zujie', 127; the original source is Li Pingshu's essay in a Shanghai gazetteer.
[109] Johnson, *Shanghai*, 96, 113–19; Xiong, 'Shanghai zujie', 132.

1843 magnified environmental pressures on the cramped city, as was the case with most medieval cities elsewhere in modern history. As an 1881 essay in *Shenbao* explains, the self-cleansing capacity of the rivers by tidal flow was outpaced by the speedy accumulation of rubbish, produced not only by the residents but also by a stream of business travellers and tourists. Inevitably, the walled city was infested with mal-odours.[110] Furthermore, new features of the economy altered the occu-pational structure of the local labour force. When farmers in or near the region were attracted by more lucrative jobs in foreign and domestic shipyards, shops, and mills, the nutrient cycles of the urban–rural symbi-osis were fractured.[111] As a Japanese traveller observed in 1862, the locals had been neglecting farming in favour of working in silk workshops, and thus the demand for night soil lowered and the city grew smellier.[112]

A more profound factor that unbalanced the pre-existing ecosystems was the spatial reorganization carried out by the foreigners to serve the colonial capitalist economy and modern sanitary ideology. As shown in the previous section, the crux of this spatial project was threefold: expunging ditches, paving roads, and building underground sewers. By the late 1860s, most ditches that had been criss-crossing the land leased to the British had vanished, replaced by a longitudinal grid of streets and a subterranean network of sewers.[113] Whilst colonial medical officers feared the border crossings of miasma, water, and disease, they rarely reflected that their man-made enclave disrupted the ecology of Jiangnan's water network, in part leading to the build up of stagnant water outside the settlements. Moreover, unlike the London system, which discharged sewage miles downstream into the Thames, the main outlet of the Shanghai drainage was Yangjing Creek, running through the city's central area.[114] In other words, stenches were relegated from the centre to the periphery only if one

---

[110] 'Shanghai chengnei difang yijia zhengdun shuo', *SB*, 18 December 1881, 1.

[111] Bergère, *Shanghai*, 58–70; Xiong, 'Shanghai zujie', 132. But night-soil businesses did not discontinue; see Huang, 'Deodorizing China', 1114–16.

[112] Mine, 'Qingguo Shanghai jianwen lu', 623–4.

[113] Chen, *Kindai Shanghai no toshi keiseishi*, 103.

[114] Jamieson, 'Memo. on the Sanitary Condition', 210; 'Report upon Drainage and Water Supply', *NCH*, 5 April 1862. For a map of the London system, see Halliday, *The Great Stink of London*, 94.

adopts the British perspective. Until 1916, when it was filled in, Yangjing Creek was a constant topic of complaint – being an 'odoriferous, open sewer', its impact on the whole waterway system of Shanghai was profound and complex.[115] The detailed contours of the environmental transfiguration warrant a separate study; suffice it to say, the festering smellscapes of the native city need to be comprehended against the backdrop of these macroscopic ecological shifts.

In response to the physical, moral, and psychological crisis of the great stink, the local Chinese elite – the gentry, merchants, and imperial officials – initiated a battle to deodorize the native city. Sanitary policing was strengthened, new regulations were announced, and novel municipal institutions were installed. In many ways the measures emulated the foreign public-health infrastructure, whilst building on existing traditions and institutions. The enhanced olfactory sensibility was addressed. The Shanghai Daotai announced a decree in 1873, stipulating that night-soil boats and buckets must be equipped with tight coverings in order to avoid 'miasmic vapours' (*huiqi xunzheng* 穢氣薰蒸), a rule that duplicated an article in the 1869 Land Regulations of the International Settlement.[116] A highway code published in 1898 gave meticulous guidance on sanitary management, 'all imitating the Settlements'.[117] Out of twenty-four articles, four contain direct references to stench prohibition: 'foul objects' (*chouwu* 臭物) or anything 'offensive to the nose' (*qiwei chubi* 氣味觸鼻) must not be left outside or stored inside individual homes, ordure pails must be fitted with lids to avoid 'disease-causing noxious emanations', and unkempt beggars who 'would cause one to cover his nose' were forbidden on public roads.[118] More groundbreaking was the establishment of a sanitary bureau (*weisheng chu* 衛生處) within the Shanghai City Council, a new municipal institution set up in 1905. It marked the dawn of institutionalized public-health

[115] 'Objectionable Creeks', *NCH*, 17 May 1913, 486–7. Also see Chen, *Kindai Shanghai no toshi keiseishi*, 117.

[116] 'Yizun fengxing chajin fenchuan fentong bujia jingai gaoshi', *SB*, 5 April 1873, 3; Article 26 in *Land Regulations and By-laws for the Foreign Settlement of Shanghai*, 16.

[117] 'Malu fakuan', *SB*, 1 February 1898, 3.

[118] 'Hunan xinzhu malu shanhou zhangcheng', *SB*, 20 January 1898, 3.

administration under Chinese jurisdiction.[119] Apart from the routine duties of hygiene maintenance, conquering Shanghai's troublesome water was high on its agenda. The dominant strategy, however, was not the traditional approach of dredging, but the modern solution of filling in, laying sewers, and paving roads. In the modern history of water, as Jean-Pierre Goubert writes, 'invisibility is indeed the height of conquest'.[120]

From the Shanghai gazetteer of 1914, we learn that between 1906 and 1913, 169 road repair or construction projects were carried out in the walled city and its adjacent suburbs, out of which fifty-four cases (32 per cent) involved filling in creeks or ponds.[121] Stench saturates the otherwise lifeless chronicle of public-works achievements: 'choked, fetid, and filthy creeks' (*yuse chuohui bang* 淤塞臭穢浜), 'stinking ditches' (*choushuibang* 臭水浜), and 'scummy pools' (*huichi* 穢池) were all noted, evoking vicarious repulsion that might have served to justify the sanitary reform.[122] The new roads were paved with flagstones (*shipian* 石片), and open brick sewers (*zhuangou* 磚溝) were replaced by earthenware pipes (*watong gou* 瓦筒溝) with a diameter of thirty centimetres (nine *cun*), forty centimetres (twelve *cun*), or one metre (three *chi*). Supervised by the City Council, large projects were sponsored by government funds, while small ones were financed collectively by local residents, businesses, and gentry-run charities (such as Fuyuantang 輔元堂). This model was a continuation of the traditional organizing mechanism of hydraulic programmes.[123]

The most spectacular, physically and symbolically, of all the projects was the demolition of the city wall and moat. Constructed in the mid-sixteenth century to defend against rampant pirate raids, Shanghai's city wall was about 4.5 kilometres (nine *li*) in circumference and 3.6 metres high, and had six gates and three watergates. It was surrounded by a moat eleven metres wide and two metres deep.[124] By the mid-nineteenth century, the pirates had long disappeared, and the dilapidated wall

---

[119] Peng, *Gonggong weisheng*, 89–90; for a comprehensive study of the Shanghai City Council, see Elvin, 'The Administration of Shanghai, 1905–1914'.

[120] Goubert, *The Conquest of Water*, 26.   [121] Yang, *Shanghai shi zizhi zhi*, 73–92.

[122] Ibid., 73, 74, 76, inter alia.   [123] Elvin, 'Market Towns and Waterways', 462–7.

[124] Johnson, *Shanghai*, 81.

remained only as a psychological barrier and had only semiotic existence. The moat was an open sewer, receiving drainage from three sides of the city, thereby a generator of *materies morbi*, according to Alexander Jamieson.[125] Under the pen of the Chinese officials, the choked moat was 'indescribably fetid' (*yuhui chou'e buke xiang'er* 淤穢臭惡不可嚮而), and the narrow roadway between the wall and the moat teemed with wretched shanties of 'unimaginable squalor' (*wochuo wanzhuang* 齷齪萬狀). All the impurities and stenches were not only 'an object of ridicule' by foreigners but also 'a disgrace and shame' to the Chinese officials in charge.[126] Pleas for action arose. In 1906, thirty-one of the local gentry submitted a petition to the Daotai, calling for the demolition of the wall in order to promote commerce.[127] Three years later, the French Concession proposed to fill in the portion of the moat adjacent to its territory for the benefit of public health.[128] Both proposals met with strong resistance from the conservative contingent of the Chinese populace, but the momentous transition to becoming a republic supplied a fresh impetus that eventually brought the walls down.

On 14 January 1912, only fourteen days after the declaration of the Republic, the newly installed mayor of Shanghai received a proposition. On behalf of the same cohort of Shanghai notables, the proposer, Li Pingshu, asserted that time was ripe for demolishing the wall as the new Republic was 'striving for progress' (*litu jinhua* 力圖進化). Three benefits were emphasized: the improvement of traffic circulation (to the advantage of commerce), the city's appearance, and public hygiene (*renmin weisheng* 人民衛生).[129] The proposal was approved expeditiously. On 19 January work commenced, starting from the section stretching from near the county *yamen* (the magistrate's office), a symbolic gesture of

---

[125] Jamieson, 'Memo. on the Sanitary Condition', 209.

[126] Yang, *Shanghai shi zizhi zhi*, 283, 'Kairui chenghe ji laowa chengnei Zhaojiabang an' (The Case of Dredging the City Moat and Zhaojia Creek), 1906.

[127] Ibid., 289, 'Yiqing chaicheng ji gaiban pimen zhulu an' (The Case of Petitioning for Demolishing the City Wall and Paving Roads), 1906.

[128] Ibid., 323, 'Yi rui Xiao dongmen zhi Ximen chenghe an' (The Case of Dredging the City Moat from Small East Gate to West Gate), 1909.

[129] Ibid., 795, 'Chaiqiang tianhao an' (The Case of Demolishing the City Wall and Filling in the Moat), 14 January 1912.

breaking away from the dynastic past.[130] The Shanghai mayoralty also signed an agreement with the French consul about drying up the city moat. The new road to be built on the site would be about 13.3 metres (four *zhang*) wide, equipped with large and deep drains, into which the small drains originally owned by the French municipality would be connected.[131] The underground sewers that replaced the moat, ironically, were constructed with the bricks of the dismantled city wall.[132] The last vestige of the ancient fortification was transfigured into the quintessentially modern facility, practically and symbolically keeping the obsolete, the malodourous, away from sight and nose.

At the centre of this olfactory revolution was likewise a spatial project of redistributing odour and capital. Colonial deodorization and ecological shifts provided the immediate catalyst for the Chinese drive to integrate its space with foreign terrains. Rhetorically, as the gentry petitioners asserted, removing the ancient wall would make the inside and outside of the native city 'integrated and aligned' (*dangping zhengzhi* 蕩平正直), and 'orderly and uniform' (*zhengli huayi* 整理劃一).[133] Technically, the new road that replaced the moat joined the adjacent road within the French concession, merging into a 'level and broad' thoroughfare, and so were the drains (by extension, waste and stench).[134] The new spatial–sensorial vocabulary overturned the Confucian order of things. The High Qing appearance of Shanghai – the well-regulated garden city inside the wall and the unplanned, meandering commercial suburbs – mirrored the Confucian hierarchy of urban organization, with governmental/scholarly affairs placed at the centre and mercantile activities on the periphery.[135] But now, with the altered urban morphology, Shanghai's centre was transposed to the foreign territory, specifically the commercial hub of Nanjing Road and the Bund.[136] This physical,

---

[130] Ibid., 795–6; 'Demolition of City Walls', *NCH*, 27 January 1912, 232.
[131] Yang, *Shanghai shi zizhi zhi*, 797; 'City-Wall Demolition Scheme', *NCH*, 17 August 1912, 478.
[132] 'The City Wall: Progress of the Scheme', *NCH*, 26 October 1912, 228.
[133] Yang, *Shanghai shi zizhi zhi*, 795.   [134] 'City-Wall Demolition Scheme', 478.
[135] Johnson, *Shanghai*, 96–7.
[136] For a *longue durée* trajectory of Nanjing Road's identity making, see Huang, 'Smellscapes of Nanjing Road'.

sensorial, and affective map of Shanghai is retained to the present day, to a large degree.

At the same time, the shifting geography of odour was coterminous with that of capital and social stratification. As was the case in Haussmann's Paris, the disinfected and deodorized zones of Shanghai likewise resulted from hierarchical operations of power and a differential division of order/disorder. A journalist of the *North-China Herald* pointed out that the land freed up by the removal of the walls should 'be of considerable value', if used 'to best advantage'.[137] The real-estate market was a major source of Shanghai prosperity. Spurred by the influx of war refugees in the 1850s and 1860s, the soaring prices of land and leases made a vast contribution to the fortunes of a coterie of speculators, banks, and commercial firms, foreign and Chinese alike.[138] Yet at the turn of the century, the average property value in the Chinese districts was only a third or a quarter of that in the foreign concessions.[139] Raising land value must have been an unstated motive of the Chinese elites in demolishing the wall. Concerns were raised in official correspondence with regard to relocating the inhabitants of the shanties from the foot of the wall, mostly 'the powerless poor' (*wuli pinmin* 無力貧民).[140] Yet little is known about the actual compensation deals and details of their new homes. When the poor were ordered to remove their shacks, fences, and materials which would 'impede the progress of the work', foreign observers expected an outcry; but the order was 'quietly accepted'.[141] This observation might be only partially true, as intensive negotiations did happen between the City Council and a committee that represented the landowners and tenants affected.[142] Nevertheless it is doubtful that the interests of the underclass were earnestly addressed. The gentry-scholar Wang Yincai 王引才 expressed his opinion at a meeting of the council's policy-making body:

> Leasing the land between the wall and the moat was an imprudent policy
> (*bizheng* 弊政), and therefore the leaseholders should not claim the same
> rights as normal landowners. I would feel uneasy to make a policy to only

---

[137] 'Demolition of City Walls', 232.   [138] Bergère, *Shanghai*, 56–8.

[139] 'Yue benbao ji malu kaigong xi er shu ci', *SB*, 14 July 1896, 1.

[140] Yang, *Shanghai shi zizhi zhi*, 283.   [141] 'Demolition of City Walls', 232.

[142] 'Chaicheng zhulu zhi jingying', *SB*, 26 July 1912, 7, and many other reports in *Shenbao* during the period.

meet the minority's interests, whilst neglecting the public interests of building the thoroughfare. It would be ideal to compensate them a piece of land on the same site if there's any available after the wall's demolition; otherwise any land elsewhere would serve the purpose.[143]

The plebeians seemed unlikely to benefit from the gentrification of this area; most probably they were dispersed elsewhere away from the centre, as Wang hinted. In late 1913 the northern sector of the project was completed and named Republic Road (Minguo lu 民國路), followed by the completion of other portions in ensuing years.[144] The native city was further modernized by the operation of a tramway on Republic Road, above the sealed pipelines that now caged miasmas and *materies morbi*.[145]

The progression of the twentieth century saw the advent of a new character in the modern history of stench in Shanghai: shanty towns, or *penghu qu* 棚户区 ('straw hut districts'). A by-product of Shanghai's rapid industrialization, large shanty towns began to emerge in the 1920s on the edges of the city, often by riversides. Poverty-stricken rural migrants squatted in clusters of settlements that ringed the urban centre – the foreign concessions and the former walled city (Figure 3.3).[146] It was on this ring around the city that the miasmic outcasts of olfactory modernity were displaced. A shanty town in Yangshupu (in 1932) had every element that public-health laws proscribe:

> Sanitary conditions are bad, garbage and sewage being left uncovered. No public facilities are used by these dwellers, even though on a main road a few yards away there may be a sewerage system and garbage collection service. Many of these dwellers in huts of straw are fond of keeping pigs as an investment, pig-pens being placed right next to and adjoining the huts. Chickens are prevalent and at night sleep under the beds. Odors of decaying garbage, excreta of pigs, or dirty dampness pervade the atmosphere in the vicinity of these human habitations.[147]

[143] 'Zai ji chaicheng zhulu wenti', *SB*, 9 July 1912, 7.

[144] 'Fenqing Hua Fa jiexian', *SB*, 9 December 1913, 10.

[145] 'Minguo lu xingshi dianche zhi xiansheng', *SB*, 28 June 1914, 10.

[146] Lu, *Beyond the Neon Lights*, 116–18; Bergère, *Shanghai*, 103.

[147] Lamson, 'The Problem of Housing for Workers in China', 147–8, quoted in Lu, *Beyond the Neon Lights*, 121.

Figure 3.3 Slum districts in Shanghai before 1949. Source: Shanghai shehui kexueyuan, *Shanghai penghuqu de bianqian.*

Legend

Boundary of
Foreign Settlements
Boundary of District
Shantytown
Railway
River
Street

Huangpu River

Yangjingzhen

Yangshupu

Pudong

Hongkou

Nanjing Road

Suzhou Creek

Chinese City

Zhabei

British race Course

Zhaojia Creek

Changning

Xujiahui

There is no question that the modern values of deodorization and hygiene were championed by all sociopolitical agents in charge of municipal duties in these tumultuous decades of the Republic. In 1926, the warlord Sun Chuanfang 孫傳芳 created the first unified public-health bureau to oversee Shanghai's Chinese sectors. The Nationalist (Guomindang, or GMD) government inaugurated a more systematic state-sponsored sanitary administration after 1928. This infrastructure was inherited by the Japanese and the collaborative government in Shanghai during the war.[148] The familiar cast of pestilential ditches and ponds was still onstage,[149] but no monumental undertakings comparable to the wall and moat removal project occurred during the period. Slum clearance was on the agenda of the Nationalist government,[150] but more sensational performances in the continuous olfactory revolution would arrive under the Communists.

SOCIALIST DEODORIZATION

Socialist deodorization picked up where the previous programmes had left off, i.e. the fringes of the city where expelled stenches gathered. A Shakespearean ditch, featured in a three-act play by Lao She 老舍, sums up the new dynamics of the redistribution of the sense-scape. Known as Dragon Beard Ditch (Longxu gou 龙须沟), it is 'full of muddy, slimy water, mixed with rubbish, rags, dead rats, dead cats, dead dogs and now and then dead children', where night soil and waste water from the nearby tannery and dyeworks accumulate. Its riverbanks are peopled by 'labourers, handcraft workers – the multifarious toiling poor'.[151] First

---

[148] Nakajima, *Body, Society, and Nation*, 76–128. For a regulation by the Health Bureau of the collaborative government in Shanghai in 1941, see 'Shanghai tebie shi huwai qingjie guize' (April 1941), SMA, R50-1-42.

[149] Sporadic public works to fill in stinky ditches can be found; see 'Pudong qingjie yundong', *SB*, 29 April 1935, 9; 'Shisan qu tianse shuibang', *SB*, 29 August 1946, 6. Further research needs to be conducted for a fuller picture of this matter.

[150] Henriot, *Shanghai, 1927–1937*, 221–5.

[151] Lao She, *Dragon Beard Ditch*, 7. For its Chinese version, see Lao She, *Longxugou*, 4.

performed in 1951 in Beijing, the play was based on the actual public-works drive to dry up the ditch in 1950. The engineering project, the play, and a film made afterwards illustrated Maoist ideology, created a socialist urban identity, and redirected the gaze of citizens, as Yomi Braester argues.[152] Malodour takes up a vital role in propaganda aesthetics, as exemplified in Sisao's words:

> [In the past] it's as if the creek has always sat there and said, 'I'm stinking, but what do you dare to do about it? I drowned your child, but what do you dare to do about it?'' Once the government started mending the creek, it's as if Ding Si talked back and said, 'You're stinking, and you drowned my child, huh? I'm going to level you, bastard!'[153]

Whilst before 'liberation' the reeking ditch has the upper hand, after 'liberation' the empowered Ding Si (representing the suppressed masses) achieves supremacy. Stench acquires an allegorical position in the teleological march of Communism. This olfactory narrative differs little from the thrust of Western olfactory modernity that centres on progress. Moreover, socialist deodorization was likewise a physical and ideological project at the same time, striving to reorganize the geography of stench.

The new regime's war with odours began in association with the Patriotic Hygiene movement (*Aiguo weisheng yundong* 爱国卫生运动, hereafter PHM), a political campaign initiated in 1952 by Mao Zedong in response to the alleged use of germ warfare by the US Army in the Korean War.[154] This mass mobilization aimed to improve personal cleanliness and environmental sanitation, to implement compulsory vaccination, and to eradicate insects and germs. As a component of environmental purification, 'stinky ditches need to be dredged and ideally transformed into drains' and 'small ponds and depressions' need

---

[152] Braester, *Painting the City Red*, 27–55.

[153] Lao She, *Longxugou*, 64. The English translation is from Braester, *Painting the City Red*, 39.

[154] For a brief study of the movement in Tianjin, see Rogaski, *Hygienic Modernity*, 293–8. For a brief overview of the movement, see Xiao, '1949–1959 nian Aiguo weisheng yundong shulun'.

to be filled in, as instructed in a propaganda pamphlet.[155] This strategy is reminiscent of the numerous previous cases in the foreign concessions and the walled city, though the notion of germs was politicized more overtly. Politically defined enemies – the American imperialists, foreign invaders, and Chinese elites of the past – acquired a biological alter ego, the stench that is a sign of contamination. Ideology trespassed on the sensorium more blatantly in this episode of the olfactory revolution coterminous with a political revolution. Let us return to Shanghai to see how the spatial schema of deodorization continued to evolve.

Responding to the central government's call, Shanghai launched its Patriotic Hygiene movement in June 1952. Under the leadership of a central committee, thirty districts set up their own PHM committees and extensive mass organizations in schools, factories, and work units.[156] In February 1953, named PHM Month (*Aiguo weisheng yundong chunji tujiyue* 爱国卫生运动春季突击月), mobilized Shanghai citizens filled in 1,798 stagnant ponds, dredged 8,182 filthy ditches, and constructed drains covering 19,245 metres.[157] For example, 1,200 residents in Zhabei volunteered to clean and dredge a stinky ditch, and the citizens from Xuhui devised an innovative method of building drainage with bamboo pipes. In a neighbourhood in Changning, 'criss-crossed by reeking ditches' and afflicted by 'an appalling sanitary condition', 3,529 inhabitants collectively filled in a ditch with coal dust and earth. In order to boost the morale of the masses, the head of Yangjing township put up a slogan: 'Most glorious is to have mud on your hands (手上有泥最光荣).' These districts were all located in the slum zones that fringed the city (Figure 3.3). According to official statistics, by the time of the Communist takeover in 1949 there were 322 shanty towns/*penghu qu* in Shanghai, inhabited by a population of 1,000,000 in 180,000 households.[158]

[155] Song et al., *Aiguo weisheng yundong*, 6.
[156] 'Shanghai shi Aiguo weisheng yundong sannian lai gongzuo baogao', SMA, B242-1-805, 1. Also see *Shanghai weisheng zhi* bianzuan weiyuanhui, *Shanghai weisheng zhi*, 218–19.
[157] 'Shanghai shi Aiguo weisheng yundong chunji tujiyue gongzuo zongjie' (February 1953), SMA, B242-1-535, n.p. Examples below are all based on this report.
[158] Shanghai shehui kexueyuan, *Shanghai penghuqu de bianqian*, 1–8.

Hengbang Creek (Hengbanghe 横浜河) was one such spot on the map of miasma, selected as a model in the socialist olfactory revolution.[159] The 1.5-kilometre river was a 'notorious fetid ditch' located in Hongkou, just north of where the colonial deodorization had taken place in the 1890s. Another incarnation of the Shakespearean pond or the cesspool near the Thomsons' Henan home, it housed heaps of rubbish and excreta on its banks, and dead cats, dogs, rats, and children on its riverbed, making it 'a breeding ground of germs and a transmission centre for diseases (细菌的大本营，疾病的传播所)'. Local cadres pinpointed several root causes: the river functioned as a sewer for local residents, as a workshop for boatmen, and as an outlet for waste water and rubbish discharged from adjacent mills. They were determined to 'clean the banks, fill up the depressions, and clean the muddy water'. Relying on a network of party organizations (a neighbourhood committee (*jumin weiyuanhui* 居民委员会), a women's association (*funü weiyuanhui* 妇女委员会), and so on), they enlisted 3,000 residents for the cleaning work, including a female manager, some factory bosses' wives, and some elderly people who were all unaccustomed to manual labour. On 25 February the volunteers gave up their routine work and gathered at 1 p.m. Carrying red banners alive with slogans, they marched in unison amid a cacophony of joyous sound: drums and gongs, Peking opera and clapper talk, speech, and revolutionary music (from a loudspeaker donated by a pharmaceutical factory). While some volunteered to jump into the noxious water, others cleaned rubbish on the banks that had reportedly been piling up for decades under Nationalist and Japanese rule. At the end of the day, 150 tons of rubbish and dozens of animal corpses were removed. The elated local residents composed a folk song to sing the praises of the PHM and the Communist Party. One of them remarked, 'The power of the masses is mind-blowing! Holding a broom per person, we can sweep away the American enemies!'

---

[159] Unless otherwise noted, this paragraph is based on an official document (SMA, B242-1-535) under the subheading 'Bei Sichuan qu zhengli Hengbanghe de jingguo' (Details of the Cleansing of Hengbang Creek in the North Sichuan Neighbourhood). The report is not paginated.

This case illuminates some key dynamics of the socialist olfactory revolution. It shared the foundation of Western olfactory modernity – the miasma-phobia buttressed by germ theory – but it replaced the 'China stinks'/Chinese-deficiency discourse with a rhetoric that stressed the inadequacy of the former regimes. It diverged from previous practices primarily in its organizing strategy: Communist cadres substituted for professional surveyors and elitist opinion leaders to conduct investigations, party organizations took over the administrative duties of municipal public-health services, and the masses stood in for skilled workers to carry out the work. And obviously, socialist olfactory modernity was more performative, unfolding as a multisensory spectacle of labour in the Hengbang Creek case. Hardly a Communist invention, sanitary carnivals and ritualized campaigns had occurred during the Republican era and elsewhere under colonial rule.[160] Nevertheless, the CCP's mass mobilization had 'a distinctive blend of coercion and normative appeals', bolstered by 'a didactive self-confidence in its own moral rightness, unique vision and claims to transform past injustices'.[161] Bodily/sensory engagement played no small part in the Communist carnivals now taking place on the reeking margins of the urban landscape, whilst Republican-era hygiene campaigns were often launched in a deodorized site at the spatial/symbolic centre of the power structure.[162]

However resolute the socialist olfactory revolution appeared to be, it was not free from ambivalence and contradiction. Being purged as an enemy aside, malodour was simultaneously glorified when associated with labour and the masses. As Mao Zedong proclaimed in his famous 1942 Yan'an talks, 'the workers and peasants are the cleanest people and, even though their hands are soiled and their feet smeared with cow-dung, they are really cleaner than the bourgeois and petty-bourgeois

---

[160] Nakajima, *Body, Society, and Nation*, 129–80, esp. 164–70; Anderson, 'Excremental Colonialism', 665–7.

[161] Strauss, 'Morality, Coercion and State Building by Campaign in the Early PRC', 893.

[162] Nakajima, *Body, Society, and Nation*, 165. The opening ceremonies of hygiene campaigns took place in the Public Recreation Grounds, the Municipal Educational Institute, the Confucian temple of the city, and the Nanjing Grand Theatre in the 1930s, all located centrally in Shanghai.

intellectuals'.[163] The rhetoric of filth veneration was further promoted by state propaganda after the founding of the PRC. In 1959 Shi Chuanxiang 时传祥, a night-soil carrier, became a 'model worker' and shortly after a household name for his dedication to his 'evil-smelling' job. This campaign valorized excrement 'as an unlikely medium for ideas of mobilization and modernization' during the Great Leap Forward.[164] The Communist meaning-making apparatus used the neural plasticity of olfaction to its own advantage. Despite its claim to address atmospheric injustice via spatial reordering, the socialist olfactory revolution was more self-serving than emancipatory in the sense of Marx's vision, one that anticipates 'the complete emancipation of all human senses and attributes' as a result of the transcendence of private property.[165] Stench that is the stranger would continue its intervention in this revolution.

If Hengbang Creek is an unknown character, much more legendary is the socialist transformation of Zhaojia Creek (Zhaojiabang 肇嘉浜) from an infamous nuisance into an elegant boulevard. Before Shanghai's opening as a treaty port, Zhaojia Creek was a major waterway that ran across the walled city, connecting in the west to the web of watercourses outside Shanghai city and in the east to the Huangpu river (Figure 3.2). The sector within the walled city was dried up and converted to streets amidst the tide of urban restructuring in the 1910s. The western sector, which bordered the French concession, slowly became a stinking ditch due to a growing population and industrial development.[166] Its sanitary condition further deteriorated during the Sino-Japanese War, with an increasing number of slums built along the creek, rendering it Shanghai's Dragon Beard Ditch.[167] Contrary to the narrative of socialist propaganda, the Nationalist government was not completely actionless. In 1935, for example, the police issued an order to ban the dumping of

---

[163] Mao, 'Talks at the Yenan Forum on Literature and Art', 73.

[164] Morris, 'Fight for Fertilizer!', 52.

[165] Marx, *Economic and Philosophic Manuscripts of 1844*, 125.

[166] Xue, *Lao Shanghai pu tang jing bang*, 160–8. For a report on dredging Zhaojia Creek in 1906, see Yang, *Shanghai shi zizhi zhi*, vol. 2, 283–8.

[167] Shanghai shehui kexueyuan, *Shanghai penghuqu de bianqian*, 15–18; Benshu bianxie zu, *Zhaojiabang de bianqian*, 3.

rubbish in the river or on its banks.[168] In 1947, the public-works department of the Shanghai municipal government filled in part of the creek near Tushanwan 土山灣 and built an indoor market. 'Extraordinary foulness of the water' was emphasized in a short news report as the rationale for the work.[169] Yet it was the Communists who dramatized the olfactory imagery of the river, carving it into an unforgettable emblem of socialist olfactory modernity.

A propaganda pamphlet painted a caricature of Zhaojia Creek in a familiar vein: at low tide, river water was as black and sticky as asphalt, decaying carcasses and waste were floating on the surface, and the exhalations were appalling. At high tide, the river often overflowed its banks, polluting the air of the whole area.[170] In this 'waterfront slum district' (*shuishang penghu* 水上棚戶), approximately 8,000 inhabitants (in 2,000 households) lived in sheds built from bamboo, wood, and straw, hanging above the water. Sickening stench, penetrating through cracks in the floorboards and walls, was inescapable for the slum residents. Moreover, thriving mosquitos, flies, and other insects transmitted diseases rapidly.[171] In short, it was a paragon of the vices of imperialism and the Nationalist Party.[172] Conquering its stench and filth, therefore, was imperative for the new regime.

Associated with the first Five Year Plan, this major public-works project was given a government budget of 754.2 million yuan and commenced on 8 October 1954.[173] The programme aimed, first, to dry up and fill in the three-kilometre creek and to lay five kilometres of sewer pipes underneath; second, to construct a waste-water treatment plant; and third, to build a boulevard and a street garden.[174] With over 300 labourers and around 1,000 volunteers working on the site per day, the work

[168] 'Shanghai shi gong'anju xunling' (24 January 1935), *Jingcha yuekan* 3, no. 2 (20 February 1935), 46.
[169] 'Zhaojiabang Tushanwan duan hebang tianzhu malu', *Huxi* 7 (30 March 1947), 10.
[170] Benshu bianxie zu, *Zhaojiabang de bianqian*, 4.
[171] Shanghai shehui kexueyuan, ed., *Shanghai penghuqu de bianqian*, 17–18.
[172] Benshu bianxie zu, *Zhaojiabang de bianqian*, 4.
[173] *Shanghai weisheng zhi* bianzuan weiyuanhui, *Shanghai weisheng zhi*, 223.
[174] Benshu bianxie zu, *Zhaojiabang de bianqian*, 36. Also see 'Shanghai shi Zhaojiabang maiguan zhulu gongcheng zhengshi kaigong', *Jiefang ribao*, 10 October 1954, 1.

was completed in December 1956: an avenue with a green zone in the middle emerged on the site, officially named Zhaojiabang Road.[175] The stark visual contrast evokes the disparate smellscapes of past and present (Figure 3.4). The ensuing propaganda campaign heavily capitalized on the opposing sensory impressions.[176] As local resident Xie Judi 谢菊娣 remarked, 'In the old society (*jiu shehui*), imperialist bandits and reactionary governments neglected people's interests and made Zhaojia Creek filthy and stinky. Today, under the leadership of Chairman Mao and the Communist Party, Zhaojia Creek has been transformed into such a desirable place.'[177]

Socialist deodorization, however, was not an absolute departure from 'the old society'. The familiar scenario – confining evil stench into underground sewers, replaced by a pleasant-smelling boulevard with a street garden – adheres to the script of olfactory modernity, followed by Georges Haussmann, the colonial officials of Shanghai, and the Confucian reformers alike. The socialist projects were just a continuation of the ongoing olfactory revolution. And this revolution produced, in China's evolving history into post-socialism, likewise a stratified urban space and atmosphere. As noxious vapours have long vanished into thin air, house prices in the gentrified Zhaojia Creek neighbourhood have rocketed. Browsing a Shanghai property website in May 2022, one finds that a 140-square-metre apartment at the eastern end of Zhaojiabang Road is priced at 18.8 million RMB (approximately 2.8 million US dollars).[178] The value per square metre (134,190 RMB) is almost four times higher than the average annual disposable income of an individual in 2021 China (35,128 RMB).[179] This 'quality luxurious home' (*pinzhi*

---

[175] 'Linyin dadao mingming', *Jiefang ribao*, 30 December 1956, 2.

[176] Dai, *Zhaojiabang de bianhua*. The book was published in 1960 in the Learning Knowledge Series (*Xue wenhua wenku* 学文化文库) for primary- and middle-school students.

[177] Benshu bianxie zu, *Zhaojiabang de bianqian*, 52.

[178] See https://shanghai.anjuke.com/prop/view/A6225036198?spread=commprop_p& position=2&click_url (accessed 19 May 2022). The apartment is located in the Huifeng Premium Garden 汇峰鼎园, a residential complex developed in 2004 at the intersection of Zhaojiabang Road and South Ruijin Road.

[179] The data are from the National Bureau of Statistics (Guojia tongjiju 国家统计局), published on 17 January 2022, at www.stats.gov.cn/tjsj/zxfb/202201/t20220117_ 1826403.html (accessed 19 May 2022).

今日的林蔭道

昔日的臭水沟

Figure 3.4 Zhaojia Creek's past and present. Source: Shanghai shehui kexueyuan, *Shanghai penghuqu de bianqian.*

haozhai 品质豪宅) at a 'premium location' (*hexin diduan* 核心地段), as the advertisement boasts, is evidently not for the masses.

After the Zhaojia Creek project, efforts in deodorizing Shanghai continued, reaching its peak in 1958. In the spirit of the Great Leap

Forward, probably the highest number of ponds and ditches were cleansed in Shanghai's modern history that year. The mobilized masses (1,590,000 people) filled in ditches totalling 153 kilometres and laid 180 kilometres of pipes during various 'weekend and holiday volunteer labour campaigns' (*jiari yiwu laodong* 假日义务劳动).[180] In connection to the political imperative of regime consolidation and mass education, the 1950s witnessed the most dramatic episode in the socialist olfactory revolution. Despite the ever-changing political climate in the 1960s and after, the overall thrust of deodorization, hygiene, and public health has always remained. However, the spectre of malodour would return, uncannily, to other realms of Mao-era political life, a topic to be explored in Chapter 6.

CODA

The buttery aroma is as if still lingering, but the tram takes Xiaomao away from the former French concession. It was his first time to sample the tantalizing, sumptuous taste of a French brioche, generously shared by a fellow teenage boy when waiting in a queue outside the cinema. As he alights, Xiaomao's gaze follows the tram's brioche-shape as it heads north, taking with it the buttery aroma from his nasal memory. Here is his familiar neighbourhood, the notorious shanty town nestling along Suzhou Creek. Looking out from the mansard roof window of his home is a view of monotonous rooftops and smokestacks, those of the cotton mills, tobacco factories, chemical plants, handkerchief manufacturers, and steel plants. A westerly breeze wafts in the scents of spearmint toothpaste, while a north-west wind blows in the paper mill's signature olfactory compounds, a rank alkaline odour, a pungent acid vapour. Every household is forced to shut its windows.[181]

Jin Yucheng 金宇澄 re-creates this multilayered smellscape of 1950s Shanghai, as an invisible substratum of urban life he artfully weaves together in his celebrated novel *Fanhua* 繁花 (Blossoms). It also sums up the sedimented history of the city's breath recounted in this chapter.

[180] *Shanghai weisheng zhi* bianzuan weiyuanhui, *Shanghai weisheng zhi*, 223.
[181] Jin, *Fanhua*, 18–19, 45.

The enticing aroma of French bread became a synecdoche of the old foreign concession only because stenches were banished in the long battle of deodorization under colonial rule. The reeking shanty towns outside the metropolitan centre were where miasmic anomalies re-gathered, a by-product of the industrial and urban restructuring concurrent with both colonial and native-city deodorizing schemes. Socialist deodorization did not succeed in revolutionizing the city's unequal smellscapes, as Xiaomao's olfactory mapping indicates. The distinction between the so-called 'lower corner' (*xiazhijiao* 下只角) and 'upper corner' (*shangzhijiao* 上只角) is deeply ingrained in the Shanghainese perception of the city still to the present day.[182]

Charting the entwined trajectories of deodorization and urban spatial reorganization, this chapter has revealed the ways in which stench was targeted as a sanitary and sociopolitical arch-enemy in the three episodes of the Chinese olfactory revolution. A colonial branch of the ongoing European olfactory revolution, Shanghai's foreign settlements relied upon legislation, institutionalization, professionalism, and coercion to perform the tasks of deodorization. The Chinese gentry acted upon a psychological urge and practical demands, reforming the native city not only by emulating the foreign model, but also by deploying traditional resources within the Confucian community. Driven by the new regime's political agenda, the Communist project of deodorization depended on a robust network of party organization, mass mobilization, manpower, and propaganda. In spite of the different (occasionally overlapping) methods, these strands of the story shared a common ideology, one that associates odour with an uncivilized or reactionary past in the frame of developmental thinking. The manifold positive effects of modern sanitary advances are beyond doubt; nevertheless, inequity and injustice were embedded in these processes of differential deodorization. The human sensorium is not a static, indifferent witness to historical changes, but a crucial site of contest for sociopolitical forces. At the opposite end, a parallel undertaking was profoundly influencing the Chinese sensorium, initiated by a different band of actors with an aim to re-perfume China.

[182] Li, *Shanghai Homes*, 27.

4

Re-perfuming China

I read an advertisement of a soap-making 'school.' . . . It was an attractive and inspiring advertisement. It told of the great social benefits of soap-making, how it would enrich the country and enrich the people. I changed my mind about the police school and decided to become a soap-maker.

Mao Zedong 毛澤東 (1893–1976)[1]

WHEN EDGAR SNOW INTERVIEWED Mao Zedong in Yan'an, the mysterious guerrilla leader talked about his innocent youthful days. It was the first year of the new Republic (1912) and he was nineteen. Undecided what to do next, he was attracted by an advertisement that boasted of 'the great social benefits of soap-making'. Mesmerized by the inspiring words and possibly the scents of foreign soap bars, the young Mao almost embarked on a career in the beauty industry. The novelist Mao Dun 茅盾 (1896–1981) offered an alternative perspective on encounters with manufactured scents. When the village gentleman Old Mr Wu sets foot in Shanghai in May 1930, in his son's Citroën, on seeing the towering skyscrapers and street lamps flashing past in quick succession, he closes his eyes in terror. Yet he cannot switch off his sense of smell. The pungent petrol fumes and the pervasive perfume worn by his daughter assail the old man's olfactory nerves like a 'nightmare on his frail spirit'.[2] Arriving at his son's mansion brings no respite either: 'an overpowering gust of rich, heady perfume' and a swirl of 'overwhelmingly fragrant scent' compete with the sound of women's enticing laughter, music from the radio, and the glimmering lights and

---

[1] Snow, *Red Star Over China*, 139.   [2] Mao Dun, *Midnight*, 17.

143

colours of this sumptuous house.[3] The old man's nerve is overwrought, and that night he dies from a stroke. The doctor's diagnosis is 'cerebral haemorrhage' caused by overexcitement. A fashionable lady in the house is bewildered: 'Fancy it being over-excitement, though!'[4]

The opening chapter of the canonical novel *Ziye* 子夜 (*Midnight*) is often quoted as an example of the allure and menace of modernity flowering in the Chinese metropolis.[5] This compelling caricature suggests that modernity wields power on every nerve via the sensory conduits, taking a toll on some members of society, such as Old Mr Wu. In Georg Simmel's famous theorization on the metropolis and mental life, we may find a sociological diagnosis differing from that of the doctor. Simmel premises that 'lasting impressions, the slightness in their differences, the habituated regularity' consume less mental energy than 'the rapid telescoping of changing images, pronounced differences within what is grasped at a single glance, and the unexpectedness of violent stimuli'.[6] The latter characterizes the modern metropolis, creating in 'the sensory foundations of mental life' a deep contrast with the slower rhythm of the pre-industrial small town and rural existence.[7] This theory is a perceptive prognosis of Old Mr Wu's malaise, illuminating a vital sociopsychological consequence of the modern olfactory revolution in the regime of the body. By virtue of transcorporeality, scents can well be 'violent stimuli', quite opposite to the young Mao Zedong's rosy vision.

This chapter explores the fragrant branch of the Chinese olfactory revolution. Alongside the grand scheme of deodorization, re-perfuming China with a miscellany of mass-manufactured scents was equally ambitious. The language of perfume is polysemous and ambiguous, and their effects on the human nervous systems are varied. Just like malodours, fragrances are likewise strangers, the meaning of which depends on the recipient of the aroma. The mission of the olfactory revolution in this episode was to tune neurons to accept strangers as friends; the soap-making advertisement that Mao came across was an exemplar. Equipped with industrialism, capitalism, consumerism, science, and nationalism, the revolution's key battlefield was none other than the human body.

---

[3] Ibid., 20.   [4] Ibid., 26.   [5] Lee, *Shanghai Modern*, 3.
[6] Simmel, 'The Metropolis and Mental Life' (1903), 11.   [7] Ibid., 11–12.

The regulation and management of its odours were intended to transform it into what Jean Baudrillard terms 'the finest consumer object'.[8] This chapter sets out to untangle the pedagogical programme, seeking a historically informed diagnosis as to why and how the heady perfumes overwhelm Old Mr Wu's nerves, but not others'.

The cosmetics industry laid the material foundation for this olfactory revolution. I first investigate the import of Western beauty products in the post-Opium War era and the rise of the Chinese beauty industry.[9] Next I focus on an element crucial to the formation of a new olfactory sensibility: the invention and adoption of artificial essences. While 'organic' is the present-day lifestyle buzzword, ironically, synthetic scents governed the aesthetics of aroma a century ago. Literal strangers that invaded and contaminated the human sensorium, artificial smells were symptomatic of high modernity in its spirit of conquering/replacing the natural. Lastly, I interrogate the techniques with which industrially manufactured fragrances induced a new set of codes, values, and aesthetics to discipline the body, reshaping the sensory foundations of modern life.

IMPORTING SCENTS

In September 1865, J. Llewellyn & Co. (Laodeji yaofang 老德記藥房), a British-run pharmacy founded in 1853 in Shanghai, sold an assortment of cosmetic products manufactured by Paris-based Pinaud's Extra Fine Perfumery, allegedly a 'perfumer to Her Majesty the Queen of England'. Items on display included 'violet vinegar, eau de cologne, lettuce juice soap, nymphean juice soap, extra fine wild flower pomade, medulline oil, hygienic elixirs and powders, Alpasine (an emulsive cream)'.[10] This was the start of the adventure of Western beauty products and their exotic fragrances in China. Buttressed by the valiant spirit of capitalism, they

---

[8] Baudrillard, *The Consumer Society*, 129–50.

[9] The types of beauty product discussed in this chapter include perfume, soap, skin, hair and body care products (face cream, hair oil, tooth powder/toothpaste, talcum powder, and so on), and make-up products (lipstick, face powder, and so on). The term 'beauty products' is used interchangeably with cosmetics (and perfumery in some cases).

[10] *NCH*, 30 September 1865, 154. For the information on Laodeji, see Shanghai shi yiyao gongsi et al., *Shanghai jindai xiyao hangye shi*, 23.

were ready to compete against the well-established Chinese perfumery tradition in this lucrative market. As we learned in Chapter 1, Cao Xueqin's *Dream of the Red Chamber* enlightens the reader on a highly sophisticated perfume culture cultivated on the basis of Chinese medical and botanical knowledge, fine craftsmanship, and the philosophy of harmony.[11] In the mid-nineteenth century, several family-run perfume shops were enjoying prosperity and nationwide popularity, including Dai Chunlin 戴春林 from Yangzhou, Kong Fengchun 孔鳳春 from Hangzhou, and Lao miaoxiang shi 老妙香室 from Shanghai.[12] Yet they increasingly found themselves in a position of remaining 'only the last breath' (*gouyan canchuan* 苟延殘喘) in the contest with their self-styled progressive rivals: the industrially manufactured products either from abroad or from modern domestic enterprises.[13] How did the latter manage to gain the upper hand and propel an olfactory revolution?

Unlike textiles, opium, and metals, cosmetics were not a product that flooded the Chinese market from the start of post-Opium War foreign trade. Annual trade reports compiled by the Chinese Maritime Customs did not initially specify the import volumes of cosmetics, categorizing them within 'unenumerated sundries'.[14] Soap and perfumery first appeared in the trade reports for 1891: their net imports were, respectively, 184,634 and 42,063 Haikwan taels, occupying 0.17 per cent of the total value of foreign imports to China (134,003,863 Haikwan taels).[15] Surging import volumes in the ensuing decades (Chart 4.1) are indicative of the diminishing influence of Chinese traditional perfumery. The

---

[11] For an overview of the traditional Chinese cosmetics culture, also see Tu and Che, *Huazhuangpin ji xiangliao zhizaofa*, 3.

[12] Shanghai shi baihuo gongsi et al., *Shanghai jindai baihuo shangye shi*, 82; 'Shanghai shangye chuxu yinhang youguan huazhuangpin ye diaocha ziliao', 1933–1952, SMA, Q275-1-1944. Some of them were still operating until the mid-twentieth century. For example, Dai Chunlin ran an advertisement in *Funü shibao* 2, 1911.

[13] Jiang, *Shanghai gongye gailan*, 26.

[14] Annual and decennial reports on foreign trade in China (compiled by the Chinese Maritime Customs) were reprinted in 2001 in 170 volumes under the title *Zhongguo jiu haiguan shiliao* 中國舊海關史料 (1859–1948). Unless otherwise noted, all trade data cited in this chapter are from this source. 'ATRC 1891' stands for the annual trade reports of 1891; 'DTRC 1882–1891' for the decennial trade reports for 1882–1891.

[15] ATRC 1892, 9. The Customs revenue and all values are stated in Haikwan/Customs taels until 1931. In 1892, 1 Haikwan tael = 4 shillings 4.25 pence.

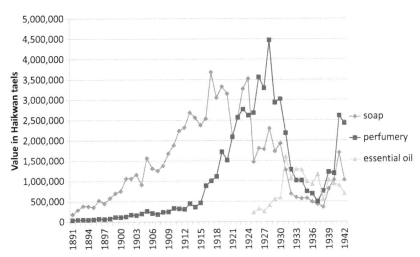

Chart 4.1 Foreign imports of soap, perfumery, and essential oil, 1891–1942. Source: ATRC. On the chart all values are shown in Haikwan taels, although from 1932 onwards they were stated in Customs gold units (one Customs gold unit = 1.184 Haikwan taels; see ATRC 1932).

global colonial operation of consumer capitalism was pivotal to the transformation of the mercantile landscape and smellscape alike.

An expanding retail network was the first driving force for the growth of the fragrant kingdom in China. The earliest stage only saw sporadic activities by individual businessmen and foreign-trade agents (*yanghang* 洋行). For example, in December 1852 Edward Hall, a 'bread and biscuit baker, and general store keeper in Shanghai', posted probably the first foreign cosmetic advertisement in the *North-China Herald* for the sale of 'a large assortment of English & French perfumery'.[16] In July 1860 a trade agent known as H. Fogg & Co. (Zhaofeng yanghang 兆丰洋行) announced an upcoming public auction to sell, among other goods, aromatic items produced by the British cosmetic manufacturer John Gosnell & Co.[17]

While fragrant items were classified under 'novel and exotic stuff' (*qiqiao* 奇巧) at auction in the early years,[18] a more systematic retail

---

[16] *NCH*, 4 December 1852, 1.

[17] *NCH*, 28 July 1860, 118. For information on the company, see www.britishmuseum.org/collection/term/BIOG142230 (accessed 8 September 2022).

[18] See advertisements for the sale of foreign soap (*SB*, 6 May 1872, 7); American perfume (*SB*, 7 May 1872, 5); perfume, fragrant soap, and fragrant oils (*SB*, 24 May 1872, 5); and various kinds of soap (*SB*, 6, 9 July 1872, 5).

channel took shape in the 1880s as a result of the burgeoning Western-run pharmacies, the most successful ones in Shanghai being the British Dispensary (Daying yiyuan 大英醫院, established 1850), Llewellyn (1853), A. S. Watson & Co. (Quchenshi 屈臣氏, 1860), and Voelkel & Schroeder Ltd (Kefa yaofang 科發藥房, 1866).[19] Flourishing pharmacy advertising in local newspapers in the 1880s and 1890s indicates that beauty products were becoming their staple source of income. It was precisely at this time when the customs statistical department made perfumery and soap a separate item on the trade reports. Facilitated by the colonial treaty port system, this fragrant kingdom expanded across China and throughout Western colonies in South East Asia. In January 1888, Watson owned thirty-three branches in twenty-seven Chinese cities, as well as in Hong Kong (its headquarters), Macau, the Philippines, and Siam (Thailand),[20] up from twenty-two branches two years earlier.[21] Pharmacies were not only a crucial site for selling cosmetics, but also proved to be a successful business modal and a thriving trade network, spreading new concepts of health, hygiene, and civility.[22] Patent medicines and beauty products teamed up, playing an instrumental role in compelling the modern demands linked to 'the narcissistic investment of the body' and 'the processes of personalization and social mobility'.[23] The olfactory revolution was rooted in the wider regime of capitalist colonial modernity's functioning at institutional and corporeal levels.

The twentieth century witnessed the advent of a glamorous new icon of consumerism in China, namely department stores. Emblems of modern material culture, they gave fresh impetus to the continuous expansion of the olfactory revolution. Between 1917 and 1936, four large-scale department stores were opened in Shanghai's commercial centre,[24] and similar stores mushroomed in other major Chinese cities.

---

[19] Shanghai shi yiyao gongsi et al., *Shanghai jindai xiyao hangye shi*, 22–3.

[20] *SB*, 20 January 1888, 7.

[21] Shanghai shi yiyao gongsi et al., *Shanghai jindai xiyao hangye shi*, 26; also see *SB*, 2 March 1886.

[22] For a detailed study of the modern Chinese medicine enterprise, see Cochran, *Chinese Medicine Men.*

[23] Baudrillard, *The Consumer Society*, 139.

[24] Chan, 'Selling goods and Promoting a New Commercial Culture', 23.

Grandiose architecture, opulent interiors, and endearing shop assistants aside, they also attended to olfactory details, by then an essential component of modern sensibility. The Sun Sun Department Store (Xinxin gongsi 新新公司), for instance, installed a perfume ball on the ceiling of its entrance, showering customers with an exquisite whiff of perfume on its opening day in January 1926.[25] Capitalizing on smell's instinctive and immersive nature, consumer capitalism was fostering the cult of the (perfumed) body for its own benefit.

This retail infrastructure, growing from random shops and auctions to pharmacy chains and department stores, laid the foundation for the olfactory revolution. Within a decade (1891–1901), the volume of soap imports increased by nearly six times and perfumery imports three times (see Chart 4.1). Soap imports continued to experience two more decades of boom and reached a peak in 1917, with an import value of 3,681,928 Haikwan taels, twenty times higher than that of 1891. Within the fifteen years from 1901 to 1915, perfumery imports maintained a slow and steady growth, while the ensuing thirteen years saw a rapid surge, hitting a peak in 1928. The total import value of 4,468,256 Haikwan taels in 1928 was 106 times higher than that of 1891. These statistics underpin Mao Dun's fictional portrayal of the smellscapes in 1930s Shanghai, the sensory foundations of modern life to which Old Mr Wu was unaccustomed. The momentous transformation in Chinese smellscapes also mirrored the global olfactory revolution in relation to the modern cosmetics industry, the second factor to be analysed in detail.

From the catalogues produced by Llewellyn, Watson, and the British Dispensary in July 1885, we learn that they introduced an array of products novel to Chinese customers: deodorant powder, tooth powder, bath gel, mouthwash, Florida water, rose ointment, rose glycerin, and perfumed soap.[26] These products reflected the latest developments of the beauty industry in Europe, which started to bloom in the mid-nineteenth century, with London and Paris as the centres. The introduction of chemical processes and the improvement of mechanical

---

[25] *NCH*, 30 January 1926, 16.   [26] *SB*, 21 July 1885, 12; 23 July 1885, 7; 23 July 1885, 10.

techniques (such as the invention of the atomizer) prompted its growth, and colonial expansion ensured it a plentiful supply of aromatic raw materials and a lucrative global market to sell its products.[27] China was one node of this global network, acting not only as a consumer market but also a supplier of musk, cassia, and other key ingredients. Around the turn of the century, the European cosmetics industry was moving into high gear. In France, production value soared from 45 million francs in 1878 to 100 million francs in 1912,[28] stimulated chiefly by 'the power of entrepreneurial agency in expanding the market for beauty'.[29] At the same time, large corporations operating on a global scale came on the scene, yielding a number of star products and brands, many of which are still to be found today. Through the following cases I probe how the Chinese olfactory revolution was interlinked with the increasingly sophisticated capitalist system.

The first case is Hazeline Snow, a legendary moisturizing cream first introduced to Chinese consumers around 1908.[30] Established in London in 1880, its manufacturer, Burroughs Wellcome & Co. Ltd (hereafter BW & Co.) was at the forefront of producing pharmaceutical preparations through the use of science and technology.[31] Hazeline Snow was one of the products that arose from its laboratory for chemical research. Introduced in 1892, it was the first commercial stearate cream containing an extract distilled from the bark of *Hamamelis virginiana* (witch hazel). BW & Co. branded this extract 'Hazeline', claiming that it had multiple medical effects against dry scalp, thin hair, eczema, acne, and so on.[32] Its Chinese advertisements stressed that Hazeline Snow was a 'wondrous elixir' (*juemiao lingdan* 絕妙靈丹), derived from 'extensive knowledge about skin physiology and chemistry'.[33] This advertising strategy once again demonstrates the mutual corroboration of health and beauty in

[27] For an overview of the modern beauty industry in the West, see Jones, *Beauty Imagined*, 15–93.
[28] Ibid., 20–1. Also see Briot, 'From Industry to Luxury'. [29] Jones, *Beauty Imagined*, 21.
[30] Its first advertisement appeared in *SB*, 25 April 1908, IV4.
[31] For the company's history, see https://wellcome.org/who-we-are/history-wellcome (accessed 23 September 2022).
[32] See 'Hazeline' publicity sheet, Wellcome Collection, EPH296.
[33] *SB*, 10 January 1913, 11.

the 'anxious, perfectionist manipulation of the sign function of the body' in modern consumer society.[34]

Medical products of BW & Co. arrived in China as early as 1886, evidenced by the company's earliest extant Chinese publicity material: an exquisitely painted Chinese-style calendar poster that lists over forty medical and cosmetic items.[35] By 1912 BW & Co. had established retail outlets in New York, Montreal, Sydney, Buenos Aires, Cape Town, Milan, Bombay, and Shanghai.[36] Standardization and globalization aside, its business model embraced localization. Its Shanghai pharmacy had an authentic Chinese name phonetically connected to Burroughs Wellcome: Baowei 寶威 ('treasure and strength'). Its branding tactics for Hazeline Snow invoked Chinese floral imageries, imparting to this medically oriented facial cream a sensual, indulgent flavour. Whilst 'snow' in the English brand name implies cool and grease-free qualities,[37] its Chinese name, Xiashilian 夏士蓮, elicits a poetic image of summer lotus, the Buddhist icon of serenity and beauty. Its English-language advertisement features a matter-of-fact depiction of the product: 'it is free from greasiness and its fragrant perfume is most refreshing', whereas an ornate couplet appears in its Chinese counterpart: it is 'as cool as snow in the high mountain, as fragrant as orchids in a tranquil valley (清涼如高山之雪，芳馥若幽谷之蘭)'.[38] The fragrance of orchids bears little resemblance to the scent of witch hazel, but it appeals to the Chinese olfactory sensibility as the orchid carries rich symbolic meaning in Chinese literati culture. This ruse attests to the ambiguous, polysemic coding of olfaction, and the manipulation of the human sensorium in the modern olfactory revolution.

Pond's Extract Vanishing Cream was another star product in China. Launched in 1907 by a New York-based company, it was one of the best-selling face creams in 1920s America and also one of the most

---

[34] Baudrillard, *The Consumer Society*, 139.

[35] The original copy of this calendar poster for 1887 is kept in the Wellcome Collection in London derived from the pharmaceutical firm. See Wellcome Collection, WF/M/A/15.

[36] See its advertisement in *SB*, 15 January 1909, I7.

[37] See its English-language publicity pamphlet, dated 22 March 1932, Wellcome Collection, WF/M/GB/01/37, 98.

[38] Ibid.; *SB*, 17 November 1910, II8.

internationalized cosmetic brands, sold in ninety-six countries worldwide by the end of the 1930s.[39] Known in Chinese as Pangshi baiyu shuang 旁氏白玉霜 (literally 'Pond's white jade cream'), it entered the Chinese market around 1917.[40] Interestingly, despite being another witch hazel skincare product, it smelled of the 'sweet perfume of rose', as promoted in Chinese advertising.[41] It is clear that the human agents of capitalism intuitively capitalized on olfactory perception's plasticity and played tricks on the neurons, with the aim of turning the stranger of manufactured scent into an affable friend.

The 1920s witnessed more American brands entering the Chinese market. Colgate, established in 1806 in New York as a starch, soap, and candle business, merged with Palmolive and Peet in 1928 and became a leading global enterprise in its field.[42] Four of its Éclat series products (perfumes, soap, and talcum powder) were advertised in *Shenbao* on 5 March 1920, proclaiming that their 'unparalleled refreshing and sensuous scents (清香芳馥無有其右)' would guarantee a radiant, fragrant, and adorable appearance.[43] Other heavily advertised products included Murray & Lanman Florida water, 4711 eau de cologne, Listerine toothpaste, and Lux toilet soap, among many others.[44] By the mid-1920s there were hundreds of foreign cosmetic brands in China.[45] As an outcome of the capitalist spirit of mass production and marketing, in conjunction with science, technology, and colonialism, the Chinese perfume revolution became integrated into the global perfume landscape.

In addition to retail and industrial growth, the third major catalyst for the olfactory revolution was advertising, which is also a fruitful site to observe how this industry affected body and mind personally and socially. Publicity is a cornerstone of cosmetics marketing worldwide; the

[39] Jones, *Beauty Imagined*, 52–4, 100, 128.
[40] See its advertisement in *SB*, 21 March 1920; 'Yichang yanghang yanke ji', *SB*, 29 May 1925, *benbu zengkan* 18.
[41] *SB*, 18 April 1920, Sunday Supplement 1.
[42] Jones, *Beauty Imagined*, 20, 34, 76, 79, 100.   [43] *SB*, 5 March 1920, 20.
[44] See *SB*, 2 September 1911, II7; *SB*, 14 August 1929, 20; *SB*, 10 August 1929, 17; *SB*, 18 July 1936, 10.
[45] Arnold, *China: A Commercial and Industrial Handbook*, 191.

common means in the early twentieth century involved newspapers and magazines, outdoor advertising (posters, painted bulletins, and walls), circular letters, calendars, and samples.[46] Naturally, local tastes were keenly attended to. According to Carl Crow (1883–1945), a guru in the field, Chinese consumers valued pleasant smells exceptionally highly, outweighing all other considerations. A bar of toilet soap (known as 'perfumed' soap in Chinese) not heavily perfumed was regarded as an anomaly, in the same way Americans would regard an odourless cologne.[47] This observation matches the frequent appearance of *xiang* in Chinese names for foreign cosmetics: 'fragrance-generating hair oil' (*fufa shengxiang shui* 敷髮生香水), 'refreshing and fragrant mouthwash' (*qingxiang xiya shui* 清香洗牙水), and 'delicate perfume powder' (*nenmian xiangshui fen* 嫩面香水粉), to name just a few.[48] Two rare copies of calendar posters for the publicity of BW & Co. goods shed further light on the evolving technology of selling beauty and promoting the cult of the scented body in China.

The calendar poster for 1888 (Figure 4.1) represents an early style of *yuefenpai* 月份牌, the thriving genre of commercial art that is almost a byword for Republican-era sensuality.[49] Not yet sensuous, with a Gregorian calendar in the middle, the poster is dominated by visual themes of the traditional Chinese New Year calendar, interspersed with a dull inventory of goods sold in the Baowei pharmacy. In the lower right corner is a Chinese circus clown, holding on the top of his nose a device with three balls, around which are listed Lundborg perfumes: Alpine Violet, Marechal Niel Rose, Lily of the Valley, and so on. Ingenious as it is to juxtapose oriental elements and European perfumery icons, it has yet to venture forth to engage the body. By contrast, Lundborg's 1894 art nouveau poster for the American market (Figure 4.2) – centring on a woman with a seductive gaze, shrouded in floral and cosmetic perfumes – is a step further into the project of fetishizing 'beauty and eroticism',

[46] For Euro-American marketing strategies, see Jones, *Beauty Imagined*, 53–4; for advertising in the Chinese market, see Crow, 'Advertising and Merchandising', 194–200.
[47] Crow, 'Advertising and Merchandising', 195.
[48] See a Llewellyn advertisement, *SB*, 21 July 1885, 12.
[49] For the early development of poster calendar art, see Laing, *Selling Happiness*, 79–93.

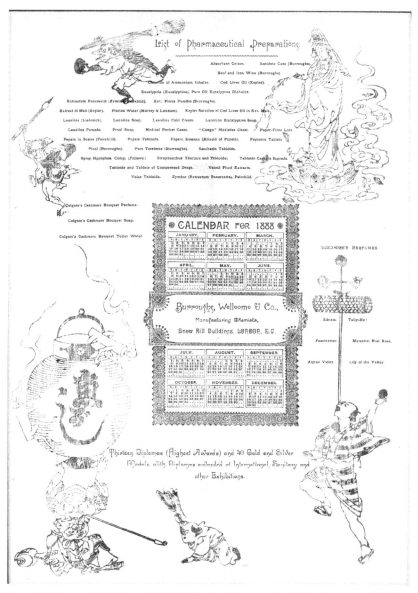

Figure 4.1 Burroughs Wellcome & Co. 1888 calendar poster for China. On paper fibre lint, 66 × 52 cm. Courtesy of Wellcome Collection, WF/M/A/16.

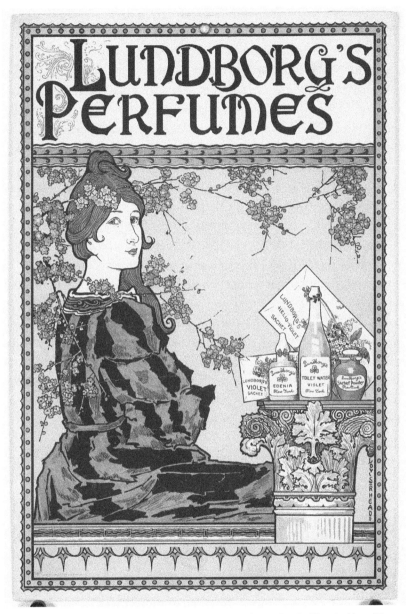

Figure 4.2 Lundborg perfume advertisement, 1894. Artist: Louis Rhead. 46 × 31 cm. Courtesy of American Art Posters 1890–1920 Collection, Boston Public Library.

and of defining the 'new ethics of the relation to the body' in the capitalist era.[50] Its Chinese counterpart would soon follow suit.

The other surviving copy of a BW & Co. advertising poster, for 1911, is a more elaborate and visually striking image, verging on a kind of visual language to entice 'the narcissistic investment of the body' (Figure 4.3). The key design concept is akin to product placement in a twenty-first-century film: visually analogous to the Prospect Garden in *Red Chamber*, the mansions and pavilions here are redolent of facial cream, cod liver oil, and quinine instead of jasmine bracelets, mimosa-flavoured samshoo, or incense. Women and children (male) are the only protagonists, pointing to the core of the modern mythology of the body 'as capital and as fetish (or consumer object)'.[51] Investing in the body means perfuming *her* face with Hazeline Snow (see the scene in the lower right corner, Figure 4.3a), and strengthening *his* health by taking cod liver oil (upper left corner, Figure 4.3b). Thus the boy's body gains capital (as a future pillar of society), and the woman's becomes a fetish (to be consumed visually/sensorially, if not physically). By decoding the gendered sensorial space of the poster, we can comprehend how the olfactory revolution was interlinked to broader social and cultural transformations of the body in modern China.[52] Driven by an innate motive to expand the market, cosmetics advertising was instrumental not only in advancing the industry economically, but also in cultivating new sensibilities and bodily codes.

To sum up, mass production, market expansion, and advertising collectively contributed to the phenomenal story of re-perfuming China with imported scents. Where were these scents from, and where did they go? This section concludes with an example of the golden year of 1927 to address these questions. Of the twenty countries or regions listed in the customs statistics (Chart 4.2), the biggest cosmetics imports were from Hong Kong (38 per cent), Japan (including Formosa/Taiwan, 30 per cent), the USA (13 per cent), France (12 per cent), and Britain

---

[50] Baudrillard, *The Consumer Society*, 132.

[51] Ibid., 129. The only adult man is at the far end of the garden, with his back facing the viewer.

[52] See Pickowicz, Shen, and Zhang, *Liangyou*, Parts II and III, among other studies.

Figure 4.3 Burroughs Wellcome & Co. 1911 calendar poster for China. On silk, 102 × 70 cm. Courtesy of Wellcome Collection, WF/M/A/5.

(a) (b)

Figure 4.3 (*cont.*)

(5 per cent). The majority of imports from Hong Kong (as an entrepôt) were most probably from Europe and North America.[53] The imports were distributed to forty-one cities and towns in sixteen Chinese provinces (Table 4.1). Although Shanghai, Dalian, and Tianjin imported 73.8 per cent of the total volume,[54] exotic fragrances pervaded China, except for a few inland provinces.

The golden age for Western cosmetics in China lasted approximately from the mid-1910s to the end of the 1920s. Import volumes fell sharply in the 1930s (see Chart 4.1) due to the booming domestic beauty industry, the Great Depression, and China's recovered tariff autonomy in the late 1920s (the tariff rate of 1934 was seven times the pre-1929 rate).[55] Yet perhaps the most important factor was the growing influence of Japan,

[53] No available source shows where Hong Kong's cosmetics exports were originally from, but Hong Hong's re-exported chemical materials were mostly from Western Europe and the USA. See Arnold, *China: A Commercial and Industrial Handbook*, 57.

[54] The total import volumes of the three cities were 2,449,317 Haikwan taels, while the total imports distributed to all of the forty-one customs houses were 3,316,944 Haikwan taels (with a small part of the gross imports re-exported to elsewhere).

[55] Gerth, *China Made*, 5–6.

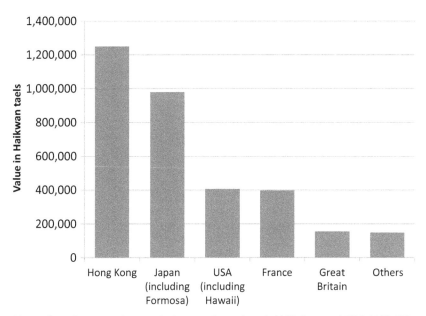

Chart 4.2 Perfumery and cosmetics imports from abroad, 1927. Source: ATRC 1927, 602. Other countries and regions include Macao, French Indo-China, Siam, Singapore and Straits, the Dutch Indies, British India, Norway, Germany, the Netherlands, Belgium, Italy, Russia, the Pacific ports, Korea, the Philippine Islands, Canada (all the country names are original).

with its military incursions into China in the early 1930s and economic encroachment. A major rival for Western cosmetics since the early twentieth century, Japanese fragrant goods dominated the north China market. Japanese cosmetics advertisements abounded in the Tianjin newspaper *Dagong bao* dating back to the mid-1900s,[56] and the late 1920s and early 1930s saw increased growth in Japan's trade with China, stimulated by its flourishing fragrance industry.[57] After the outbreak of the full-scale Sino-Japanese War in 1937, Japanese products virtually monopolized the Chinese fragrance market, with Japanese toilet soap imports making up 90.3 per cent, 71.9 per cent, and 93.2 per cent of

[56] Advertised Japanese products included Lion tooth powder, Lion Florida water, a type of toilet water named Beautifying Water (Huayanshui 花顏水), and an insecticide powder. See *Dagong bao*, 21 February 1908, 9 June 1910, 19 May 1911, 27 June 1906.

[57] See Chart 4.2. For a study of the Japanese cosmetics industry, see Tu, 'Japan's Empire of Scents'.

Table 4.1 Distribution of imported perfumery and cosmetics in China, 1927

Province	Custom House	Custom House Import Value	Province Total Import Value
Heilongjiang 黑龍江	Aihun 愛琿	3,850	3,850
Jilin 吉林	Huichun 琿春	4,791	65,378
	Longjing 龍井	18,404	
	Andong 安東	42,183	
Liaoning 遼寧	Dalian 大連	804,909	942,793
	Niuzhuang 牛莊	137,844	
Hebei 河北	Qinwangdao 秦王島	180	567,758
	Tianjin 天津	567,578	
Shandong 山東	Longkou 龍口	9,728	117,590
	Yantai 煙台	399	
	Jiaozhou 膠州	107,463	
Sichuan 四川	Chongqing 重慶	51,771	58,352
	Wanxian 萬縣	6,581	
Hubei 湖北	Yichang 宜昌	2,517	66,374
	Shashi 沙市	819	
	Hankou 漢口	63,038	
Hunan 湖南	Changsha 長沙	4,519	5,160
	Yuezhou 岳州	641	
Jiangxi 江西	Jiujiang 九江	26,566	26,566
Anhui 安徽	Wuhu 蕪湖	38,920	38,920
Jiangsu 江蘇	Nanjing 南京	31,566	87,807
	Zhenjiang 鎮江	30,827	
	Suzhou 蘇州	25,414	
Shanghai 上海	Shanghai 上海	1,076,790	1,076,790
Zhejiang 浙江	Hangzhou 杭州	271	27,877
	Ningbo 寧波	20,307	
	Wenzhou 溫州	7,299	
Fujian 福建	Sanduao 三都澳	108	48,685
	Fuzhou 福州	17,903	
	Xiamen 廈門	30,674	
Yunnan 雲南	Mengzi 蒙自	22,873	30,426
	Tengyue 騰越	7,553	

Table 4.1 (*cont.*)

Province	Custom House	Custom House Import Value	Province Total Import Value
Guangdong 廣東	Jiulong 九龍	281	86,620
	Shantou 汕頭	34,078	
	Guangzhou 廣州	42,561	
	Gongbei 拱北	3,086	
	Jiangmen 江門	6,624	
Guangxi 廣西	Wuzhou 梧州	27,368	65,998
	Qiongzhou 瓊州	25,706	
	Beihai 北海	12,512	
	Longzhou 龍州	412	
		Grand Total	3,316,944

Source: ATRC 1927, 602-3. Value in Haikwan taels.

the total import volumes in 1940, 1941, and 1942 respectively.[58] The same tendency can be seen in the import of face cream and powder.[59] The Japanese factor is of such significance that it deserves a separate study, which is beyond the scope of this chapter.

MANUFACTURING SCENTS

The modern Chinese perfume industry began with Feng Futian 馮福田 (Fook Tien Fung) and his legendary firm Kwong Sang Hong 廣生行 (Guangsheng hang, hereafter KSH). Founded in Hong Kong in 1898, KSH was born within an atmosphere of surging Chinese nationalism. According to its own company history, Fung 'spotted an opportunity' when observing that exquisite foreign cosmetics were unaffordable to most locals, and therefore he decided to manufacture 'fine perfumery at

[58] ATRC 1942, 418. The volumes of Japanese toilet soap imports were 736,836 Customs gold units (GU) (for a total of 815,360 GU) in 1940, 997,836 GU (for a total of 1,387,036 GU) in 1941, and 703,574 GU (for a total of 754,682 GU).
[59] ATRC 1942, 561.

an affordable price'.[60] He started humbly, trademarking his products as Shuangmei 雙妹 (Two Girls), an unpretentious name, sweet, endearing, and accessible. His business never looked back. In April 1910, two years after Hazeline Snow landed in China, KSH opened its Shanghai flagship store in Nanjing Road, the deodorized commercial hub and symbolic epicentre of consumerism in China.[61] Its Tianjin branch was set up in October 1910, vying with Japanese brands for the northern China market.[62] At that time, KSH's fragrant kingdom was operating via an extended retail network, with sixteen branch offices and more than a thousand shops across China and South East Asia.[63] In the 1920s, Two Girls was firmly established as one of the leading native brands. KSH further scaled up its business by moving its Shanghai store to a more grandiose building in Nanjing Road in 1924.[64] Its remarkable history in mainland China only came to an end in 1958 when it was merged with other cosmetics companies into a state-run firm known as the Mingxing Chemical Company (Mingxing huagongchang 明星化工廠) based in Shanghai.[65] While KSH still exists in Hong Kong today, the Shanghai firm has revived the Two Girls brand recently and coined a new brand name, Shanghai Vive, drawing on the popular nostalgia for the city's golden 1930s.[66]

Built on the same bedrock of capitalist mass production and marketing, KSH commanded a resource unattainable to its foreign rivals: nationalism. It proclaimed in 1910, 'Our products follow Western models, but all are manufactured by the Chinese. Our fellow country-men have been displaying fervent patriotism and determination to pro-mote national goods. [Patriotic customers] from near and far all come to

---

[60] See the company history on its website: http://twogirls.hk/en/about_us.php (accessed 17 July 2022). Because of its self-styled Chinese identity, I consider KSH a Chinese cosmetics company, though it was based in the British colony.

[61] *SB*, 29 April 1910, I5.

[62] *Dagong bao*, 3 October 1910; 'Dongsheng jinwen', *SB*, 12 June 1915, 6.

[63] *SB*, 29 April 1910, I5.

[64] In 1920, KSH invested 1,200,000 yuan in building a lemonade factory, a glass factory, and a print factory in Shanghai. See 'Nanjing lu Guangshenghang qianyi xishou kaizhang', *SB*, 26 February 1922, 16; 'Guangshenghang xinwu luocheng', *SB*, 18 April 1924, 19.

[65] SMA, B163-1-710-6.   [66] See www.jahwa.com.cn/en/vive (accessed 11 May 2020).

buy our perfume articles.'[67] Nationalist/Chinese elements were spelled out more elaborately in an advertisement for Two Girls Florida water.[68] The text starts by highlighting the popularity of Florida water and the considerable revenues it has generated for foreign companies, revenues that would be better spent with a Chinese brand. It goes on to assure customers of the supreme quality of this perfume: KSH's founder is a leader in chemical research and his formula is unrivalled. Distilled from an assortment of rare exquisite flowers (*qihua yihui* 奇花異卉), this essence (*lu* 露) has the power to transpose one instantly to a fragrant kingdom comparable to the ancient orchid chamber abided in by noble ladies. To further promote the national fervour of the product, the label features the Chinese dragon flag.

Referencing the classical perfumery lexicon (*lu, qihua yihui*), the advertisement evokes an olfactory imagery reminiscent of *l'essence de fleurs* in *Red Chamber* (Chapter 1). Whereas Cao Xueqin's master perfume is a metaphorical blend of the female protagonists' bodily scents, the industrially crafted Florida water drew on cultural heritage for the sake of enhancing its commodity value and appeal to patriotic buyers. In other words, the former expresses the individual bodies, whilst the latter addresses the abstract bodies of the consuming masses and the national body of China simultaneously. In this light, we understand why the soap-making advertisement that attracted the young Mao Zedong under-scored the mission to 'enrich the *country* and enrich the *people*' (emphasis mine). Nationalism was enlisted to turn the domestically manufactured scents from 'strangers' into 'friends' via technologies of engaging the body. KSH's strategy paid off. Being a national brand, it benefited from the National Products movement (*Guohuo yundong* 國貨運動) raging throughout China at the time.[69] KSH cosmetics were enthusiastically introduced in newspaper columns about *guohuo*,[70] and in product lists compiled by organizations to promote domestic goods.[71] In September

---

[67] *SB*, 29 April 1910, I5. [68] Ibid.

[69] For an overview of the *Guohuo* movement, See Gerth, *China Made*, 5–19.

[70] See 'Guohuo diaocha' (National Goods Survey), *SB*, 12 April 1915, 11; 'Jieshao guohuo' (Introducing National Goods), *SB*, 8 July 1916, 11.

[71] 'Wujin tuiguang guohuo tuan jianzhang', *SB*, 7 November 1915, 17; 'Shimin tichang guohuo hui zhaoji huiyuan dahui', *SB*, 13 July 1929, 16.

1934, KSH and fifteen other local manufacturers attended the National Cosmetic Products Exhibition held in Nanjing Road in Shanghai, with over 1,300 items on display in a hall packed with high-spirited customers.[72]

Another vital technology that interlinked smell, body, and commodity was visuality and synaesthesia, in particular through the *yuefenpai* calendar poster. Having been employed by BW & Co. to sinicize its products, this commercial art form reached the pinnacle of its popularity in the 1920s and 1930s. Two Girls was the first cosmetic brand to make extensive use of the visual form.[73] Painted by the foremost commercial artists of the day (such as Guan Huinong 關蕙農 and Zheng Mantuo 鄭曼陀), Two Girls calendar posters spun variations on an iconic formula: two alluring women in the centre of a landscape, bordered by exuberant flowers and fine bottles and jars as ornaments (Figure 4.4).[74] By this time the plebeian 'two girls' had morphed into the seductresses par excellence, beguiling buyers with beauty and eroticism impeccably wrapped in a mist of perfumes – the flowers and jars are imbricated, the natural and the manufactured mingled. By animating the sensorium synaesthetically, these advertising posters not only bolstered the brand value but also partook in a broader shift in the ethics of the body. Compared to the 1888 and 1911 BW & Co. calendars (Figures 4.1 and 4.3), the bodies of the 1930s 'two girls' appear to be 'liberated' (sexually and sensorially). If we juxtapose this 1932 *yuefenpai* with the 1894 Lundborg advertisement (Figure 4.2), the confluence of style in representing body and fragrance is evident. In this regard, domestically manufactured perfumes also contributed to the cult of the (scented) body that was evolving globally

---

[72] 'Guohuo huazhuangpin zhanlan kaimu', *SB*, 12 September 1934, 12; 'Guohuo huazhuangpin zhan shengkuang', *SB*, 15 September 1934, 15.

[73] Widely employed by medicine, tobacco, and many other industries, calendar posters strangely did not become a major publicity channel for such prominent Western cosmetics brands as Pond's and Colgate. But as early as 1910, KSH's complimentary calendar posters were already distributed in its Hong Kong store and attracted a large crowd. See 'Guangshenghang yuefenpai zhi tese', *Huazi ribao*, 29 January 1910; quoted in Chen, 'Guanyu Guan Huinong', 7.

[74] Laing, *Selling Happiness*, 132. For the status of Guan Huinong and Zheng Mantuo, see Cochran, *Chinese Medicine Men*, 122, 51–3.

Figure 4.4 Two Girls calendar poster, 1932. Artist: Kwan Wai-nung (Guan Huinong). 74.5 × 51 cm. Courtesy of the Hong Kong Heritage Museum 香港文化博物館藏品.

in partnership with commodity culture. But Chinese olfactory modernity had its own idiosyncrasies with regard to the body, an aspect to be explored in Chapter 5.

Following KSH's lead, many aspiring Chinese entrepreneurs dabbled in the beauty industry. The 1910s witnessed the emergence of two major cosmetics firms, both based in Shanghai. Founded by Fang Yexian 方液仙 (1893–1940) in 1912 as a small-scale family business, China Chemical Industries (Zhongguo huaxue gongye she 中國化學工業社) flourished after the large-scale boycott of foreign goods in the aftermath of the May Fourth movement in 1919, and its trademark Three Stars (Sanxing 三星) soon became another icon of *guohuo*.[75] Household Industries (Jiating gongye she 家庭工業社), founded in 1918 by the popular writer Chen Diexian 陳蝶仙 (1878–1940), had a similar trajectory. Growing from a household workshop to an industrial powerhouse, it survived the Sino-Japanese War and the Communist takeover in 1949. Although it was eventually merged into a state-run firm, products under its legendary Butterfly brand remained on the socialist market for a number of decades.[76] Eugenia Lean has argued that Chen's unconventional cultural–industrial pursuits constituted a form of 'vernacular industrialism', which was local, informal, artisanal in spirit, and family-run (as opposed to imperialist and state-sponsored industrialism), whilst overlapping with the nationalistic *guohuo* initiative and the global circuits of law, science, and commerce.[77] The playful approach of vernacular industrialism was exemplified by Chen's ingenious idea for his cosmetic trademark Wudi 無敵: with a literal meaning of 'peerless', it bears a phonetic resemblance to *hudie* (butterfly) in the Shanghai dialect and implies the *die* 蝶 in Chen's own name and the so-called Mandarin Duck and Butterfly school he was associated with.[78] In a word, the brand is an unlikely combination of sentiment-infused literary trope and science-based industrial pursuit. By addressing a particular taste of the Chinese

[75] Gerth, *China Made*, 180; for the boycott of 1919, see 146–57.

[76] 'Jiating gongyeshe gufen youxian gongsi', SMA, Y9-1-99-46, 43; Shanghai shi jiayong huaxuepin gongye tongye gonghui, *Shanghai shi jiayong huaxuepin gongye chanpin zhishi jieshao*, 49.

[77] Lean, *Vernacular Industrialism in China*, 3.   [78] Lean, 'The Butterfly Mark', 62–91.

consuming masses, Chen's cultural entrepreneurialism represented yet another approach to tuning the neurons in the olfactory revolution.

Inspired by the phenomenal success of Two Girls, Three Stars, and Butterfly, China's local beauty industry boomed like 'sprouting bamboo shoots in spring' (*yuhou chunsun* 雨後春筍) after 1919.[79] Pharmacies and department stores, previously acting as retailers, began to create their own cosmetic brands, such as the Sincere Department Store (Xianshi gongzi 先施公司), the Great China–France Drugstore (Zhong Fa dayaofang 中法大藥房, established 1890), the Great Five Continents Drugstore (Wuzhou da yaofang 五洲大藥房, 1907), and the Talow Dispensary (Dalu yaofang 大陸藥房, 1912).[80] In 1928, a trade association (*tongye gonghui* 同業公會) was formed by around thirty cosmetics firms in Shanghai, and its membership had grown to seventy by 1930 and over a hundred by 1935. At the end of 1949 there were 126 registered cosmetics companies, with a total of 4,437 staff.[81] Shaped by global forces and vernacular industrialism, domestic and imported cosmetics re-perfumed Chinese bodies and spaces to an unprecedented level. As a female author observed in 1920, manufactured beauty products penetrated not only big cities but also small towns and even village peddlers' carts, rendering 'every civilized woman a synonym for "fragrant beauty (*xiang meiren* 香美人)"'.[82] The next section turns to the true 'essence' of this olfactory revolution; that is, the actual fragrances exuding from these products.

THE VOCABULARY OF SCENT, NATURAL AND ARTIFICIAL

By the time Western perfume articles made their foray into China in the mid-nineteenth century, perfume fashion in Europe had been going

---

[79] Jiang, *Shanghai gongye gailan*, 26; Shanghai shi baihuo gongsi et al., *Shanghai jindai baihuo shangye shi*, 84.

[80] For the advertisments for Sincere's Tiger Florida Water, see *SB*, 8 April 1923, 4; Sincere Snow Cream (Xianshi bailanshuang 先施白蘭霜), *SB*, 25 November 1931, 9. For Talow's hair oil, face cream, and Florida water, see *SB*, 10 July 1921, 9; 1 October 1927, 2; 8 July 1936, *benbu zengkan* 1. For talcum powder and perfume manufactured by Five Continents, see *SB*, 1 July 1936, 13; 31 July 1936, 9.

[81] Shanghai shi baihuo gongsi et al., *Shanghai jindai baihuo shangye shi*, 85; Ge, 'Shanghai shi jiayong huaxue gongye tongye gonghui lishi yange', December 1952, SMA, C48-1-44-36.

[82] Miao, 'Xiang yu funü', *Funü zazhi* 6, no. 3 (1920), 3. For an account of beauty products' trajectory in early twentieth-century China, see Dikötter, *Exotic Commodities*, 205–13.

through a revolution. Codified as expressions of the elegance and respectability of the rising bourgeoisie, 'fleeting country odors' of violets, roses, and lavenders held sway as a new vocabulary of scent, replacing the heavy animal scents of musk, civet, and ambergris.[83] The earliest types of beauty products imported to China (such as violet vinegar, wild-flower pomade, rose tooth powder, and lavender water) reflected this shifting aesthetic. Colonial expansion diversified this vocabulary as plantations and trade agencies in Africa and Asia supplied the industry with an exotic array of raw materials: geranium, orange, cassia, eucalyptus, and so on.[84]

China was located within these global circuits of transaction that characterized the nineteenth-century capitalist mode of production. Specifically it contributed to the vocabulary of scent with musk, cassia, and rhubarb, the 'principle articles of Chinese produce' for export for a long period.[85] A captivating oriental smellscape was depicted in a poem *à la* Byron by an American trader in 1820s Canton: 'Know'st thou the land where the nankin and tea-chest, / With cassia and rhubarb and camphor, abound?'[86] Oriental scents thus wafted into the European sensorium. Brown Windsor Soap was one such embodiment of the early globalization of fragrance and commodity. With Chinese musk and cassia as key ingredients, the soap was allegedly a favourite of Queen Victoria and Napoleon; these scents (or their spectres abiding in the commodity), interestingly, travelled back to China in the 1860s.[87] A new (or renewed) aromatic vocabulary imported from abroad notwithstanding, the 'essence' of the Chinese olfactory revolution had retained, to a degree, its own vocabulary before the reign of the homogenizing force of artificial compounds.

A Two Girls perfume advertisement in 1910 casts some valuable light on local tastes. Supplementary to the rhetorical claim of using *qihua yihui*

---

[83] Corbin, *The Foul and the Fragrant*, 182, 199.   [84] Jones, *Beauty Imagined*, 22.

[85] See 'Forty Years Values of the Principle Articles of Chinese Produce' (1862–1901), in DTRC 1892–1901, vol. 2, xxiv; DTRC 1912–1921, 434. Contemporary Western perfumery books also noted that musk and cassia were mainly imported from China. See Piesse, *The Art of Perfumery*, 99; Rimmel, *The Book of Perfumes*, 265–6.

[86] Hunter, *The 'Fan Kwae' at Canton before Treaty Days*, 67.

[87] For a recipe for Brown Windsor Soap (which includes thyme, cassia, caraway, and lavender), see Piesse, *The Art of Perfumery*, 166. For the use of musk in the making of Paris's original Windsor soap, see Piesse, *The Art of Perfumery*, 100. For Brown Windsor Soap's advertisement in China, see *NCH*, 28 July 1860, 118.

(rare, exquisite flowers) was a list of sixteen floral essences employed in their products: white rose (*bai meigui* 白玫瑰), yulan magnolia (*bai yulan* 白玉蘭), *Jasminum grandiflorum* (*suxin* 素馨), osmanthus (*guihua* 桂花), gardenia (*baichan* 白蟾, *Gardenia jasminoides* var. *fortuniana*), rose (*tuwei* 荼薇, a rose species), magnolia coco (*yehe* 夜合), *Daphne odora* (*ruixiang* 瑞香), orchid (*suxinlan* 素心蘭), daffodil (*shuixian* 水仙), tuberose (*yuzan* 玉簪), wintersweet (chimonanthus, *lamei* 臘梅), *Telosma cordata* (*yexiang* 夜香), jasmine (*moli* 茉莉), and violet (*zilan* 紫蘭).[88] Among them, none but rose, violet, and jasmine were common ingredients of European perfumery of the day.[89] However, many of the species can be found in the fourteenth-century *New Book on Perfume* (*Xinzuan xiangpu*), including jasmine, *Jasminum grandiflorum*, osmanthus, *Daphne odora*, rose (*tuwei*), and gardenia, all under the classification of 'southern flowers' (*nanfang hua* 南方花). Their essences can be extracted by the method of distillation imported from the Middle East.[90] It is not surprising that the Hong Kong-based KSH relied on the indigenous 'southern flowers' sourced from its Chinese suppliers at a lower cost.[91] Moreover, it agrees with the biological logic that dictates the olfactory aesthetic: mere exposure affects odour perception through 'the passive acquisition and storage of odor percept' with minimal conscious awareness.[92] That is to say, the Chinese penchant for magnolia, osmanthus, gardenia, orchid, and wintersweet is surely a result of neural wiring influenced by exposure and sedimented cultural values.[93] We are reminded of Baoyu's impromptu gifts to his mother and grandmother: a few sprays of osmanthus flowers arranged in elegant vases. However, it was the same exposure logic, allied with other factors, that facilitated the re-education of the nerves for a favourable reception of laboratory-born aromatic compounds.

[88] *SB*, 29 April 1910, I5.
[89] Rimmel, *The Book of Perfumes*, 265–6. Daffodil (*Narcissus*) and tuberose are also in Rimmel's list, but were not frequently used in perfumery.
[90] Chen, *Xinzuan xiangpu*, 111–15.
[91] Tong, 'Guangshenghang diaocha baogao', SMA, Q78-2-13341.
[92] Wilson and Stevenson, *Learning to Smell*, 153.
[93] Chen, *Xinzuan xiangpu*, 92, 96, 97, 192. For more pomade recipes that include osmanthus, see Hu, *Xianglian runse*, 25, 27.

The development of synthetic organic chemistry in the first half of the nineteenth century laid the foundation for this change. Following German chemist Friedrich Wöhler's successful production of urea by synthesis in the laboratory in 1828, thousands of organic compounds were formed by artificial processes.[94] The late nineteenth century witnessed the harvest of key synthetic fragrances, including bitter almonds (benzoic aldehyde), wintergreen (methyl salicylate), vanilla (vanillin), musk ketone, and violet (ionones).[95] Easy availability of these crucial perfume ingredients in chemical form transformed the beauty industry in both olfactory and economic terms. The iconic perfume Chanel No. 5, purely based on a chemical formula, sums up modern myth making that knits together science, capitalism, and the commodification of the body. Its commercial success in the 1920s engendered the synthetic revolution of the perfume industry.[96] From then on, synthetics were 'indispensable in every perfumer's laboratory',[97] and methods of making them were available to both professionals and the general public via popular cosmetics handbooks.[98]

Unsurprisingly, chemical scents quickly set off to tour the world, including China. How did they smell to Chinese noses? A Chinese author writes, 'In this era of science and civilization, Chinese cosmetics, which carry natural floral scents, are far inferior to synthetic ones. Synthetic perfumes are elegant, refreshing, and fragrant (*youya qingfen* 幽雅清芬), hundreds of times better than natural floral scents.'[99] It is difficult to gauge whether this account represented the general Chinese perception of artificial scents. Yet it indubitably exemplified a particular mentality in association with 'the cult of chemistry', which had swept Chinese life since the late Qing amid a tide of introducing Western

[94] Von Isakovics, *Synthetic Perfumes and Flavors*, 6.
[95] Johnston, *The Chemistry of Common Life*, 418–26; also see von Isakovics, *Synthetic Perfumes and Flavors*, 22.
[96] Fortineau, 'Chemistry Perfumes Your Daily Life', 46–7.
[97] Askinson, *Perfumes and Cosmetics*, 148.
[98] Parry, *The Chemistry of Essential Oils and Artificial Perfumes*; Deite, *A Practical Treatise on the Manufacture of Perfumery*; Charabot, *Les parfums artificiels*, and so on.
[99] Fan, 'Zhongguo huazhuang pin jishi Qin Xichou', *SB*, 7 January 1929, 19.

learning (*xixue* 西學). The English missionary John Fryer (1839–1928, aka Fu Lanya 傅蘭雅) played a key role. He translated or compiled a number of influential books on chemistry in the 1870s and 1880s, including 'Huaxue weisheng lun 化學衛生論' (On Chemistry and Hygiene) translated from Scottish chemist James Johnston's *The Chemistry of Common Life* (1855).[100] While the concept of *weisheng* (hygiene) elucidated in this seminal text shaped Chinese olfactory modernity in the direction of environmental deodorization, the notion of *huaxue* (chemistry) revolutionized the realm of fragrance. Stemming from circles of scholars, the cult of chemistry spread far and wide, from the imperial court to common life.

In his memoir, the last Chinese emperor, Aisin-Gioro Pu Yi (1906–1967) recalled his indulgence in 'the combined odours of Max Factor lotions, eau-de-Cologne and mothballs'. Foreign candies delighted him too, 'their tin box, silver wrapping-paper and different fruit flavours'.[101] His English tutor, Reginald Fleming Johnston, explained to him how the fruity tastes were produced by new chemical techniques and how the neat shapes were made by machines. By associating sensory pleasure with chemistry and machine, Johnston's lessons – as well as their impact on the young emperor's sensorial response and memory – were a vivid illustration of the confluence of epistemic and affective shifts, supporting modern scientists' conviction that odour perception is affected by learning.[102]

Lessons to rewire the Chinese olfactory nervous system, so to speak, were orchestrated in more concrete ways in industrial and commercial sectors. When a British firm (Imperial Chemical Industries) set up a plant in Shanghai in 1899, it also acted as an apostle of chemistry, promulgating the benefits of replacing 'natural products by the manufactured article'.[103] When Chinese entrepreneurs ventured in the

---

[100] 'Huaxue weisheng lun' first appeared in *Gezhi huibian* 格致彙編 (*Chinese Scientific Magazine*) 3 (1880), 10. For the original version, see Johnston, *The Chemistry of Common Life*. For a detailed discussion of John Fryer and his translations, See Rogaski, *Hygienic Modernity*, 109–18; Wright, *Translating Science*, 50.

[101] Pu Yi, *From Emperor to Citizen*, 212, 112; quoted in Dikötter, *Exotic Commodities*, 189, 220.

[102] Wilson and Stevensen, *Learning to Smell*, 142–53.

[103] Kwan, 'Market and Network Capitalism', 95.

nascent cosmetics industry, they brazenly inserted *huaxue*/chemistry and *gongye*/industry in their company names.[104] The scientific flavour is in stark contrast to the poetic vibe that traditional perfume brands convey. Dai Chunlin 戴春林, for example, conjures up a sweet medley of aromas in a springtime forest. The capitalist ethic preferred scientific authority to sentimentalism. KSH boasted that the fragrance of Two Girls Florida water can last for twelve days according to a test conducted by a 'British royal chemist' (*Yingguo huangjia huaxueshi* 英國皇家化學師).[105] A 1930s advertisement for Palmolive soap features a test tube, whereas today's product of the same brand uses '98% natural origin' as the catchphrase (Figures 4.5 and 4.6). In the light of twenty-first-century organic fever, the impassioned cultivation of the chemistry-friendly olfactory disposition a century ago feels ironic, a testament to the plasticity of sensory neurons and the forces behind the scenes (re)moulding them.

In short, the alliance of intellectual and popular discourse and mercantile drive fed new conceptual data to olfactory perceptual learning, preparing the ground for the inexorable march of artificial scents in China (and elsewhere). In 1925 a mounting demand for essential oils led the Chinese Maritime Customs to include them as a separate field in foreign-imports statistics.[106] While the 1925 import value (228,816 Haikwan taels) remained modest – compared to soap and perfumery imports (Chart 4.1) – a steep rise occurred in 1931, reaching 1,604,948 Haikwan taels, seven times higher than the 1925 value (Chart 4.3). Moreover, imports of essential oils exceeded those of soap (1,274,159 Haikwan taels) and came close to those of perfumery (2,182,794 Haikwan taels) in 1931. Starting in 1932, essential oils are classified under the subcategories of natural oils, artificial oils, and mixtures.[107] As Chart 4.3 shows, the proportion of synthetic essences quickly outnumbered that of natural oils. Britain, the Netherlands, France, Germany, and Switzerland were the top five countries exporting to China both for synthetic oils and in total volume (Chart 4.4), while Netherlands India

---

[104] Examples include China Chemical Industries, Household Industries, Oriental Chemical Industries (Dongfang huaxue gongyeshe 東方化學工業社), and others. See Shanghai shi baihuo gongsi et al., *Shanghai jindai baihuo shangye shi*, 83–4; Jiang, *Shanghai gongye gailan*, 321–3.

[105] *SB*, 29 April 1910, I5.   [106] ATRC 1926, 181.   [107] ATRC 1932, vol. 2, 54.

Figure 4.5 Palmolive soap advertisement, *Dagongbao*, 17 August 1933, 8.

Figure 4.6 Palmolive soap bar, 2021. Author's photograph.

and British India provided a large proportion of natural oils, mirroring the geopolitical landscape of the world at that time: Europe was at the forefront of science and industry, whilst their colonies contributed natural resources to the economy.

Apart from professional manufacturers, individuals and households also participated in this chemical olfactory revolution, not only as consumers but also as active practitioners of vernacular industrialism. Starting in the 1910s, popular journals and newspapers ran how-to columns to

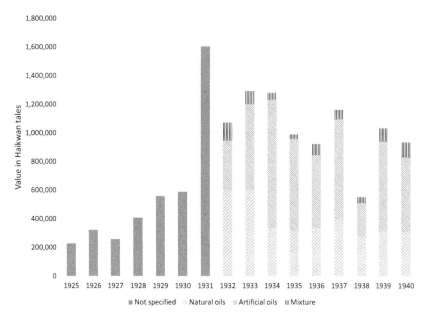

Chart 4.3 Essential-oil imports, 1925–1940. Source: ATRC. On the chart all values are shown in Haikwan taels, although from 1932 onwards they were stated in Customs gold units (one Customs gold unit = 1.184 Haikwan taels; see ATRC 1932).

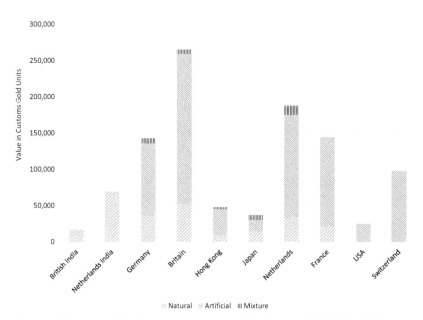

Chart 4.4 Major essential-oil importing countries, 1934. Source: ATRC 1935, 451–2.

promote new domestic knowledge,[108] and perfume manuals were sought-after on the book market in the 1920s, many of which were either translated from or based on Western books.[109] Artificial scents were part of this new body of knowledge. A perfume manual published by the Commercial Press in 1927 (and reprinted four times thereafter) introduced nine artificial essences (neroli, lilac, camphor, bitter almond, and some fruit ethers) and popular recipes involving synthetic ingredients.[110] Curious readers of such books and columns had easy access to perfume ingredients at pharmacies.[111] Artificial smells entered multiple social locales and as a consequence, the vocabulary of scent in China was homogenized to a degree thanks to the standardization of chemical fragrance. In fact, no better word than 'contamination' can characterize the intrusion of artificial chemicals (true strangers) into the nervous system. Yet once framed as a developmental fairy tale, acts of intrusion became a revolution. For the unprepared nerves, like Old Mr Wu's, this revolution could be fatal.

RE-PERFUMING THE BODY IN TIME AND SPACE

If deodorizing fundamentally concerns the sensorial reorganization of *space*, re-perfuming is essentially about the management of the *body*. The material foundation of such an intrusive modern project has been laid out; questions remain with regard to the implications of this revolution, the technologies it employed, and new norms that were internalized.

Referencing *Red Chamber* lends us a perspective to grasp how the body was perceived and represented differently in the modern era. As

---

[108] Lean, *Vernacular Industrialism in China*, Chapter 2, 77–119.

[109] For example, an influential perfume book entitled *Xiangliao ji huazhuangpin* (Perfumes and Cosmetics), edited by Zheng Zunfa, was translated from George Askinson's *Perfumes and Cosmetics* (1922). Several major perfume books (by A. Poucher, Ernest Parry, among others) are mentioned in Tu and Che, *Huazhuangpin ji xiangliao zhizaofa*.

[110] Guo, *Zuixin huazhuangpin zhizaofa*, 27–30, 36, 121. It was reprinted in 1928, 1932, 1937, and 1940. For example, a Florida water recipe includes synthetic musk essences, and a British soap recipe includes artificial bitter almond oils.

[111] See an advertisement for the sale of chemical materials by a Shanghai pharmacy: *SB*, 8 April 1921, 15.

discussed in Chapter 1, Cao Xueqin crafts an olfactory imagery to convey the *distinctive* essence of each female character: the otherworldly 'ethereal fragrance' *youxiang* for Lin Daiyu, the sophisticated 'cold fragrance' *lengxiang* for Xue Baochai, the sensual 'sweet fragrance' *tianxiang* for Qin Keqing, and the spiritual 'chilly fragrance' *hanxiang* for Adamantina. The transcendant *essence des fleurs* is an organic synthesis of them all in an allegorical sense. Aroma is likewise a powerful trope in work by authors of the New Sensationalism school (*xin ganjue pai* 新感覺派), a Chinese modernist literary school of the 1930s. Comparable to the keen-scented Baoyu, male protagonists created by Liu Na'ou 劉吶鷗 (1905–1940) are equally discerning: he can unmistakably capture a message of seduction coded in 'a whiff of cyclamen perfume'; he can effortlessly recognize 4711 eau de cologne amid a 'cocktail' of aromas as he embarks on a sexual liaison.[112] What differs is that the modern women are objectified in these stories, with the homogenizing manufactured scents as a synecdoche of their beauty and eroticism. A striking demonstration of this logic can be found in a cartoon, which is a simple juxtaposition of a bride and a bottle of perfume (Figure 4.7).

Its satirical message is encrypted in the title 'Yuanfenghuo 原封貨' (Sealed Goods), punning on virginity. Francesca Dal Lago interprets this cartoon as a portrayal of women as 'both subject *and* object of market and sexual consumption'.[113] Her consumer (subject) status functions to enhance her 'exchange value' as an object on the marriage market – a spray of perfume can even perform the magic of smoothing over her doubtful virginity, as the cartoon hints. In this dual mockery, consumerism is fused with hypocritical traditionalist morality. Mass-produced perfumes enabled the 'mechanical reproduction' of sensuality and further encouraged narcissistic investment in the body, heeding 'a *normative* principle of enjoyment and hedonistic profitability' as well as 'an enforced instrumentality', as Baudrillard puts it.[114] By these means, the sociopolitical forces of capitalism–industrialism and the private spheres of the body and sense perception were intertwined in the currents of China's olfactory

---

[112] Liu, 'Liangge shijian de buganzheng zhe', 11; Liu, 'Fengjing', 29.
[113] Dal Lago, 'Crossed Legs in 1930s Shanghai', 111 (emphasis original).
[114] Baudrillard, *The Consumer Society*, 131 (emphasis original).

作澄漢　The parcel goods. By　貨封原
Chang Hau-tsing.

Figure 4.7 'Yuanfenghuo' (Sealed Goods), by Chang Hau-tsing, *Liangyou* 76 (31 May 1933), 36.

modernity. This seemingly compelling narrative, globally applicable to a large degree, only tells part of the story, however. The next chapter will put forward a counterargument; the body is complex and olfactory perception ambivalent, defying any totalizing theorization. For now let us stay with this thread of the plot and take a deeper sniff of the technologies of perfuming, or how culture retuned neurons.

Referencing *Red Chamber* once again brings up some underexplored avenues, beyond the well-trodden territory of smell's engagement with femininity, sexuality, and hygiene.[115] I will demonstrate that commodity

---

[115] Needless to day, these are the dimensions of modern life with which perfume culture most intensely engaged. For an illuminating study of the global Modern Girl icon in the interwar period, see Weinbaum et al., *The Modern Girl around the World*, especially Chapter 9 (by Madeleine Dong) and Chapter 13 (by Tani Barlow). Also see Peng,

culture strategized to turn manufactured perfumes into amicable friends not only by directly addressing the body, but also by tending to the situatedness of the body in time and space. Incense and floral scents permeate the Jia mansions, giving times and spaces embodied forms of meaning. Twentieth-century advertisers intuitively capitalized on the efficacy of embodied knowledge, providing consumers with new parameters within which to experience time and space. Time is the key frame in an advertisement run by Chen Diexian's Household Industries (Figure 4.8). In the comic strip in which commodities are embedded, the reader's gaze (and nose) is guided to relish 'four summer delights' (*qu shu si miao* 祛暑四妙) demonstrated by an elegant bourgeois woman. In the morning, brushing her teeth with Peerless (Wudipai) whitening toothpaste kicks off the day with refreshing coolness and fragrance (*qingliang fenfang* 清涼芬芳), the first delight. The second delight follows as she applies Butterfly moisturizer and Peerless powder before work, a guarantee of lasting radiance all day long. After dinner, drinking Peerless orange juice refreshes her mind and aids digestion, the third delight. The day is consummated with the fourth delight: after a soothing bath scented with Peerless Florida water, she perfumes her body with Peerless talcum powder, indulging in a divine sensation of smoothness and fragrance (*huani youxiang* 滑膩幽香).

An art of titillation and an art for emulation, this advertisement preaches a prototype of ideal life, a modern myth. The passage of time is no longer an agonizing experience analogous to the burning of incense – 'and year by year my heart consumes away', as Lin Daiyu writes. Rather, the passage of time is imbued with sensual gratification afforded by the commodities, to indulge your senses, to soothe your body and mind. If you follow the rhythmic flow, your body vicariously merges with the woman's body, healthy and fit, sexually appealing, and professionally successful. In short, the objective of this product placement comic strip is to rewire the consumer's nervous system, and to internalize the preached lifestyle that rests on the particular package of sensorial–temporal experience.

'Selling a Healthy Lifestyle in Late Qing Tianjin', 211–30; Luo Wanxian, 'Cong Liangyou huabao de huazhuangpin guanggao kan Shanghai funü de meirong qingkuang, 1926–1941'.

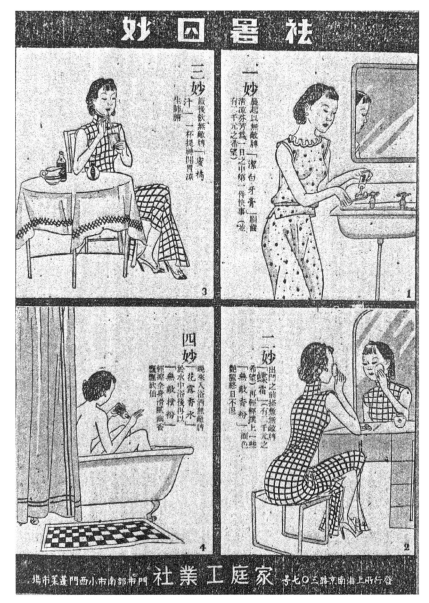

Figure 4.8 'Qu shu si miao' (Four Summer Delights), *Shenbao*, 18 July 1936, 15.

Space was also mobilized in new ways to anchor the body sensorially. In *Red Chamber*, a diverse array of incense is applied to define religious, ceremonial, scholarly, and intimate spaces. Many of the practices diminished in the modern era, whilst spaces of consumption arose as a prime locus to be perfumed. The aforementioned perfume ball installed on the ceiling of the Sun Sun Department Store in 1926 is a case in point. A Shanghai film theatre adopted the same practice in 1927, putting in place ten 'anti-miasma perfume boxes' (*fenfang biyi xia* 芬芳避疫匣).[116] Imagine the uncanny experience of watching a film adaptation of *Red Chamber* (screening at that time, coincidentally) while inhaling the synthetic compounds of almond scent wafting in the air! A perfuming device was also installed in a luxury hotel, enchanting the olfactory nerves of its guests with costly French perfume.[117] These technologized perfuming tactics belong to what contemporary scholars call 'marketing semiotics'.[118] Smell's liminal, instinctive attributes help consumers associate specific spatial experience with brand value and naturalize the link in the unconscious.

Physical consumer spaces aside, the beauty industry elicited spatial imaginations to reposition the modern body. Advertising for 4711 eau de cologne stages a *mise en scène* at the train station: a fond adieu is personified by the sign function of rose and eau de cologne, the latter 'a fine companion for travel' (*lüxing liangban* 旅行良伴, Figure 4.9). A scented mobile space filled with excitement is conjured up to accommodate idealized femininity abiding in her perfect body. Spaces of mobility zoomed out to also include the nation and the globe. When a Chinese American founded a cosmetics company in San Francisco in 1915, he implanted a global vision into his brand Xiangya 香亞 (Hang Ah, 'Perfuming Asia'): from a bird's-eye view, a Chinese woman is seen to be pouring a bottle of Florida water to scent Asia and the globe (Figure 4.10).[119] When *Dongfang zazhi* 東方雜誌 (Eastern Miscellany) launched the New Year special issue for 1933, its cover image likewise stages an overhead view: a chubby boy is seen to be washing China and the globe with Lysol and soap (Figure 4.11). His body,

---

[116] 'Zhongyang zhuangshe fenfang biyi xia', *SB*, 18 July 1927, 18. Zhongyang refers to the Palace Theatre (Zhongyang daxiyuan).

[117] 'Shenzhou da lüshe kaishi yingye', *SB*, 19 October 1928, 15.

[118] Oswald, *Marketing Semiotics*, especially Chapter 6, 'The Semiotics of Consumer Space'.

[119] The company moved its headquarters to Shanghai and built stores and factories there in 1919. Its cosmetic products were under the trademark of 'Golden Bell' (Jinzhong 金鍾). See 'Xiangya gongsi', SMA, Q90-1-940; 'Xiangya gongsi yingye jinxing ji', *SB*, 17 December 1919, 11.

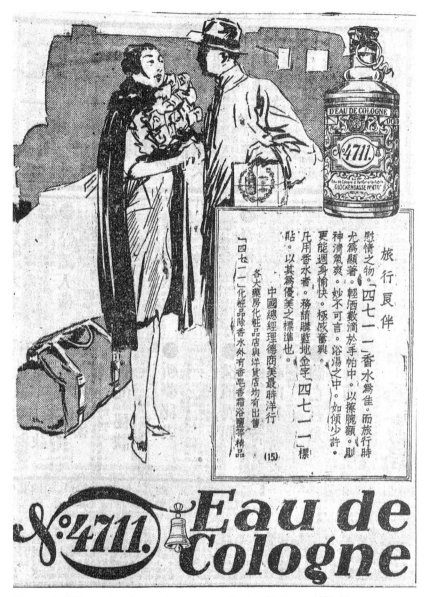

Figure 4.9 4711 eau de cologne advertisement, *Shenbao*, 14 August 1929, 20.

the 'object' to be washed in the traditional New Year bath custom, gains agency in this fable of hygienic modernity. In comparison to the BW & Co. calendar poster for 1911 (Figure 4.3), the female and young male bodies here are repositioned in a globally homogenizing smellscape, beyond the

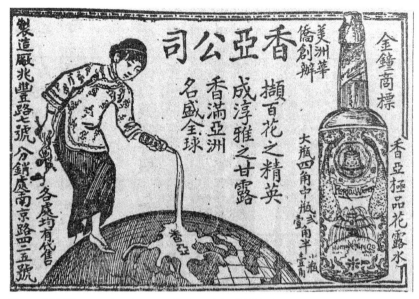

Figure 4.10 Xiangya advertisement, *Shenbao*, 3 April 1919, 4.

Figure 4.11 The cover of *Dongfang zazhi* 30, no. 1 (1 January 1933).

private garden. A new spatial relationship of Self, China, Asia, and the globe was envisioned, and brand value and moral value (of hygiene and progress) were sutured.

Despite all the cleverly choreographed tactics, the perfume culture invited a flurry of moralistic criticisms, invariably placing women (not capitalism) in the limelight for scrutiny. Writing for the *Ladies' Journal*, female author Miao Cheng Shuyi opines that women's emancipation cannot be truly realized if women are preoccupied with perfume and make-up, 'degrading themselves to be men's plaything' (*zishi wei wanwu* 自飾為玩物). Being an unnecessary extravagance, cosmetics are also detrimental to the cause of national salvation. Hence she calls on her women readers to pay more attention to cultivating 'scholarly and moral fragrance' (*hanmo xiang* 翰墨香, *daode de fangxiang* 道德的芳香).[120] This kind of moral charge against (scented) women was often politicized to serve different ends. In the 1930s, during the New Life movement (*Xin shenghuo yundong* 新生活運動), Chiang Kaishek concocted a rhetoric against perfume for its alleged role in undermining frugality and discipline: 'Nowadays the more perfume people wear, the more malodourous they are and the more unclean they become!'[121] Communist propaganda was not short of similar discourse, framing perfume as a synonym for the depraved 'old society' and its tenacious grip.[122] The colonial capitalist thread of the Chinese olfactory revolution reverberated far beyond its initial terrain of acts.

A DIAGNOSIS

Regarding the death of Old Mr Wu on his first night in Shanghai, a historically informed diagnosis can now be added to the medical and sociological ones. Simply put, the colonial capitalist circuits of manufactured fragrances (among other commodities) can be held culpable for overburdening the village gentleman's nervous system, one that has been ill-prepared for the hyperbolic sensorial stimulation and cultural shock. This chapter unveils the breadths and depths of this olfactory revolution in quantitative, qualitative, and cultural terms.

The scale of the revolution is best demonstrated by Chart 4.1, which shows that in less than forty years (from 1891 to 1928), the value of

[120] Miao, 'Xiang yu funü', 4–5. I thank Rachel Hui-chi Xu for sharing with me this source.
[121] Chiang, 'Xin shenghuo yundong zhi yaoyi' (19 February 1934), 79.
[122] Huang, 'Smellscapes of Nanjing Road', 86–9.

imported perfumery increased 106-fold, an astounding figure if we envisage it as the actual amount of fragrance permeating cities, towns, and villages throughout China. Adding to it was the exponential growth of the native industry, exemplified by Household Industries, developed from a family business to a modern firm with 130 types of cosmetics and toiletries on the market in 1937, less than twenty years after its establishment.[123] In qualitative terms, this industry, overseas and domestic, revolutionized the sensory foundations of modern life by introducing novel aromas, especially synthetic scents non-existent in the taxonomy of smells up until that time. While it is the scientists' mission to gauge the precise impact of chemical odours on our human physiopsychological system, my inquiry illuminates the historical milieu for this human invention to thrive. Lastly, this olfactory revolution not only occurred materially, but also took root in the very human body. Concurrent with its expansion was the shaping of an ingenious system of (self-)disciplining, through the mechanisms of commodity culture and redefined moral–aesthetic norms.

To what extent did it 'enrich the country and enrich the people' (as proclaimed by the advertisement that attracted the young Mao)? No conclusion can be reached if 'people' is framed as an abstract entity. For the bourgeois woman who relishes the 'four summer delights' (Figure 4.8), she may well believe – or has been convinced – that her life has been enriched by the bounty of perfumes at her disposal, or by the pleasure of shopping in an elegantly scented department store located in the deodorized zone of the city. But how about Xiaomao, the teenage boy in the novel *Blossoms*, who has to inhale reeking emanations of the mills, many of which are manufacturing none other than the bounty of perfume articles? We are reminded that Xiaomao lives near the renowned slum called Yaoshui nong 藥水弄 (Lotion Lane), the name of which derived from a lotion factory around which the slum formed in the 1920s.[124] The two fictitious figures had innumerable

---

[123] 'Jiating gongyeshe gufen youxian gongsi', 43.
[124] For the reference to Yaoshuinong in Xiaomao's story, see Jin, *Fanhua*, 19. For the history of Lotion Lane, see Lu, *Beyond the Neon Lights*, 118–21.

human incarnations in real history. Our story comes full circle, showing that deodorizing and perfuming cannot be separated in our parable of contamination. Bringing together the two sides of the Chinese olfactory revolution prompts further meditation on the thesis about the uneven distribution of sense-scapes in the past and present.

PART THREE

A WHIFF OF ALTERITY

5

The Bouquet of *Eros*

A few steps along the second floor he came into a dark corridor; immediately his nostrils were assaulted by the provocative perfume of face powder, mixed with a unique scent of Japanese woman's flesh, and the fragrance of hair tonic. He felt dizzy and sparks floated before his eyes, which made him reel.

走了幾步，經過一條暗暗的夾道的時候，一陣惱人的粉花香氣，同日本女人特有的一種肉的香味，和頭髮上的香油氣息合作了一處，撲上他的鼻孔裏來。他立刻覺得頭暈起來，眼睛裏看見了幾顆火星，向後面跌也似的退了一步。

Yu Dafu, 'Sinking'[1]

NO STUDENT OF MODERN CHINESE literature fails to be 'amused' by the melancholic, hypersensitive protagonist of Yu Dafu's 郁達夫 1921 short story 'Chenlun 沈淪' ('Sinking'). After lengthy scrutiny of his tormented psyche fraught with anguish, sexual yearning, self-pity, self-curse, and lamentation for the weakness of his motherland, the above passage about his olfactory enchantment appears at a critical moment leading up to the crescendo of the story. His visit to the Japanese brothel brings all his mental agonies to the fore. After waking in the prostitute's bed 'scented with a strange perfume', he walks to the seaside and resolves to drown himself in the sea, murmuring his last words: 'O China, my China, you are the cause of my death!'[2]

Needless to say, much has been said about 'Sinking', the canonical work that represents the May Fourth generation's ardent probing of

---

[1] Yu, 'Chenlun', 46; Yu, 'Sinking', 64 (modified). [2] Yu, 'Sinking', 67, 69.

selfhood.[3] Yet no study has offered a reading of the olfactory dimension of the modern sexual subject explored in this story. But just as a virgin girl's magnificent scent makes Jean-Baptiste Grenouille 'sick with excitement' in *Perfume*, and Lin Daiyu's ethereal fragrance *youxiang* renders Jia Baoyu 'intoxicated and limp' in *Red Chamber*, it is 'the fragrance emanating from the Japanese woman's mouth, hair, face, and body' that inebriates the twenty-one-year-old Chinese youth to such a degree that it foreshadows his demise.[4] Reading Yu Dafu's powerful portrayals of scents as merely a naturalistic representation of sensual stimulation is inadequate in capturing, as I will argue, a paradigm shift in bodily/sensorial relations to selfhood in May Fourth China. The private language of smell, lurking in the most intimate corner of *eros*, made a daring appearance in collective public articulations of the modern body and individuality. Ironically, the radically modern expressions in the Chinese context smell strange to the nose trained in the classroom of Western olfactory modernity. According to the doctrine of deodorization, sexual odour is an archetypal transgressor that contaminates the hygienic body, physically and morally. This contradiction points to the stranger status of the intimate aroma of sexuality. Neither foul nor fragrant, its perception depends on the communication between neurons and cultures. This chapter sets out to investigate the enigma of the bouquet of *eros* in the Chinese olfactory revolution.

Yu Dafu is merely one of the plethora of May Fourth writers who displayed traits of olfactophilia, a term borrowed from Victorian medical discourse, referring to a pronounced, 'perverted' interest in odours with regard to sexual behaviour.[5] Sex psychologist Havelock Ellis (1859–1939) asserts that olfaction plays a considerable role for neurasthenics, 'inverts', and 'primitives', while 'the majority of refined and educated people' do not fit the profile of the 'olfactory type'.[6] And Freud famously

---

[3] Denton, 'Romantic Sentiment and the Problem of the Subject'; Lee, *The Romantic Generation of Modern Chinese Writers*, 81–123; Chow, *Woman and Chinese Modernity*, 138–45, among others.

[4] Yu, 'Sinking', 64.

[5] Drobnick, *The Smell Culture Reader*, 257. I use the term in a neutral, non-pathological sense.

[6] Ellis, *Studies in the Psychology of Sex*, vol. 4, 111.

claims that the devaluation of olfactory stimuli marks civilization, resulting from human's adoption of an upright posture that removes the olfactory organ from the ground and from the genitals.[7] Collectively, to quote David Howes, 'this animalization of the sense of smell pushed it beyond the pale of culture' in the civilizing West.[8] Against this backdrop, the Chinese modernist writers' olfactophilia begs many questions. Why did the modern self wish to be associated with or expressed by smell, the arguably animalistic sense? How could the allegedly 'unsublimated pleasure' evoked by odours dovetail with the earnest quest for 'the sublime figure' in modern Chinese history?[9] What did this 'anomalous' fascination mean for the global history of olfactory modernity and the commodified body?

Fiction serves as a prism that refracts subtle dynamics of perception and subjectivity in this episode of the olfactory revolution. As we know, Liang Qichao 梁啟超 (1873–1929) and his fellow intellectuals elevated modern Chinese fiction to a critical position for individual soul-searching and national salvation. While advertising manifests the engineering of the scented body, as discussed in the preceding chapter, fiction's role is complementary, shedding light on the inner construct of the sexual subject through the nose. Based on my reading of a much longer list of novels and short stories, I have selected three sets of texts that reflect the genealogy of the May Fourth olfactophiliac fascination. The first section examines several early works by members of the Creation Society (Chuangzao she 創造社) published in the early 1920s. These works functioned as a trendsetter for overt sexual depictions in olfactory terms. The second section focuses on Lu Xun's 1924 short story 'Feizao 肥皂' ('Soap'), which is an artful anatomy of the ambivalent modern psyche wrapped in an ambiguous whiff of olive aroma. In the third section, Mao Dun's early fictional *oeuvre* of the late 1920s is analysed, inquiring into the meanings of libidinal odours impregnated with revolutionary vigour.

---

[7] Freud, *Civilization and Its Discontents*, 45–7.   [8] Howes, *Sensual Relations*, 202.

[9] For the term 'unsublimated pleasure' (acquired through smell and taste), see Marcuse, *Eros and Civilization*, 39; for 'the sublime figure of history', see Wang, *The Sublime Figure of History*.

THE ORGANIC ODOURS OF SEXUALITY

The earliest cluster of olfactophiliac writers in modern Chinese literary history are members of the Creation Society (hereafter 'Creationists'). It was formed in 1921 in Tokyo by a small coterie of Chinese students (including Yu Dafu, Guo Moruo 郭沫若, and Zhang Ziping 張資平, among others), in the wake of Hu Shih's 胡適 call for a literary revolution (1917) and the epoch-making May Fourth movement (1919). It represents 'a predominant force in the shaping of modern Chinese literature', epitomizing May Fourth romanticism and individualism in the early and mid-1920s. Their literary experimentalism involves a crucial aspect – the elevation of sex as a serious concern.[10] The olfactory emerged as an expressive mode within this context.

Explicit sexual depictions are rare in late Qing and early Republican popular fiction (excluding erotic literature).[11] Nor is the sense of smell a vital literary device.[12] In the renowned courtesan novel *Haishang hua liezhuan* 海上花列傳 (*The Sing-Song Girls of Shanghai* by Han Bangqing 韓邦慶, 1892), a typical allusion to sex reads like this: 'so Mama Zhao made the bed, blew out the lamp, and closed the door as she left the room. But Prosperity [the guest] had to wait until Green Phoenix [the courtesan] returned before going to bed with her.'[13] Scents abound in the works of Zhou Shoujuan 周瘦鵑, but the Mandarin Duck and Butterfly popular writer favoured an aesthetic invocation of perfume to depict 'virtuous sentiments'. In a short story of 1915, his protagonist seals her lover's postcards in a jewellery box, scented with violet perfume, as a token of

---

[10] Hsia, *A History of Modern Chinese Fiction, 1917–1957*, 93, 105. Also see Keaveney, *The Subversive Self in Modern Chinese Literature*.

[11] For example, Leo Ou-fan Lee comments, 'Lin shu and Su Man-shu had either side-stepped the problem of sex or submerged it in a stream of sentiment.' Lee, *The Romantic Generation of Modern Chinese Writers*, 111. As Chen Pingyuan puts it, most Mandarin Duck and Butterfly fiction focuses only on 'spiritual attachment rather than physical intimacy (只有思念之意而无肌肤之亲)'. See Chen, *Zhongguo xiandai xiaoshuo de qidian*, 223. Quoted in Chen, *Revolution and Form*, 76.

[12] Fragrance is extensively featured in other literary genres, for example in a subgenre of sentimental–erotic poetry known as *xiangliang* 香匲 (perfumed cosmetic case) style or *xiangyan* 香艷 (fragrant and bedazzling) style. See Li, *The Poetics and Politics of Sensuality in China*.

[13] Han, *The Sing-Song Girls of Shanghai*, 61–2.

her chaste love.[14] Just a few years later, however, the Creationists initiated a divergent approach, indexed in part by a spurt of sexual odours that stimulated, I dare say, a different bundle of nerves of the modern reader. Zhang Ziping, Guo Moruo, and Yu Dafu spearheaded this olfactory revolution in literature.

Best known as a master of hackneyed love-triangle fiction, Zhang Ziping (1893–1959) published his first short story in 1920 prior to the existence of the Creation Society.[15] The autobiographical story, entitled 'Yuetanhe zhi shui 約檀河之水' (The Water of the Jordan River), features a Chinese student in Japan who falls in love with a Japanese girl and makes her pregnant, both eventually seeking redemption through conversion to Christianity. It all starts with a fateful encounter on a rainy day – the girl offers to share her umbrella with him. The exhilarating sensation of sexual arousal is triggered by scent: 'Her in-breath and out-breath assailed his nostrils, smelling like a weak type of yeast. Inhaling her gentle breath, his whole body became hot as if it were fermented (她一呼一吸吹到他的鼻孔裏，好像弱醇性的酵母。他感受了她微微的呼吸，覺得全身發了酵似的，脹熱起來).'[16]

The scent of breath is not unusual as a sexual stimulus in Chinese erotic fiction. In *Jin ping mei* 金瓶梅 (*The Plum in the Golden Vase*), the sixteenth-century masterpiece which 'set the standards against which later novels focusing on desire were judged',[17] Ximen Qing uses the tip of his tongue to pass 'breath-sweetening lozenges flavored with fragrant tea and osmanthus' (*xiangcha muxi bing* 香茶木樨餅) into his mistress Pan Jinlian's mouth. The two of them then start to hugging and embracing 'like snakes darting out their tongues'.[18] The aphrodisiac usage of scented lozenges is common in traditional Chinese perfume culture, as the bond between sexual desire and aroma is

---

[14] Zhou, 'Duanchang riji', *Libailiu* 52 (May 1915), 29. For a study of Zhou's obsession with violet, see Chen, 'Zhou Shoujuan yu ziluolan', 253–85.

[15] For studies of Zhang Ziping, see Chen, *Revolution and Form*, 94–106; Peng, *Haishang shuo qingyu*, 27–63.

[16] Zhang, 'Yuetanhe zhi shui', *Xueyi* 2, no. 8 (1920), 5. Its autobiographical nature is mentioned in Zhang, 'Wo de chuangzuo jingguo', 6–8.

[17] Huang, *Desire and Fictional Narrative in Late Imperial China*, 67.

[18] Xiaoxiao sheng, *Jin ping mei*, 50; Xiaoxiao sheng, *The Plum in the Golden Vase*, vol. 1, 90.

anything but surprising.[19] What sets Zhang Ziping apart is his 'scientific' portrayal of the girl's *organic* aroma that sparks romance. This shift – from cultured flavours of *ars erotica* to yeast-like odours of sexuality – marks a divergence in the individual's relation to his/her body. In another short story by Zhang, the private language of smell registers the stirrings of emotion exchanged between the lovers who have long drifted apart: 'The two of them stood in front of a fireplace, both lowering their heads. A fragrance that he had not smelled for a long while wafted along, provoking a profound feeling inside him (兩個人低首站在室隅的火爐前。有種許久不聞，耐人尋味的香氣不時撲進他的鼻孔裏來).'[20]

This fragrance is distinctly individual – it belongs only to *this* woman, and elicits memories only attached to her. In other words, her body is not abstracted in orchid and musk, the clichéd scents that represent female sensuality in classical vernacular literature.[21] The latter is duplicable, whilst the former is unique, carrying the individual's biological codes. If she smells of her biological body, how does he smell to her? Zhang Ziping toyed with the subject of female sexual desire as well. 'Meiling zhi chun 梅嶺之春' (Spring on the Plum Mountain) is an early exploration of female sexuality in the May Fourth literary repertoire.[22] It tells a coming-of-age story about the fifteen-year-old Baoying, who lives with her uncle's family in a small town and attends the missionary school where her uncle Ji Shu is employed as a teacher. An incestuous attraction sprouts between the two at a time when Baoying senses an inkling of sexual desire in her body. On a spring morning, Baoying marvels at the

---

[19] Fu, *Zhongguo xiang wenhua*, 65.

[20] Zhang, 'Ai zhi jiaodian', *Chuangzao jikan* 1, no. 4 (1923), 41.

[21] Orchid and musk are the most common aromatics used to scent clothes. For example, the appearance of Meng Yulou (Ximen Qing's future wife) is described as such: 'Wherever she sits, the aroma of orchid and musk assails the nostrils (坐下時，一陣麝蘭香噴鼻).' See Xiaoxiao sheng, *Jin ping mei*, 75 (Chinese), 133 (English). A poem line in *The Romance of the Western Chamber* reads, 'The fragrance of orchid and musk left by her is still here, while the tinkling sound of her jade ornaments becomes gradually more remote (蘭麝香仍在，佩環聲漸遠).' See Wang, *Xixiang ji*, Act 1, scene i, 9; *The Romance of the Western Chamber*, 14.

[22] Zhang, 'Meiling zhi chun', *Dongfang zazhi* 21, no. 20 (1924), 85–100. For brief analyses of this story, see Chen, *Revolution and Form*, 101–2; Peng, *Haishang shuo qingyu*, 33–5.

flowering peach blossoms in the family garden, not noticing that Uncle Ji is behind her:

> Her nostrils were assailed by the aroma of cigar smoke drifting over from behind. She felt a force pressing upon her, but she didn't dare turn around. He, meanwhile, was excited by her fragrance – a fragrance only a virgin girl has and that becomes more alluring when she has just arisen.

> 雪茄的香味由她的肩後吹進鼻孔裏來。她給一種重力壓着了，不敢再翻轉頭來看。處女特有的香氣—才起床時尤更濃厚的處女的香氣，給了他一個奇妙的刺激。[23]

Unable to resist 'the allure of her fragrance', he holds her tightly. This embrace eases Baoying's repressed sexual yearnings, but her desire only intensifies thereafter and she becomes melancholic. After the death of Uncle Ji's wife, they eventually consummate their relationship, but they are expelled by the community after the birth of their illicit child.

A blend of the favourite May Fourth themes, the story testifies to Zhang's experimentalism in invoking smell to encode the female sex drive biologically, instead of sentimentally. Female sexual awakening aroused by scents is not unprecedented in classical Chinese literature. Cui Yingying in *The Romance of the Western Chamber* can be conceived as an archetype: in one act, she agonizes over her amorous cravings stirred by 'the air of late spring' – falling fragrant petals, incense aromas wafting in the wind, and fumes of orchid and musk drifting from the bed.[24] *Mudan ting* 牡丹亭 (*The Peony Pavilion*) features an analogous scene, in which Du Liniang's 'stirrings of the spring's passions' evolve into an erotic dream.[25] Notably, despite the profusion of olfactory stimuli (flowers, incense, and perfumed clothes and boudoirs), there is no masculine scent in the two canonical plays. In Liniang's erotic dream, Liu Mengmei holds an odourless willow branch as a token of love, an emblem of male affection. Clearly, aroma is a highly gendered instrument in the art of *amour* in classical Chinese cultural imaginings.

---

[23] Zhang, 'Meiling zhi chun', 94. The translation is quoted from Chen, *Revolution and Form*, 102 (modified).

[24] Wang, *Xixiang ji*, Act 2, scene i, 33–4 (Chinese), 50–2 (English).

[25] See Tang, *Mudan ting*, scene x, 'Jingmeng 驚夢' (The Interrupted Dream), 53–7; Tang, *The Peony Pavilion*, 42–53.

Seen in this light, Zhang Ziping's portrayal of Uncle Ji's aroma of cigar smoke is revolutionary in that it anchors female sexuality not in cultural symbolism but in the physical basis of being human. Despite the cigar being a clichéd signifier of masculinity, it is an aroma attached to the male body. Eileen Chang 張愛玲 (a self-admitted 'olfactophile') also embeds masculinity and infatuation in the scent of tobacco. In 'Hong meigui yu bai meigui 紅玫瑰與白玫瑰' ('Red Rose, White Rose'), Zhenbao catches an unexpected glimpse of his mistress Jiaorui 'sitting near his coat and letting the cigarette scent from his clothes waft down over her', and 'as if that weren't enough, she'd lit his used cigarette butts'.[26] Biological masculine odours are only occasionally invoked. Ding Ling 丁玲 depicts a sweet moment of enticement for Mengke when her cousin's breath tickles the back of her neck.[27] An overt account can be found in *Xingshi* 性史 (History of Sex), Zhang Jingsheng's 張競生 collection of allegedly real-life sexual experiences. The only female author recalls her sexual feelings ignited by 'a faint fragrance' (*xiangze weiwen* 香澤微聞) exuding from her mathematics teacher's body when he leans towards her. Her heartbeat quickens, and that night she has a dream in which she is held tightly by a man.[28]

The variety of personal sexual odours under Zhang Ziping's pen heralded the rise of a new sensibility and expressive modality in relation to the body. Zhang's fellow Creationists also contributed to this shift. Guo Moruo's early fictional works teem with olfactory imageries, tying in with his keen interest in Freudian psychoanalysis.[29] His early short story 'Canchun 殘春' (Late Spring) exemplifies the ways in which he wove olfactory cues in his narrative to explore the interlinked psychical and physical regimes of humankind.[30] The story's first-person narrator,

---

[26] Chang (Zhang Ailing), 'Red Rose, White Rose', 279. I thank Yang Chia-hsien 楊佳嫻 for drawing my attention to this source.

[27] Ding, 'Mengke', *Xiaoshuo yuebao* 18, no. 12 (1927), 20.   [28] Zhang, *Xingshi*, 5.

[29] Celebrated as a poet, Guo's fictional work has been largely overlooked. In fact Guo was an avid fiction writer between 1919 and 1925, and produced three volumes of fiction with the exploration of sexual desire as its main theme. See Shih, *The Lure of the Modern*, 98.

[30] Guo, 'Canchun', *Chuangzao jikan* 1, no. 2 (1922), 126–38. Subsequent page references are given parenthetically in the text. For an analysis of the story, see Shih, *The Lure of the Modern*, 103–5. Some English translations cited here are Shih's, with modification.

Aimou, a Chinese student in Japan, lives with his wife and two children. Informed by Mr Baiyang of a mutual friend's failed suicide attempt, they go to visit the friend, Mr He, in a small hospital in Moji. Upon arrival, this olfactophiliac narrator is greeted by a 'repellent odour characteristic of hospital wards' (132). But his sensitive nose is soothed instantly by 'a heady perfume of rouge and powder' (*zhifen de nongxiang* 脂粉的濃香) when he enters the adjacent nurse's room (132). This sensual aroma, together with the sight of the nubile nurse Miss S, plants the seeds of desire in Aimou's unconscious. That night he has an amorous dream about a rendezvous with Miss S on a moonlit mountaintop. Silence is broken when Miss S 'opens her flower-bud-like lips' (134), seeking advice from the medical-student narrator for her tuberculosis or neurasthenia, both linked to the strong sex drive in medical discourse of the time. This conversation leads to the crescendo of the erotic dream, a 'medical examination' of her body: 'she slowly bared her upper body and walked towards me. Her body was like a marble statue, her [naked] shoulder like peeled lychees, and her breasts, slightly pointing upward, like rosebuds not yet in bloom (說著便緩緩地袒出她的上半身來，走到我的身畔。她的肉體就好像大理石的雕像，她[裸]著的兩肩，就好像一顆剝了殼的荔枝，胸上的[兩]個乳房微微傾向上，就好像兩朵未開苞的薔薇花蕊)' (135).

Despite the absence of direct olfactory references, this scene is filled with sensual aromas, especially that of rosebuds. From this point, the dream turns into a Freudian nightmare: Mr Baiyang arrives at the scene with the news that Aimou's wife has killed their two sons and gone insane. The sexually charged aromatic metaphor of rose remains alive in the rest of the story. Next morning Aimou brings a bunch of roses to Mr He's ward, and, to his surprise, Miss S picks one to put in her hair. A few days after he has returned home, he receives a letter from Mr Baiyang, with three dry rose petals that Miss S has enclosed in the envelope as a farewell gift. Feeling 'a melancholic emotion' (*shanggan de qinghuai* 傷感的情懷) arising, Aimou places the rose petals inside his favourite book of Shelley's poetry, and writes a postcard to the nurse, with a short poem about roses.

The allegorical linkage of flower and romance is anything but new, and a virgin girl's sweet-smelling boudoir is commonplace in classical

Chinese literature. Whilst evidently drawing on traditional tropes, Guo's writing is quintessentially modern in two regards. First, the olfactory cues in this story function biologically, not sentimentally or symbolically. The cosmetic perfume in Miss S's room signifies her bodily allure, not the traditional cultural code attached to the orchid chamber. The rosebud is a vaginal metaphor, not a symbol of romantic love. Thereby the sense of smell secured new psychological significance in May Fourth China, mediating the articulation of the unconscious on behalf of the modern sexual subject. Second, the olfactory imageries themselves are modern. While erotic bedchambers are invariably scented by orchid and musk traditionally,[31] it is the modern cosmetic perfume that is floating in the air of Miss S's room. The globally growing beauty industry was rewiring the human nervous system and redefining sensuality, as discussed in Chapter 4. The rose is also a modern emblem in China. In the classical literary repertoire, plum blossoms and peach blossoms are far more common amorous icons, and a woman's sensuous mouth is convention-ally likened to a cherry.[32] The rosebud analogy (of her mouth and breasts) is more sexually charged.[33] A cartoon (Figure 5.1) published in the heyday of urban decadence in 1930s Shanghai illustrates the entangled rose metaphor, odour, and sexuality. Guo Moruo and his fellow Creationists are forerunners of these new sensorial–amorous expressions.

The most olfactophiliac of the Creationists is probably Yu Dafu. Odours often transmit the anguish of his protagonists or his autobio-graphical self. Sexually repressed youths in his work have cultivated not only sensitive noses, but also olfactophiliac minds capable of aromatic fantasizing. In 'Yinhuise de si 銀灰色的死' (Silver Death) (1921), the

---

[31] For example, the first line of a poem in *The Plum in the Golden Vase*: 'The scent of orchid and musk pervades the gauze netting (紗帳輕飄蘭麝).' See Xiaoxiao sheng, *Jin ping mei*, 110 (Chinese), 203 (English).

[32] Pan Jinlian's 'fragrant cherry-like mouth (香噴噴櫻桃口)' is underscored in Xiaoxiao sheng, *Jin ping mei*, 26.

[33] A similar expression, 'lips that resemble rosebuds (薔薇花苞似的嘴唇)', can be found in Yu Dafu's 'Yinhuise de si', 2. For a genealogy of breasts as a trope in modern Chinese literary imagination, see Chen, *Revolution and Form*, Chapter 8, 280–327; for a study of rose, see Classen, 'The Odor of the Rose'.

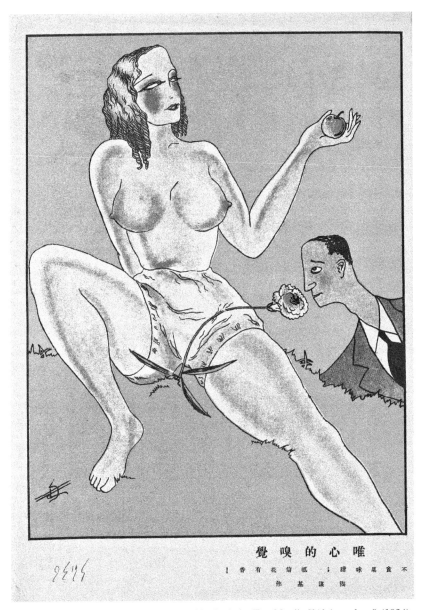

Figure 5.1 'Weixin de xiujue' (Idealist Olfaction), by Tao Mouji, *Shidai manhua* 5 (1934). Courtesy of the Special Collections and University Archives, Colgate University Libraries.

Chinese student in Japan repents of his acts of debauchery and is determined to discipline himself. Sitting in the library, however, when the street lights come on at dusk, he slips into reverie: 'aromas of rouge and powder, hair tonic, fried fish, cigarette and wine' drift into his nose, music and women's smiling faces tantalize his ears and eyes.[34] Sensorial stimulants, real or otherwise, are directly fed into the psyche. Another sentimental young man, in 'Nanqian 南遷' (Moving to the South) (1921), is tormented by imagining the lovemaking scene of his secret lover and her husband: 'her hair spreading on the pillow, her lips and the tip of her tongue, the fragrance from a mixture of her face powder and sweat, the tremble of her lower body (散在枕上的她的頭髮，她的嘴唇和舌尖，她的那一種粉和汗的混合的香氣，下體的顫動)'.[35]

The multisensory imagination, unbearably vivid in his mind, agonizes him deeply. Zhifu, another neurotic young man, faces a different kind of challenge. On a stormy night in a spa sanatorium, his neighbour knocks on his door to seek 'refuge' in his room. When the sixteen- or seventeen-year-old girl falls asleep on his bed, he is distressed by uncontrollable sexual impulses evoked by her naked body in his mind: 'a marble statue of a virgin girl, with warm, sweet-smelling blood running in her veins, now lying in front of him'.[36]

It is reminiscent of the same marble statue metaphor for Miss S's naked body in Guo Moruo's 'Late Spring'. By adding 'warm, sweet-smelling blood running in her veins', Yu Dafu brings the body alive, making it a more appealing sexual object (as well as subject). Interestingly, the two budding Chinese writers seemingly shared a philosophical premise with eighteenth-century French sensualists, notably Étienne Bonnot de Condillac. In order to illustrate his theory concerning senses and sensations, Condillac devised the conceit of a marble statue (*homme-statue*) coming alive in a series of stages, in the course of which it receives the five senses in order of smell, hearing, taste, sight, and touch.[37] In the context of May Fourth China, we can argue that the

---

[34] Yu, 'Yinhuise de si', 2.   [35] Yu, 'Nanqian', 85.

[36] Yu, 'Kongxu', 159; first published in *Chuangzao jikan* 1, no. 2 (1922) under 'Fengling 風鈴' (Wind Chimes).

[37] Condillac, *Treatise on the Sensations*, 289–90. Quoted in Jütte, *A History of the Senses*, 129–30.

cognate metaphor – the marble statue of a woman's body being brought to life by means of sensual imagining – is emblematic of the discovery of selfhood in a modern, scientific, and humanist fashion. By engaging the senses and the biological body, the Creationists breathed new life into the arguably static, marble-statue-like Confucian culture.[38] The revitalization of individualized sexual odours played out in a subversive manner on the path of self-awakening. Following the lead of these young Creationists, other writers started to take an attentive sniff of modernity and its consequences, including Lu Xun, the father of modern Chinese literature.

THE INDETERMINATE SCENT OF MODERNITY

It is well-known that the sense of sight was pivotal in Lu Xun's awakening to the question of 'what it means to "be Chinese" in the modern world'.[39] Scholars have examined his fiction *oeuvre*, which throws reflexive light on gaze and seeing in the construction of modern subjectivity.[40] Yet few, if any, have probed Lu Xun's use of smell to meditate on the complexities of experiencing the modern. 'Soap' is a story that tackles this theme and, in many ways, encapsulates the central thesis of this book – about smell as the stranger, the ambivalence of odour perception, and embedded pitfalls of olfactory modernity. First published in 1924 in *Chenbao fukan* 晨報副刊 (Morning Post) and subsequently included in the short-story collection *Panghuang* 彷徨 (*Wandering*, 1926), 'Soap' has not gained as much attention as his other canonical stories, probably owing to its apparently trivial subject matter in the domestic sphere. But Lu Xun himself was fond of it, and scholars have recently rediscovered its value from less political perspectives, focusing on its psychoanalytical orientation and literary experimentation.[41]

---

[38] To be sure, premodern Chinese culture should not be essentialized. There are examples about women's natural fragrance in late imperial popular literature, though the expressive mode is different. *Red Chamber* is a case in point. Also see Santangelo, 'The Culture of Smells'.

[39] Chow, *Primitive Passions*, 5.

[40] Braester, *Witness against History*, 38–9; Lee, *Revolution of the Heart*, 231.

[41] For an overview of the publication and reception of 'Soap' in China, see Yang, '1924–1949: luexian jimo de "Feizao" yanjiu'; Chen, 'Shangpin, jiating yu quanqiu xiandaixing', 135–7.

Technically speaking, it is an exquisitely crafted story, with 'economy of plot, finely chosen detail, and subtle observation of human behaviour'.[42] Notably, two smell-related phrases recur multiple times like melodic motifs that impart structure and cohesion to a piece of music. Inspired by the musicality of the story, I adopt an analytical strategy that is to envision the story as a concerto comprising three movements, with the two olfactory motifs running throughout. This approach grants the elusive sense of smell a recognizable shape, pointing to the possibility of synaesthesia in understanding sensorial literary expressions.

I ADAGIO: 'THE INDETERMINATE SCENT – THAT MIGHT OR MIGHT NOT HAVE BEEN OLIVE'

The first movement is an adagio, quietly unfolding in a humdrum domestic space on a late afternoon 'beneath the sun's slanting rays'.[43] Siming arrives home and presents his wife with a bar of perfumed soap, readily purchasable in most 1920s Chinese cities, as we learned in the preceding chapter. As she takes it from him, she smells 'a scent she couldn't quite put her finger on – that might or might not have been olive' (195). Lu Xun's original phrase, '似橄欖非橄欖的說不清的香味', has an untranslatable quality in terms of rhythm and subtlety. It ingeniously captures the ambiguous nature of smell and smelling, as well as the indeterminate desires and anxieties deep in the psyche of Siming, his wife, and the modern subject in general, as the story will unravel.

She pushes away their daughter Xiu'er who has dashed over to have a look, and opens the wrapper. The olfactory motif, 'the indeterminate scent – that might or might not have been olive', appears a second time following an elaborate description of the sensuality of the soap bar and the pattern, texture, and colour of the wrapper.[44] Once it is unwrapped, the fragrance intensifies. She lifts the soap carefully to her nose and sniffs. At that moment she catches a glimpse of her husband's eyes falling

---

[42] Brown, 'Woman as Trope', 58.

[43] Lu Xun, 'Soap', 195. Further page references are given parenthetically in the text. English translations are Julia Lovell's, with modifications.

[44] Wen Rumin offers an insightful Freudian reading of the visual and olfactory portrayal of the soap, arguing that it may allude to the sensual naked body of the filial girl (who will appear soon in the story). See Wen, '"Feizao" de jingshen fenxi jiedu', 13.

on to the back of her neck, where there is 'a certain roughness', some long-accumulated dirt 'she'd never minded much' (196). His 'inquisitorial scrutiny', in the company of this 'green, extraordinarily fragrant foreign soap' (葵綠異香的洋肥皂), prompts a hot flush (196).

This is the crescendo of the movement, preparing for the gradual unfolding of the drama. On the part of Siming's wife, the gaze and the fragrance seem to have triggered some sort of awakening of her sexual self, a dimension absent in the Confucian structure of 'good wife and wise mother' (*xianqi liangmu* 賢妻良母). Since being sexually attractive is not part of the gendered role of a married woman in this traditional framework, 'she'd never minded much' about the dirt; that is, her sexual appeal. On the part of Siming, this gaze could have directed to a courtesan had he been born a few decades earlier. However, by the mid-1920s the nuclear family and monogamy had been a new norm for the urban educated class, and thereby the legitimate sexual relationship should only happen, in principle, between husband and wife. The exchange of the respective covert thoughts and feelings between the married couple is transmitted by the 'indeterminate scent'. Seen in this light, *shuobuqing* is more than a qualifier to describe the ephemeral soap fragrance; rather, it indicates that the existential, embodied dimension of modern life is ambivalent and indeterminate. One question that remains at this point of reading is whether Siming embraces modernity wholeheartedly, through the gesture of perfuming his wife's body and converting her into a hygienic and sexually alluring one. There is no easy answer, as we will see from the second movement.

II ANDANTE TO ALLEGRO: 'GEZHI GEZHI A GOOD SCRUBBING'

Entering the second movement, the tempo speeds up. It starts with Siming's impatient summoning of his son Xuecheng to solve a question. The question is about the meaning of an English word that sounds like e-du-fu (old fool), a word he has picked up earlier at the soap shop from some schoolboys' teasing comments. Unable to provide an immediate answer, Xuecheng falls prey to his father's explosion of inexplicable rage, accompanied by a lengthy fulmination about numerous problems of 'the youth of today', the new education system, the 'poisonous' preaching of freedom and liberty in new schools, and the uselessness of their half-Chinese half-Western curricula. He goes on to accuse the 'schoolgirls with bobs' parading along the street: 'It's not the warlords and bandits that're the problem – it's the women who've brought the country to its knees' (198). Perplexed by his capricious mood, Siming's wife urges him to explain what has happened, bringing us to the kernel of the drama, compressed in the second olfactory motif.

It all started with buying the soap bar at the shop. Siming's narrative circles back to the schoolboys' mockery, moves on to some grand-sounding grumbles, and finally brings the central figure, a beggar girl, to the fore. Outside the shop there was a seventeen- or eighteen-year-old girl begging with her blind grandmother. 'Whenever she got given something, she'd give it to her grandmother straightaway and go hungry herself', Siming says. But his rage returns when he recalls that no bystander gave a penny, and worse yet, 'I heard one lowlife say to another, "Don't worry about all that dirt. Reckon she'd scrub up lovely with a couple of bars of soap"' (200). The sexually charged phrase '*gezhi gezhi* a good scrubbing (咯吱咯吱遍身洗一洗)' is the second olfactory motif, which appears seven times in this movement.

Through the Freudian prism, we may argue that Siming's anger towards his son, new-style schools, girl students, and China is entirely a cover for his frustration caused by the repression of his sexual impulse. Whilst covertly desiring the beggar girl and an imaginary good scrubbing of her body with perfumed soap, his persona as a Confucian patriarch and moralist restrains the free will of his sexual self.[45] And yet there is something more. The full circle of apathetic spectators is reminiscent of the famed slide show episode that awakened the young Lu Xun to the realization of the Chinese characteristic of indifference.[46] Whereas the

---

[45] For a discussion of Lu Xun's interest in Freud, see Brown, 'Woman as Trope', 67–8. For a more comprehensive study of Freud's influence in modern China, see Larson, *From Ah Q to Lei Feng*.

[46] In the preface to Lu Xun's first short-story collection, *Nahan* 吶喊 (*Call to Arms*, 1922), he recalls a slide show he watched in Japan, in which a crowd of apathetic Chinese spectators watched an execution of an alleged Chinese spy by a squadron of Japanese soldiers during the Russo-Japanese war (1904–5). Lu Xun was mortified by the indifference of his countrymen, and decided to discontinue medical study and take up literature because he reckoned that it was more important to change Chinese people's spirit than to cure their illness. As Haiyan Lee notes, this passage has become 'not only

young Lu Xun in Japan stood on a moral high ground, Siming finds himself involuntarily associated with that 'lowlife' and his lewd imagination. Judged by his Confucian superego, Siming is overwhelmed by shame, guilt, and dejection, all blended in a whiff of indeterminate fragrance.[47]

Siming's wife intuitively gets a good grip on the issue. At the family dinner, Siming's continuous scolding of their son gets on her nerves: 'He's not a mind-reader. If he was, he'd have skipped dinner to go and fetch that girl of yours back home. One more bar of soap, and she'd scrub up nicely' (202). From this point the tempo further quickens, from andante to allegro, and the motif *gezhi gezhi* recurs three times in her sarcastic remarks. She is forthright: 'You men are the problem. When you're not bad-mouthing girl students, you're eyeing up girl beggars. "Scrub up lovely"! You're all disgusting' (202). This remark summarizes another layer of self-contradiction in Siming's olfactory perception and moral judgement.

Siming's accusation of fashionable schoolgirls was not uncommon at that time.[48] As discussed in Chapter 4, the perfumed bodies of Modern Girls were at once the target of capitalist commodification and moralistic allegations. Siming's conscious mind would like to summarize the problem this way: modern schoolgirls are physically fragrant and morally foul; the filial beggar girl is the reverse. This unambiguous dyadic framework, however, is disturbed by the dissonant chord '*gezhi gezhi* a good scrubbing'. Whilst glorifying the beggar girl's fragrance of virtue, his unconscious mind fantasizes the fragrance of her body. But there is a paradox. What would be the prospective life path for the beggar girl if she were cleansed and perfumed, and transformed into a sensual Modern Girl? Republican-era literature and films supplied a plenitude of possible scenarios: she could become a dance hostess, film actress, shop assistant, waitress, prostitute, concubine, and girl student (if she were lucky). All of these Modern Girls, however, were cursed as morally foul in one way or

---

the founding text of modern Chinese literature, but also the mission statement of modern Chinese intellectuals'. See Lee, *Revolution of the Heart*, 231–2.

[47] Wen Rumin has a similar reading, see Wen, '"Feizao" de jingshen fenxi jiedu', 14.

[48] Judge, 'The Culturally Contested Student Body'; Brown, 'Woman as Trope', 60.

another in dominant social discourse.[49] In other words, physical and moral fragrances are antithetical, and Siming's desire entails an irresolvable aporia. All the contradictions rise to the surface, and are simultaneously suppressed in the unconscious. No wonder Siming is agitated.

The visit of two friends rescues him from the predicament, but the topic they bring up circles back to the dilemma of the fragrant and the foul. They come to settle on a subject for a poetry contest for the sake of 'improving social mores' in the Confucian moral structure. Siming's thoughts wander back to the filial girl, and he proposes a topic to extol her virtues. He repeats the story, including the mantra of '*gezhi gezhi* a good scrubbing'. His Confucian gentlemen friends erupt in laughter, and they repeat the phrase a few more times, unable to hold back their chuckles. The reader can envision his wife's attentive ears behind the door. The generous repetition of the motif is a stinging satire on male hypocrisy. After seeing his friends off, Siming returns to the sitting room and sees the packet of soap lying right in the centre of the dining table. His daughter Xiu'er mutters, '"Scrub up lovely"! Shameless, shameless.' This motif dies away, and Siming feels 'overwhelmed by sorrow – forsaken, alone, like the virtuous beggar-girl' (205).

III ADAGIO: 'THE INDETERMINATE SCENT – THAT MIGHT OR MIGHT NOT HAVE BEEN OLIVE'

The finale is a short adagio, probably too short for a concerto, but it works powerfully as a thoughtful end to the story, adding yet another layer of nuance through the recurrence of the first motif. The next morning, the soap bar is officially put to use by Siming's wife. 'For little less than half a year, his wife's skin took on a scent that might or might not have been olive, after which (according to everyone who smelt it) the fragrance changed to sandalwood' (205). Interpreting the ending as a form of female surrender to male sexual demands may be too simplistic.[50] To me, this tale is more than a straightforward critique of the objectification of the female body facilitated by the compound of capitalist production and Confucian morality. Reading it as a 'pragmatic solution' taken by

---

[49] Sang, 'Failed Modern Girls in Early-Twentieth-Century China'.
[50] Zhu, '"Feizao" yinyu de qianxing yu pojie', 62.

Siming's wife, who 'neither rejects [tradition] nor submits [to marriage] but finds personal space within the givens of her life', sounds reductionist as well.[51] Juxtaposing it with the sensorial expressions of female sexuality in the Creationist works, I propose a reading that centres on her agency, her sexual awakening. Just like the marble statue brought to life by sweet-smelling blood, the soap fragrance may function to animate her body, subverting her de-sexualized identity as a wise mother and good wife. Her daily application of soap indicates a process of internalizing the new sexual identity by tuning her olfactory neurons. From Siming's perspective, this scenario offers a hopeful reconciliation between the moral and bodily regimes. A virtuous wife and a sexual being can be one and the same. It seems consistent with Lu Xun's habit of ending his sombre stories with a dim light of hope, but at the same time we should not forget that the smell is indeterminate, and so, I believe, is Lu Xun's stance.

Unlike some of his literary peers, Lu Xun does not show any obvious sign of olfactophilia in his work. But in 'Soap' he deftly mobilizes the primitive sense of smell to conduct an anatomy of what it means to be a modern individual (woman and man) biologically, psychologically, and socially. In other words, Lu Xun perceptively realizes that the indeterminate/*shuobuqing* nature of scent – the stranger – could be a potent tool to explore the most complex question of being human. Ambivalence threads its way through the rhythmic recurrence of the two smell motifs. While 'the indeterminate scent – that might or might not have been olive' – is mainly concerned with the redefined sexual dimension of a married woman, encoded in '*gezhi gezhi* a good scrubbing' is the ambivalent male identity between a Confucian *junzi* and a modern sexual self, as well as the (im)possibility for a Modern Girl to be fragrant both morally and physically. All the contradictions occurred in the times of transition, and odours offered a conduit for probing and articulating the complexities. Yet things were changing rapidly alongside tumultuous political developments from the mid-1920s onwards. The air of melancholia and uncertainty gave way to a more vigorous spirit under the sweeping notion of revolution. This shift was also registered by aroma. Mao Dun was a prominent spokesman for the passionate union of revolution and libido.

[51] Brown, 'Woman as Trope', 66.

THE LIBIDINAL AROMAS OF REVOLUTION

Another olfactophiliac May Fourth writer, Mao Dun, invented a unique type of revolutionary woman, who is vivacious, desirable, and, more often than not, alluringly aromatic. Mao Dun started to write novels in 1927 as he withdrew from politics in the aftermath of the disintegration of the Communist–Nationalist alliance. Within a few years, he completed the trilogy *Shi* 蝕 (Eclipse) (1927–1928), the novel *Hong* 虹 (Rainbow) (1929), and some short stories collected in *Ye qiangwei* 野薔薇 (Wild Roses) (1929). These works are the focus of analysis in this section. While his 1930s novels (such as *Midnight*, *Linjia puzi* 林家鋪子 (The Lin Shop), and *Nongcun sanbuqu* 農村三部曲 (Village Trilogy)) have been widely acclaimed as the canon of modern Chinese realist fiction, his early fictional *oeuvre* on petty-bourgeois life has only recently received closer scrutiny.[52]

Written at a moment of political and personal crisis, these works paint a complex picture of 'bourgeois revolutionary psychology', a 'panoramic portraiture of political upheavals in town and country', and 'acute presentation of history on the move', as David Der-wei Wang aptly summarizes.[53] Moreover, as Chen Jianhua points out, Mao Dun was probably the first modern Chinese writer who consciously 'tried to make the modern woman into a vehicle for historical movement'. In so doing, he quested after the meanings of 'timeliness' (*shidaixing* 時代性).[54] Endowing his zestful female protagonists with various aromas, Mao Dun's late 1920s fiction marks the peak of the May Fourth quest for individual subjectivity. If the Creationists and Lu Xun were at an experimental stage of sensorial–literary expression, it seems as if Mao Dun had reached a carnivalesque state, celebrating his revolutionary women's agency in libidinal terms. A prototype emerges in 'Chuangzao 創造' (Creation) (1928), one of the short stories in *Wild Roses*.

Like the opening scene of a film, 'Creation' begins with a long take panning over an urban middle-class apartment, scanning inquisitively through the furniture and miscellaneous items that reveal the identity of

---

[52] For a short literature review, see Chen, *Revolution and Form*, 2–5.
[53] Wang, *Fictional Realism in Twentieth-Century China*, 25.
[54] Chen, *Revolution and Form*, 9–10.

its occupants: a young couple. The camera then zooms in on the bed, where Junshi is awakened by a car horn from the street. When he opens his eyes, his senses are awakened by 'a waft of heady fragrance' from his wife's hair. His gaze falls upon the attractive woman still asleep, her 'rosy cheeks', her tight-fitting vest that exposes her arms and legs under the caress of the morning sunlight.[55] The smell and sight of his young wife Xianxian, however, bring disturbing thoughts back to Junshi's consciousness. A series of flashbacks inform the reader about his efforts to *create* Xianxian to be an ideal woman (*lixiang de nüzi* 理想的女子, 104). His project is threefold: first, he instructs her to read books on a variety of topics covering 'science, history, literature, philosophy, and modern thoughts', as well as political theories ranging from Plato and Hobbes, to Marx and Lenin for a 'balanced and sensible' political view (107). Second, considering the 'toxic' Daoist influence of her father, Junshi introduces Darwinism, Nietzsche, and Marxist historical materialism to counterbalance Daoist nihilism and idealism. The third area concerns her shy and passive disposition that is characteristic of 'old-fashioned women' (*jiushi nüzi* 舊式女子). A firm believer in eugenics, Junshi is determined to transform her nature for the sake of their future children.

Junshi reaps the harvest of the well-designed curriculum: Xianxian flowers into his ideal woman, and yet she continues to grow and he loses his grip on her 'development'. Weary of 'the grace of quietness' (*jing de youya* 静的優雅), she is hunting for 'strong stimuli' (*qianglie de ciji* 強烈的刺激, 101). Her exceedingly sensual (*rougan* 肉感) body and strong sex drive put her creator, Junshi, at unease. More disturbing to him are her increasingly radical political views and passionate involvement in political activism, under the influence of a feminist friend and progressive magazines. These are the ruminations that agitate Junshi when he wakes up that morning. In contrast to Junshi's dark thoughts is the warm and bright ambience of this late spring morning: everything in the room is bathed in sunlight, full of life (*yuanqi miman* 元气弥漫), including his wife. She is now sitting on the sofa pulling on her stockings, and the

---

[55] Mao Dun, 'Chuangzao', *Dongfang zazhi* 25, no. 8 (April 1928), 100. Further page references are given parenthetically in the text.

'warm aroma of her flesh' (*rou de rexiang* 肉的热香, 109) is exuding from the hem of her vest. Torn by the opposing forces of her tantalizing body and unfathomable mind, Junshi's pain intensifies. There is an existential quandary posed to the May Fourth youth of Junshi's kind: 'beneath the dynamic and stimulating modern life are fatigue, distress, and boredom' (110). And a predominant source of their distress is the emancipated New Woman. The warm libidinal aroma allegorizes the at once alluring and threatening New Woman. Not surprisingly, the ultimate outcome of Junshi's creation is that Xianxian becomes Ibsen's Nora and leaves home. It is up to Junshi 'to keep up with her'; otherwise she will not wait (114).

Composed in a playful tone, this satirical parable presents a caricature of May Fourth-generation male intellectuals, their hypocrisy and ambivalence. It can also be read as a prehistory of how 'revolutionary femmes fatales' are born and evolve.[56] In a nutshell, he suggests that the sexual power of New Woman is not inborn, but created by men; however, once born, it quickly spirals out of the creator's control. Smell registers the profound male ambivalence towards female sexuality and agency. Building on early work, Mao Dun probes more deeply the genealogy of women's emancipation in 1920s China. A technique he intuitively deploys is what I term a dynamic–static duo: vis-à-vis the sexualized woman, a quiet and delicate woman is often in place, and they smell different.

Two such women are featured in 'Huanmie 幻灭' (Disillusionment), Mao Dun's first novella in the *Eclipse* trilogy. Jing, the delicate type, is born with 'exquisite beauty' (*youli* 幽麗) that 'soothes your stressed nerves and charms you'. Her body seems to exude an 'ethereal fragrance' (*youxiang* 幽香) and sends out electric waves.[57] Interestingly, Mao Dun uses the same word *youxiang* that Cao Xueqin applies to Lin Daiyu, the classical aroma of de-sexualized femininity. On the other side of the spectrum is Hui, a stereotypical New Woman. She is independent, robust, outgoing, and confident, 'exciting you with her magic power'

---

[56] Hilary Chung has an insightful analysis of the femme fatale type of New Woman in Mao Dun's early fiction. See Chung, 'Questing the Goddess'.

[57] Mao Dun, 'Huanmie', 20.

(20). Her olfactory embodiment is 'a distinctively sweet feminine fragrance, mixed with the aroma of wine', which leads to a passionate kiss with the male protagonist on one summer evening (27). Yet this sweet fragrance (*tianxiang* 甜香) only serves as an alluring catalyst, not a token of love, since Hui declares that she has no faith in men – she only wants to 'play' with them. Intriguingly, Mao Dun references *Red Chamber* once again, as we know *tianxiang* is attributed to Qin Keqing, the sexually transgressive woman who undermines social norms. Subconsciously or otherwise, the use of the two olfactory codes discloses a deep-rooted contradiction in the mentality of May Fourth males. The subversive libidinal odour is worshipped and feared simultaneously. But Mao Dun reserves a space for his New Women to thrive, a space that is called revolution, whereas no legitimate space is available for Qin Keqing in the Confucian social structure.

Despite his taste for the dynamic–static duo,[58] Mao Dun's true passion falls on the dynamic type he terms 'women of the times' (*shidai nüxing* 時代女性).[59] A prime example is Sun Wuyang, a cadre at a government-affiliated Women's Association in an anonymous town.[60] Her first appearance in the novella assumes the form of a heady waft of 'sweet fragrance' (*tianxiang*), registered by a local gentleman's nose when he passes her on the street (118). The trope of 'sweet fragrance' is already indicative of her revolutionary femme fatale status. Nicknamed 'model communal wife' (*gongqi bangyang* 公妻榜樣, 170), she is 'promiscuous, sensuous, and skilled in love triangles' (150). To her admirer and lover Fang Luolan, she is 'charming, intelligent, optimistic, and glowing with energy' (255). Compared to Fang's wife, a woman of the static type, Sun Wuyang is 'the light of hope' (138). The sensuality of her body is portrayed in granular detail: 'her pert nipples moving up and down beneath the violet silk *qipao*' (159), 'her voluptuous bottom and slender waist' (168), the 'fair skin of her thighs' (170), and her 'warm fleshy aroma' (*routi de rexiang* 肉體的熱香, 216).

On his first visit to her apartment, Fang Luolan catches a 'peculiar scent' (*qite de xiang* 奇特的香) hanging in the air, though she claims that

[58] There are more examples, such as Mao Dun's short story 'Semang'.
[59] Chung, 'Questing the Goddess', 168. [60] Mao Dun, 'Dongyao'.

she has never worn perfume (171). It transpires that the odour comes from a jar of contraceptive pills known as Neolides-H.B. (174). A discreet statement of sexual liberty, the peculiar smell can be construed as equivalent to the traditional aphrodisiac aromas of musk and orchid, titillating the olfactory nerves of her sexual partners and eliciting their fantasies. In this regard Mao Dun and the Creationists are of the same olfactophiliac pedigree, both replacing cultural symbolism with natural, scientific-oriented sexual odour. Furthermore, this modern aphrodisiac aroma signals the breaking of the sex–reproduction bond, setting women free to pursue sexual pleasure. Encoded in this peculiar scent is in fact a provocative manifesto of women's emancipation announced by Sun and her fellow 'women of the times'. Mao Dun ingeniously engages the private language of smell to illustrate May Fourth discourses about sex and love.

Freely accepting her biological self, Sun shares Hui's view on affairs of the heart: 'Sexual impulses never restrict me. Not a man has ever won my love; they were only my playthings' (213). The scent of her breath tickles Fang Luolan's fancy (*xinjin yaoyao* 心旌搖搖, 212), but her heart is not willing to be conquered. Where do the men position themselves vis-à-vis the New Woman? From Junshi to Fang Luolan, and perhaps the author himself, male voices are equivocal. Revolutionary femmes fatales are no different to conventional femmes fatales in any culture. They are both an attraction and a menace, echoing the time-honoured trope of love and death. The theme has a more dramatic exemplar in 'Zhuiqiu 追求' (Pursuit), through the medium of smell perceived by Shi Xun, a sickly and suicidal young man.

Having lost all hope of life and suffering from depression, Shi Xun decides to commit suicide by taking an overdose of chloroform. The drug is stored in an exquisite perfume bottle, the lingering fragrance of which evokes painful memories of a woman who has broken his heart. His ensuing fanatical pursuit of carnal pleasure with prostitutes has drowned him even deeper in scepticism and pessimism. 'Farewell, dreams of life, riddles of life', he murmurs as he covers his mouth with a handkerchief soaked with the drug. Inhaling its 'chilly sweet fragrance', he sinks into unconsciousness until a strong odour of ammonia brings him back to life. He hears a soft voice from a woman's 'warm fragrant' (*wenxiang* 溫香) mouth, calling his name.[61] The woman is his former classmate, Zhang Qiuliu, yet another revolutionary femme fatale. She likewise exudes an 'exceedingly sweet fleshy aroma' (*qitian de rouxiang* 奇甜的肉香, 356) and holds the view that '[sensual] stimulation is sacred, moral, and legitimate!' (360) Zhang's 'vigorous life force' (398) rescues Shi Xun temporarily from the dark abyss of love and death, but fails to prevent the final demise of his sickly body. After drinking half a bottle of wine at a party, he suddenly collapses:

> He closed his eyes and took a deep breath, trying to vomit up something from his chest, but suddenly his nose caught a whiff of *indeterminate perfume*; when he reopened his eyes, he saw Zhang Qiuliu standing by his head, throwing an empty bottle into the sky. His eyebrows were gently caressed by the hem of her cylindrical-shaped dress, from which wafted the *peculiar perfume*. He saw two legs moving swiftly within the silk wall; his heartbeat quickened and he wished to hold her sensuous ankles in his arms. All of a sudden a sensation of dizziness engulfed him as if the earth under his body had cracked in two; he tried hard to turn over his body but to no avail, and blood suddenly spewed forth from his mouth.

> 他閉了眼，用力呼吸一下，想嘔出胸間的什麼東西，同時猛嗅得一股似香非香的氣味；他再睜開眼來，卻見章秋柳站在他頭旁，也把空酒瓶向空擲去。他的眉毛被章秋柳的衣緣輕輕地拂著，就從這圓筒形的衣殼中飄來了那股奇味。他看見兩條白腿在這綢質的圍墻裏很伶俐地動著，他心裏一動，伸臂想抱住這撩人的足踝。驟然一陣暈眩擊中了他，似乎地在他身下裂了縫；他努力想翻個身，但沒有成功，腥血已經從他嘴裏噴出來。(403, emphasis mine)

Shi Xun dies three days later, leaving Zhang Qiuliu infected with his syphilis. This story epitomizes Mao Dun's rhapsodic invocation of the vital forces of revolution and libidinal energy, but the messages sealed in scent seem to divulge his indeterminacy towards both revolution and woman. Aroma plays a part in Shi Xun's two (near-)death experiences. The perfume bottle used to store the anaesthetic drug is an intriguing

---

[61] Mao Dun, 'Zhuiqiu', 310–13. Subsequent page references are given parenthetically in the text.

prop. We are reminded of the cartoon 'Sealed Goods' (Figure 4.7), and hearsay goes that Paris perfumers would offer lovelorn customers a tomb-shaped flask to imprison the perfume of the vanished woman.[62] If the fatal 'chilly sweet fragrance' enclosed in the bottle signifies doomed bourgeois love, then Zhang Qiuliu's sweet fleshy aroma stands in for the revolutionary energy that breezes life into Shi Xun's body. And yet libido's 'indeterminate perfume' (*si xiang fei xiang* 似香非香) proves to be equally deadly, escorting him into the final stretch of life. Coincidentally, Lu Xun used the same semantic structure 'si ... fei ...' (might be ... or might not be ...) to encrypt the gist of his message. Smells are enigmatic strangers, thereby a conduit for the articulation of the inexpressible. Mao Dun's ambivalence symbolically marks the end of the May Fourth search for individuality in sensorial terms. With the advance of the Communist revolution and hegemonizing left-wing culture from the 1930s onwards, revolution was subjected to deodorization and re-odorization from other directions, shrinking the grey zone of ambivalence, a topic to be discussed in Chapter 6 and elsewhere.[63]

SEXUAL ODOUR IN CONTEXT

Zoologist D. Michael Stoddart claims, 'All the evidence of anatomy, chemistry and psychology suggests that human beings are indeed the most highly scented of the apes.' And the highly active scent-producing apparatus is principally 'geared to reproductive biology'.[64] Seen in this light, the copious sexual odours documented in May Fourth literature may be conceived as a naturalistic reflection of human biology. And yet, seen against the backdrop of both Chinese perfume tradition and Western olfactory modernity, the phenomenon of olfactophilia invites further scrutiny. In this concluding section, I inquire into the sociocultural context of May Fourth China and the broader implications of the olfactory–literary modality. Why did the modern Chinese self wish to be associated with or expressed by the animalistic sense of smell? The theoretical scheme of Western olfactory modernity cannot offer an

---

[62] Corbin, *The Foul and the Fragrant*, 286, footnote 19.
[63] Huang, 'Smellscapes of Nanjing Road', 83–92.   [64] Stoddart, *The Scented Ape*, 72, 75.

answer to this question. Instead, I posit that knowledge, ideology, and sensibility shifting at the particular juncture of Chinese history joined forces to bring about the olfactory turn.

Echoing the overarching pursuit of modernization and national strengthening in the late Qing and the early Republican era, a new body of knowledge about sex and the biological body was imported from the West and Japan, circulating via elite and professional discourses, popular print culture, education, and commercial enterprises.[65] Popular scientific essays on olfaction proliferated, and one of their favourite theorists was none other than Havelock Ellis, the mastermind of modern sexology. But, interestingly, Chinese intellectuals selectively introduced his theory. His claim about the perverted nature of olfactophilia seems not to have grasped the attention of Chinese translators. Instead, a 1918 essay on smell's sexual functioning was perhaps his first appearance in China.[66] His elaborate theory on the sexual aspect of olfaction, in his canonical *Studies in the Psychology of Sex* (volume 4), was also partially translated into Chinese in 1927.[67] Some of the texts surveyed above read almost like a literary illustration of his treatise.

According to Ellis, 'every person has ... a distinguishing odor', exuding from different parts of the body: the skin, hair and scalp, breath, armpit, feet, the perineum, and genitals.[68] Some odours tend to become exaggerated in resonance with sexual or other emotional states, evidenced by scientific and anecdotal texts that chronicle the goaty smell of women, the chloroform-like odour of men, an indescribable special scent during sexual excitement, and so on (63–5). Sexual odours of 'a healthy and sexually desirable person' tend to be agreeable, even irresistible, because 'many odors, including some bodily odors, are nervous

---

[65] Dikötter, *Sex, Culture and Modernity in China.*
[66] Gu, 'Xiujue yu xingyu zhi guanxi', *Dongfang zazhi* 15, no. 9 (1918), 99–104. It is Rachel Hsu's conjecture according to her extensive research. See Hsu, 'The "Ellis Effect"', 190 (her unpublished Chinese version makes this point more explicit).
[67] Ellis (Ai Lisi 靄理思), 'Xiujue yu xingmei de guanxi', trans. Peng Zhaoliang, *Xin Wenhua* 1, no. 5 (1927), 35–47. The original text is Ellis, *Studies in the Psychology of Sex*, vol. 4, 57–81.
[68] Ellis, *Studies in the Psychology of Sex*, vol. 4, 62, Peng's Chinese translation, 42. In the subsequent discussion, I only give page references to the original version, parenthetically.

stimulants' (66–7). Ellis's theory finds compelling examples in the Chinese literary imagination: the Japanese girl's breath in 'The Water of the Jordan River', the heady fragrance from Xianxian's hair in 'Creation', warm aromas of women's flesh/skin in multiple novellas by Mao Dun, the peculiar perfume drifting from the hem of Zhang Qiuliu's dress (implying her genitalia) in 'Pursuit', and the mixed scents of face powder and sweat from a woman in coitus in 'Moving to the South'.

Ellis's sexology and an extensive corpus of imported scientific knowledge undergirded the writing of smells into modern Chinese literature. But a stronger impetus was from ideology; that is, the May Fourth generation's rejection of what Haiyan Lee terms 'the Confucian structure of feeling' that champions 'virtuous sentiments'.[69] Instead, the May Fourth 'enlightenment structure of feeling' favours 'an expressivist or physicalist understanding of emotion and other universalizing norms of enlightenment humanism and naturalism'.[70] Within this scheme, the sexualization of individuals and the naturalization of sexual desire became imperative.[71] Or, as Lee puts it, romantic individuals were 'no longer enmeshed in a web of social ties and obligations', but were wrapped in 'glorious isolation in our libido'.[72] Indescribable libidinal impulses found vibrant utterance in odours. Contrary to the European repression of olfaction during the civilizing process, Chinese May Fourth iconoclasts discovered in smell the true essence of being human, a device to fight against the arguably doctrinaire Confucian culture.

Sensibility played a subtle role as well, and the pseudo-illness of sexual neurasthenia (*shenjing shuairuo* 神經衰弱) was a key player. Deemed *maladie d'époque*, sexual neurasthenia was often associated with the cultivated urban youth, whose sensitive nervous systems suffered from overwhelming stimulations from modern civilization.[73] As part of the imported knowledge, it aroused intense medical discussion and keen public interest in Republican China.[74] Yu Dafu's melancholic youths are typical sufferers from neurasthenia. According to Victorian sexology,

---

[69] Lee, *Revolution of the Heart*, 16.   [70] Ibid., 15–16.
[71] Dikötter, *Sex, Culture and Modernity in China*, 62–9.   [72] Lee, *Revolution of the Heart*, 137.
[73] Beard, *Sexual Neurasthenia (Nervous Exhaustion)*.
[74] Dikötter, *Sex, Culture and Modernity in China*, 162–4.

there is a close tie between neurasthenia and olfactophilia. As Havelock Ellis notes, 'a great many neurasthenic people, and particularly those who are sexually neurasthenic, are particularly susceptible to olfactory influences'.[75] He names several eminent writers as examples, including Baudelaire, Zola, Nietzsche, and Goethe. Most were avidly read in 1920s China, and their works acted as literary bibles for all our olfactophiliac authors, particularly during their student years in Japan.[76] Chinese literature of the period was thereby permeated by neurasthenic sensibilities and aesthetics.

Our revisit to the tumultuous 1920s through the nose attests to the interpenetration of the epistemic, affective, and sociopolitical spheres. What does this literary chapter in the Chinese olfactory revolution mean for the global history of olfactory modernity and the commodified body? Let us return to the physical sites of the olfactory revolution that Part Two of this book maps. The fleshy aromas investigated in this chapter complicate the universalizing discourse of deodorization, propelling us to take seriously the heterogeneity of the human sensorium that teems with strangers.[77] These smells particularly point to the chemical nature of olfaction and the animalistic core of humankind. What did it mean to these authors to see humans as animals? What *else* (texts and interpretations) will surface if we shift away from the anthropocentric frame of inquiry? These questions demand research in new directions which I shall leave to the future.

The perfuming thread of the olfactory revolution calls for a dialogue with the literary smellscape as well. The two terrains overlap on the focal point of the body. As we discussed in Chapter 4, capitalist commodity culture endeavoured to foster the cult of the hygienic and perfumed

---

[75] Ellis, *Studies in the Psychology of Sex*, vol. 4, 72.

[76] Hsia, *A History of Modern Chinese Fiction, 1917–1957*, 103; Liu, *Transcultural Lyricism*, 123–4, 169–78; Zhang, 'Wo de chuangzuo jingguo'.

[77] The Enlightenment bodily code is also challenged by *fin de siècle* European modernist literature (decadence and aestheticism in particular). The olfactory penetrated into 'the libidinal–aesthetic realm', emerging in literature as 'the instrument of exquisite individuality' and subverting the olfactory norms governed by medical and moral discourses. See Rindisbacher, *The Smell of Books*, Chapter 3. Chinese May Fourth literature's connection to European modernism in terms of olfactory expressions and their challenge to the deodorization discourse warrants further research.

body. In Baudrillard's frame of critique, capitalist society's liberation of the body is accompanied by *repressive solicitude* (caring in the form of repressing), with hygiene as a vital technique. As a consequence, the body is sanctified in its hygienic abstraction as 'a disincarnated signifier' of 'forgotten, censored desire'. Or, put differently,

> the preoccupation with hygiene founds a morality based not on pathos, but on play: it 'eludes' deep fantasies in favour of a superficial, cutaneous religion of the body. Taking care of, being 'loving' towards the body, that morality prevents any collusion between the body and desire.[78]

This frame illuminates the apparatus of beauty advertising (consider the 'Four Summer Delights' comic strip, Figure 4.8). The method of repressive solicitude conjures away the organic body and its desire, whilst propagating a superficial religion of the body that is cleansed and perfumed by beauty products. In contrast, the May Fourth olfactory texts seem to be the opposite, valorizing the (overall) organic smells of the human and her/his desire. For all the insights Baudrillard's critique offers, the binary of the organic and commodified body can be called into question. Desire and sexual awakening can well be embedded in a manufactured soap bar and its indeterminate scent, as Lu Xun's 'Soap' shows. So are the perfumes of modern cosmetics in Yu Dafu's and Guo Moruo's texts. Once inhaled, and processed by the neurons, the odour molecules, natural or artificial, fuse with the body and interlock with the memories, desires, and emotions of the individual. As much as the capitalist colonial enterprise of re-perfuming China deserves critical interrogation, we are warned against making simplified postulations by the essentially ambivalent odour perception. And yet, by virtue of the very same ambiguous nature, the olfactory is harnessed in the moral–political realm as an instrument of manipulation. A whiff of alterity wafts in, this time not in the private body of the May Fourth youth, but in the collective body in Mao-era politics.

[78] Baudrillard, *The Consumer Society*, 141–2.

6

The Politics of Smell

I was here with a hundred companions 携来百侣曾游

Vivid still the months and years, full of youthful pride 忆往昔峥嵘岁月稠

Schoolmates we were, altogether young 恰同学少年

Upright and honest, in the bloom of our lives 风华正茂

Impetuous students, full of enthusiasm 书生意气

Boldly we cast all restraints aside 挥斥方遒

Pointing to China, its mountains and rivers 指点江山

Setting the people afire with our words 激扬文字

And counted for muck all those ranking high 粪土当年万户侯

Do you still remember 曾记否

How, venturing midstream, our oars lashed the waters 到中流击水

And the waves stayed the flight of our speeding boats 浪遏飞舟

Mao Zedong, 'Changsha' (Stanza 2)[1]

S TANDING ALONE IN THE CHILL AUTUMN, the thirty-three-year-old Mao Zedong watches the Xiang river flow northward. On the shores of Orange Island, he sees 'the ten thousand hills all crimson, and the forests all stained with red'. Alone in the desolate vastness, he asks of the ageless earth, 'Who is the ruler of the universe?'[2]

---

[1] Mao, 'Qin Yuan Chun – Changsha', *Shikan* 1 (1957), 4–5. The English translation is by A.W.T. with modifications, at www.infopartisan.net/archive/maowerke/mao_006.htm (accessed 3 August 2022). Other English translations include 'At Changsha' (in Mao, *Reverberations*, 7–9); 'Ch'angsha, to the melody of Shen Yüan Ch'un' (in Ch'ên, Bullock, and Mao, *Mao and the Chinese Revolution, with Thirty-Seven Poems by Mao Tse-tung*, 320–1); 'Qin Yuan Chun – Changsha' (in Payne, 'Poems by Mao Tse-Tung', 82).

[2] Mao, 'Qin Yuan Chun – Changsha', in Payne, 'Poems by Mao Tse-Tung', 82.

This moment, enveloped in an aura of melancholy, is depicted by Mao Zedong in the first stanza of his famous poem 'Qin Yuan Chun – Changsha 沁园春 长沙' ('Changsha, to the melody of Qin Yuan Chun'). Mao wrote the poem in the autumn of 1925, thirteen years after considering a career in soap-making. It was an unheroic phase of his revolutionary roller coaster. Because of his humble cultural position, he was a 'negligible figure' in the small circle of the fledgling Chinese Communist Party dominated by elite intellectuals.[3] Discontented with his work in Shanghai and having fallen ill, he returned to his home town in Hunan Province in the winter of 1924. During his active participation in the local peasant movement in 1925, he developed a keen interest in the peasant as an alternative revolutionary agent, an idea hardly deemed pertinent or progressive by his orthodox peers. However, as we now know, that aspect would play a pivotal role in the unfolding history of both the party and the revolution.[4] This newly acquired vision inspired Mao and boosted his spirits, a trace of which can be found in the second stanza of the poem. The tinge of sorrow in the first stanza is replaced by a dash of audacity. He reminisces about his student years when he and his schoolmates, in the bloom of their youth, cast all restraints boldly aside. They gazed upon rivers and mountains, wrote vibrant words, and 'counted for muck all those ranking high (粪土当年万户侯)'.

The term *fentu* (dung, muck), used unconventionally here as a verb, stands out dissonantly in this otherwise ornate, sentimental verse. Robert Payne, one of the earliest translators of Mao's poetry, translated this sentence, 'They despised the ancient feudal lords.' But he admitted that 'the blow has been softened', while Mao's original term *fentu* conveys 'a fierce contempt'.[5] Given Mao's situation as a partial exile from the party centre, we can gather where the rebellious, anti-intellectual undercurrent came from. I consider Mao's use of the faecal word a critical rhetorical moment in the Chinese Communist revolution and the

---

[3] Apter and Saich, *Revolutionary Discourse in Mao's Republic*, 100.

[4] Ch'ên, Bullock, and Mao, *Mao and the Chinese Revolution*, 96–8; Peng, *Mao Zedong nianpu 1893–1949*, vol. 1, 140–7.

[5] Payne, 'The Poetry of Mao Tse-Tung', 22.

Chinese olfactory revolution alike: on the one hand, it summarizes the core of Mao's political ambition 'to reach out to the bottom of society to turn the world upside down';[6] on the other, this word heralds the mighty symbolic power that malodour would command in the moral–political regime of Maoist China. In short, excreta allegorizes the revolt of the pungent peasants against the perfumed landlords, bourgeoisie, intellectuals, and all of those in power at the time. This was exactly the kind of peasant revolution Mao began to envisage in 1925.

Mao's intuitive utilization of the term *fentu* distinguishes him as an astute politician rather than merely an enthusiastic poet.[7] This knack, or tactic, inadvertently prompted a wave of olfactory revolution teeming with malodour during his reign. This chapter analyses the blasphemous olfactory lexicon in Maoist propaganda, and ponders its jarring relationship with the teleology of olfactory modernity. Essentially, it is a whiff of alterity against the tenet of deodorizing and perfuming, an unapologetic gesture to contaminate. Furthermore, a different attitude towards smell as the stranger is forged. While Western modernity purges the stranger to ease the discomfort of ambivalence, Mao seems poised to embrace her, to dance with her. Smell's ambiguity enabled him to manoeuvre deftly in a capricious political climate, fashioning odour metaphors into a potent tool of persuasion and mobilization. In short, Mao's olfactory revolution was yet another round of retuning the neurons; the power of smell went far beyond the private realm of sensations and reached the sophisticated terrain of public life through the mediation of language.

Reflecting on the tumultuous trajectory of the twentieth century, towering thinkers such as Raymond Williams, Hannah Arendt, and George Orwell have all contemplated the intricate nexus between politics and language.[8] Rhetoric and discourse are of immense significance in the Chinese Communist revolution too. As David Apter and Tony Saich claim, 'perhaps no other major revolution relied more heavily on revolutionary discourse than the Chinese'.[9] China was a laboratory in which

[6] Apter and Saich, *Revolutionary Discourse in Mao's Republic*, 108.
[7] For a study of Mao's poetry, see Ng, 'The Poetry of Mao Tse-tung'.
[8] Williams, *Keywords*; Orwell, *Nineteen Eighty-Four*; Arendt, *Eichmann in Jerusalem*.
[9] Apter and Saich, *Revolutionary Discourse in Mao's Republic*, x.

Mao conducted 'the biggest experiment in linguistic engineering in world history, and one of the most rigorously controlled', as Ji Fengyuan asserts.[10] Many studies point to the power of words, symbols, metaphors, and rituals in forging a 'discourse community', a moral space knitted together by meaning and discipline, emerging in Yan'an and consolidated in post-1949 China.[11] Various techniques of revolutionary engineering evolved, resting on the common foundation of 'the emotional roots of political power'.[12] A dominant emotion was, as Lucian Pye notes, 'a preoccupation with hatred coupled with an enthusiasm for singling out enemies'.[13]

The olfactory interfaced with the linguistic and emotional formations of revolutionary discourses. While Mao's famed dictum goes that one should 'make revolution in the depths of your soul (灵魂深处闹革命)', we may argue that smell metaphors can even help embed revolution deep in the neurons. By studying the underexplored sensory dimension of Communist propaganda, this chapter untangles the encounters of language, emotion, and body through smell. Raymond Williams's keywords approach offers a useful methodology.[14] Sifting through Mao's writings, party documents, official newspapers and magazines, literature, and memoirs,[15] I identified four sets of smell-related keywords: 'the political sense of smell' (zhengzhi xiujue 政治嗅觉), a range of scatological

---

[10] Ji, *Linguistic Engineering*, 2–3.

[11] The 'discourse community' is a central concept in Apter and Saich's study. For the definitions of the concept, see Apter and Saich, *Revolutionary Discourse in Mao's Republic*, 6, 35. For other major studies of this subject, see Schoenhals, *Doing Things with Words in Chinese Politics*; Lu, *Rhetoric of the Chinese Cultural Revolution*; Wang, *Words and Their Stories*.

[12] Apter and Saich, *Revolutionary Discourse in Mao's Republic*, 5. These overlapping techniques include storytelling, myth making, coded narratives, sacred texts, moral/ethical persuasion, deductive reasoning, the use of metaphors, neologism, conspiracy theories, dehumanization, radicalization, alienation, negation, verbal aggression, linguistic dichotomies, self-criticism, confession, and so on. See the aforementioned studies by Ji, Lu, Apter and Saich.

[13] Pye, *The Spirit of Chinese Politics*, 67.

[14] Williams, *Keywords*; Ban Wang also applies this approach to his volume on the language of Chinese revolution. See Wang, *Words and Their Stories*.

[15] Two databases are immensely helpful for this study: The Contemporary Chinese Political Movements Database (Zhongguo dangdai zhengzhi yundongshi shujuku 中國當代政治運動史數據庫, hereafter CCPMD) and the *People's Daily* database (*Renmin ribao* 人民日報, hereafter *RMRB*).

utterances (fart/*pi* 屁, shit/*shi* 屎, and muck/*fen* 糞), 'to *stinken*' (*douchou* 斗臭, *pichou* 批臭), and 'fragrant breezes' versus 'fragrant blossoms' (*xiangfeng* 香风 versus *xianghua* 香花). Bridging the biological and the moral–political, this olfactory glossary maps the emotional states of paranoia, rudeness, ruthlessness, and love–hate, all necessary ingredients of the Communist revolution.

THE POLITICAL SENSE OF SMELL 政治嗅觉:
ON REVOLUTIONARY PARANOIA

Mao must have possessed a keen sense of smell. In a speech delivered during the Yan'an Rectification Campaign in 1942, he instructed his comrades to 'develop a good nose' (*tigao xiujue* 提高嗅觉) and to 'take a sniff at everything and distinguish the good from the bad'.[16] Metaphorical references to the olfactory faculty would become a leitmotif in the Maoist art of political rhetoric. A variation of the 1942 usage appeared in 1955, this time referencing the nose's ability to detect risk and threat. The threat was allegedly from the so-called Hu Feng Clique, and Mao alerted his people to the hazard.[17] Given the enemy's 'pretty good counter-revolutionary nose', Mao emphasized, 'We must study and heighten our class vigilance and make our political sense of smell keener.'[18] The judging and alerting nose aside, Mao enlisted the feeling nose as well to educate his cadres. At a party conference in 1955, he urged his officials to go to the masses; otherwise, 'you won't be able to smell the political climate, your nose will become insensitive and you will catch a cold politically. Once your nose is blocked up, you can't tell what the climate is at a given time'.[19]

Interestingly, Mao's smell metaphors correspond neatly with what scientists have said about olfaction's primal role in species-survival

[16] Mao, 'Zhengdun dang de zuofeng', *MXJ* 3, 827; *SWM* 3, 49.
[17] The Hu Feng incident marks the first massive political purge of intellectuals in the Mao era. See Denton, *The Problematic of Self in Modern Chinese Literature*, 2–4.
[18] Mao, '*Guanyu Hu Feng fangeming jituan de cailiao* de xuyan he anyu', *MXJ* 5, 167; *SWM* 5, 182.
[19] Mao, 'Nongye hezuohua de yichang bianlun he dangqian de jieji douzheng', *MXJ* 5, 210; *SWM* 5, 226 (modified).

abilities: to detect food (by judgement), predators (by alertness), and mates (by instinctive feelings).[20] Certainly, the nose's judging, alerting, and feeling functions imbricate in their realms of ruling, to the effect that they sometimes negate or contradict each other. Similarly, Mao's application of the 'political sense of smell' is not short of aporia. Sometimes he highlighted the sagacity of the nose. For example, during the fervent campaign to denounce Hu Feng, Mao spoke of Hu's correspondence with Shu Wu (as evidence of Hu's 'counter-revolutionary' deeds): 'Can we sniff out a tiny tinge of revolutionary smell (*geming qiwei* 革命气味) there? Don't the letters smell exactly the same as those Nationalist Party's counterrevolutionary journals ...?'[21] On another occasion, when informed by his confidant Kang Sheng of signs of scepticism within the party (about his Hundred Flowers policy), Mao responded, 'No wonder I've caught a whiff of this odour.'[22] But he did not always put trust in olfactory perception; sometimes he stressed the polysemy of odour. For example, he said to the provincial-level party secretaries at a conference in 1957, 'A fart from above is not necessarily fragrant. There's contradiction here too. Some are fragrant and some are foul (including those from Beijing). You must take a good sniff.'[23] Mao left his cadres themselves to work out how to interpret the meaning of their sniff. Ambiguity was tactically necessary and smell the stranger served the purpose superbly.

Thereby 'the political sense of smell' entered the standard lexicon of official language, or *Maospeak* (*Maoti* 毛体) – a term coined by Geremie Barmé and Li Tuo to denote the political and social lingua franca in Maoist China.[24] Consequently, the masses and officials, low and high, all needed to sharpen their political sense of smell. An increasingly vigilant revolutionary nervous system and the emotion of paranoia were growing symbiotically. If Victorian travellers sensitized their nerves by treating the strangers of repugnant stenches as enemies, socialist nerves, in contrast, needed to befriend them and to learn to dance with them. Odours in the

[20] See Axel, 'Scents and Sensibility', 234–6.   [21] Mao, 'Bianzhe an'.

[22] 'Mao Zedong he wenyijie renshi de tanhua' (8 March 1957), CCPMD.

[23] 'Mao Zedong zai sheng, shi, zizhiqu dangwei shuji huiyi shang de chahua huiji' (January 1957), CCPMD.

[24] Barmé, *Shades of Mao,* 224–7; Barmé, 'New China Newspeak'.

moral–political regime are even more indeterminate. Innumerable political campaigns and 'incidents' were veritable hands-on training sessions for the political noses of the socialist subjects.

In the early 1950s, the fledgling Communist regime felt a great sense of insecurity, with GMD spies, American imperialists, and internal enemies lurking in every corner. As a consequence, state media constantly called on the Chinese people to 'raise the political sense of smell', a phrase that recurred in propaganda texts surrounding a variety of 'counterrevolutionary incidents', ranging from a minor arson attack known as the 'Lingling incident' (*Lingling shijian* 零陵事件) in 1951,[25] to a major party factional struggle linked to the alleged 'Gao Gang and Rao Shushi Anti-Party Alliance' (*Gao Gang Rao Shushi fandang lianmeng* 高岗、饶漱石反党联盟) in 1955,[26] to the influential Hu Feng incident in 1955.[27]

The most crucial phase in the training process is the Anti-Rightist campaign of 1957, customarily understood as Mao's 'vengeance' towards the outspoken intellectuals during the preceding Hundred Flowers campaign (1956–July 1957), a campaign arguably designed to invite frank criticisms of the party. As Perry Link points out, the Anti-Rightist campaign was 'the crucial turning point of the Mao era: it was then that public language was subverted, ideals destroyed, and political cynicism set onto a course that has extended to the present day'.[28] There was widespread mental confusion caused by Mao's contradictory policies, and the actual consequence for many intellectuals was catastrophic. The nose proved to be a convenient tool to identify – that is, to sniff out – the rightists (*youpai* 右派) since they were ill-defined and amorphous. As early as April 1957, veteran party leader Li Weihan 李维汉 said that his nose had captured a 'rightist' odour emanating from certain

---

[25] 'Duiyu fangeming de kuanrong jiushi dui renmin de canren' (editorial), *RMRB*, 7 March 1951, 1.

[26] 'Dang de lishi shang de zhongda shengli' (editorial), *RMRB*, 10 April 1955, 1. For a study of the incident, see Teiwes, *Politics at Mao's Court*.

[27] Mao Dun, 'Tigao jingti, wajin yiqie qiancang de diren', *RMRB*, 15 June 1955, 3.

[28] See 'Comments from Scholars' in the preface to the subsection '中國反右運動數據庫' in CCPMD.

liberal opinions, a sign of his keen political sense of smell.[29] In June, a newspaper editorial notes, 'We took a sniff ... and found out that they were exactly the small coterie of ambitious rightists who had been attempting to topple the socialist system.'[30] At the same time, if something went wrong, the 'irrational' nose could be easily made a scapegoat. During the Hundred Flowers campaign, *Wenhuibao* 文汇报 (Wenhui Daily) published an essay in praise of the honest critical voices from students and staff of Peking University. Yet the essay soon fell victim to the political backlash that followed. The university's radical student group swiftly followed the new direction and claimed, 'At that time, we did feel that the essay reeked of rightist views, but we failed to see through their cunning scheme. However, the unfolding events have eventually sharpened our eyes.'[31]

These exercises of smelling bear witness to the influence of the Maoist philosophy of 'slippage', so to speak, and all the examples show a lack of evidence-based reasoning. The feeling nose is malleable, and therefore it was imperative to constantly train it to enable it to comprehend the fluctuating political currents. This imperative bore hard on the psyche, giving rise to the symptoms of paranoia that haunted Chinese society from the Anti-Rightist campaign to the Cultural Revolution. And yet, another thread of propaganda rhetoric sought to fix the slippage by rationalizing the nose and correlating the political sense of smell with one's political stance. In an influential speech delivered at the peak of the Anti-Rightist campaign, Zhou Yang 周扬 (the vice minister of the Propaganda Department) asserted, 'When one's political stance changes, his sense of smell and vision change accordingly.'[32] A more elaborate elucidation appeared in a lengthy article selected as study material during the campaign. The author, Yang Er 杨耳, claims that emotions and the political sense of smell are determined by one's

---

[29] 'Li Weihan zai quanguo tongzhan gongzuo huiyi shang de fayan' (4 April 1957), CCPMD.

[30] 'Jianjue fensui youpai de jingong', *Dazhong ribao*, 18 June 1957, CCPMD.

[31] Beijing daxue xuesheng hui, 'Beijing daxue xueshenghui kangyi *Wenhuibao* waiqu zhenxiang, daochu dianhuo', *Wenhuibao*, 7 July 1957.

[32] Zhou, 'Wenyi zhanxian shang de yichang da bianlun' (16 September 1957), *RMRB*, 28 February 1958.

political stance, which explains why workers and peasants are more vigilant about rightists' attacks than intellectuals. He concludes that in order to take a true socialist stance, one must transform non-proletarian emotions to proletarian ones, and transform the numb political sense of smell into a sensitive one.[33]

Both Zhou and Yang seem to have mastered the theory of neural plasticity, and the thrust of both texts was the party's pedagogical mission to create the socialist New Man (*xinren* 新人), a mission that depended upon the synchronization of the biological, the moral, and the ideological.[34] By the time of the Cultural Revolution, the feeling nose had grown more assertive; henceforth, this metaphor gained more momentum in both discourse and practice. For example, in an editorial of *Jiefangjun bao* 解放军报 (PLA Daily), the author states adamantly, 'The truth is in our hands. Our cadres and soldiers take a firm stand, hold a red flag, our sense of smell is keen, our eyes are sharp, and we can distinguish between enemies and comrades, the correct and the wrong.'[35] *Wenhui Daily* published a famous editorial to eulogize Mao's supreme order to the Red Guards ('To Rebel is Justified', *zaofan youli* 造反有理), in which 'revolutionary rebels' (*geming zaofan pai* 革命造反派) are described as those who possess 'the sharpest eyes, most acute noses, and most unflagging zeal to struggle'.[36] At the same time, 'a lack of the political sense of smell' became a clichéd label found in confessional writings and self-criticisms by intellectual 'rightists', including the eminent sociologist Fei Xiaotong 费孝通, physicist Qian Xuesen 钱学森, mathematician Su Buqing 苏步青, and artist Huang Yaomian 黄药眠, among others.[37]

[33] Yang, 'Tan lichang wenti' (1957), CCPMD.

[34] For studies of the Socialist New Man, see Cheng, *Creating the 'New Man'*; Yu, *Xingsu 'xinren'*.

[35] 'Qianwan buyao wangji jieji douzheng' (editorial), *Jiefangjun bao*, 4 May 1966.

[36] Wenhuibao bianjibu, 'Geming zaofan youli wansui', *Wenhuibao*, 6 January 1967. For the slogan 'To rebel is justified', see Li, *A Glossary of Political Terms of the People's Republic of China*, 559–61.

[37] Fei, 'Fei Xiaotong gei Zhongyang minzu xueyuan Su Keqin fu yuanzhang de yifeng jiancha xin' (August 1957), CCPMD; Xinhua she, 'Kexuejia men tongchi youpai', *RMRB*, 22 June 1957, 3; Ge, 'Xuesheng fenfen jihui, jiaoshi lianri baogao', *Jiefang ribao*, 1 July 1957; Huang, 'Wo de jiantao', *RMRB*, 19 July 1957, 10.

Alongside the noses/neurons, odorants were also implicated into the biological–political nexus of the communist olfactory revolution.

MUCK 粪, SHIT 屎, AND FART 屁: ON REVOLUTIONARY RUDENESS

Every major speech by Mao exemplifies 'a strategy of intimacy', as David Apter and Tony Saich note.[38] His predilection for barnyard humour, classical allusions, and earthy remarks boosts performativity, producing a strong emotional effect of persuasion. Excremental metaphors belong to this strategy. Given excreta's bond with foul language (often associated with the lower classes), its high-profile appearance in Maospeak is hardly surprising, acting as an embodied illustration of the mass-line concept developed by Mao and the CCP. The young Mao's poetic line 'And counted for muck all those ranking high' was a herald. Against the tide of the civilizing mission of olfactory modernity, the idiosyncratic figure of excrement defiantly cultivated the vogue of 'revolutionary rudeness'.[39] What follows is a study of the uncanny encounters of muck/*fen*, shit/*shi*, and fart/*pi* with a diverse set of people, ranging from the highest echelon of leadership, to its highest educated class, to the young Red Guards.

As early as August 1933 in Jiangxi, in a speech aimed at strengthening the party to resist Chiang Kaishek's onslaughts, Mao said, 'The ugly evil of bureaucracy, which no comrade likes, must be thrown into the cesspit (*fengang* 粪缸).'[40] In July 1945, the same metaphor was employed to accuse American ambassador Patrick Hurley's policy in favour of Chiang and the GMD: if this policy continued, Mao warned, the US government would get trapped in 'a deep stinking cesspool' (*you chou you shen de fenkeng* 又臭又深的粪坑).[41] Mao was also fond of 'dog shit' (*goushi* 狗屎) for disparaging opponents. He labelled Zhang Guotao 张国焘, his nemesis within the party, as a bullheaded man destined to become 'dog shit beneath contempt by all human beings' (*bu chiyu renlei de goushi dui* 不齿于人类的狗屎堆).[42] The Maoist art of impudence teems with 'fart' (*pi, fangpi*) as well. In response to

[38] Apter and Saich, *Revolutionary Discourse in Mao's Republic*, 87.
[39] This concept was studied in Perry and Li, 'Revolutionary Rudeness', 221–36.
[40] Mao, 'Bixu zhuyi jingji gongzuo', *MXJ* 1, 124; *SWM* 1, 134.
[41] Mao, 'Ping He'erli zhengce de weixian', *MXJ* 3, 1115; *SWM* 3, 336.
[42] Mao, 'Xin minzhu zhuyi de xianzheng', *MXJ* 2, 737. My translation.

criticisms from other political parties (*minzhu dangpai* 民主党派), Mao retorted, 'If they want to fart, let them. It's actually to our advantage because everyone can tell whether the smell is fragrant or foul.'[43] With hindsight, this caustic remark, made in January 1957 at the height of the Hundred Flowers campaign, perhaps foreshadowed the imminent storm. Although critical voices were compared to the hundred flowers, they were de facto a fart. The dialectic of the fragrant and the foul characterizes the Maoist olfactory revolution, a topic we shall return to later.

As the personality cult of Mao forged ahead, revolutionary rudeness came to be *à la mode*. Odours of waste matter wafted into the fabric of political texts – official speeches, media articles, wall posters, Red Guards' writings, and confessional materials. Senior officials spoke in the fashion of Maospeak or simply parroted Mao. Madame Mao (Jiang Qing 江青) was no longer restrained by bourgeois decorum. Responding to an alleged attack on her work regarding film production, she said, 'This is just a fart (*fangpi*). We've been working very hard.'[44] The PLA marshal He Long 贺龙 instructed his comrades, 'Dog shit can be used to fertilize soil, and human waste to feed the dog. But how about dogmas? They can neither fertilize the soil nor feed the dog. What's the use of them?'[45] Official media further fuelled the vogue for profanity. A *People's Daily* editorial quoted Vladimir Lenin's alleged saying about the so-called revisionists – they are like 'the chicken living around the dung in the backyard of the Proletarian Movement'.[46] Media language grew more vulgar during the Cultural Revolution, strewn with Mao's stinky aphorisms. While a *Beijing Daily* editorial called on its readers to struggle against 'capitalist roaders' until they become 'dog shit beneath contempt by all human beings', the same phrase figured in a *Red Flag* editorial to warn those against the Thought of Chairman Mao.[47]

[43] Mao, 'Zai sheng shi zizhiqu dangwei shuji huiyi shang de jianghua', *MXJ* 5, 355; *SWM* 5, 375.

[44] 'Jiang Qing tingqu Shanghai yuetuan yinyuehui shi de jianghua' (29 October 1973), CCPMD.

[45] 'He Long guanyu gaijin xuexi Mao zhuxi zhuzuo de zhishi' (August 1965), CCPMD.

[46] *Renmin ribao* bianjibu, 'Guanyu Sidalin wenti', *RMRB*, 13 September 1963, 1.

[47] *Beijing ribao* bianjibu, 'Hongweibing xiaojiang yao zuo geming da pipan de ji xianfeng', *Beijing ribao*, 21 July 1967; *Hongqi* zazhi bianjibu, 'Xiang renmin de zhuyao diren menglie kaihuo', *Hongqi* 12 (1 August 1967).

Now that the revered Chairman Mao, his wife, senior leaders, and official media were all speaking foul language, the masses followed suit. A 'big-character poster' (*dazibao* 大字报) reads, 'Chairman Mao teaches us . . . that even poisonous weeds can be utilized to fertilize soil. Why did Commander Liu consider erroneous thoughts simply a fart?'[48] Even the time-honoured art of couplets (*duilian* 对联) reeked of the sulphury odour. A Red Guard compiled a revolutionary couplet: 'My Dad is a revolutionary and so am I, that's the fact; Your Mum farts and so do you, that's foul (老子革命我革命事实如此， 你娘放屁你放屁臭气冲天).'[49] Invoking Mao's 'And counted for muck all those ranking high', a Red Guard group proclaimed in their anti-Confucian manifesto, 'We'd like to shit and piss on the shoulders of the "sage"!'[50] This sinister encounter between the sage (*shengren* 圣人, i.e. Confucius) and the scatological odour appears even more eerie if we consider the scented space of reverence to enshrine sages and ancestors in *Red Chamber*. Condensed in this striking expression is the spirit of the socialist olfactory revolution, a revolution 'to turn the world upside down' even in the private realm of smell.

The snowball effect of revolutionary rudeness reached intellectual circles, too. How did they adjust their sensibilities, already moulded by the dictums of bourgeois olfactory modernity? The renowned writer Shao Yanxiang 邵燕祥 expounded his reasoning in a confessional 'thought report' (*sixiang huibao* 思想汇报). He reflected on his attitudes towards getting dirty when working in a labour camp. Mao's Yan'an talks were quoted – the passage on the 'cleanliness' of the workers and peasants despite their soiled hands and feet smeared with cow dung. Subsequently he underscored the importance of this realization: 'my own bourgeois world views and reactionary thoughts are filthier and smellier than all filth and sewage, all cow dung, shit, and piss'. Only with this realization can an intellectual be ready for a fundamental transformation of thought, he concluded.[51]

[48] Li, 'Xiang Liu Silingyuan chui xie hefeng xiyu', CCPMD.

[49] Shoudu dazhuan yuanxiao hongweibing silingbu xuanchuanchu, *Geming duilian xuan*, CCPMD.

[50] Beijing shifan daxue Mao Zedong sixiang hongweibing jingangshan zhandoutuan, 'Huoshao Kongjia dian' (7 November 1966), CCPMD.

[51] Shao, *Rensheng baibi*, 169.

Shao's writing illustrates the slippery attribute of Mao's olfactory rhetoric, the dialectic of the fragrant and the foul. In Chapter 3, I illuminated the paradox of filth veneration (through the propaganda campaign valorizing the night-soil carrier Shi Chuanxiang) and socialist deodorization (as part of the Patriotic Hygiene movement). Here, excremental stench was deployed to revile and dehumanize opponents on the one hand; yet, on the other, it was sublimated as an embodied technology to rewire intellectual brains. Intellectuals were thus sent to labour camps named 'cowsheds' (*niupeng* 牛棚), and toilet cleaning became a metonymic punitive measure.[52] They were physical–symbolic means of humiliation and education simultaneously, enacted by the slippage of the private language of smell. When people from all walks of life spoke (were compelled to speak) a language reeking of fart, we know that it is more than a behavioural matter; it points to the biological foundation of Maoist ideology. It is hard to gauge the actual somatic impact of such linguistic bombardment on the recipients. If Jia Baoyu were living through this olfactory revolution, how would his olfactory nerves react? Yet the truth is that he perhaps would not have had a chance to voice his opinions before he had been *stinkened* (*douchou*), a unique technique of political purge characteristic of the era.

TO STINKEN 斗臭 / 批臭: ON REVOLUTIONARY RUTHLESSNESS

I coin the neologism 'stinken' to translate *douchou/pichou*, a terminology of Maospeak that denotes 'to denunciate someone and make them stink'. Thus, for example, the typical Mao-era slogan 'Douchou Liu Shaoqi 斗臭刘少奇!' can be translated as 'Stinken Liu Shaoqi!' The birth of *douchou* and *pichou* was concurrent with the notion of *pidou* 批斗 ('to struggle'), an act of publicly denouncing class enemies.[53] As is widely known, 'struggle sessions' (*pidou hui* 批斗会) were a hallmark political spectacle of high Maoism, and a swathe of rhetorical and practical

---

[52] Ji, *The Cowshed*; Yang, *Xizao*. Also see Larson, 'The Pleasures of Lying Low'.

[53] *Pidou* related slogans include *yidou erpi sangai* 一斗二批三改 (To struggle, criticize, and transform), *dousi pixiu* 斗私批修 (Combat selfishness and repudiate revisionism). See Li, *A Glossary of Political Terms of the People's Republic of China*, 520, 70.

techniques were designed to humiliate enemies mercilessly.[54] The ingenious invention of *pichou* and *douchou* embraced the spirit of revolutionary ruthlessness, whilst leveraging the biological–moral power of stench. In this section, I track the genealogy of the two interchangeable terms in cultural and political contexts.

Their invention was built on pre-existing linguistic usage of *chou/* stink. Mao's own writings include a few oft-quoted phrases/terms that contain *chou*. In his important essay 'Fandui dang bagu 反对党八股' (Oppose Stereotyped Party Writing), he draws an analogy between the so-called 'eight-legged essay' (characterized by empty verbiage) and foot bindings of a slattern which are 'long and smelly' (*you chou you chang* 又 臭又长), and requires his comrades to throw this writing style into the dustbin.[55] Mao also gave intellectuals a derogatory moniker, 'Stinking Number Nine' (*chou laojiu* 臭老九), indicating their status at the bottom of the nine categories of political–social undesirables (landlords, rich peasants, counterrevolutionaries, and so on).[56] In addition, several stink-related idioms (*chengyu* 成语) acquired renewed importance in Mao-era vocabulary. *Yichou wannian* 遗臭万年 is one such example. It derives from a line in the fifth-century book, *Shishuo xinyu* 世説新語 (A New Account of the Tales of the World): 'If one could not hand down a good/fragrant name to posterity, one should at least leave a foul reputation for a million years.'[57] Propaganda texts employed this idiom to disgrace political undesirables, claiming that people like Hu Shi and Liu Shaoqi were doomed to 'leave a foul reputation for a million years'.[58] Another idiom, *chouming zhaozhu* 臭名昭著 ('notorious, foul reputation') appeared 828 times in *People's Daily* between 1946 and 1976. *Chouwei xiangtou* 臭味相投 (or *chouqi xiangtou* 臭气相投) was often used to

---

[54] Lu, *Rhetoric of the Chinese Cultural Revolution*, 140–2.

[55] Mao, 'Fandui dang bagu', *MXJ* 3, 834; *SWM* 3, 56.

[56] Li, *A Glossary of Political Terms of the People's Republic of China*, 27–8.

[57] See the online idiom dictionary at https://dict.idioms.moe.edu.tw (accessed 13 September 2022).

[58] Wang et al., 'Pipan Hu Shi de fandong zhengzhi sixiang', *RMRB*, 17 December 1954, 3. A 1922 essay by Hu Shi was described as 'a manifesto of his high treason which should have left a foul reputation for a million years'. Also see 'Ba da pantu Liu Shaoqi pide yichou wannian', *RMRB*, 7 February 1969, 3.

discredit 'anti-revolutionary' factions, though it originally means kindred spirits attracted to each other's scents.

An immediate inspiration for the coinage of *pichou* and *douchou* was probably *gaochou* 搞臭, a colloquial phrase that denotes 'to ruin someone's reputation by making them stink'. Only sporadically seen in political texts in the early 1950s,[59] its frequency of use rocketed in *People's Daily* from 1957 to 1959 during the Anti-Rightist campaign, being used seventy times in contrast to two before 1957 and ten from 1960 to 1965.[60] The *gaochou* logic and methodology are spelled out in an editorial entitled 'Gaochou zichan jieji de geren zhuyi 搞臭资产阶级的个人主义' (Make Bourgeois Individualism Stink). Since bourgeois individualism stinks, the author explains, we must expose the filth and stink under the sun so that its repulsive odour will cause every passer-by to hold their nose. Only by this means can we awaken those who have been poisoned and paralysed by bourgeois individualism.[61] Mimicking Mao's strategy of intimacy, the author seeks to animate the reader's nose, granting it agency to level a moral–political charge against the bourgeoisie. To a degree, it heralded the arrival of a more aggressive language during the Cultural Revolution, such as *pichou* and *douchou*.

Neither *pichou* nor *douchou* was popular in Maospeak vocabulary prior to the Cultural Revolution. Yet an early reference to *pichou* by Mao divulged his desire to stinken intellectuals. In January 1957, Mao said informally at a conference that the best way to punish dissident intellectuals (such as Xiao Jun and Ding Ling) was neither to kill them, nor to jail them, nor to control them; instead it was best to find out their shortcomings and 'stinken them'.[62] In other words, the mind overtook

---

[59] For example, in the Five-Anti campaign (*Wufan yundong* 五反運動) in 1952, an internal document stated that the first step of the campaign was aimed at making the bourgeoisie stink and isolated. See 'Zhongyang zhuanfa huadong ju guanyu wufan de quanmian celue guandian he bushu jihua' (22 March 1952), CCPMD.

[60] The statistics are based on my search in the *People's Daily* database. An early example is 'Jianjue ba fan youpai douzheng jingxing daodi', *RMRB*, 13 September 1957, 3. Mao also used the term in a speech: 'Mao Zedong zai wuhan huiyi shang de jianghua' (6 April 1958), CCPMD.

[61] 'Gaochou zichan jieji de geren zhuyi', *RMRB*, 13 April 1958, 1.

[62] 'Mao Zedong zai sheng, shi, zizhiqu dangwei shuji huiyi shang de chahua huiji' (January 1957), CCPMD.

the body in the Maoist hierarchy of control. To stinken means to shame, to stigmatize, through a biological–moral code that is legible to everyone. We now circle back to the verb form of muck (*fentu*) in Mao's poem 'Changsha', a form of empowerment given to stench to instigate a revolution in the soul and the nervous system.

The beginning of the Cultural Revolution saw an explosion of *pichou* and *douchou* in the media: In *People's Daily* alone, *pichou* occurred 972 times from 1966 to 1969 (out of 1,350 in total between 1946 and 2012), and *douchou* 568 times (out of 586). *Douchou* first appeared in a game-changing article on 19 April 1966, which was arguably the trigger of Mao's official launch of the Cultural Revolution. In this essay to denounce Wu Han 吴晗, the author writes, 'We must struggle all anti-Party, anti-people, and anti-socialist monsters and demons (*niu gui she shen* 牛鬼蛇神) and stinken them.'[63] *Pichou* emerged two months later: 'Anyone who violates or objects to Mao Zedong Thought, regardless of his rank or status, must be uncovered, exposed under the sunlight, debunked, and stinkened.'[64] Navigating this reeking complex of texts, we find that the two terms are often assembled in rhythmic patterns, inlaid with other phrases.

Douchou is normally paired with *doudao* 斗倒 (to make someone fall) and *doukua* 斗垮 (to make someone collapse). For example, an open letter written by the students from Qinghua University is entitled 'Struggle against All Black Gangs until They Fall, Collapse, and Stink' ('Doudao doukua douchou yiqie heibang 斗倒斗垮斗臭一切黑帮').[65] *Pichou* is also coupled with its own regular set of words. In the campaign to denounce Liu Shaoqi, a *People's Daily* report asserts that Red Guards are determined to mobilize their fellow students and teachers to debunk Liu Shaoqi's counterrevolutionary theories thoroughly until they collapse and stink (*pishen, pitou, pidao, pichou* 批深、批透、批倒、批臭).[66] Mao's aphorisms sometimes adjoin them to amplify the rhetorical

[63] 'Doukua Wu Han de fandong de zichanjieji sixiang', *RMRB*, 19 April 1966, 5.
[64] 'Gaoju Mao Zedong sixiang weida hongqi, ba wuchan jieji wenhua dageming jinxing daodi', *RMRB*, 6 June 1966, 1.
[65] 'Doudao doukua douchou yiqie heibang', *RMRB*, 10 August 1966, 2.
[66] 'Gaoju Mao Zedong sixiang de geming pipan qizhi jiji touru zhandou', *RMRB*, 3 April 1967, 1.

effects. It is of vital importance, as is proclaimed, 'to struggle against the small group of capitalist roaders within our party deeply and thoroughly until they collapse and stink, turning them into dog shit beneath contempt by all human beings.'[67] Another author writes, 'We must struggle against the Number One capitalist roader until he collapses and stinks; let him "cultivate" himself in the dustbin of history!'[68]

What is lost in translation is the rhythm and punch of the *pi* or *dou* phrases. Maoist political texts are anything but insipid. They thrive on the use of classical rhythms and parallelism, and it is ironic that their political efficacy hinges upon old-culture roots.[69] They also build on an intuitive mastery of synaesthesia, pairing stink with black, the colour of counterrevolutionary evil.[70] Their invocation of the olfactory is linked to the sensorial–moral bond of *xing* 腥 (rank) and corruption in ancient Chinese thinking. However, the fragrant *xin* 馨, tied to virtue and sagacious governance, scarcely breezes into the propaganda texts, with a few exceptions.

FRAGRANT BREEZES 香风 AND FRAGRANT BLOSSOMS 香花: ON REVOLUTIONARY DIALECTIC

The iconography of Chairman Mao is replete with visual signs and haptic associations of the sun – redness, brightness, and warmth – yet he rarely emits fragrance.[71] Although virtuous rulers are endowed with sweet scents in ancient China, perfume is too intimately bound to the bourgeois lifestyle thanks to the capitalist advancement of the olfactory revolution that we explored in Chapter 4. Perhaps for this reason, the positive side of the smell spectrum is cautiously shunned in socialist propaganda, but 'fragrant breezes' (*xiangfeng*) and 'fragrant blossoms' (*xianghua*) are two exceptions: the former acts as a synecdoche of bourgeois decadence and the latter stands for politically commendable art and literary work.

---

[67] 'Geming da pipan de mofan', *RMRB*, 21 July 1967, 2.

[68] Ye, 'Ba woguo xiuzheng zhuyi zong houtai saodao lishi lajidui li qu', *RMRB*, 11 April 1967, 4.

[69] Link, *An Anatomy of Chinese*, 5, 33, 42, 105.

[70] Perry and Li, 'Revolutionary Rudeness', 228.

[71] Mittler, *A Continuous Revolution*, 272–3.

While fragrant breezes are considered poisonous (to the socialist subject), fragrant blossoms are positioned vis-à-vis 'poisonous weeds' (*ducao* 毒草), inviting admiration and praise. The opposing values attached to the supposedly kindred chemicals remind us, once again, of the ambivalence of smell, the stranger. This slippery trait enabled the propaganda apparatus to manipulate signification, and enables us to reflect on the contradiction of revolutionary discourse.

The political life of 'fragrant breezes' began in *Nihongdeng xia de shaobing* 霓虹灯下的哨兵 (Sentinels under the Neon Lights) (hereafter *Sentinels*), a stage play first performed in 1962 (with a film version released in 1964).[72] It was a product of a political campaign that promoted emulating the Good Eighth Company of Nanjing Road (Nanjing lu shang hao balian 南京路上好八連), an army unit that had participated in Shanghai's 'liberation' and had since guarded the city.[73] *Sentinels* tells a story of the soldiers stationed along the symbolic Nanjing Road, centring on 'their struggle against counterrevolutionary activities and other more subtly subversive elements'.[74] Several idioms arose from this play and entered the vocabulary of Maospeak: the 'big dying vat' (*da rangang* 大染缸), 'sugar-coated bullets' (*tangyi paodan* 糖衣炮弹), and 'fragrant breezes', all alluding to the insidious erosive effects of the residual capitalist culture. The politicized whiff of 'fragrant breezes' summarizes the preceding chapters of the olfactory revolution, now leaving the socialist state to redraw an affective map and to imbue it with new meanings.

Political messages are encoded in dialogues, stage design, and visual cues in both the play and the film. When commenting on a PLA soldier's surrender to materialist allures, the regiment commander, Lu Hua, says, 'The die-hard capitalists in Nanjing Road are indeed detestable, but more disturbing is the perfume that assails our nostrils.'[75] Put differently, the peril resides in the fact that '[t]he fragrant breeze has blown into his bone'.[76] Stage design interprets the olfactory trope visually and acoustically. The second act takes place in 'a peaceful atmosphere of Nanjing Road', saturated

[72] For a detailed analysis of the play and film, see Huang, 'Smellscapes of Nanjing Road', 83–92.
[73] Braester, 'A Big Dying Vat', 424–34.   [74] Ibid., 435.
[75] Shen, Mo, and Lü, 'Nihong deng xia de shaobing', *Juben* 2 (1963), 13.   [76] Ibid., 17.

Figure 6.1 A screenshot of *Sentinels.*

with 'revolutionary songs, jazz, glittering neon lights, and the fragrant breeze that caresses your face'. As the set designer explained, the indulging ambience throws into stark relief 'the complexity of class struggle' behind the scene: spectres of the imperialists are haunting the city, harnessing the poisonous 'fragrant breezes' to debilitate the Communists' revolutionary resolve.[77] The film version features a few signature scenes of the bourgeois Nanjing Road, evocative of the tantalizing 'fragrant breezes' (Figure 6.1).

Soon after, 'fragrant breezes' blew into the lexicon of Maospeak, featuring in such standard phrases as 'bourgeois "fragrant breeze"-cum-noxious gas' (*zichan jieji 'xiangfeng' duqi* 资产阶级'香风'毒气) or 'bourgeois "fragrant breeze"-cum-stinking air' (*zichan jieji 'xiangfeng' chouqi* 资产阶级'香风'臭气). Notably, the phrase was invariably placed in quotation marks, as if alarming the reader not to take the fragrant quality at face value. A reviewer of the play wrote, 'Our soldiers have toughened themselves up in the storm of bullets, but they will equally toughen themselves up in front of covert enemies and the bourgeois "fragrant

---

[77] Gui, 'Qiantan huaju *Nihongdeng xia de shaobing* wutai meishu sheji', *RMRB*, 17 March 1963, 5.

breeze"-cum-noxious gas.'[78] A slight variation figured in an army official's speech: the Good Eighth Company of Nanjing Road 'has equipped the minds of their cadres and soldiers with Mao Zedong Thought ... enabling them to withstand the test of the bourgeois "fragrant breeze"-cum-stinking air.'[79] Fragrant breeze was even invoked in a semi-scientific, semi-political study of wind: the breeze blown from bourgeois class enemies 'is at times rank and foul going up on high (*xingchou xuntian* 腥臭熏天), at times "fragrant and sweet" to tantalize your nose (*'xiangqi' pubi* '香气'扑鼻)'.[80] Mao's dialectic of the fragrant and the foul seems to have taken root deeply in the minds of these writers.

'Fragrant breezes' transcended the realm of political rhetoric and wafted into physical spaces alike. At the peak of the social havoc of the Cultural Revolution, a group of Red Guards in Shanghai went to the streets to smash the so-called 'Four Olds' (old thought, old culture, old customs, and old habits). In Nanjing Road, they proclaimed, 'Today we're instigating a revolution (*nao geming* 闹革命). We will thoroughly sweep away the bourgeois "fragrant breeze" and stinking air with our iron broom.' One of their methods was to rename those 'stinky brands' (*chou zhaopai* 臭招牌) which they considered to be the soul of the deodorized zone of colonial modernity, the index of bourgeois commodity culture. They suggested renaming the Yong'an 永安 (literally, eternal peace) department store 'Yonghong 永红' (eternal red), 'Yongdou 永斗' (eternal struggle), or 'Hongwei 红卫' (red guard).[81] Thereby revolutionary flavours would replace bourgeois tastes, implanting revolution in every cell of the socialist *flâneurs*.

While 'fragrant breezes' were treated with caution, 'fragrant blossoms' were outright on the positive pole of the Manichean value system. Mao introduced the concept at a party conference in January 1957 as he expounded on the policy of the Hundred Flowers campaign: 'Some comrades hold the opinion that only fragrant flowers should be allowed to blossom while poisonous weeds should not be allowed to grow. This

[78] Fengzi, 'Zai huaju wutai shang de xin shouhuo', *RMRB*, 10 March 1963, 5.
[79] 'Jiti de Lei Feng, Sihao liandui de dianxing', *RMRB*, 6 April 1963, 1.
[80] Sha, 'Zatan "feng"', *RMRB*, 1 June 1963, 5.
[81] 'Shanghai Tianjin geming xiaojiang he shangye zhigong xiang boxue jieji "Sijiu" fadong zonggong', *RMRB*, 25 August 1966, 2.

approach reflects an inadequate understanding of the policy of letting a hundred flowers blossom and a hundred schools of thought contend.' Only by allowing poisonous weeds to grow can one 'wage struggles' against them. Moreover, poisonous weeds can be useful because 'when ploughed under they can be turned into manure'. In short, 'fragrant flowers stand in contrast to poisonous weeds and develop in struggle with them'.[82] This argument is typical of Mao's dialectic thought. The flower/ weed metaphor appeared later in a more significant speech, 'On the Correct Handling of Contradictions among the People' (February 1957), a speech that presaged the imminent Anti-Rightist campaign. Mao gave six criteria to distinguish 'fragrant flowers' from 'poisonous weeds', but ultimately he underscored the vital importance of the party's leadership.[83] The speech sent a signal that Mao would not grant liberal soil for a hundred flowers to blossom any more; rather, he would wield authority on defining what is fragrant and what is foul or poisonous by his own standards under the name of the party's leadership.

Following Mao's speeches, 'fragrant blossoms' and 'poisonous weeds' came to be in vogue in the discourse of Maospeak, inciting the polarized emotions of love and hate essential to the upcoming political turmoil. Ouyang Yuqian 欧阳予倩 was among the first cultural officials to use the trope in writing. As he remarks, 'as long as we know how to cultivate fragrant flowers and how to deal with poisonous weeds, we should not pull up all the weeds, allowing only one flower to blossom'.[84] Ouyang's liberal thought betrays his weak 'political sense of smell', failing to grasp the gist of Mao's talk. Fortunately, it happened prior to the Anti-Rightist hurricane. In the rising tide of radical thinking and action, the liberal space of interpretation drastically shrank, and the dividing line between foul and fragrant had to be definitively drawn. In an influential article that was to trigger a domino effect leading up to the Cultural Revolution, the author Yao Wenyuan 姚文元 asserts his uncompromising position: 'Our view is *Hai Rui Dismissed from Office* is not a fragrant blossom, but a

---

[82] Mao, 'Zai sheng shi zizhiqu dangwei shuji huiyi shang de jianghua', *MXJ* 5, 338; *SWM* 5, 359.

[83] Mao, 'Guanyu zhengque chuli renmin neibu maodun de wenti', *MXJ* 5, 393; *SWM* 5, 412.

[84] Ouyang, 'Tingle Mao Zhuxi de baogao de jidian tihui', *RMRB*, 19 March 1957, 7.

poisonous weed.'[85] A *PLA Daily* editorial instructs that 'only by applying class analysis can one distinguish fragrant blossoms from poisonous weeds, and distinguish proletarian thought from bourgeois "fragrant breeze"-cum-stinking air and "sugar-coated bullets"'.[86] Once 'class analysis' had become the only benchmark, liberal voices were silenced. In the cultural flowerbed of the Cultural Revolution, what were the fragrant flowers? Not surprisingly, the model performance (*yangbanxi* 样板戏) *Baimao nü* 白毛女 (White-Haired Girl) was hailed as 'a fragrant flower cultivated by Mao Zedong Thought on Literature and Art'.[87] *Hongdeng ji* 红灯记 (The Legend of the Red Lantern) was praised as 'an adorable fragrant flower of proletarian art'.[88]

Why should fragrant breezes be considered foul and noxious, but fragrant blossoms sweet-smelling and adorable? What would the olfactory neurons say about the scents? These are not the questions people would ask at the time even if they were confused. Most of them were conscious that it was not a matter of truth; it was simply rhetoric. Yet if one would like to 'seek truth from facts', one's nose knows that this does not make sense. The coexistence of the two fragrance-oriented terms pokes fun at the aporia of Mao-era politics, bearing amusing testimony to Mao's philosophy of contradiction.[89] Capitalizing on the ambiguity of odour perception, this philosophy was but a tactic of manipulation. The olfactory revolution and the socialist revolution intertwined.

CODA

A poem in *Chuci* 楚辭 (*Songs of the South*), the ancient Chinese poetry anthology, features an olfactory allegory:

> The daphne and lily-magnolia die in the wild wood's tangle.
> Stinking weeds find a position: fragrant flowers may not come near.

[85] Yao, 'Ping xinbian lishiju *Hairui baguan*', *Wenhui bao*, 10 November 1965; *RMRB*, 30 November 1965.
[86] 'Bu wang jieji douzheng', *RMRB*, 3 August 1963, 2.
[87] Ding, 'Wenhua dageming zhong de yiduo xianghua', *RMRB*, 12 June 1966, 6.
[88] 'Yangguang yulu yu xinhua', *RMRB*, 4 July 1968, 3.
[89] The concept of contradiction is 'central to Mao's Marxism'. See Dirlik, *The Origins of Chinese Communism*, 85–92.

For the Dark and Light have changed places: the times are out of joint.
露申辛夷，死林薄兮。
腥臊並御，芳不得薄兮。
陰陽易位，時不當兮。 [90]

Chu nobleman Qu Yuan wrote these poems during his exile. As a victim of slander and royal folly, his conception of honour and purity set him 'at odds with a society fallen into evil ways', and poetry was a vehicle for 'expressing his personal sorrow and resentment'.[91] Therefore 'stinking weeds' (*xingsao*, rank and gamy) stand for the evil forces who take senior positions at court, and 'fragrant flowers' (*fang*) represent noble people who are banished. A poignant lament for the misfortunes of himself and his country, the undertone of this olfactory allegory is analogous to that of Mao's poem: 'And counted for muck all those ranking high.' Yet Mao sets himself apart from Qu Yuan by making the evil-smelling muck a weapon to defy those who rank high. Both Qu Yuan and Mao seem to have an acute awareness of the allegorical–affective power of smell, but Mao goes a step further by leveraging the power to his own advantage. By cultivating a keen political sense of smell, Mao orchestrated a culture of paranoia to distort rational judgement. By circulating scatological terms and stink-based neologisms, Mao encouraged rudeness and ruthlessness to legitimize revolutionary violence. Drawing on contradiction in olfactory perception, Mao developed tactics of confusion for the benefit of monopolizing political discourse. By these means, he and his cadres trained and re-trained the revolutionary olfactory systems of the Chinese people, making olfaction a potent component of the emotional roots of political power.

In relation to smell's innate discriminating capacity, moral–political sniffing is hardly uncommon in human history. Adverse odours are utilized to stigmatize social groups, to attack enemies, and to shape negative social judgement across cultures. As we know, hellish stink is ubiquitous in most religious cultures.[92] Odoriferous metaphors pervaded

---

[90] Qu Yuan, *Chuci*, 'Jiuzhang/Shejiang'; English version: Qu Yuan, *Ch'u Tz'u*, 63.
[91] David Hawkes's introduction in Qu Yuan, *Ch'u Tz'u*, 21.
[92] Classen, 'The Breath of God', 382–4.

the increasingly vituperative party politics of England of the long eighteenth century. While the Whigs were accused of having inherited
'Naaman's crime, more odious and stinking than his leprosy', the Whig
news organ retorted by suggesting that the critic's 'breath stinks so vilely
it will make the whole cause smell of it, and he will in time grow nauseous
to the whole world and especially to his Party'.[93] These words are strik-
ingly redolent of Maoist propaganda texts. Mao's favourite 'dog shit'
metaphor is not unusual either. Late nineteenth-century anti-Christian
propaganda in China besmirched Christian texts in this way: 'Their "dog
fart" monstrous books stink like dung (狗屁妖書如糞臭).'[94] Fast-
forwarding to our contemporary time, during his 2010 election campaign to be the Republican nominee for governor of New York, Tea
Party candidate Carl Paladino mailed out campaign flyers impregnated
with the smell of garbage. He obviously shared Mao's intuition, sending
out a political message coded in smell: 'Something really stinks in
Albany.' And this strategy seems to have worked as he won his primary
(although he was defeated by the Democratic candidate to become
governor).[95]

Scientific research sheds more light on the biological underpinnings
of smell's moral–political intervention. Combining behavioural manipulation with neuroimaging, a team of psychologists and neuroscientists
tested how 'evaluative smell conditioning' influences processes of drawing personality attributions, liking, and morality judgements. Their conclusion was that negative smell associations do not simply induce a
negative perception of the target person but rather bias the attribution
style. In other words, once we have associated a person with an unpleasant smell, we tend to perceive and judge this person based on this
preceding association regardless of different behaviours and situations.
Whole-brain analysis of stimulus indicates neural involvement in this
process.[96] What happened to the neurons of the masses who had been
told to stinken the landlord? What did their neural activities look like

[93] Quoted in Tullett, *Smell in Eighteenth-Century England*, 109 (emphasis removed). More analysis is provided in Chapter 5.
[94] Quoted in Clark, 'Rape, Baptism, and the "Pig" Religion', 61.
[95] Sapolsky, 'Metaphors Are Us'.
[96] Homan et al., 'Aversive Smell Associations Shape Social Judgment', 86–95.

when they saw an image of Liu Shaoqi, who had been likened to dog shit? If we were able to conduct an FMRI (functional magnetic resonance imaging) scan of their brains, we might find out that negative smell associations in propaganda did rewire certain neural connectivity. Neural plasticity of olfaction is a consistent underlying mechanism of the olfactory revolution. Despite the apparent alterity of Mao's olfactory revolution, it in fact shared with Western olfactory modernity the same impulse – a desire to superimpose ideology onto the body.

Let us end this chapter with Jean-Baptiste Genouille's story, with which Chapter 1 started. After a two-year journey collecting ingredients from a dozen maids he has murdered, his *great* perfume is ready. A mere drop of it makes captives of the people around him; it makes the world admire him, love him, desire him, idolize him. In a word, he makes himself a god. Within the scent of his perfume hides power, 'the invincible power to command the love of mankind'.[97] In his 'Anthropology from a Pragmatic Point of View', Kant underscores the inescapability of smells and condemns olfaction as 'opposed to freedom', but precisely for this reason Genouille – perhaps Mao as well – considers 'olfactory sensations the most effective medium for influencing and manipulating sensate creatures'.[98] Genouille's reasoning for his 'olfactory programme of tyranny' is as follows:

> For people could close their eyes to greatness, to horrors, to beauty, and their ears to melodies or deceiving words. But they could not escape scent. For scent was a brother to breath. Together with breath it entered human beings, who could not defend themselves against it, not if they wanted to live. And scent entered into their very core, went directly to their hearts, and decided for good and all between affection and contempt, disgust and lust, love and hate. He who ruled scent ruled the hearts of men.[99]

This manifesto points to the interpenetration of body and power, sensorium and politics, an uncanny echo of Mao's politics of smell. The Chinese olfactory revolution is connected to the shared sensorial experiences of humankind.

---

[97] Süskind, *Perfume*, 235–55, quote at 252.
[98] Gray, 'The Dialectic of "Enscentment"', 239.   [99] Süskind, *Perfume*, 155.

Epilogue

The Smell of Winter White Cabbage

Andrew Thomson, the co-creator of the cesspool rose garden which opens this book, was forced to leave China as a prisoner of war in 1942 by the Japanese. Yet his roses survived the violence and turmoil of those years. New China under Mao's rule tore down the city wall and the church buildings, and the stinking cesspool was replaced by a small, clear pool of water, surrounded by a park where the thriving Thomson roses were still perfuming the air.[1] Amid the ruins of the past, can the scents of the roses bear, in Proust's words, 'in the tiny and almost impalpable drop of their essence, the vast structure of recollection'?[2] If they can, then the most enduring of memories must be of their faithful companion: the reeking breath of the cesspool. Inspired by the peculiar mix of odours, this book has tracked a chaotic assemblage of olfactory vestiges of recent Chinese history. Let us conclude the book by returning to the questions posed at the outset: could the sweet scent of the Irish roses offset the effluvia from the indigenous cesspool? Or did the latter overpower the effect of the former? Answers vary, reflecting the strands of thinking this book has explored.

Scientists may challenge the legitimacy of the questions themselves. Odours are 'the vast universe of molecular structures', and an odour image is not 'the sum of its molecular parts'.[3] Since every inhalation takes in a blend of smells, the olfactory receptors do not unambiguously

[1] Thomson, *A Daring Confidence*, 174, 9.
[2] Proust, *In Search of Lost Time*, vol. 1, *Swann's Way*, 64.
[3] Axel, 'Scents and Sensibility', 236; Barwich, *Smellosophy*, 199.

determine the individual components. Odorants in a mix sometimes block each other and sometimes amplify each other (known as *inhibition* and *enhancement* effects). The nose thus measures odours not only in terms of what they are, but also in relation to other smells as part of an olfactory landscape.[4] Once mixtures of chemicals are translated into olfactory signals and enter the brain, more complexities arise when neurons interpret the signals. Entering the olfactory cortex, as Barwich pictures it, 'is like walking into a vastly distributed neural firework of combinatorial activity'.[5] Therefore the floral scents and the festering stenches in the cesspool rose garden were not two separate components that competed with each other, but a cloud of odorants, the perception of which depended on the variable conditions of the environments and people. There is no such thing as absolutely foul or fragrant.

This answer through the lens of molecular biology, to a degree, is in alignment with Zen Buddhism. The Vietnamese Zen master Thich Nhat Hanh (1926–2022) elucidates the concept of interbeing with the metaphor of rose and garbage. Whilst a beautiful rose smells sweet, a garbage can smells horrible. Yet as time goes by, the rose will become part of the garbage, and the garbage will be transformed into a rose. Thereby he writes, 'Defiled or immaculate. Dirty or pure. These are concepts we form in our mind . . . The rose and the garbage are equal. The garbage is just as precious as the rose. If we look deeply at the concepts of defilement and immaculateness, we return to the notion of interbeing.'[6] This philosophy on (im)purity is also condensed in Cao Xueqin's *Red Chamber* (see Chapter 1). Through the Buddhist nose, when sniffing the Thomson roses one can smell the cesspool (which supplied fertilizer), and when sniffing the cesspool one can smell the roses. In spite of their disparate methodologies, modern science and Buddhism both endorse the non-binary nature of olfactory perception. In other words, they echo Bauman's sociological understanding of smell as the stranger, a member of the family of *undecidables*. When odour molecules intermingle, contamination is inevitable, pointing to contaminated diversity as a

---

[4] Barwich, *Smellosophy*, 186–201.   [5] Ibid., 244.
[6] Thich Nhat Hanh, *Peace Is Every Step*, 96–7.

common condition of human existence in relation to nonhumans and environments.

Yet the modern olfactory revolution overall produced a different answer to the above questions, one that centres on the dichotomy of the foul and the fragrant. If one of the Victorian travellers (in Chapter 2) had visited the cesspool rose garden, under his/her pen the sewage would smell repugnant and the flowers would likely have gone unmentioned. Built on the 'China stinks' discourse, deodorizing China (through the eradication of cesspools and so on) became imperative to the 'developmental fairy tales' contrived by the Western colonizers, the Confucian gentry, and the Communists alike (Chapter 3). Conversely, a rose by any other name would smell as sweet, even in the form of a synthetic essence in manufactured perfumery articles (Chapter 4). The mighty sociopolitical forces of imperialism, nationalism, and capitalism superimposed power onto the sensorium. Whilst the master narrative of progress has strived to silence voices of the strangers, such strangers as smells are persistent intruders contaminating uniformity and order. Whiffs of alterity were unexpected characters that took the stage in the Chinese olfactory revolution. Libidinal odours superseded the cultured scents of musk and orchid and disregarded the modern Western norm of olfactory repression, declaring their agency in the May Fourth articulations of selfhood (Chapter 5). The rhapsodic outburst of stinking words in Maoist propaganda polluted the deodorized and perfumed zones of the olfactory revolution (Chapter 6). Although power, in its manifold forms, has capitalized on the malleability of olfactory nerves to exercise its influence, the faculty of smell has exposed the fallacy of theory and the contingency of history. Revisiting modern Chinese history through the nose, I contend that the Chinese olfactory revolution was neither a faithful mimicry of Western olfactory modernity nor a Marxist emancipation of the senses,[7] but a series of discursive formations of new sensual relations, a process that involved coercion, negotiation, ambivalence, and many other indeterminable factors.

This Chinese history of smell propels further reflection on several master narratives about olfactory modernity in existing scholarship.

---

[7] Marx, *Economic and Philosophic Manuscripts of 1844*, 124–31.

First, the claim that the lower senses are downgraded in the post-Enlightenment sense hierarchy needs to be reassessed. Seeing and hearing are instrumental in knowledge production and transmission, but the lower senses more actively engage with the affective domain, the role of which is equally important in modern history. As Chapters 2 and 3 demonstrate, emotions and visceral sensations through smelling were profoundly entangled with grand historical undertakings under the banner of modernity. The lower senses deserve more attention for comprehending the undercurrents of history that the intellect cannot always grasp. Second, the leitmotif of deodorization begs rethinking. Although its remarkable contribution is undeniable when operating alongside public-health initiatives, deodorization was only one thread of modern experience, one that was closely allied with developmental thinking. Critical reflections might focus on unravelling unevenly reallocated smellscapes under the veneer of progress, as illustrated in Chapter 3. Another direction can be taken in inquiring into 're-odorization' caused by, for example, pervasive synthetic aromas in modern life. Third, the cultural-construction thesis about sensory perception invites re-evaluation. Whilst this study has attested that culture does persistently strive to tune neurons, the chaotic and flexible neural wiring constantly resists the imposition of cultural tuning, producing experiences of incoherence, contradiction, and indeterminacy, as summed up by the metaphor of the stranger. This book calls for a more acute consciousness about operations of power underlying such tunings, a more humble awareness of human inadequacy, and a more tolerant attitude towards contaminated diversity, whether it concerns odours, ethnicities, genders, classes, or nations.

The book will conclude with four snapshots that recapture key moments of the long smell tour it has undertaken. I want to emphasize that the many characters we have encountered in this study were caught up in their own temporalities, unaware of their positions in the tour, and their individual experiences and thoughts should not be abstracted simply as a component of grand history. The snapshots will document some of the irreducible olfactory experiences that point to the private language of smell and its public articulations.

THE SMELL DETECTIVE

Alexander Jamieson, the Shanghai-based colonial officer we encountered in Chapter 3, can be justly deemed a 'smell detective', a phrase coined by the New York-based chemist and health officer Charles Frederick Chandeler in 1878. Chandeler urged the use of properly trained chemists as smell detectives in place of lay citizens, who were only able to identify the superficial sources of foul emanations, rather than their true origins.[8] Jamieson was doubtless qualified as a professional smell detective ahead of the coinage of the term. He recounted an investigation of Shanghai's newly built sewerage system in September 1869:

> Suspecting that the accumulations of filth [in the drainpipes] must pollute the air of the streets, I have, during the past few weeks, exposed strips of paper moistened with a saturated solution of acetate of lead, to the action of whatever gases might be found escaping from the gully holes in the Foochow and Kiangse Roads … In all cases, the paper was rapidly blackened, showing the generation and escape of at least one necessarily deleterious gas—Sulphuretted Hydrogen.[9]

He went on to suggest several remedial measures and employed the very word 'de-odorize': carbolic acid should be brought into general use in Shanghai 'for the purpose of disinfecting and de-odorizing private drains, house closets and such like'.[10] His undisguised anxieties about miasmic pollution, his earnest sense of duty, and his scrupulous scientific attitudes were shared by many smell detectives during the modern olfactory revolutions in different parts of the globe. Therefore his smell tour in the Shanghai autumn of 1869 deserves to be captured here as a snapshot of the long history of deodorization chronicled in this book.

COMING TO THE SENSES

Forty years after Jamieson's smell tour, at the time when the Shanghai gentry were clamouring for the demolition of the city wall and reeking

[8] Kiechle, *Smell Detectives*, 13.
[9] Jamieson, 'Memo. on the Sanitary Condition', *NCH*, 22 March 1870, 210.   [10] Ibid.

moat, the journalist and popular writer Lengxue 冷血 published a short story in a fiction magazine.[11] The 1909 story features an 'I' who is placed by a sorcerer into a magical mental state of 'awakening', as opposed to hypnotism. All of a sudden, 'I was amazed: my heart/mind was clear, my eyes, ears, mouth, nose, hands, and feet all became keen (*huoran* 豁然).' However, with his awakened senses, he sees the omnipresence of filth and squalor, hears the cries of people in despair, tastes the disgusting sourness of bad food, feels the irritating itch of insect bites, and smells the nauseating odours:

> I heaved a sigh, but I was soon provoked again by a putrid smell assailing my nostrils. I looked around and found soured leftovers at a corner of the street, inviting a bevy of flies around them. I held my nose and ran away. After a few steps, a dead rat came to my sight, with worms crawling out of its mouth, and a ghastly reek assaulted my head. I held my nose and ran away. After a few steps, a peculiar sound and a pungent stench made me sick to my stomach. I saw a man urinating in front of a wall, where those reddish, yellowish marks told its long history as a urinal. Yet, apart from me, passers-by on the street all seemed to be at ease as if their noses were non-existent.

> 予方叹息，似有秽气触予鼻，予又勃然起，四方审视，见巷内宿菜若干，蝇声哄哄然。予急掩鼻，疾走。走数步，又见一死鼠，弃路侧，蛆自其口出，毁败之气，直入脑。予又急掩鼻，疾走。走又不数步，其声凄然，臭气又阵阵来，胸间作恶数四不能忍。予急四视，见有一人，方对墙而溲，溲处已有宿渍，若红若白若黄。斑斓墙上，知系久溲者。然而除予之外，行道之人，均甚安然若无鼻。[12]

After these traumatic sensory experiences, he lets out a heavy sigh:

> I would have never expected that my possession of the acute senses could bring me such trouble, such pain! Reminiscing my past, I now realize what a jovial time it was; looking at others, I now envy what merry lives they have. It is all my sharp senses to blame, my awakening to blame …

[11] Lengxue, 'Cuixingshu', *Xiaoshuo shibao* 1 (October 1909), 1–4. I thank Guan Kean-fung 颜健富 for drawing my attention to this story. For studies of the short story, see Guan, *Cong 'shenti' dao 'shijie'*, 240–3.
[12] Lengxue, 'Cuixingshu', 3.

不意予有此灵敏之感觉，而予乃劳若是，予乃苦若是。予回忆他日，是
他日之予逸，而今日之予劳也。予外观他人，是他人之予乐，而予之予
苦也。此皆予之感觉灵敏为之也，此皆予之醒之故也。¹³

Surprisingly akin to Lu Xun's canonical 'Kuangren riji 狂人日記' ('A
Madman's Diary', 1918) with regard to the theme of awakening, this
long-forgotten story is a commentary on 'China asleep', a key metaphor
in the tide of late Qing political discourse.[14] The series of sensorial
metaphors of China asleep is ironically redolent of the Western travel
literature that teems with stenches and comments on the blunt Chinese
nerves. Undertaken by the awakened nerves of a Chinese man, this
sensory tour powerfully sums up the collective Chinese drive to deodorize China, as part of the grand scheme of development to invigorate the
Chinese nation. At the same time, we can also discern a sense of irony
and ambivalence in this parable of contamination. Coming to the senses,
what is awaiting? Lengxue seems equivocal about the consequences
of awakening.

THE FOUL AND THE FRAGRANT

A shift in olfactory perception happens to another fictional character in
a mini-story (*xiao xiaoshuo* 小小説) published in a tabloid newspaper in
1932. A year ago, as the story begins, he seemingly disliked her and
avoided her whenever possible. If they were cast in the same movie, after
shooting he often left immediately with a frown on his face. Many people
were puzzled. She was pretty and vivacious, and a league of men were
eager to get close to her. When they asked him, he said, 'Can't you smell
that? Her "fox stench" (*huchou* 狐臭) is appalling.' He must have possessed an exceptionally acute nose because not everyone had the same
aversion to her body odour. This year, mysteriously, he and she somehow
have become very close, or they might have become lovers. Has her 'fox
stench' disappeared? Can love and hate shift so quickly? Someone asks
him again. 'All I can smell is her fragrance', he replies humorously,

[13] Ibid., 4.
[14] For a study of its connection to 'A Madman's Diary', see Fan, 'Cuixingshu'; for the
'China asleep' metaphor, see Wagner, 'China "Asleep" and "Awakening"'.

because he does not know what to say. That might be true, because love and hate do shift.[15]

Entitled 'Fox Stench and Sweet Aroma', the mini-story captures the ambiguity and plasticity of odour perception supervised by the chaotic olfactory cortex. Or, given that the early 1930s was the pinnacle of capitalist perfume culture in Shanghai, is it possible that she has simply applied an imported deodorant and perfumed herself profusely to mask the stigmatized 'fox stench'?[16] Or, just like the olfactophiliac youths fascinated by libidinal odours in May Fourth literature, is it likely that he has subconsciously rewired his olfactory nerves under the influence of other chemicals and neural activities in his brain? This snapshot encapsulates the dialectic of the foul and the fragrant and the complexities of corporeal and sensorial practices.

THE SMELL OF WINTER WHITE CABBAGE

Between the foul and the fragrant, there lies a vast zone of unnameable scents. They are private, bearing intimate feelings, emotions, and memories of an individual person, regardless of how grandiose the external history is. 'When I think about Beijing, the first thing that recurs in my mind are smells, smells that change with the changing seasons.' Thus begins a chapter in Bei Dao's memoir.[17] The acclaimed dissident poet was born in 1949; when talking about the sweet smells that suffuse his childhood memories, he talks about a time when Mao and his comrades were relentlessly stinkening class enemies and bombarding the Chinese sensorium with excremental odours. Yet what lingers in Bei Dao's private memories are none of those smells. Instead, they are 'the smell of winter white cabbage', the odour of coal smoke and dust, 'a subtle pungent scent' of spring willow trees, the faint fragrance of pagoda tree blossoms

---

[15] Di, 'Huchou he xiangwei', *Kaimaila* 108 (1932), n.p.

[16] *Huchou* is a pseudoscientific term referring to the disease of exuding strong body odour. The dual reference to the barbarian's odour and the alluring fox spirit's odour demonstrates the ancestral fear of the other and misogynous anxiety about women. See Santangelo, 'The Culture of Smells', 46.

[17] Bei Dao, *City Gate, Open Up*, 13. I thank Julian Ward for drawing my attention to this book.

'that travel great distances like the notes of a xiao flute', and the mix of 'formalin, bleaching power, urine' of the summer swimming pool. Then autumn arrives:

> Autumn rains fall in bursts, leaves turn and whirl away, damp, then soaked, the bitter aroma of strong tea, over-steeped, gives way to the aroma of fermenting mold. Which, in mutual correspondence, is soon succeeded by the aroma of stored winter white cabbage.[18]

If we take a sniff through Marx's nose, we may venture to claim that the aroma of winter white cabbage conceals the 'entire richness of his being'.[19] This snapshot discloses smell's miraculous power in recollecting and reconstructing the past in the private realm.

****

From the heavenly fragrance of incense, the heady perfume of manufactured cosmetics, and the alluring aroma of a Modern Girl, to the sickly sweet fumes of opium, the ghastly reek of stagnant water, and the pungent stench of class enemies, this book has chronicled an eclectic array of odours and explored how microscopic molecular processes of smelling ran deeply beneath everyday social interactions, comprising an invisible layer of material life in modern Chinese history. Let us end this book with a passage with which Claude Lévi-Strauss ends his *Tristes tropiques*:

> And instead, during the brief intervals in which humanity can bear to interrupt its hive-like labours, let us grasp the essence of what our species has been and still is, beyond thought and beneath society: an essence that may be vouchsafed to us in a mineral more beautiful than any work of Man; *in the scent, more subtly evolved than our books, that lingers in the heart of a lily*; or in the wink of an eye, heavy with patience, serenity, and mutual forgiveness, that sometimes, through an involuntary understanding, one can exchange with a cat.[20]

---

[18] Ibid., 17.   [19] Marx, *Economic and Philosophic Manuscripts of 1844*, 127.

[20] Lévi-Strauss, *Tristes tropiques*, 398 (emphasis mine).

I concur with Lévi-Strauss and I believe that the essence of the history navigated in this book was vouchsafed in the many aromas captured by our characters: for Bei Dao, in the smell of winter white cabbage; for Andrew Thomson, in the peculiar odour of the cesspool rose garden; and hopefully for you, in a fleeting scent that drifts your way when you close the book.

Bibliography

'Ba da pantu Liu Shaoqi pide yichou wannian 把大叛徒刘少奇批得遗臭万年' (Struggle against Liu Shaoqi and Make Him to Leave a Foul Reputation for Ages). *RMRB*, 7 February 1969, 3.

'Bu wang jieji douzheng: *Jiefangjun bao* bayue yiri shelun zhaiyao 不忘阶级斗争《解放军报》八月一日社论摘要' (Never Forget Class Struggle: An Excerpt from *PLA Daily*'s Editorial on 1 August). *RMRB*, 3 August 1963, 2.

'Chaicheng zhulu zhi jingying 拆城築路之經營' (The Management of the City Wall Demolition and Road Construction Project). *SB*, 26 July 1912, 7.

'The City Wall: Progress of the Scheme'. *NCH*, 26 October 1912, 228.

'City-Wall Demolition Scheme'. *NCH*, 17 August 1912, 478.

'Dang de lishi shang de zhongda shengli 党的历史上的重大胜利' (A Major Victory in the History of the Party). *RMRB*, 10 April 1955, 1.

'Demolition of City Walls'. *NCH*, 27 January 1912, 232.

'Dongsheng jinwen 東省近聞' (Recent News from Manchuria). *SB*, 12 June 1915, 6.

'Doudao doukua douchou yiqie heibang 斗倒斗垮斗臭一切黑帮' (Struggle against All Black Gangs until they Fall, Collapse, and Stink). *RMRB*, 10 August 1966, 2.

'Doukua Wu Han de fandong de zichanjieji sixiang 斗垮吴晗的反动的资产阶级思想' (Struggle against Wu Han's Reactionary Bourgeois Thoughts). *RMRB*, 19 April 1966, 5.

'Duiyu fangeming de kuanrong jiushi dui renmin de canren 对于反革命的宽容就是对人民的残忍' (The Tolerance of Anti-revolutionaries is Cruelty for the People). *RMRB*, 7 March 1951, 1.

'Fenqing Hua Fa jiexian 分清華法界限' (The Boundary Demarcated between the Chinese City and the French Concession). *SB*, 9 December 1913, 10.

'Gaochou zichan jieji de geren zhuyi 搞臭资产阶级的个人主义' (Make Bourgeois Individualism Stink). *RMRB*, 13 April 1958, 1.

'Gaoju Mao Zedong sixiang de geming pipan qizhi jiji touru zhandou 高举毛泽东思想的革命批判旗帜积极投入战斗' (Raise the Revolutionary Flag of Mao Zedong Thought and Actively Engage in the Battle). *RMRB*, 3 April 1967, 1.

'Gaoju Mao Zedong sixiang weida hongqi, ba wuchan jieji wenhua dageming jinxing daodi 高举毛泽东思想伟大红旗 把无产阶级文化大革命进行到底' (Raise the Great Red Flag of Mao Zedong Thought, Carry Out the Great Proletarian Cultural Revolution to the End). *RMRB*, 6 June 1966, 1.

'Geming da pipan de mofan 革命大批判的模范' (A Model of the Great Revolutionary Struggle). *RMRB*, 21 July 1967, 2.

'Guangshenghang xinwu luocheng 廣生行新屋落成' (The New Building for Kwong Sang Hong Is Completed). *SB*, 18 April 1924, 19.

'Guangshenghang yuefenpai zhi tese 廣生行月份牌之特色' (Features of Kwong Sang Hong Calendar Posters). *Huazi ribao* 華字日報, 29 January 1910, n.p.

'Guohuo diaocha 國貨調查' (National Goods Survey). *SB*, 12 April 1915, 11.

'Guohuo huazhuangpin zhan shengkuang 國貨化妝品展盛况' (A Spectacular Scene of the National Cosmetic Goods Exhibition). *SB*, 15 September 1934, 15.

'Guohuo huazhuangpin zhanlan kaimu 國貨化妝品展覽開幕' (National Cosmetic Goods Exhibition Opens). *SB*, 12 September 1934, 12.

Guoyu 國語, https://ctext.org/guo-yu.

'He Long guanyu gaijin xuexi Mao zhuxi zhuzuo de zhishi 贺龙关于改进学习毛主席著作的指示' (He Long's Directive on How to Improve the Learning of Chairman Mao's Works). *Zhongguo renmin jiefangjun zong zhengzhibu gongzuo tongxun* 中国人民解放军总政治部《工作通讯》 (PLA Bulletin) 159 (August 1965). CCPMD.

Huangdi neijing 黃帝內經 (Inner Canon of the Yellow Emperor). https://ctext.org/huangdi-neijing.

'Hunan xinzhu malu shanhou zhangcheng 滬南新築馬路善後章程' (A By-law about the Use of the Newly Constructed Road in the Southern City of Shanghai). *SB*, 20 January 1898, 3.

'Jiang Qing tingqu Shanghai yuetuan yinyuehui shi de jianghua 江青听取上海乐团音乐会时的讲话' (Jiang Qing's Speech at the Concert of the Shanghai Orchestra). 29 October 1973. Ministry of Culture. CCPMD.

'Jianjue ba fan youpai douzheng jingxing daodi 坚决把反右派斗争进行到底' (Resolutely Carry Out the Anti-Rightist Struggle to the End). *RMRB*, 13 September 1957, 3.

'Jianjue fensui youpai de jingong 坚决粉碎右派的进攻' (Resolutely Smash Rightists' Attack). *Dazhong ribao* 大众日报, 18 June 1957. CCPMD.

'Jiating gongyeshe gufen youxian gongsi 家庭工業社股份有限公司' (Household Industries and Co.). SMA, Y9-1-99-46.

'Jieshao guohuo 介紹國貨' (Recommendation of National Goods). *SB*, 8 July 1916, 11.

'Jiti de Lei Feng, Sihao liandui de dianxing 集体的雷锋　四好连队的典型' (Collective Lei Feng, a Model 'Four Goods' Company). *RMRB*, 6 April 1963, 1.

Land Regulations and By-laws for the Foreign Settlement of Shanghai. Shanghai: North-China Herald Office, 1907.

'Li Weihan zai quanguo tongzhan gongzuo huiyi shang de fayan 李维汉在全国统战工作会议上的发言' (Li Weihan's Speech at the National United Front Conference). 4 April 1957. CCPMD.

Liji 禮記 (*Book of Rites*). https://ctext.org/liji.

'Linyin dadao mingming 林蔭大道命名' (The Naming of the Boulevard). *Jiefang ribao* 解放日報, 30 December 1956, 2.

'Lun chengnei ruihe huiqi niang sha shi 論城內濬河穢氣釀痧事' (On the River Dredging Project in the Native City That Caused Miasma and Disease). *SB*, 13 June 1873, 2.

'Lun Jingshi jiedao 論京師街道' (On Beijing's Streets). *SB*, 30 September 1879, 1.

'Malu fakuan 馬路罰欵' (Penalties on the Streets). *SB*, 1 February 1898, 3.

'Mao Zedong he wenyijie renshi de tanhua 毛泽东和文艺界人士的谈话' (Mao Zedong's Conversation with Writers and Artists). 8 March 1957. Internal material. CCPMD.

'Mao Zedong zai sheng, shi, zizhiqu dangwei shuji huiyi shang de chahua huiji 毛泽东在省、市、自治区党委书记会议上的插话汇集' (A Collection of Mao Zedong's Interruptions at the Meeting of Party Secretaries). January 1957. CCPMD.

'Mao Zedong zai Wuhan huiyi shang de jianghua 毛泽东在武汉会议上的讲话' (Mao Zedong's Speech at the Wuhan Conference). 6 April 1958. CCPMD.

'Minguo lu xingshi dianche zhi xiansheng 民國路行駛電車之先聲' (The Herald of Running a Tram on Republic Road). *SB*, 28 June 1914, 10.

'The Municipal Report, 1870–71'. *NCH*, 5 May 1871, 317.

'Municipal Report for the Half Year Ending 30th September, 1863'. Shanghai Municipal Council, 1863.

'Municipal Report for the Year 1862'. *NCH*, 11 April 1863, 58–9.

'Municipal Report for the Year Ending 31st March 1864'. Shanghai Municipal Council, 1864.

'Nanjing lu Guangshenghang qianyi xishou kaizhang 南京路廣生行遷移西首開張' (Kwong Sang Hong Relocated Further West along Nanjing Road and Reopened). *SB*, 26 February 1922, 16.

'Objectionable Creeks'. *NCH*, 17 May 1913, 486–7.

'Pudong qingjie yundong 浦東清潔運動' (The Sanitary Campaign in Pudong). *SB*, 29 April 1935, 9.

'Qianwan buyao wangji jieji douzheng 千万不要忘记阶级斗争' (Never Forget Class Struggle). *Jiefangjun bao*, 4 May 1966.

'Report upon Drainage and Water Supply'. *NCH* (Supplement), 5 April 1862, n.p.

'Shanghai chengnei difang yijia zhengdun shuo 上海城内地方宜加整頓說' (On the Necessity of Improving the Native City of Shanghai). *SB*, 18 December 1881, 1.

'Shanghai Land Regulations (29 Nov. 1845)'. *NCH*, 17 January 1852, 99.

'Shanghai shangye chuxu yinhang youguan huazhuangpin ye diaocha ziliao 上海商業儲蓄銀行有關化妝品業調查資料' (Surveys on the Cosmetics Industry by the Shanghai Commercial Savings Bank). 1933–1952. SMA, Q275-1-1944.

'Shanghai shi Aiguo weisheng yundong chunji tujiyue gongzuo zongjie 上海市爱国卫生运动春季突击月工作总结' (A Report on Shanghai's Patriotic Hygiene Movement Month). February 1953. SMA, B242-1-535.

'Shanghai shi Aiguo weisheng yundong sannian lai gongzuo baogao 上海市爱国卫生运动三年来工作报告, 1953–1955' (A Report on Work of the Shanghai Patriotic Hygiene Movement in the Past Three Years, 1953–1955). SMA, B242-1-805.

'Shanghai shi gong'anju xunling 上海市公安局訓令' (Decrees of the Shanghai Municipal Public Security Bureau). *Jingcha yuekan* 警察月刊 3, no. 2 (20 February 1935): 46.

'Shanghai shi Zhaojiabang maiguan zhulu gongcheng zhengshi kaigong 上海市肇嘉浜埋管筑路工程正式开工' (The Zhaojia Creek Drainage and Road Construction Project Officially Started). *Jiefang ribao*, 10 October 1954, 1.

'Shanghai tebie shi huwai qingjie guize 上海特別市戶外清潔規則' (Shanghai Special City Outdoor Cleaning Rules). April 1941. SMA, R50-1-42.

'Shanghai Tianjin geming xiaojiang he shangye zhigong xiang boxue jieji "Sijiu" fadong zonggong 上海天津革命小将和商业职工向剥削阶级"四旧"发动总攻' (Revolutionary Youths and Commercial Employees in Shanghai and Tianjin Launched an Attack against the 'Four Olds' of the Exploiter Classes). *RMRB*, 25 August 1966, 2.

Shangshu 尚書 (*Book of Documents*). https://ctext.org/shang-shu.

'Shenzhou da lüshe kaishi yingye 神州大旅社開始營業' (The Shenzhou Hotel Opened). *SB*, 19 October 1928, 15.

'Shimin tichang guohuo hui zhaoji huiyuan dahui 市民提倡國貨會召集會員大會' (The Citizens' Association for Promoting National Goods Convened a Meeting). *SB*, 13 July 1929, 16.

'Shisan qu tianse shuibang 十三區填塞水浜' (Ditches Filled in the Thirteenth District). *SB*, 29 August 1946, 6.

'Wujin tuiguang guohuo tuan jianzhang 武進推廣國貨團簡章' (Guidelines of the National Goods Association in Wujin). *SB*, 7 November 1915, 17.

'Xiangya gongsi 香亞公司' (Xiangya & Co.). SMA, Q90-1-940.

'Xiangya gongsi yingye jinxing ji 香亞公司營業進行紀' (The Progress of Xiangya & Co.). *SB*, 17 December 1919, 11.

'Yangguang yulu yu xinhua 阳光雨露育新花' (Sunshine, Rain, and Dew Grow New Flowers). *RMRB*, 4 July 1968, 3.

Yi Jing 易經 (*Book of Changes*), https://ctext.org/book-of-changes.

'Yichang yanghang yanke ji 怡昌洋行宴客紀' (Yichang & Co. Hosted a Banquet). *SB*, 29 May 1925, benbu zengkan 18.

'Yizun fengxing chajin fenchuan fentong bujia jingai gaoshi 邑尊奉行查禁糞船糞桶不加緊盖告示' (The Magistrate's Notice on Banning Manure Boats and Buckets without Tight Covers). *SB*, 5 April 1873, 3.

'Yue benbao ji malu kaigong xi er shu ci 閱本報紀馬路開工喜而書此' (Writing upon Learning from *Shenbao* the Great News about Road Construction). *SB*, 14 July 1896, 1.

'Zai ji chaicheng zhulu wenti 再紀拆城築路問題' (Further on the Issue of City Wall Demolition and Road Construction). *SB*, 9 July 1912, 7.

'Zhaojiabang Tushanwan duan hebang tianzhu malu 肇嘉浜土山灣段河浜填築馬路' (Road Construction at the Tushanwan Section of Zhaojia Creek). *Huxi* 滬西 7 (30 March 1947): 10.

'Zhongyang zhuanfa huadong ju guanyu wufan de quanmian celue guandian he bushu jihua 中央转发华东局关于五反的全面策略观点和部署计划' (The Central Committee Forwards the East China Bureau's Comprehensive Strategies and Deployment Plans for the Five-Antis Campaign). 22 March 1952. Anonymous archive in Sichuan. CCPMD.

'Zhongyang zhuangshe fenfang biyi xia 中央裝設芬芳避疫匣' (The Palace Theatre Installed Anti-miasma Perfume Boxes). *SB*, 18 July 1927, 18.

'Zujie jiedao qingjie shuo 租界街道清潔說' (On the Cleanliness of the Streets in the Foreign Settlements). *SB*, 20 July 1872, 1.

Abel, Clarke. *Narrative of a Journey in the Interior of China.* London: Longman, Hurst, Rees, Orme, and Brown, 1819.

Ackerman, Diane. *A Natural History of the Senses.* New York: Random House, 1990.

Almagor, Uri. 'Odors and Private Language: Observations on the Phenomenology of Scent'. *Human Studies* 13, no. 3 (1990): 253–74.

Anderson, Warwick. 'Excremental Colonialism: Public Health and the Poetics of Pollution'. *Critical Inquiry* 21, no. 3 (1995): 640–69.

Apter, David, and Tony Saich. *Revolutionary Discourse in Mao's Republic.* Cambridge, MA: Harvard University Press, 1994.

Arendt, Hannah. *Eichmann in Jerusalem: A Report on the Banality of Evil.* Harmondsworth: Penguin, 1994.

Armstrong, Alexander. *In a Mule Litter to the Tomb of Confucius.* London: James Nisbet, 1896.

Arnold, Julean et al., eds. *China: A Commercial and Industrial Handbook.* Washington, DC: Government Printing Office, 1926.

Askinson, George William. *Perfumes and Cosmetics: Their Preparation and Manufacture.* New York: The Norman W. Henley, 1922.

Axel, Richard. 'Scents and Sensibility: A Molecular Logic of Olfactory Perception'. Nobel Lecture (8 December 2004), 234–56. www.nobelprize .org/uploads/2018/06/axel-lecture.pdf. Accessed 15 September 2020.

Ball, James Dyer. *Things Chinese: Or, Notes Connected with China.* New York: C. Scribner's Sons, 1906.

Ban Gu 班固. *Baihu tongde lun* 白虎通德論 (Discussions from the White Tiger Hall). https://ctext.org/bai-hu-tong.

Barlow, Tani E. 'Buying In: Advertising and the Sexy Modern Girl Icon in Shanghai in the 1920s and 1930s'. In *The Modern Girl around the World: Consumption, Modernity, and Globalization,* edited by Alys Eve Weinbaum and Modern Girl Around the World Research Group, 288–316. Durham, NC: Duke University Press, 2008.

Barmé, Geremie. 'New China Newspeak 新華文體'. *China Heritage Quarterly.* http://chinaheritage.net/archive/academician-archive/geremie-barme/ grb-essays/china-story/new-china-newspeak-%E6%96%B0%E5%8D%8E% E6%96%87%E4%BD%93. Accessed 15 September 2020.

Shades of Mao: The Posthumous Cult of the Great Leader. Armonk: M. E. Sharpe, 1996.

Barnes, David S. *The Great Stink of Paris and the Nineteenth-Century Struggle against Filth and Germs.* Baltimore: Johns Hopkins University Press, 2006.

Barthes, Roland. 'Toward a Psychosociology of Contemporary Food Consumption'. In *European Diet from Pre-industrial to Modern Times,* edited by Elborg Forster and Robert Forster, 47–60. New York: Harper and Row, 1975.

Barwich, Ann-Sophie. *Smellosophy: What the Nose Tells the Mind.* Cambridge, MA: Harvard University Press, 2020.

Baudrillard, Jean. *The Consumer Society: Myths and Structures.* London: Sage, 1998.

Bauman, Zygmunt. *Modernity and Ambivalence.* Cambridge: Polity Press, 1991.

Modernity and the Holocaust. Ithaca, NY: Cornell University Press, 1989.

'The Sweet Scent of Decomposition'. In *Forget Baudrillard?,* edited by Chris Rojek and Bryan S. Turner, 22–46. London: Routledge, 1993.

Beard, George M. *Sexual Neurasthenia (Nervous Exhaustion): Its Hygiene, Causes, Symptoms, and Treatment, with a Chapter on Diet for the Nerves.* New York: E. B. Treat, 1884.

Bei Dao. *City Gate, Open Up: A Memoir.* Translated by Jeffrey Yang. Manchester: Carcanet Press, 2017.

Beijing daxue xuesheng hui 北京大学学生会 (Peking University Student Union). 'Beijing daxue xueshenghui kangyi *Wenhuibao* waiqu zhenxiang, daochu dianhuo 北京大学学生会抗议《文汇报》歪曲真相、到处点火' (Peking University Student Union Protested against *Wenhui Daily* for Its Distorting the Truth). *Wenhuibao,* 7 July 1957, n.p.

Beijing ribao bianjibu 《北京日报》编辑部 (*Beijing Daily* Editorial Board). 'Hongweibing xiaojiang yao zuo geming da pipan de ji xianfeng 红卫兵小将要做革命大批判的急先锋' (Young Red Guards Must Be the Vanguard of the Great Revolutionary Struggle). *Beijing ribao,* 21 July 1967, n.p.

Beijing shifan daxue Mao Zedong sixiang hongweibing jingangshan zhandou-tuan 北京师范大学毛泽东思想红卫兵井冈山战斗团 (Beijing Normal University Mao Zedong Thought Mount Jingang Red Guard Regiment). 'Huoshao Kongjia dian: tao Kong xuanyan 火烧孔家店:讨孔宣言' (Burn the Confucius Family Shop: A Declaration of Denouncing Confucius). *Tao Kong zhanbao* 讨孔战报, 10 November 1966. CCPMD.

Belsky, Richard D. 'Bones of Contentions: Siming Gongsuo Riots of 1874 and 1898'. *Papers on Chinese History* 1, no. 1 (1992): 56–73.

Benshu bianxie zu 本书编写组. *Zhaojiabang de bianqian* 肇家浜的变迁 (The Transformation of Zhaojia Creek). Shanghai: Shanghai renmin chubanshe, 1976.

Bergère, Marie-Claire. *Shanghai: China's Gateway to Modernity.* Translated by Janet Lloyd. Stanford, CA: Stanford University Press, 2009.

Birch, John Grant. *Travels in North and Central China.* London: Hurst and Blackett, 1902.

Bird-Bishop, Isabella L. *The Yangtze Valley and Beyond,* vol. 2. London: John Murray, 1900.

Bodde, Derk. *Peking Diary: A Year of Revolution.* New York: Schuman, 1950.

Bonnard, Abel. *In China, 1920–1921.* Translated by Veronica Lucas. London: Routledge, 1926.

Boulnois, H. Percy. *The Municipal and Sanitary Engineer's Handbook.* 2nd ed. London: E. & F. N. Spon, 1892.

Bradley, Mark, ed. *Smell and the Ancient Senses.* London: Routledge, 2015.

Braester, Yomi. '"A Big Dying Vat": The Vilifying of Shanghai during the Good Eighth Company Campaign'. *Modern China* 31, no. 4 (2005): 411–47.

Painting the City Red: Chinese Cinema and the Urban Contract. Durham, NC: Duke University Press, 2013.

Witness against History: Literature, Film, and Public Discourse in Twentieth-Century China. Stanford, CA: Stanford University Press, 2003.

Briot, Eugénie. 'From Industry to Luxury: French Perfume in the Nineteenth Century'. *Business History Review* 85, no. 2 (2011): 273–94.

Brown, Arthur Judson. *New Forces in Old China: An Unwelcome but Inevitable Awakening*. New York: F. H. Revell Co., 1904.

Brown, Carolyn T. 'Woman as Trope: Gender and Power in Lu Xun's "Soap"'. *Modern Chinese literature* 4, nos. 1–2 (1988): 55–70.

Buck, Linda B. 'Unraveling the Sense of Smell'. Nobel Lecture (8 December 2004), 267–83. www.nobelprize.org/uploads/2018/06/buck-lecture.pdf. Accessed 15 September 2020.

Bushdid, C., M. O. Magnasco, L. B. Vosshall, and A. Keller. 'Humans Can Discriminate More than 1 Trillion Olfactory Stimuli'. *Science* 343, no. 6177 (2014): 1370–72.

Cai Yuanpei 蔡元培. 'Zai Shaoxing gejie dahui yanshuo ci 在紹興各界大會演說詞' (Speech at a Public Meeting in Shaoxing). In *Cai Yuanpei Quanji* 蔡元培全集 (Complete Works of Cai Yuanpei), edited by Gao Pingshu 高平叔, 478–82. Beijing: Zhonghua shuju, 1984.

Cain, William. *Sanitary Engineering*. Raleigh, NC: P. M. Hale & Edward Broughton, 1880.

Cameron, Nigel. *Barbarians and Mandarins: Thirteen Centuries of Western Travelers in China*. New York: Walker/Weatherhill, 1970.

Cao Xueqin 曹雪芹 and Gao E 高鶚. *Hongloumeng* 紅樓夢 (Dream of the Red Chamber). Beijing: Renmin wenxue chubanshe, 2000.

　The Story of the Stone. Translated by David Hawkes. 5 vols. London: Penguin Books, 1973.

Cao Xueqin 曹雪芹 and Zhiyanzhai 脂硯齋. *Zhiyanzhai piping ben Hongloumeng* 脂硯齋批評本紅樓夢 (Dream of the Red Chamber with Red Inkstone's Commentaries). Changsha: Yuclu shushe, 2015.

Carl, Katharine. *With the Empress Dowager*. New York: The Century Co., 1905.

Carlisle, Janice. *Common Scents: Comparative Encounters in High-Victorian Fiction*. Oxford: Oxford University Press, 2004.

Chadwick, Edwin. *Report on the Sanitary Condition of the Labouring Population of Gt. Britain: 1842*. Edited by M. W. Flinn. Edinburgh: Edinburgh University Press, 1965.

Chan, Wellington K. K. 'Selling Goods and Promoting a New Commercial Culture: The Four Premier Department Stores on Nanjing Road, 1917–1937'. In *Inventing Nanjing Road: Commercial Culture in Shanghai, 1900–1945*, edited by Sherman Cochran, 19–36. Ithaca, NY: Cornell University Press, 1999.

Chang, Che-chia. 'Health and Hygiene in Late Qing China as Seen through the Eyes of Japanese Travelers'. In *Print, Profit, and Perception: Ideas, Information and Knowledge in Chinese Societies, 1895–1949*, edited by Pei-yin Lin and Weipin Tsai, 40–63. Leiden: Brill, 2014.

Chang, Eileen (Zhang Ailing 張愛玲). 'Red Rose, White Rose'. Translated by Karen Kingsbury. In *Love in a Fallen City*, 253–312. New York: New York Review Books, 2007.

Chang, Elizabeth Hope, ed. *British Travel Writing from China, 1798–1901*. 5 vols. London: Routledge, 2016.

Charabot, Eugène. *Les parfums artificiels*. Paris: Librairie J.-B. Baillière et fils, 1900.

Chau, Adam Yuet. 'The Sensorial Production of the Social'. *Ethnos* 73, no. 4 (2008): 485–504.

Chen Duxiu 陳獨秀. 'Wo zhi aiguo zhuyi 我之愛國主義' (My Patriotism). *Xin qingnian* 新青年 2, no. 2 (1916): 1–6.

Ch'ên, Jerome, and Michael Bullock. *Mao and the Chinese Revolution, with Thirty-Seven Poems by Mao Tse-Tung*. Oxford: Oxford University Press, 1965.

Chen Jianhua. *Revolution and Form: Mao Dun's Early Novels and Chinese Literary Modernity*. Translated by Carlos Rojas, Max Bohnenkamp, Todd Foley, Poshek Fu, Nga Li Lam, and Meng Li. Leiden: Brill, 2018.

'Shangpin, jiating yu quanqiu xiandaixing: lu Lu Xun de 'Feizao' 商品、家庭 与全球现代性：论鲁迅的《肥皂》' (Commodity, Family and Global Modernity: A Reading of Lu Xun's 'Soap'). *Xueshu yuekan* 学术月刊 52, no. 7 (2020): 135–45.

'Zhou Shoujuan yu Ziluolan: wenben jiangou yu minguo shiqi aiqing, hunyin yu jiating 周瘦鵑與紫羅蘭：文本建構與民國時期愛情、婚姻與家庭' (Zhou Shoujuan and Violet: Textual Construction and Love, Marriage and Family during the Republican Era). *Qinghua zhongwen xuebao* 清華中文學報 10 (December 2013): 253–85.

Chen Jichun 陳繼春. 'Guanyu Guan Huinong 關於關蕙農' (On Guan Huinong). www.mam.gov.mo/ws/ShowFile.ashx?p=mam2013/pdf_theses/635525900745148.pdf. Accessed 2 March 2015.

Chen Jing 陳敬. *Xinzuan xiangpu* 新纂香譜 (New Book on Perfume), edited by Yan Xiaoqing. Beijing: Zhonghua shuju, 2012.

Chen Lianqing 陳連慶. 'Han Jin zhiji shuru Zhongguo de xiangliao 漢晉之際輸 入中國的香料' (Imported Aromatics during the Han and Jin Dynasties). *Shixue jikan* 史學集刊 no. 2 (1986): 8–17.

Chen Pingyuan 陈平原. *Zhongguo xiandai xiaoshuo de qidian: Qing mo Min zhu xiaoshuo yanjiu* 中国现代小说的起点—清末民初小说研究 (The Origins of Modern Chinese Fiction: A Study of Fiction in the Late Qing and Early Republican Era). Beijing: Peking University Press, 2005.

Chen Yunlian 陳雲蓮. *Kindai Shanghai no toshi keiseishi: kokusai kyōsōka no sokai kaihatsu* 近代上海の都市形成史：国際競争下の租界開発 (The History of

Urban Development in Modern Shanghai: Foreign Settlements in the Context of International Competition). Tokyo: Fūkyōsha, 2018.

Cheng, Yinghong. *Creating the 'New Man': From Enlightenment Ideals to Socialist Realities.* Honolulu: University of Hawaii Press, 2009.

Chiang, Connie Y. 'Monterey-by-the-Smell: Odors and Social Conflict on the California Coastline'. *Pacific Historical Review* 73, no. 2 (2004): 183–214.

'The Nose Knows: The Sense of Smell in American History'. *Journal of American History* 95, no. 2 (2008): 405–16.

Chiang Kaishek 蔣介石. 'Xin shenghuo yundong zhi yaoyi 新生活運動之要義' (Essential Instructions on the New Life Movement). 19 February 1934. In *Zongtong Jiang Gong sixiang yanlun zongji* 總統蔣公思想言論總集 (A Collection of President Chiang's Thoughts and Speeches), vol. 12, edited by Qin Xiaoyi 秦孝儀, 70–80. Taipei: Zhongguo Guomindang zhongyang weiyuanhui dangshi weiyuanhui 中國國民黨中央委員會黨史委員會, 1984.

Chiu Chung-lin 邱仲麟. 'Fengchen, jierang yu qiwei: Ming Qing Beijing de shenghuo huanjing yu shiren de didu yinxiang 風塵、街壤與氣味：明清北京的生活環境與士人的帝都印象' (Dirt, Streets, and Smells: The Environment of Beijing and Scholars' Impressions of the Imperial Capital in the Ming and Qing Dynasties). *Qinghua xuebao* 34, no. 1 (2004): 181–225.

'Mingdai Beijing de gouqu shurui jiqi xiangguan wenti 明代北京的溝渠疏濬及其相關問題' (Dyke Dredging and Relevant Issues in Beijing during the Ming Dynasty). Guoli zhengzhi daxue lishi xuebao 國立政治大學歷史學報, no. 41 (2014): 43–104.

Chow, Rey. *Primitive Passions: Visuality, Sexuality, Ethnography, and Contemporary Chinese Cinema.* New York: Columbia University Press, 1995.

Woman and Chinese Modernity: The Politics of Reading between West and East. Minneapolis: University of Minnesota Press, 1991.

Chung, Hilary. 'Questing the Goddess: Mao Dun and the New Woman'. In *Autumn Floods: Essays in Honour of Marián Gálik,* edited by Raoul Findeisen and Robert Gassmann, 165–83. Bern: Peter Lang, 1998.

Cipolla, Carlo M. *Miasmas and Disease: Public Health and the Environment in the Pre-industrial Age.* Translated by Elizabeth Potter. New Haven, CT: Yale University Press, 1992.

Claridge, Claudia. *Hyperbole in English: A Corpus-Based Study of Exaggeration.* Cambridge: Cambridge University Press, 2011.

Clark, Anthony E. 'Rape, Baptism, and the "Pig" Religion: Chinese Images of Foreign Missionaries during the Late Nineteenth Century'. In *Beating Devils and Burning Their Books: Views of China, Japan, and the West,* edited by Anthony E. Clark, 43–81. Ann Arbor: Association for Asian Studies, 2010.

Classen, Constance. 'The Breath of God: Sacred Histories of Scent'. In *The Smell Culture Reader*, edited by Jim Drobnick, 375–90. Oxford: Berg, 2006.

ed. *A Cultural History of the Senses*. 6 vols. London: Bloomsbury, 2014.

'The Odor of the Rose'. In *Worlds of Sense: Exploring the Senses in History and across Cultures*, edited by Constance Classen, 15–36. London: Routledge, 1993.

Worlds of Sense: Exploring the Senses in History and across Cultures. London: Routledge, 1993.

Classen, Constance, David Howes, and Anthony Synnott. *Aroma: The Cultural History of Smell*. London and New York: Routledge, 1994.

Claudel, Paul. *The East I Know*. Translated by Teresa Benét and William Benét. New Haven and London: Yale University Press and Oxford University Press, 1914.

Clifford, Nicholas. *'A Truthful Impression of the Country': British and American Travel Writing in China, 1880–1949*. Ann Arbor, MI: University of Michigan Press, 2001.

Cochran, Jean Carter. *Foreign Magic: Tales of Every-Day China*. New York: Missionary Education Movement of the United States and Canada, 1919.

Cochran, Sherman. *Chinese Medicine Men: Consumer Culture in China and Southeast Asia*. Cambridge, MA: Harvard University Press, 2006.

Condillac, Étienne Bonnot de. *Treatise on the Sensations*. Translated by Geraldine Carr. London: Favil Press, 1930.

Cooke, George Wingrove. *China*. London and New York: Routledge, 1859.

Corbin, Alain. *The Foul and the Fragrant: Odor and the French Social Imagination*. Translated by Miriam L. Kochan. Cambridge, MA: Harvard University Press, 1986.

Cornaby, William Arthur. *Rambles in Central China*. London: Charles H. Kelly, 1896.

A String of Chinese Peach-Stones. London: Charles H. Kelly, 1895.

Cowan, Alexander, and Jill Steward, eds. *The City and the Senses: Urban Culture since 1500*. Aldershot: Ashgate, 2007.

Crespi, John A. *Manhua Modernity: Chinese Culture and the Pictorial Turn*. Berkeley: University of California Press, 2020.

Crow, Carl. *400 Million Customers: The Experiences – Some Happy, Some Sad – of an American in China and What They Taught Him*. Norwalk: EastBridge, 2003.

'Advertising and Merchandising'. In *China: A Commercial and Industrial Handbook*, edited by Julean Arnold, 191–205. Washington, DC: Government Printing Office, 1926.

The Travelers' Handbook for China (Including Hongkong). New York and Shanghai: Dodd, Mead & Co. and Carl Crow, 1921.

Dai Zhongfu 戴中孚. *Zhaojiabang de bianhua* 肇嘉浜的變化 (The Transformation of Zhaojia Creek). Shanghai: Shanghai jiaoyu chubanshe, 1960.

Dal Lago, Francesca. 'Crossed Legs in 1930s Shanghai: How "Modern" the Modern Woman?'. *East Asian History* 19 (2000): 103–44.

Daly, Emily Lucy. *An Irishwoman in China*. London: T. W. Laurie, 1915.

Deite, Carl. *A Practical Treatise on the Manufacture of Perfumery*. Philadelphia, PA: Henry Carey Baird & Co., 1892.

Denton, Kirk A. *The Problematic of Self in Modern Chinese Literature: Hu Feng and Lu Ling*. Stanford, CA: Stanford University Press, 1998.

 'Romantic Sentiment and the Problem of the Subject: Yu Dafu'. In *The Columbia Companion to Modern Chinese Literature*, edited by Kirk A. Denton, 145–51. New York: Columbia University Press, 2016.

De Pee, Christian, Joseph Sui Ching Lam, Shuen-fu Lin, and Martin Joseph Powers, eds. *Senses of the City: Perceptions of Hangzhou and Southern Song China, 1127–1279*. Hong Kong: The Chinese University of Hong Kong Press, 2017.

Di Zhaofu 第兆夫. 'Huchou he xiangwei 狐臭和香味' (Fox Stench and Sweet Aroma). *Kaimaila* 開麥拉 108 (1932), n.p.

Dikötter, Frank. *Exotic Commodities: Modern Objects and Everyday Life in China*. New York: Columbia University Press, 2006.

 Sex, Culture and Modernity in China: Medical Science and the Construction of Sexual Identities in the Early Republican Period. Honolulu, HI: University of Hawaii Press, 1995.

Ding Ling 丁玲. 'Mengke 夢珂' (Mengke). *Xiaoshuo yuebao* 小説月報 18, no. 12 (1927): 14–38.

Ding Wei 丁謂. *Tianxiang zhuan* 天香傳 (On Heavenly Perfumes). Reprinted in Chen Jing, *Xinzuan xiangpu* 新纂香譜 (New Book on Perfume), 233–49. Beijing: Zhonghua shuju, 2012.

Ding Yi 丁毅. 'Wenhua dageming zhong de yiduo xianghua 文化大革命中的一朵香花' (A Fragrant Flower in the Cultural Revolution). *RMRB*, 12 June 1966, 6.

Dingle, Edwin John. *Across China on Foot: Life in the Interior and the Reform Movement*. New York: Henry Holt, 1911.

Dirlik, Arif. *The Origins of Chinese Communism*. Oxford: Oxford University Press, 1989.

Dong Shaoxin 董少新, ed., *Gantong shenshou: Zhongxi wenhua jiaoliu beijing xia de ganguan yu ganjue* 感同身受—中西文化交流背景下的感官与感觉 (The Senses and Sensations in the Context of Cultural Exchanges between China and the West). Shanghai: Fudan daxue chubanshe, 2018.

Donkin, Robert A. *Dragon's Brain Perfume: An Historical Geography of Camphor*. Leiden: Brill, 1999.

Douglas, Mary. *Purity and Danger: An Analysis of Concepts of Pollution and Taboo.* London: Routledge, 2002.

Drobnick, Jim. *The Smell Culture Reader.* Oxford and New York: Berg, 2006.

Duburquois, Alexandre. *Notes sur les maladies des européens en Chine et au Japon.* Paris: A. Parent, 1872.

Dugan, Holly. *The Ephemeral History of Perfume: Scent and Sense in Early Modern England.* Baltimore: Johns Hopkins University Press, 2011.

Dukes, Edwin Joshua. *Everyday Life in China; or, Scenes along River and Road in Fuh-Kien.* London: Religious Tract Society, 1885.

Dupée, Jeffrey N. *British Travel Writers in China: Writing Home to a British Public, 1890–1914.* Lewiston: Edwin Mellen Press, 2004.

Dyce, Charles M. *Personal Reminiscences of Thirty Years' Residence in the Model Settlement Shanghai, 1870–1900.* London: Chapman & Hall, 1906.

Edwards, Louise P. *Men and Women in Qing China: Gender in the Red Chamber Dream.* Leiden: Brill, 1994.

Elias, Norbert. *The Civilizing Process: Sociogenetic and Psychogenetic Investigations.* Malden: Blackwell Publishers, 2000.

Ellis, Havelock. *Studies in the Psychology of Sex,* vol. 4. Philadelphia: F. A. Davis, 1931.

  (Ai Lisi 靄理思). 'Xiujue yu xingmei de guanxi 嗅覺與性美的關係' (The Relationship between Olfaction and Sexuality), translated by Peng Zhaoliang 彭兆良. *Xin Wenhua* 新文化 1, no. 5 (1927): 35–47.

Elvin, Mark. 'The Administration of Shanghai, 1905–1914'. In *The Chinese City between Two Worlds,* edited by Mark Elvin and G. William Skinner, 239–62. Stanford, CA: Stanford University Press, 1974.

  'Market Towns and Waterways: The County of Shang-hai from 1480 to 1910'. In *The City in Late Imperial China,* edited by G. William Skinner, 441–73. Stanford: Stanford University Press, 1977.

  The Retreat of the Elephants: An Environmental History of China. New Haven, CT: Yale University Press, 2004.

Engels, Friedrich. *The Condition of the Working-Class in England in 1844.* Translated by Florence Kelly Wischnewetzky. London: Allen and Unwin, 1952.

Enzinger, Irmgard. *Ausdruck und Eindruck: Zum Chinesischen Verständnis der Sinner.* Wiesbaden: Harrassowitz, 2006.

Eyles, Desmond. *Royal Doulton 1815–1965: The Rise and Expansion of the Royal Doulton Potteries.* London: Hutchinson, 1965.

Fan Boqun 范伯群. '"Cuixingshu": 1909 nian fabiao de "Kuangren riji", jiantan "ming baoren" Chen Jinghan zai zaoqi qimeng shiduan de wenxue chengjiu 《催醒术》： 1909 年发表的"狂人日记"—兼谈"名报人"陈景韩在早期启蒙时段的文学成就' ('The Magic of Awakening': 'A Madman's Diary' of 1909, and the Famous Journalist Chen Jinghan's Achievement in the Early Phase of Literary Enlightenment). *Jiangsu daxue xuebao* 江蘇大學學報 6, no. 5 (2004): 1–8.

Fan Fengyuan 范鳳源. 'Zhongguo huazhuang pin jishi Qin Xichou 中國化妝品技師秦錫疇' (Chinese Cosmetics Expert Qin Xichou). *SB*, 7 January 1929, 19.

Fei Xiaotong 费孝通. 'Fei Xiaotong gei Zhongyang minzu xueyuan Su Keqin fu yuanzhang de yifeng jiancha xin 费孝通给中央民族学院苏克勤副院长的一封检查信' (A Letter from Fei Xiaotong to Su Keqin, Vice President of the Minzu University for China). In *Jielu he pipan Zhang Luo lianmeng de junshi: Fei Xiaotong* 揭露和批判章罗联盟的军师—费孝通 (Expose and Criticize the Military Adviser of the Zhangluo Alliance: Fei Xiaotong), edited by Zhongyang minzu xueyuan zhengfeng bangongshi, August 1957. CCPMD.

Fengzi 凤子. 'Zai huaju wutai shang de xin shouhuo: tuijian huaju *Nihongdeng xia de shaobing* 在话剧舞台上的新收获—推荐话剧《霓虹灯下的哨兵》' (New Achievement on the Stage of Spoken Drama: Recommending *Sentinels under the Neon Lights*). *RMRB*, 10 March 1963, 5.

Fogel, Joshua A. *The Literature of Travel in the Japanese Rediscovery of China, 1862–1945*. Stanford, CA: Stanford University Press, 1996.

Forman, Ross G. *China and the Victorian Imagination: Empires Entwined*. Cambridge: Cambridge University Press, 2013.

'Eating Out East: Representing Chinese Food in Victorian Travel Literature and Journalism'. In *A Century of Travels in China: Critical Essays on Travel Writing from the 1840s to the 1940s*, edited by Julia Kuehn and Douglas Kerr, 63–73. Hong Kong: Hong Kong University Press, 2007.

Fortineau, Anne-Dominique. 'Chemistry Perfumes Your Daily Life'. *Journal of Chemical Education* 81, no. 1 (2004): 45–50.

Fox, Jasmine. 'The Nose Knows'. *Psychology Today* 32, no. 1 (1999): 22.

Freud, Sigmund. *Civilization and Its Discontents*. Translated by David McLintock. London: Penguin Books, 2004.

'The Uncanny'. In *The Uncanny*, translated by David McLintock, 121–62. London: Penguin Books, 2003.

Fu Jingliang 傅京亮. *Zhongguo xiang wenhua* 中國香文化 (Chinese Culture of Incense and Aromatics). Jinan: Qilu shushe, 2008.

Galle, Paul-Édouard. *Shang-hai au point de vue médical: Contributions à la climatologie médicale*. Paris: Adrien Delahaye, 1875.

Ge 戈. 'Xuesheng fenfen jihui, jiaoshi lianri baogao: Fudan daxue shisheng fanyoupai douzhi angyang 学生纷纷集会 教师连日报告: 复旦大学师生反右派斗志昂扬' (Students Gathered Together; Teachers Reported for Days: Fudan University Teachers and Students are Fighting against the Rightists). *Jiefang ribao*, 1 July 1957.

Ge Bingjian 葛丙劍. 'Shanghai shi jiayong huaxue gongye tongye gonghui lishi yange 上海市家用化學工業同業公會歷史沿革' (The History of the Shanghai Household Chemical Industry Association). December 1952. SMA, C48-1-44-36.

Geaney, Jane. *On the Epistemology of the Senses in Early Chinese Thought*. Honolulu: University of Hawaii Press, 2002.

Gerth, Karl. *China Made: Consumer Culture and the Creation of the Nation*. Cambridge, MA: Harvard University Asia Center, 2003.

Glen, W. Cunningham. *The Law Relating to the Public Health and Local Government, in Relation to Sanitary and Other Matters*. London: Butterworths, 1858.

Gong, Huanan. 'Senses and Cognition in Early Chinese Thought'. *Social Sciences in China* 38, no. 4 (2017): 28–44.

Gordon, Charles Alexander. *China from a Medical Point of View in 1860 and 1861, to Which Is Added a Chapter on Nagasaki as a Sanitarium*. London: J. Churchill, 1863.

Gordon-Cumming, Constance. *Wanderings in China*. Edinburgh: W. Blackwood, 1888.

Gotteland, R. P. '30e lettre, le R. P. Gotteland, supérieure des missions de la compagnie de Jésus en Chine, aux scholastiques de Vals, Kiangnan, 20 novembre 1844'. *Lettres des nouvelles missions de la Chine* 1 (1844): 177–83.

Goubert, Jean-Pierre. *The Conquest of Water: The Advent of Health in the Industrial Age*. Translated by Andrew Wilson. Princeton: Princeton University Press, 1989.

Gray, Richard. 'The Dialectic of "Enscentment": Patrick Süskind's *Perfume* as Critical History of Enlightenment Culture'. In *The Smell Culture Reader*, edited by Jim Drobnick, 235–53. Oxford: Berg, 2006.

Gu Shaoyi 顧紹衣. 'Xiujue yu xingyu zhi guanxi 嗅覺與性慾之關係' (The Relationship between Smell and Sexual Desire). *Dongfang zazhi* 東方雜誌 15, no. 9 (1918): 99–104.

Gu, Yi. *Chinese Ways of Seeing and Open-Air Painting*. Cambridge, MA: Harvard University Press, 2020.

Guan Kean-fung 顏健富. *Cong 'shenti' dao 'shijie'*: Wan Qing xiaoshuo de xin gainian ditu 從「身體」到「世界」: 晚清小說的新概念地圖 (From the 'Body' to the 'World': A New Conceptual Map of New Fiction in the Late Qing Dynasty). Taipei: Taiwan daxue chubanshe, 2014.

Gui Zhongsheng 桂中生. 'Qiantan huaju *Nihongdeng xia de shaobing* wutai meishu sheji 浅谈话剧《霓虹灯下的哨兵》舞台美术设计' (On the Stage Design of the Spoken Drama *Sentinels under the Neon Lights*). *RMRB*, 17 March 1963, 5.

Guo Benlan 郭本瀾, ed. *Zuixin huazhuangpin zhizaofa* 最新化妝品製造法 (Latest Cosmetic Manufacturing Methods). Shanghai: Shangwu yinshuguan, 1927.

Guo Moruo. 'Canchun 残春' (Late Spring). *Chuangzao jikan* 創造季刊 1, no. 2 (1922): 126–38.

Halliday, Stephen. *The Great Stink of London: Sir Joseph Bazalgette and the Cleansing of the Victorian Metropolis.* New York: History Press, 2013.

Hamlin, Christopher. *Public Health and Social Justice in the Age of Chadwick: Britain, 1800–1854.* Cambridge: Cambridge University Press, 1998.

Han Bangqing. *The Sing-Song Girls of Shanghai.* Translated by Zhang Ailing and Eva Hung. New York: Columbia University Press, 2005.

Han Fei 韓非. *Han Feizi* 韓非子, https://ctext.org/hanfeizi.

Han Fei, and Burton Watson. *Han Fei Tzu: Basic Writings.* New York: Columbia University Press, 1964.

Harris, Jonathan. 'The Smell of *Macbeth*'. *Shakespeare Quarterly* 58, no. 4 (2007): 465–86.

Harvey, Susan Ashbrook. *Scenting Salvation: Ancient Christianity and the Olfactory Imagination.* Berkeley: University of California Press, 2006.

Hauser, Jeanette (Mrs. I. L. Hauser). *The Orient and Its People.* Milwaukee: I. L. Hauser & Co., 1876.

Hay, Jonathan. *Sensuous Surfaces: The Decorative Object in Early Modern China.* Honolulu: University of Hawaii Press, 2010.

Hayot, Eric. *The Hypothetical Mandarin: Sympathy, Modernity, and Chinese Pain.* Oxford: Oxford University Press, 2009.

Henriot, Christian. *Scythe and the City: A Social History of Death in Shanghai.* Stanford: Stanford University Press, 2017.

   Shanghai, 1927–1937: Municipal Power, Locality, and Modernization. Berkeley: University of California Press, 1993.

Henriot, Christian, and Wen-Hsin Yeh, eds. *History in Images: Pictures and Public Space in Modern China.* Berkeley: University of California Press, 2012.

Henshaw, John M. *A Tour of the Senses: How Your Brain Interprets the World.* Baltimore: Johns Hopkins University Press, 2012.

Homan, Philipp, Benjamin A. Ely, May Yuan, Tobias Brosch, John Ng, Yaacov Trope, and Daniela Schiller. 'Aversive Smell Associations Shape Social Judgment'. *Neurobiology of Learning and Memory* 144 (2017): 86–95.

Hongqi zazhi bianjibu 《红旗》杂志编辑部 (*Red Flag* Editorial Board). 'Xiang renmin de zhuyao diren menglie kaihuo 向人民的主要敌人猛烈开火' (Fire Fiercely at the Main Enemies of the People). *Hongqi* 12, 1 August 1967.

Howes, David. *Empire of the Senses: The Sensual Culture Reader.* Oxford: Berg, 2005.

   'The Expanding Field of Sensory Studies'. www.sensorystudies.org/sensorial-investigations/the-expanding-field-of-sensory-studies/. Accessed 23 September 2022.

   'Olfaction and Transition'. In *The Varieties of Sensory Experience: A Sourcebook in the Anthropology of the Sense*, edited by David Howes, 128–47. Toronto: University of Toronto Press, 1991.

ed. *Senses and Sensation: Critical and Primary Sources*. 4 vols. London: Bloomsbury, 2018.

Sensual Relations: Engaging the Senses in Culture and Social Theory. Ann Arbor: University of Michigan Press, 2003.

Howes, David, and Constance Classen. *Ways of Sensing: Understanding the Senses in Society*. London: Routledge, 2014.

Howes, David, and Marc Lalonde. 'The History of Sensibilities: Of the Standard of Taste in Mid-Eighteenth Century England and the Circulation of Smells in Post-revolutionary France'. *Dialectical Anthropology* 16, no. 2 (1991): 125–35.

Hsia, Chih-tsing. *The Classic Chinese Novel: A Critical Introduction*. Bloomington: Indiana University Press, 1980.

A History of Modern Chinese Fiction, 1917–1957. New Haven: Yale University Press, 1961.

Hsu, Hsuan L. *The Smell of Risk: Environmental Disparities and Olfactory Aesthetics*. New York: New York University Press, 2020.

Hsu, Rachel Hui-Chi. 'The "Ellis Effect": Translating Sexual Science in Republican China, 1911–1949'. In *A Global History of Sexual Science, 1880–1960*, edited by Veronika Fuechtner, Douglas E. Haynes, and Ryan M. Jones, 186–210. Berkeley, CA: University of California Press, 2017.

Hu Cheng 胡成. '"Bu weisheng" de Huaren xingxiang: Zhongwai jian de butong jiangshu – Yi Shanghai gonggong weisheng wei zhongxin de guancha, 1860–1911 "不衛生"的華人形象：中外間的不同講述—以上海公共衛生為中心的觀察，1860–1911' (The Image of the 'Filthy' Chinese: Chinese and Foreign Discourses – An Observation on Public Health in Shanghai, 1860–1911). *Zhongyang yanjiuyuan jindaishi yanjiusuo jikan* 中央研究院近代史研究所集刊 56 (June 2007): 1–43.

Huang, Martin, W. *Desire and Fictional Narrative in Late Imperial China*. Cambridge, MA: Harvard University Asia Center, 2001.

Huang Ruizhen 黃瑞珍. 'Xiangliao yu Ming dai shehui shenghuo 香料與明代社會生活' (Spice and Daily Life of the Ming Dynasty). Master's thesis, Fujian Normal University, 2012.

Huang, Xuelei. 'Deodorizing China: Odour, Ordure, and Colonial (Dis) Order in Shanghai, 1840s–1940s'. *Modern Asian Studies* 50, no. 3 (2016): 1092–122.

'Smellscapes of Nanjing Road: Cognitive and Affective Mapping'. In *Sensing China: Modern Transformations of Sensory Culture*, edited by Shengqing Wu and Xuelei Huang, 71–98. Abingdon: Routledge, 2022.

Huang Yaomian 黃药眠. 'Wo de jiantao 我的检讨' (My Self-Criticism). *RMRB*, 19 July 1957, 10.

Hunter, William C. *Bits of Old China: Being a Few Chapters upon the Customs, Language, & Condition of the Chinese.* Beverley and London: Green & Son and Kent & Co., 1884.

The *'Fan Kwae' at Canton before Treaty Days, 1825–1844.* Shanghai: The Oriental Affairs, 1938.

Inglis, David. 'Sewers and Sensibilities: The Bourgeois Faecal Experience in the Nineteenth-Century City'. In *The City and the Senses: Urban Culture since 1500,* edited by Alexander Cowan and Jill Steward, 105–30. Aldershot: Ashgate, 2007.

A *Sociological History of Excretory Experience: Defecatory Manners and Toiletry Technologies.* Lewiston: Edwin Mellen Press, 2001.

Isakovics, Alois von. *Synthetic Perfumes and Flavors: A Lecture Delivered at Columbia University.* Monticello: Synfleur scientific laboratories, 1908.

Jackson, Isabella. *Shaping Modern Shanghai: Colonialism in China's Global City.* Cambridge: Cambridge University Press, 2018.

Jamieson, Alexander. 'Dr Alexander Jamieson's Report on the Health of Shanghai for the Half-Year Ended 30th September, 1871'. *Customs Gazette* 11 (1871): 33–43.

'Memo. on the Sanitary Condition of the Yang-King-Pang and Hongque Settlements at Shanghai'. *NCH*, 22 March 1870, 208–11.

Jenner, Mark. 'Civilization and Deodorization? Smell in Early Modern English Culture'. In *Civil Histories: Essays Presented to Sir Keith Thomas,* edited by Peter Burke, 127–44. Oxford: Oxford University Press, 2000.

'Follow Your Nose? Smell, Smelling, and Their Histories'. *American Historical Review* 116, no. 2 (2011): 335–51.

'Tasting Lichfield, Touching China: Sir John Floyer's Senses'. *Historical Journal* 53, no. 3 (2010): 647–70.

Ji, Fengyuan. *Linguistic Engineering: Language and Politics in Mao's China.* Honolulu: University of Hawaii Press, 2004.

Ji Xianlin. *The Cowshed: Memories of the Chinese Cultural Revolution.* New York: New York Review Books, 2016.

Jiang Naiyong 蔣乃鏞. *Shanghai gongye gailan* 上海工業概覽 (An Overview of Industry in Shanghai). Shanghai: Xuezhe shuju, 1947.

Jin Yi 金易. *Gongnü tan wang lu* 宮女谈往录 (An Imperial Maid's Reminiscences of the Past). Beijing: Zijincheng chubanshe, 2004.

Jin Yucheng 金宇澄. *Fanhua* 繁花 (Blossoms). Shanghai: Shanghai wenyi chubanshe, 2013.

Johnson, Linda Cooke. *Shanghai: From Market Town to Treaty Port, 1074–1858.* Stanford: Stanford University Press, 1995.

Johnston, James F. *The Chemistry of Common Life.* New York: D. Appleton, 1880.

Jones, Andrew F. *Developmental Fairy Tales: Evolutionary Thinking and Modern Chinese Culture*. Cambridge, MA: Harvard University Press, 2011.

Jones, Geoffrey. *Beauty Imagined: A History of the Global Beauty Industry*. Oxford: Oxford University Press, 2011.

Judge, Joan. 'The Culturally Contested Student Body: Nü Xuesheng at the Turn of the Twentieth Century'. In *Performing 'Nation': Gender Politics in Literature, Theater, and the Visual Arts of China and Japan, 1880–1940*, edited by Doris Croissant, Joshua S. Mostow, and Catherine Vance Yeh, 105–32. Boston, MA: Brill, 2008.

  Republican Lens: Gender, Visuality, and Experience in the Early Chinese Periodical Press. Berkeley: University of California Press, 2015.

Jütte, Robert. *A History of the Senses: From Antiquity to Cyberspace*. Oxford: Polity, 2005.

Kant, Immanuel. *Anthropology from a Pragmatic Point of View*. Translated and edited by Robert B. Louden. Cambridge: Cambridge University Press, 2006.

  'Physische Geographie'. In *Kant's Gesammelte Schriften*, vol. 9, edited by Königlich Preußische Akademie der Wissenschaften. Berlin: Georg Reimer, 1907.

  'Reflexionen zur Anthropologie'. In *Kant's Gesammelte Schriften*, vol. 15, edited by Königlich Preußische Akademie der Wissenschaften. Berlin: Georg Reimer, 1907.

Kazantzakis, Nikos. *Japan, China: Journey of Two Voyages to the Far East*. Berkeley, CA: Creative Arts Book Company, 1982.

Keaveney, Christopher. *The Subversive Self in Modern Chinese Literature: The Creation Society's Reinvention of the Japanese Shishō Setsu*. New York: Palgrave Macmillan, 2004.

Kettler, Andrew. *The Smell of Slavery: Olfactory Racism and the Atlantic World*. Cambridge: Cambridge University Press, 2020.

Kiechle, Melanie A. *Smell Detectives: An Olfactory History of Nineteenth-Century Urban America*. Seattle: University of Washington Press, 2017.

Konishi, Shino. 'Discovering the Savage Senses: French and British Explorers' Encounters with Aboriginal People'. In *Discovery and Empire: The French in the South Seas*, edited by John West-Sooby, 99–140. Adelaide: University of Adelaide Press, 2013.

Kuehn, Julia, and Douglas Kerr, eds. *A Century of Travels in China: Critical Essays on Travel Writing from the 1840s to the 1940s*. Hong Kong: Hong Kong University Press, 2007.

Kwan Man Bun 關文斌. 'Market and Network Capitalism: Yongli Chemical Co. Ltd. and Imperial Chemical Industries, Ltd., 1917–1937'. *Zhongyang yan-jiuyuan jindaishi yanjiusuo jikan* 49 (September 2005): 93–126.

Laing, Ellen Johnston. *Selling Happiness: Calendar Posters and Visual Culture in Early-Twentieth-Century Shanghai.* Honolulu: University of Hawaii Press, 2004.

Lamson, Herbert Day. 'The Problem of Housing for Workers in China'. *Chinese Economic Journal* 11, no. 2 (August 1932), 139–62.

Lao She. *Dragon Beard Ditch: A Play in Three Acts.* Translated by Liao Hung-ying. Beijing: Foreign Languages Press, 1956.

    Longxugou 龙须沟 (Dragon Beard Ditch). In *Lao She juzuo xuan* 老舍剧作选 (Selected Plays by Lao She), 1–72. Beijing: Renmin wenxue chubanshe, 1978.

Largey, Gale, and Rod Watson. 'The Sociology of Odors'. In *The Smell Culture Reader*, edited by Jim Drobnick, 29–40. Oxford: Berg, 2006.

Larson, Wendy. *From Ah Q to Lei Feng: Freud and Revolutionary Spirit in 20th Century China.* Stanford: Stanford University Press, 2008.

    'The Pleasures of Lying Low: Yang Jiang and Chinese Revolutionary Culture'. In *China's Literary Cosmopolitans: Qian Zhongshu, Yang Jiang, and the World of Letters*, edited by Christopher G. Rea, 133–56. Leiden: Brill, 2015.

Lateiner, Donald. 'Olfactoring Ancient Fictions: Fair and Foul Fragrances in Ancient Novels'. In *Re-wiring the Ancient Novel*, edited by Edmund Cueva, Stephen Harrison, Hugh Mason, William Owens, and Saundra Schwartz, 319–54. Eelde: Barkhuis, 2019.

Lean, Eugenia. 'The Butterfly Mark: Chen Diexian, His Brand, and Cultural Entrepreneurism in Republican China'. In *The Business of Culture: Cultural Entrepreneurs in China and Southeast Asia, 1900–65*, edited by Christopher G. Rea and Nicolai Volland, 62–91. Vancouver: UBC Press, 2015.

    Vernacular Industrialism in China: Local Innovation and Translated Technologies in the Making of a Cosmetics Empire, 1900–1940. New York: Columbia University Press, 2020.

Lee, Haiyan. *Revolution of the Heart: A Genealogy of Love in China, 1900–1950.* Stanford, CA: Stanford University Press, 2007.

    The Stranger and the Chinese Moral Imagination. Stanford, CA: Stanford University Press, 2014.

Lee, Leo Ou-fan. *The Romantic Generation of Modern Chinese Writers.* Cambridge, MA: Harvard University Press, 1973.

    Shanghai Modern: The Flowering of a New Urban Culture in China, 1930–1945. Cambridge, MA: Harvard University Press, 1999.

Legge, James, and Confucius. *The Chinese Classics: With a Translation, Critical and Exegetical Notes, Prolegomena, and Copious Indexes.* 2nd ed. Oxford: Clarendon Press, 1893.

Le Guérer, Annick. *Scent, the Mysterious and Essential Powers of Smell.* New York: Turtle Bay Books, 1992.

Lengxue 冷血. 'Cuixingshu 催醒術' (The Magic of Awakening). *Xiaoshuo shibao* 小説時報 1 (October 1909): 1–4.

Leung, Angela Ki Che, and Charlotte Furth, eds. *Health and Hygiene in Chinese East Asia: Policies and Publics in the Long Twentieth Century*. Durham, NC: Duke University Press, 2010.

Lévi-Strauss, Claude. *Tristes tropiques*. Translated by John Russell. New York: Criterion Books, 1961.

Lewis, Richard Albert. *Edwin Chadwick and the Public Health Movement, 1832–1854*. New York: Longmans, Green, 1952.

Li, Jie. *Shanghai Homes: Palimpsests of Private Life*. New York: Columbia University Press, 2015.

Li, Kwok-sing, ed. *A Glossary of Political Terms of the People's Republic of China*. Hong Kong: Chinese University Press, 1995.

Li Ling 李凌. 'Xiang Liu Silingyuan chui xie hefeng xiyu 向刘司令员吹些和风细雨' (Blow Some Gentle Rain on Commander Liu). Big-character poster, May 1957. CCPMD.

Li Shangjen 李尚仁. 'Fuwu yu angzang gan: shijiu shiji xifangren dui Zhongguo huanjing de tiyan 腐物與骯髒感：十九紀西方人對中國環境的體驗' (Filthy Matters and the Feeling of Filthiness: Western Experiences of Chinese Environments in the Nineteenth Century). In *Tiwu ruwei: wu yu shenti gan de yanjiu* 體物入微：物與身體感的研究 (Experiencing the Subtlety of Things: Studies on Objects and the Body), edited by Yu Shunde 余舜德, 45–82. Taiwan: Tsinghua University Press, 2008.

Li, Xiaorong. *The Poetics and Politics of Sensuality in China: The 'Fragrant and Bedazzling' Movement (1600–1930)*. Amherst, NY: Cambria Press, 2019.

Li Yu 李漁. *Xianqing ouji* 閑情偶寄 (Casual Expressions of Feelings of Leisure). In *Li Yu quanji* 李漁全集 (Complete Works of Li Yu), vol. 3. Hangzhou: Zhejiang guji chubanshe, 1992.

Liddell, Thomas Hodgson. *China, Its Marvel and Mystery*. London: G. Allen, 1909.

Link, Perry. *An Anatomy of Chinese: Rhythm, Metaphor, Politics*. Cambridge, MA: Harvard University Press, 2013.

Little, Archibald. *Gleanings from Fifty Years in China*. London: S. Low, Marston, 1910.

Little, Alicia (aka Mrs Archibald Little). *Intimate China: The Chinese as I Have Seen Them*. London: Hutchinson & Co., 1899.

    Round about My Peking Garden. London: T. Fisher Unwin, 1905.

Liu, Lydia. *The Clash of Empires: The Invention of China in Modern World Making*. Cambridge, MA: Harvard University Press, 2004.

Liu Na'ou. 'Fengjing 風景' (Scenery). In *Dushi fengjing xian* 都市風景線 (*Scène*), 107–41. Shanghai: Shuimo shudian, 1930.

'Liangge shijian de buganzheng zhe 兩個時間的不感症者' (Two Men Impervious to Time). In *Xin ganjue pai xiaoshuo xuan* 新感覺派小說選 (An Anthology of New Sensationalist Fiction), edited by Yan Jiayan 严家炎, 10–16. Beijing: Renmin wenxue chubanshe, 2011.

Liu, Qian. *Transcultural Lyricism: Translation, Intertextuality, and the Rise of Emotion in Modern Chinese Love Fiction, 1899–1925*. Leiden: Brill, 2017.

Liu Xiang 劉向. *Shuoyuan* 說苑, https://ctext.org/shuo-yuan.

Low, Kelvin E. Y. 'Theorising Sensory Cultures in Asia: Sociohistorical Perspectives'. *Asian Studies Review* 43, no. 4 (2019): 618–36.

Lu, Di, and Vivienne Lo. 'Scent and Synaesthesia: The Medical Use of Spice Bags in Early China'. *Journal of Ethnopharmacology* 167 (2015): 38–46.

Lu, Hanchao. *Beyond the Neon Lights: Everyday Shanghai in the Early Twentieth Century*. Berkeley: University of California Press, 1999.

Lu, Xing. *Rhetoric of the Chinese Cultural Revolution: The Impact on Chinese Thought, Culture, and Communication*. Columbia: University of South Carolina Press, 2004.

Lu Xun 魯迅. 'Soap'. Translated by Julia Lovell. In *The Real Story of Ah-Q and Other Tales of China: The Complete Fiction of Lu Xun*, 195–205. London: Penguin, 2009.

Luo Wanxian 羅婉嫻. 'Cong *Liangyou huabao* de huazhuangpin guanggao kan Shanghai funü de meirong qingkuang, 1926–1941 從《良友畫報》的化妝品廣告看上海婦女的美容情況 (1926–1941)' (Shanghai Women's Make-Up and Fashion Seen from Cosmetic Advertisements in the *Young Companion*). In *Dongya shijie: zhengzhi, junshi, wenhua* 東亞世界：政治，軍事，文化 (The World of East Asia: Politics, Military, and Culture), edited by Zhou Jiarong 周佳榮 and Fan Yongcong 范永聰, 114–45. Hong Kong: Sanlian shudian, 2014.

McGee, Harold. *Nose Dive: A Field Guide to the World's Smells*. New York and London: Penguin and John Murray, 2020.

McHugh, James. *Sandalwood and Carrion: Smell in Indian Religion and Culture*. Oxford: Oxford University Press, 2013.

Mackerras, Colin. *Western Images of China*. Oxford: Oxford University Press, 1989.

MacPherson, Kerrie L. *A Wilderness of Marshes: The Origins of Public Health in Shanghai, 1843–1893*. Oxford: Oxford University Press, 1987.

Mann, Susan. *Precious Records: Women in China's Long Eighteenth Century*. Stanford: Stanford University Press, 1997.

Mao Dun 茅盾. 'Chuangzao 創造' (Creation). *Dongfang zazhi* 25, no. 8 (April 1928): 99–114.

'Dongyao 動搖' (Vacillation). In *Mao Dun quanji* 茅盾全集 (Complete Works of Mao Dun), vol. 1, 101–258. Beijing: Renmin wenxue chubanshe, 1984.

'Huanmie 幻滅' (Disillusionment). In *Mao Dun quanji* 茅盾全集 (Complete Works of Mao Dun), vol. 1, 3–100. Beijing: Renmin wenxue chubanshe, 1984.

Midnight (*Ziye* 子夜). Translated by M.-h. Hsu. Beijing: Foreign language press, 1957.

'Semang 色盲' (Colour Blindness). In *Mao Dun quanji* 茅盾全集 (Complete Works of Mao Dun), vol. 8, 100–44. Beijing: Renmin wenxue chubanshe, 1984.

'Tigao jingti, wajin yiqie qiancang de diren 提高警惕，挖尽一切潜藏的敌人' (Raise Your Vigilance and Find Out All Hidden Enemies). *RMRB*, 15 June 1955, 3.

'Zhuiqiu 追求' (Pursuit). In *Mao Dun quanji* 茅盾全集 (Complete Works of Mao Dun), vol. 1, 259–422. Beijing: Renmin wenxue chubanshe, 1984.

Mao Zedong 毛泽东. 'Bianzhe an 编者按' (Editor's Notes). *RMRB*, 13 May 1955, 2.

'Bixu zhuyi jingji gongzuo 必须注意经济工作' (Pay Attention to Economic Work) (12 August 1933). *MXJ* 1, 119–26; *SWM* 1, 129–36.

'Fandui dang bagu 反对党八股' (Oppose Stereotyped Party Writing) (8 February 1942). *MXJ* 3, 830–46; *SWM* 3, 53–68.

'*Guanyu Hu Feng fangeming jituan de cailiao* de xuyan he anyu 《关于胡风反革命集团的材料》的序言和按语' (Preface and Editor's Notes to *Material on the Counter-revolutionary Hu Feng Clique*) (May and June 1955). *MXJ* 5, 160–67; *SWM* 5, 176–83.

'Guanyu zhengque chuli renmin neibu maodun de wenti 关于正确处理人民内部矛盾的问题' (On the Correct Handling of Contradictions among the People) (27 February 1957). *MXJ* 5, 363–402; *SWM* 5, 384–421.

Mao Zedong xuanji 毛泽东选集 (Selected Works of Mao Zedong). 4 vols. 2nd ed. Beijing: Renmin chubanshe, 1991.

Mao Zedong xuanji 毛泽东选集 (Selected Works of Mao Zedong), vol. 5. 1st ed. Beijing: Renmin chubanshe, 1977.

'Nongye hezuohua de yichang bianlun he dangqian de jieji douzheng 农业合作化的一场辩论和当前的阶级斗争' (The Debate on the Co-operative Transformation of Agriculture and the Current Class Struggle) (11 October 1955). *MXJ* 5, 195–217; *SWM* 5, 211–34.

'Ping He'erli zhengce de weixian 评赫尔利政策的危险' (On the Danger of Hurley's Policy) (12 July 1945). *MXJ* 3, 1114–16; *SWM* 3, 335–6.

'Qin Yuan Chun – Changsha 沁园春—长沙' (Changsha, to the Melody of Qin Yuan Chun). *Shikan* (1957): 4–5.

Reverberations: A New Translation of Complete Poems of Mao Tse-Tung. Translated by Nancy Lin. Hong Kong: Joint Pub. Co., 1980.

Selected Works of Mao Tse-tung. Beijing: Foreign Languages Press, 1961.

'Talks at the Yenan Forum on Literature and Art'. *SWM* 3, 69–98.

'Xin minzhu zhuyi de xianzheng 新民主主义的宪政' (New Democratic Constitutional Government) (20 February 1940). *MXJ* 2, 731–40; *SWM* 2, 407–16.

'Zai Sheng shi zizhiqu dangwei shuji huiyi shang de jianghua 在省市自治区党委书记会议上的讲话' (Talks at a Conference of Secretaries of Provincial, Municipal and Autonomous Region Party Committees) (January 1957). *MXJ* 5, 330–62; *SWM* 5, 350–83.

'Zhengdun dang de zuofeng 整顿党的作风' (Rectify the Party's Style of Work) (1 February 1942). *MXJ* 3, 811–29; *SWM* 3, 35–51.

Marcuse, Herbert. *Eros and Civilization: A Philosophical Inquiry into Freud*. London: Sphere, 1969.

Marks, Robert B. *China: An Environmental History*. 2nd edition. Lanham, MD: Rowman & Littlefield, 2017.

Marx, Karl. *Economic and Philosophic Manuscripts of 1844*. Translated by Martin Milligan. New York: Dover Publications, 2007.

Maxwell, Catherine. *Scents and Sensibility: Perfume in Victorian Literary Culture*. Oxford: Oxford University Press, 2017.

Mendoza, Juan González de. *The History of the Great and Mighty Kingdom of China and the Situation Thereof*. Translated by R. Parke. 2 vols. London: The Hakluyt Society, 1853–1854.

Meng Hui 孟晖. *Huatang xiangshi* 画堂香事 (Fragrances in Scholar's Studios). Nanjing: Nanjing daxue chubanshe, 2012.

Menninghaus, Winfried. *Disgust: Theory and History of a Strong Sensation*. Translated by Howard Eiland and Joel Golb. Albany: State University of New York Press, 2003.

Miao Cheng Shuyi 繆程淑儀. 'Xiang yu funü 香與婦女' (Aromas and Women). *Funü zazhi* 婦女雜誌 6, no. 3 (1920): 1–5.

Milburn, Olivia. 'Aromas, Scents, and Spices: Olfactory Culture in China before the Arrival of Buddhism'. *Journal of American Oriental Society* 136, no. 3 (2016): 441–64.

Miller, William Ian. *The Anatomy of Disgust*. Cambridge, MA: Harvard University Press, 1998.

Mine, Kiyoshi 峰潔. 'Qingguo Shanghai jianwen lu 清國上海見聞録' (My Observations of Shanghai in Qing China). In *Shanghai gonggong zujie shigao* 上海公共租界史稿 (The History of the Shanghai International Settlement), 621–7. Shanghai: Shanghai renmin chubanshe, 1980.

Mittler, Barbara. *A Continuous Revolution: Making Sense of Cultural Revolution Culture*. Cambridge, MA: Harvard University Asia Center, 2012.

Møller-Olsen, Astrid. *Sensing the Sinophone: Urban Memoryscapes in Contemporary Fiction*. New York: Cambria Press, 2022.

Molz, Jennie Germann. 'Cosmopolitan Bodies: Fit to Travel and Travelling to Fit'. *Body & Society* 12, no. 3 (2006): 1–21.

Morris, Andrew. '"Fight for Fertilizer!" Excrement, Public Health, and Mobilization in New China'. *Journal of Unconventional History* 6, no. 3 (1995): 51–77.

Morris, Thomas M. *A Winter in North China*. London: The Religious Tract Society, 1892.

Morrison, George Ernest. *An Australian in China: Being a Narrative of a Quiet Journey across China to British Burma*. London: Horace Cox, 1895.

Moule, Arthur Evans. *New China and Old: Personal Recollections and Observations of Thirty Years*. London: Seeley and Co., 1891.

Muchembled, Robert. *Smells: A Cultural History of Odours in Early Modern Times*. Translated by Susan Pickford. Cambridge: Polity, 2020.

Nakajima, Chieko. *Body, Society, and Nation: The Creation of Public Health and Urban Culture in Shanghai*. Cambridge, MA: Harvard University Asia Center, 2018.

Naquin, Susan, and Evelyn S. Rawski. *Chinese Society in the Eighteenth Century*. New Haven: Yale University Press, 1987.

Needham, Joseph. *Science and Civilisation in China*, vol. 5, part II. Cambridge: Cambridge University Press, 1974.

   The Shorter Science and Civilisation in China: An Abridgement of Joseph Needham's Original Text. Edited by Colin A. Ronan. Cambridge: Cambridge University Press, 1978.

Ng, Yong-Sang. 'The Poetry of Mao Tse-Tung'. *China Quarterly* 13 (1963): 60–73.

Nylan, Michael. *The Five 'Confucian' Classics*. New Haven: Yale University Press, 2001.

Orwell, George. *Nineteen Eighty-Four*. London: Secker & Warburg, 1997.

   The Road to Wigan Pier. London: Penguin, 2001.

Oswald, Laura. *Marketing Semiotics: Signs, Strategies, and Brand Value*. Oxford: Oxford University Press, 2012.

Ouyang Yuqian 欧阳予倩. 'Tingle Mao Zhuxi de baogao de jidian tihui 听了毛主席的报告的几点体会' (Some Thoughts after Hearing Chairman Mao's Speech). *RMRB*, 19 March 1957, 7.

Pang, Laikwan. *The Distorting Mirror: Visual Modernity in China*. Honolulu, HI: University of Hawaii Press, 2007.

   'The Pictorial Turn: Realism, Modernity and China's Print Culture in the Late Nineteenth Century'. *Visual Studies* 20, no. 1 (2005): 16–36.

Parry, Ernest John. *The Chemistry of Essential Oils and Artificial Perfumes*. London: Scott, Greenwood and Son, 1921.

Payne, Robert. 'Poems by Mao Tse-Tung'. *Literary Review* 2, no. 1 (1958): 82–92.

'The Poetry of Mao Tse-Tung'. *Literary Review* 60, no. 3 (2017): 19–23.

Peng Hsiao-yen 彭小妍. *Haishang shuo qingyu: cong Zhang Ziping dao Liu Na'ou* 海上說情欲：從張資平到劉吶鷗 (On Lust of Shanghai: From Zhang Ziping to Liu Na'ou). Taipei: Zhongyang yanjiuyuan wenzhe yanjiusuo, 2001.

Peng, Juanjuan. 'Selling a Healthy Lifestyle in Late Qing Tianjin: Commercial Advertisements for Weisheng Products in the *Dagong Bao*, 1902–1911'. *International Journal of Asian Studies* 9, no. 2 (2012): 211–30.

Peng Shanmin 彭善民. *Gonggong weisheng yu Shanghai dushi wenming, 1898–1949* 公共卫生与上海都市文明 (1898–1949) (Public Health and Urban Civilization in Shanghai, 1898–1949). Shanghai: Shanghai renmin chubanshe, 2007.

Peng Xianzhi 逄先知. *Mao Zedong nianpu* 毛泽东年谱 (A Chronology of Mao Zedong), vol. 1. Beijing: Zhongyang wenxian chubanshe, 2003.

Perry, Elizabeth, and Xun Li. 'Revolutionary Rudeness: The Language of Red Guards and Rebel Workers in China's Cultural Revolution'. In *Twentieth-Century China: New Approaches*, edited by Jeffrey N. Wasserstrom, 221–36. London: Routledge, 2003.

Picard, Liza. *Victorian London: The Life of a City, 1840–1870*. London: Phoenix, 2006.

Pickowicz, Paul, Kuiyi Shen, and Yingjin Zhang, eds. *Liangyou: Kaleidoscopic Modernity and the Shanghai Global Metropolis, 1926–1945*. Leiden: Brill, 2013.

Piesse, G. W. Septimus. *The Art of Perfumery, and the Methods of Obtaining Odours of Plants*. London: Longmans, Brown, Green, and Longmans, 1855.

Pike, David L. 'Sewage Treatments: Vertical Space and Waste in Nineteenth-Century Paris and London'. In *Filth: Dirt, Disgust, and Modern Life*, edited by William A. Cohen and Ryan Johnson, 51–77. Minneapolis, MN: University of Minnesota Press, 2004.

Plamper, Jan. 'Sounds of February, Smells of October: The Russian Revolution as Sensory Experience'. *American Historical Review* 126, no. 1 (2021): 140–65.

Pratt, Mary Louise. *Imperial Eyes: Travel Writing and Transculturation*. 2nd ed. London: Routledge, 2008.

Proust, Marcel. *In Search of Lost Time*, vol. 1, *Swann's Way*. Translated by C. K. Scott Moncrieff and Terence Kilmartin. Revised by D. J. Enright. New York: The Modern Library, 1992.

Pu Yi. *From Emperor to Citizen: The Autobiography of Aisin-Gioro Pu Yi*. Translated by William Jenner. Beijing: Foreign Languages Press, 1964.

Pye, Lucian W. *The Spirit of Chinese Politics: A Psychocultural Study of the Authority Crisis in Political Development*. Cambridge, MA: MIT, 1968.

Qu Yuan 屈原. *Chuci* 楚辭 (The Songs of the South), https://ctext.org/chu-ci/zh.

Ch'u Tz'u: The Songs of the South, an Ancient Chinese Anthology. Translated by David Hawkes. Oxford: Clarendon Press, 1959.

Qureshi, Sadiah. *Peoples on Parade: Exhibitions, Empire, and Anthropology in Nineteenth-Century Britain*. Chicago, IL: University of Chicago Press, 2011.

Ramos, Sergio López. *History of the Air and Other Smells in Mexico City, 1840–1900*. Bloomington: Palibrio, 2016.

Reinarz, Jonathan. *Past Scents: Historical Perspectives on Smell*. Urbana, IL: University of Illinois Press, 2014.

Reinders, Eric Robert. *Borrowed Gods and Foreign Bodies: Christian Missionaries Imagine Chinese Religion*. Berkeley: University of California Press, 2004.

Renmin ribao bianjibu (*People's Daily* Editorial Board). 'Guanyu Sidalin wenti 关于斯大林问题' (On the Problem of Stalin). *RMRB*, 13 September 1963, 1.

Rimmel, Eugene. *The Book of Perfumes*. London: Chapman and Hall, 1865.

Rindisbacher, Hans J. *The Smell of Books: A Cultural-Historical Study of Olfactory Perception in Literature*. Ann Arbor: University of Michigan Press, 1992.

Roe, Alfred Seelye. *Chance & Change in China*. London: W. Heinemann, 1920.

Rogaski, Ruth. *Hygienic Modernity: Meanings of Health and Disease in Treaty-Port China*. Berkeley: University of California Press, 2004.

Ross, Edward Alsworth. *The Changing Chinese: The Conflict of Oriental and Western Cultures in China*. New York: Century, 1911.

Rotter, Andrew J. *Empires of the Senses: Bodily Encounters in Imperial India and the Philippines*. Oxford: Oxford University Press, 2019.

Russell, Bertrand. *The Problem of China*. London: George Allen & Unwin, 1922.

Said, Edward W. *Orientalism*. New York: Vintage Books, 1979.

Salisbury, Laura, and Andrew Shail, eds. *Neurology and Modernity: A Cultural History of Nervous Systems, 1800–1950*. Basingstoke: Palgrave Macmillan, 2010.

Sang, Tze-lan D. 'Failed Modern Girls in Early-Twentieth-Century China'. In *Performing 'Nation': Gender Politics in Literature, Theater, and the Visual Arts of China and Japan, 1880–1940*, edited by Doris Croissant, Joshua S. Mostow, and Catherine Vance Yeh, 179–202. Boston: Brill, 2008.

Santangelo, Paolo. 'The Culture of Smells: Taboo and Sublimation from *Huchou* to *Tianxiang*'. In *Sensing China: Modern Transformations of Sensory Culture*, edited by Shengqing Wu and Xuelei Huang, 42–67. Abingdon: Routledge, 2022.

Sapolsky, Robert. 'Metaphors Are Us: War, Murder, Music, Art. We Would Have None without Metaphor'. *Nautilus* 75 (2019).

Schaefer, William. *Shadow Modernism: Photography, Writing, and Space in Shanghai, 1925–1937*. Durham, NC: Duke University Press, 2017.

Schlögel, Karl. *The Scent of Empires: Chanel No. 5 and Red Moscow*. Translated by Jessica Spengler. Medford MA: Polity Press, 2021.

Schoenhals, Michael. *Doing Things with Words in Chinese Politics: Five Studies.* Berkeley, CA: University of California Press, 1992.

Sha Ying 沙英. 'Zatan "feng": Sixiang zhaji 杂谈"风"—思想札记' (On 'Wind': Notes of Some Thoughts). *RMRB*, 1 June 1963, 5.

Shakespeare, William. *King Lear.* Stansted: Wordsworth, 1994.

Shanghai Municipal Council. 'Report for the Year Ended 31st December 1879 and Budget for the Year Ending 31st December 1880'. Shanghai, 1880.

Report for the Year Ended 31st December 1892 and Budget for the Year Ending 31st December 1893. Shanghai: Kelly & Walsh, 1893.

Report for the Year Ended 31st December 1895 and Budget for the Year Ending 31st December 1896. Shanghai: Kelly & Walsh, 1896.

Shanghai shehui kexueyuan 上海社會科學院, ed. *Shanghai penghuqu de bianqian* 上海棚户区的变迁 (The Changes in Shanghai's Slum Districts). Shanghai: Shanghai renmin chubanshe, 1962.

Shanghai shi baihuo gongsi 上海市百貨公司 et al., eds. *Shanghai jindai baihuo shangye shi* 上海近代百货商业史 (A History of Shanghai's Modern Department Stores). Shanghai: Shanghai shehui kexueyuan chubanshe, 1988.

Shanghai shi dang'an guan 上海市檔案館, ed. *Gongbuju dongshihui huiyilu* 工部局董事會會議錄 (Minutes of the Shanghai Municipal Council). Shanghai: Shanghai guji chubanshe, 2001.

Shanghai shi jiayong huaxuepin gongye tongye gonghui 上海市家用化學品工業同業公會, ed. *Shanghai shi jiayong huaxuepin gongye chanpin zhishi jieshao* 上海市家用化學品工業產品知識介紹 (Introduction to the Products of the Shanghai Household Chemical Industry). July 1955. SMA, S86-4-101.

Shanghai shi yiyao gongsi 上海市医药公司 et al., eds. *Shanghai jindai xiyao hangye shi* 上海近代西药行业史 (A History of Western Medicine in Modern Shanghai). Shanghai: Shanghai shehui kexueyuan chubanshe, 1988.

Shanghai tongzhi bianzuan weiyuanhui《上海通志》編纂委员会, ed. *Shanghai tongzhi* 上海通志 (Encyclopedia of Shanghai), 10 vols. Shanghai: Shanghai renmin chubanshe, 2005; online version: www.shtong.gov.cn/difangzhi-front/book/detailNew?oneId=1&bookId=2247. Accessed 7 September 2022.

Shanghai weisheng zhi bianzuan weiyuanhui《上海卫生志》編纂委员会, ed. *Shanghai weisheng zhi* 上海卫生志 (Encyclopedia of Public Health in Shanghai). Shanghai: Shanghai shehui kexueyuan chubanshe, 1998.

Shao Yanxiang 邵燕祥. *Rensheng baibi: yige miedingzhe de zhengzha shilu* 人生败笔—一个灭顶者的挣扎实录 (Failures in My Life: A True Record of My Struggle). Zhengzhou: Henan renmin chubanshe, 1997.

Shen Ximeng 沈西蒙, Mo Yan 漠雁, and Lü Xingchen 吕兴臣. 'Nihong deng xia de shaobing 霓虹灯下的哨兵' (Sentinels under the Neon Lights). *Juben* 剧本 2 (1963): 2–41.

Shih, Shumei. *The Lure of the Modern: Writing Modernism in Semicolonial China, 1917–1937*. Berkeley: University of California Press, 2001.

Shoudu dazhuan yuanxiao hongweibing silingbu xuanchuanchu 首都大专院校红卫兵司令部宣传处. *Geming duilian xuan* 革命对联选 (A Collection of Revolutionary Couplets). 22 September 1966. CCPMD.

Shoudu Xinshenghuo yundong cujinhui 首都新生活運動促進會, ed. *Shoudu Xinshenghuo yundong gaikuang* 首都新生活運動概況 (An Overview of the New Life Movement in the Capital). Nanjing Municipal Government, 1935.

Simmel, Georg. 'The Metropolis and Mental Life'. In *The Blackwell City Reader*, edited by Gary Bridge and Sophie Watson, 11–19. Malden and Oxford: Blackwell Publishers, 2002.

'Sociology of the Senses'. Translated by Mark Ritter and David Frisby. In *Simmel on Culture: Selected Writings*, edited by David Frisby and Mike Featherstone, 109–20. London: Sage, 1997.

Smith, Arthur H. *Chinese Characteristics*. Norwalk: EastBridge, 2003.

Smith, Mark. *Sensing the Past: Seeing, Hearing, Smelling, Tasting, and Touching in History*. Berkeley: University of California Press, 2007.

Sensory History. Oxford: Berg, 2007.

A Sensory History Manifesto. Philadelphia: Pennsylvania University Press, 2021.

Smell and History: A Reader. Morgantown: West Virginia University Press, 2019.

Smith, Richard J. *The Qing Dynasty and Traditional Chinese Culture*. Lanham: Rowman & Littlefield, 2015.

Snow, Edgar. *Red Star over China*. New York: The Modern Library, 1944.

Song Zhichao 宋志超 et al., eds. *Aiguo weisheng yundong* 爱国卫生运动 (The Patriotic Hygiene Movement). Beijing: Renmin weisheng chubanshe, 1953.

Soothill, Lucy. *A Passport to China: Being the Tale of Her Long and Friendly Sojourning amongst a Strangely Interesting People*. London: Hodder and Stoughton, 1931.

Spence, Jonathan D. *The Chan's Great Continent: China in Western Minds*. New York: W.W. Norton, 1998.

The Search for Modern China. New York: Norton, 1990.

Staunton, George L. *An Authentic Account of an Embassy from the King of Great Britain to the Emperor of China*. 2 vols. London: G. Nicol, 1797.

Stoddart, D. Michael. *The Scented Ape: The Biology and Culture of Human Odour*. Cambridge: Cambridge University Press, 1990.

Stokes, Edward, and Hedda Morrison. *Hong Kong As It Was: Hedda Morrison's Photographs 1946–47*. Hong Kong: Hong Kong University Press, 2009.

Stoller, Paul. *The Taste of Ethnographic Things: The Senses in Anthropology*. Philadelphia, PA: University of Pennsylvania Press, 2010.

Strauss, Julia. 'Morality, Coercion and State Building by Campaign in the Early PRC: Regime Consolidation and after, 1949–1956'. *China Quarterly* 188, no. 1 (2006): 891–912.

Su Jizu 蘇繼祖. *Qingting Wuxu chaobian ji* 清廷戊戌朝變記 (On the Hundred Days' Reform). Guilin: Guangxi shifan daxue chubanshe, 2008.

Sun Baoxuan 孫寶瑄. *Wangshanlu riji* 忘山盧日記 (Diaries from Wangshan Studio), vol. 2. Shanghai: Shanghai guji chubanshe, 1983.

Sun Qian 孙倩. *Shanghai jindai chengshi gonggong guanli zhidu yu kongjian jianshe* 上海近代城市公共管理制度与空间建设 (Municipal Management and Urban Planning in Modern Shanghai). Nanjing: Dongnan daxue chubanshe, 2009.

Süskind, Patrick. *Perfume: The Story of a Murderer*. Translated by John Woods. New York: Vintage International, 2001.

Swislocki, Mark. *Culinary Nostalgia: Regional Food Culture and the Urban Experience in Shanghai*. Stanford: Stanford University Press, 2009.

Tang Xianzu 湯顯祖. *Mudan ting* 牡丹亭 (The Peony Pavilion). Beijing: Renmin wenxue chubanshe, 2005.

   The Peony Pavilion. Translated by Cyril Birch. Bloomington, IN: Indiana University Press, 1980.

Teiwes, Frederick C. *Politics at Mao's Court: Gao Gang and Party Factionalism in the Early 1950s*. New York: M. E. Sharpe, 1990.

Thich Nhat Hanh. *Peace Is Every Step: The Path of Mindfulness in Everyday Life*. London: Rider, 1995.

Thomson, Murray. *A Daring Confidence: The Life and Times of Andrew Thomson in China, 1906–1942*. Ottawa: M. M. Thomson, 1992.

Tong Shilin 童士林. 'Guangshenghang diaocha baogao 廣生行調查報告' (An Investigation of Kwong Sang Hong). SMA, Q78-2-13341.

Treves, Frederick. *The Other Side of the Lantern: An Account of a Commonplace Tour around the World*. New York: Funk & Wagnalls Company, 1904.

Tsing, Anna Lowenhaupt. *The Mushroom at the End of the World: On the Possibility of Life in Capitalist Ruins*. Princeton, NJ: Princeton University Press, 2015.

Tu, Feng-en. 'Japan's Empire of Scents: Commerce, Science, and the Modern Senses of Health and Cleanliness'. PhD dissertation, Harvard University, 2019.

Tu Xianglin 屠祥麟 and Che Zhiyi 車志義. *Huazhuang pin ji xiangliao zhizao fa* 化妝品及香料製造法 (Methods of Making Cosmetics and Perfumes). Nanjing: Zhengzhong shuju, 1937.

Tullett, William. *Smell in Eighteenth-Century England: A Social Sense*. Oxford: Oxford University Press, 2019.

Tullett, William, Inger Leemans, Hsuan Hsu, Stephanie Weismann, Cecilia Bembibre, Melanie A. Kiechle, Duane Jethro, Anna Chen, Xuelei Huang,

Jorge Otero-Pailos, and Mark Bradley. 'Smell, History, and Heritage'. *American Historical Review* 127, no. 1 (2022): 261–309.

Vigarello, Georges. *Concepts of Cleanliness: Changing Attitudes in France since the Middle Ages.* Translated by Jean Birrell. Cambridge: Cambridge University Press, 1988.

Wagner, Rudolf. 'China "Asleep" and "Awakening." A Study in Conceptualizing Asymmetry and Coping with It'. *Journal of Transcultural Studies* 2, no. 1 (2011): 4–139.

Wang, Ban. *The Sublime Figure of History: Aesthetics and Politics in Twentieth-Century China.* Stanford: Stanford University Press, 1997.

——— ed. *Words and Their Stories: Essays on the Language of the Chinese Revolution.* Leiden: Brill, 2010.

Wang, David Der-Wei. *Fictional Realism in Twentieth-Century China: Mao Dun, Lao She, Shen Congwen.* New York: Columbia University Press, 1992.

Wang Shifu 王實甫. *The Romance of the Western Chamber.* Translated by S. I. Hsiung. New York: Columbia University Press, 1968.

——— *Xixiang ji* 西廂記 (The Romance of the Western Chamber). Shanghai: Shiji chuban jituan, 2003.

Wang Zisong 汪子嵩, Wang Qingshu 王庆淑, Zhang Enci 张恩慈, Tao Yang 陶阳, and Gan Lin甘霖. 'Pipan Hu Shi de fandong zhengzhi sixiang 批判胡适的反动政治思想' (A Criticism of Hu Shi's Reactionary Political Thought). *RMRB*, 17 December 1954, 3.

Weinbaum, Alys Eve, Lynn M. Thomas, Priti Ramamurthy, Uta G. Poiger, Madeleine Yue Dong, and Tani Barlow, eds. *The Modern Girl around the World: Consumption, Modernity, and Globalization.* Durham, NC: Duke University Press, 2008.

Wen Rumin 温儒敏. '"Feizao" de jingshen fenxi jiedu 《肥皂》的精神分析解读' (A Psychoanalytic Reading of 'Soap'). *Luxun yanjiu dongtai* 鲁迅研究动态 2 (1989): 12–17.

Wen Zhenheng 文震亨. *Zhangwuzhi* 長物志 (Treatise on Superfluous Things). Hang Zhou: Zhejiang renmin meishu chubanshe, 2016.

Wenhuibao bianjibu《文汇报》编辑部. 'Geming zaofan youli wansui 革命造反有理万岁' (Long Live Revolutionary Rebellions). *Wenhuibao*, 6 January 1967, n.p.

Williams, Raymond. *Keywords: A Vocabulary of Culture and Society.* Oxford: Oxford University Press, 2015.

Wilson, Donald A., and Richard J. Stevenson. *Learning to Smell: Olfactory Perception from Neurobiology to Behavior.* Baltimore: Johns Hopkins University Press, 2006.

Wilson, James Harrison. *China: Travels and Investigations in the 'Middle Kingdom'. A Study of Its Civilization and Possibilities, with a Glance at Japan.* New York: D. Appleton, 1901.

Withey, Lynne. *Grand Tours and Cook's Tours: A History of Leisure Travel, 1750 to 1915*. London: Aurum, 1998.

Woolgar, Christopher M. *The Senses in Late Medieval England*. New Haven: Yale University Press, 2006.

Wright, Arnold, and Henry A. Cartwright. *Twentieth Century Impressions of Hong Kong, Shanghai and Other Treaty Ports of China: History, People, Commerce, Industries, and Resources*. London: Lloyd's Greater Britain Publishing Company, 1908.

Wright, David. *Translating Science: The Transmission of Western Chemistry into Late Imperial China, 1840–1900*. Leiden: Brill, 2000.

Wu Jen-shu 巫仁恕. *Youyou fangxiang: Mingqing Jiangnan chengshi de xiuxian xiaofei yu kongjian bianqian* 優游坊廂：明清江南城市的休閑消費與空間變遷 (Wandering across the City: Leisure Consumption and Spatial Changes in Jiangnan in the Ming and Qing Dynasties). Taipei: Academia Sinica, 2013.

Wu Juanjuan 吳娟娟. 'Xiangliao yu Tangdai shehui shenghuo 香料與唐代社會生活' (Spice and Daily Life of the Tang Dynasty). Master's thesis, Anhui University, 2010.

Wu, Shengqing. *Photo Poetics: Chinese Lyricism and Modern Media Culture*. New York: Columbia University Press, 2020.

Wu, Shengqing, and Xuelei Huang, eds. *Sensing China: Modern Transformations of Sensory Culture*. Abingdon: Routledge, 2022.

Wu, Shih-ch'ang. *On The Red Chamber Dream: A Critical Study of Two Annotated Manuscripts of the XVIIIth Century*. Oxford: Clarendon Press, 1961.

Xiao Aishu 肖爱树. '1949–1959 nian Aiguo weisheng yundong shulun 1949–1959 年爱国卫生运动述论' (On the Patriotic Hygiene Movement in 1949–1959). *Dangdai zhongguo shi yanjiu* 当代中国史研究 10, no. 1 (January 2003): 97–102.

Xiaoxiao sheng 笑笑生. *Jin ping mei* 金瓶梅 (The Plum in the Golden Vase). Taipei: Sanmin, 2017.

The Plum in the Golden Vase, or, Chin P'ing Mei. Translated by David Tod Roy. 5 vols. Princeton: Princeton University Press, 1993–2011.

Xinhua she 新华社. 'Kexuejia men tongchi youpai 科学家们痛斥右派' (Scientists Condemned the Rightists). *RMRB*, 22 June 1957, 3.

Xu Jinxiong 許進雄. *Zhongguo gudai shehui: Wenzi yu renleixue de toushi* 中國古代社會：文字與人類學的透視 (Ancient Chinese Society: Through the Looking Glass of Chinese Script and Anthropology). Taipei: Shangwu yinshuguan, 1988.

Xu Shen 許慎. *Shuowen jiezi* 說文解字 (Explaining Graphs and Analysing Characters). https://ctext.org/shuo-wen-jie-zi.

Xu, Yamin. 'Policing Civility on the Streets: Encounters with Litterbugs, "Nightsoil Lords," and Street Corner Urinators in Republican Beijing'. *Twentieth-Century China* 30, no. 2 (2005): 28–71.

Xue Liyong 薛理勇. *Lao Shanghai pu tang jing bang* 老上海浦塘泾浜 (Rivers, Ponds and Creeks in Old Shanghai). Shanghai: Shanghai shudian chubanshe, 2015.

Xunzi 荀子. *Xunzi* 荀子. https://ctext.org/xunzi.

Xunzi, and John Knoblock. *Xunzi: A Translation and Study of the Complete Works*. Stanford: Stanford University Press, 1988.

Yan Xiaoqing 严小青. 'Qianyan 前言' (Foreword). In Chen Jing 陳敬, *Xinzuan xiangpu* 新纂香譜 (New Book on Perfume), edited by Yan Xiaoqing, 1–6. Beijing: Zhonghua shuju, 2012.

Yan Yan 闫艳. 'Gudai xiangnang de xingzhi jiqi wenhua yiyi 古代香囊的形制及其文化意义' (The Shapes and Cultural Meanings of Perfumed Sachets in Ancient China). *Neimenggu shifan daxue xuebao* 内蒙古师范大学学报 35, no. 2 (March 2006), 119–22.

Yang Er 杨耳. 'Tan lichang wenti 谈立场问题' (On Political Stance). *Zhongguo qingnian* 中国青年 14 (1957). CCPMD.

Yang Huali 楊華麗. '1924–1949: luexian jimo de "Feizao" yanjiu 1924–1949: 略顯寂寞的《肥皂》研究' (1924–1949: The Underdeveloped Field of Research on 'Soap'). *Mianyang shifan xueyuan xuebao* 绵阳师范学院学报 37, no. 6 (2018): 14–21.

Yang Jiang 楊絳. *Xizao* 洗澡 (Bath). Beijing: Renmin wenxue chubanshe, 2004.

Yang Yi 楊逸, ed. *Shanghai shi zizhi zhi* 上海市自治志 (Gazetteer of Shanghai under Self-Governance). Reprinted in *Zhongguo fangzhi congshu* 中國方志叢書 (Local Gazetteers Collection). Taipei: Chengwen chuban gongsi, 1974.

Yao Wenyuan 姚文元. 'Ping xinbian lishiju *Hairui baguan* 评新编历史剧《海瑞罢官》' (Review of the New Historical Play *Hai Rui Dismissed from Office*). *Wenhui bao*, 10 November 1965, n.p.; *RMRB*, 30 November 1965, 5.

Ye Wenyuan 鄢文远. 'Ba woguo xiuzheng zhuyi zong houtai saodao lishi lajidui li qu 把我国修正主义总后台扫到历史垃圾堆里去' (Sweep the Big Boss of the Revisionists in Our Country into the Trash Bin of History). *RMRB*, 11 April 1967, 4.

Yu, Anthony C. *Rereading the Stone: Desire and the Making of Fiction in Dream of the Red Chamber*. Princeton: Princeton University Press, 1997.

Yu Dafu 郁達夫. 'Chenlun 沈淪' (Sinking). In *Yu Dafu wenji* 郁達夫文集 (An Anthology of Yu Dafu), vol. 1, 16–53. Hong Kong: Sanlian shudian, 1982.

'Kongxu 空虛' (Emptiness). In *Yu Dafu wenji* 郁達夫文集 (An Anthology of Yu Dafu), vol. 1, 153–72. Hong Kong: Sanlian shudian, 1982.

'Nanqian 南遷' (Moving to the South). In *Yu Dafu wenji* 郁達夫文集 (An Anthology of Yu Dafu), vol. 1, 54–99. Hong Kong: Sanlian shudian, 1982.

'Sinking'. Translated by Joseph Lau and C. T. Hsia. In *The Columbia Anthology of Modern Chinese Literature*, edited by Joseph Lau and Howard Goldblatt, 44–69. New York: Columbia University Press, 1995.

'Yinhuise de si 銀灰色的死' (Silver Death). In *Yu Dafu wenji* 郁達夫文集 (An Anthology of Yu Dafu), vol. 1, 1–15. Hong Kong: Sanlian shudian, 1982.

Yu Miin-ling 余敏玲. *Xingsu 'xinren': Zhonggong xuanchuan yu Sulian jingyan* 形塑'新人'：中共宣傳與蘇聯經驗 (Shaping the 'New Man': Propaganda of the Chinese Communist Party and Soviet Experience). Taipei: Academia Sinica, 2015.

Yu, Xingzhong. 'The Treatment of Night Soil and Waste in Modern China'. In *Health and Hygiene in Chinese East Asia: Policies and Publics in the Long Twentieth Century*, edited by Angela Ki Che Leung and Charlotte Furth, 51–72. Durham, NC: Duke University Press, 2010.

'Qingdai Jiangnan de weisheng guannian yu xingwei jiqi jindai bianqian chutan: yi huanjing he yongshui weisheng wei zhongxin 清代江南的卫生观念与行为及其近代变迁初探—以环境和用水卫生为中心' (A Preliminary Investigation of the Concept and Practice of Hygiene in the Qing-Era Lower Yangtze Delta and Its Modern Transformation, with a Focus on the Environment and Water). *Qing shi yanjiu* 清史研究 2 (May 2006): 12–26.

Yuan Xieming 袁爕銘. 'Gongbuju yu Shanghai luzheng 工部局與上海路政 (1854–1911)' (The Municipal Council and Road Construction in Shanghai, 1854–1911). In *Shanghai yanjiu luncong* 上海研究论丛 (A Compendium of Shanghai Studies), edited by Shanghai shi difangzhi bangongshi, 169–205. Shanghai: Shanghai shehui kexue chubanshe, 1989.

Zhang Deyi 張德彝. 'Hanghai shuqi 航海述奇' (Strange Things on My Voyage). In *Zouxiang shijie congshu* 走向世界叢書, vol. 1, edited by Zhong Shuhe 鍾叔河, 405–608. Changsha: Yuelu shushe, 1985.

'Ou Mei huanyou ji 歐美環遊記' (Round Trip across Europe and America). In *Zouxiang shijie congshu* 走向世界叢書, vol. 1, edited by Zhong Shuhe 鍾叔河, 609–831. Changsha: Yuelu shushe, 1985.

'Suishi Faguo ji 隨使法國記' (My Diplomatic Mission to France). In *Zouxiang shijie congshu* 走向世界叢書, vol. 2, edited by Zhong Shuhe 鍾叔河, 287–600. Changsha: Yuelu shushe, 1985.

Zhang Jingsheng 張競生. *Xingshi* 性史 (History of Sex). Beijing: Shijie tushu chuban gongsi, 2014.

Zhang Rui 张瑞. 'Muyu yu weisheng: Qing ren dui muyu renshi de fazhan he zhuanbian 沐浴与卫生：清人对沐浴认识的发展和转变' (Bathing and Hygiene: The Development and Transformation of the Understanding of Bathing in the Qing Dynasty). In *Qing yilai de jibing, yiliao he weisheng: yi shehui wenhuashi wei shijiao de tansuo* 清以来的疾病, 医疗和卫生: 以社会文化史为视

角的探索 (Disease, Medicine, and Hygiene: An Investigation from the Perspective of Social and Cultural History), edited by Yu Xingzhong, 281–99. Beijing: Sanlian shudian, 2009.

Zhang Ziping 張資平. 'Ai zhi jiaodian 愛之焦點' (The Focal Point of Love). *Chuangzao jikan* 創造季刊 1, no. 4 (1923): 26–42.

'Meiling zhi chu 梅嶺之春' (Spring on the Plum Mountain), *Dongfang zazhi* 東方雜誌 21, no. 20 (1924): 85–100.

'Wo de chuangzuo jingguo 我的創作經過' (My Path of Fiction Writing). In *Zhang Ziping xuanji* 張資平選集 (Selected Works of Zhang Ziping), edited by Xu Chensi 徐沉泗 and Ye Wangyou 葉忘憂, 1–10. Shanghai: Wanxiang shuwu, 1936.

'Yuetanhe zhi shui 約檀河之水' (The Water of the Jordan River). *Xueyi* 學藝 2, no. 8 (1920): 1–12.

Zheng Guanying 鄭觀應. 'Xiulu 修路' (Street Paving). In *Zheng Guanying ji* 鄭觀應集 (Selected Works of Zheng Guanying), edited by Xia Dongyuan 夏東元, vol. 1. Shanghai: Shanghai renmin chubanshe, 1982.

Zheng, Yangwen. *The Social Life of Opium in China*. Cambridge: Cambridge University Press, 2005.

Zheng Zunfa 鄭尊法. *Xiangliao ji huazhuangpin* 香料及化妝品 (Perfumes and Cosmetics). Shanghai: Shangwu yinshuguan, 1931.

Zhongguo jiu haiguan shiliao bianji weiyuanhui 《中國舊海關史料》編輯委員會 et al., eds. *Zhongguo jiu haiguan shiliao* 中國舊海關史料 (Archival Materials of the Chinese Maritime Customs). 170 vols. Beijing: Jinghua chubanshe, 2001.

Zhou Jiazhou 周嘉冑. *Xiang sheng* 香乘 (Book of Perfume). In *Jing yin wenyuange siku quanshu* 景印文淵閣四庫全書, vol. 844. Taipei: Shangwu yinshuguan, 1983.

Zhou Shoujuan 周瘦鵑. 'Duanchangren riji 斷腸人日記' (The Diary of a Heartbroken Man). *Libailiu* 52 (May 1915): 25–48.

Zhou Yang 周扬. 'Wenyi zhanxian shang de yichang da bianlun 文艺战线上的一场大辩论' (A Big Debate on the Front Line of Literature and Art) (16 September 1957). *RMRB*, 28 February 1958, 2.

Zhu Chongke 朱崇科. '"Feizao" yinyu de qianxing yu pojie <肥皂>隱喻的潛行與破解' (An Interpretation of the Allegories in 'Soap'). *Mingzuo xinshang* 名作欣賞, no. 11 (2008): 61–5.

Zhuangzi 莊子. *Zhuangzi* 莊子. https://ctext.org/zhuangzi.

Zhuangzi, and Burton Watson. *The Complete Works of Chuang Tzu*. New York: Columbia University Press, 1968.

Zhuquan jushi 珠泉居士. *Xu Banqiao zaji* 續板橋雜記 (A Sequel to *The Miscellaneous Notes of Banqiao*), vol. 1. Nanjing: Nanjing chubanshe, 2006.

Index

4711 eau de cologne, 152, 176, 180
A. S. Watson & Co., 148
Abel, Clarke, 68, 71, 74, 89
Aisin-Gioro Pu Yi, 171
ambivalence, 3, 11–13, 18, 51, 65, 73, 78, 92, 136, 201, 207, 210, 214, 221, 236, 247, 251. *See also* indeterminacy
'Anthropology from a Pragmatic Point of View' (Kant), 243
Anti-Rightist Campaign, 225–7, 233, 239
Apter, David, 221, 228
Arendt, Hannah, 221
Axel, Richard, 5–7

baihe zhi xiang (Hundred Blend incense), 44, 58–9
Baimao nü (White-haired Girl), 240
Ball, James, 68, 70
Barmé, Geremie, 224
Barthes, Roland, 79
Barwich, Anne-Sophie, 7, 246
Baudrillard, Jean, 145, 176, 218
Bauman, Zygmunt, 3, 11–12
Bei Dao, 252
Birch, John G., 84, 90
Bird-Bishop, Isabella, 77
Bonnard, Abel, 76, 85–6
Braester, Yomi, 133
British Dispensary, 148
Brown Windsor Soap, 168
Buck, Linda, 5
Buddhism, 42–3, 51, 151
    emptiness and, 54
    olfactory perception and, 246
    perfume culture and, 23
Burroughs Wellcome & Co. Ltd., 150–1, 153–6

Butterfly (*Wudi*) moisturizer, 166, 178. *See also Wudi* (Peerless)

Cai Yuanpei, 96
calendar posters, 151, 153, 164, 181
'Canchun' (Late Spring) (Guo Moruo), 196–7
Cao Xueqin, 31–4, 50–1, 61. *See also Dream of the Red Chamber* (Hongloumeng) (Cao Xueqin)
Chadwick, Edwin, 69, 105–6, 119
Chandeler, Charles Frederick, 249
Chanel No. 5 170
Chang, Eileen, 196
The Chemistry of Common Life (Johnston), 171
Chen Diexian, 166, 178
Chen Duxiu, 96
Chen Jianhua, 208
'Chenlun' (Sinking) (Yu Dafu), 189
Chiang, Connie Y., 76
'China stinks' discourse, 66, 84, 89, 92, 94, 96, 112, 123, 247
China Chemical Industries, 166
'Chinese deficiency' rhetoric, 112, 123, 136
Chinese exotic, cult of, 86
Chinese Studies, 16
    'visual turn' in, 17
chou (smell, stink), 5, 9, 104, 127, 228, 232, 238
choufu (foul and rotten), 21
'Chuangzao' (Creation) (Mao Dun), 208–10
Chuci (The Songs of the South) (Qu Yuan), 240
Cixi, Empress Dowager, 58
Classen, Constance, 14, 17
Claudel, Paul, 87

Cochran, Jean, 63
Cold Fragrance Pill, 54–5
Colgate, 152
Condillac, Étienne Bonnot de, 200
The Condition of the Working-Class in England in 1844 (Engels), 69
contamination
    bad smells and, 41–2
    of beauty, 61
    beauty and, 55
    by the other, 83
    chemical frangrances and, 175
    discourse of, 64–6, 94, 96
    of European modernity, 32
    lust and, 56
    parables of, 184, 251
    purity and, 13, 25–6, 34, 50, 58, 60, 62, 89, 102, 116, 246
    sanctified space and, 44
    sexual intimacy and, 47
    sexual odour and, 190
    social, 4
    stagnant water and, 101
    stench and, 134
    strangers as smells and, 247
Cooke, George, 73, 82, 88
Corbin, Alain, 2–3, 14, 63, 92, 105
Cornaby, William, 68, 84
Creation Society, 192–201, 208
Crow, Carl, 153
Cui Yingying, 195
cultural construction theory, 17
Cultural Revolution, 226–7, 229, 233–4, 238–9
culture, space of, 45–6

Dai Chunlin, 146, 172
Dal Lago, Francesca, 176
Daly, Emily, 77
Daxue (The Great Learning), 20
de (virtue), 23
de Guignes, Joseph, 90
deodorization
    colonial, 107–20, 128
    fengshui and, 116
    Public Health Act and, 110–11
    sanitary engineering and, 105–6
    sexual odour and, 190
    Shanghai Land Regulations (SLR) and, 110–11
    Shanghai Municipal Council (SMC) and, 111–16

social stratification and, 129–30
socialist, 132–41
stagnant water trope and, 103–7
techniques of, 102–3
Ding Wei, 23, 46n65
Dingle, Edwin, 92
douchou/pichou (stinken), 231–5
Douglas, Mary, 89
Dragon Beard Ditch, 132, 137
Dream of the Red Chamber (Hongloumeng) (Cao Xueqin)
    aroma in, 32–4
    authorship debate and, 34
    femininity in, 177
    L'Essence de Fleurs and, 50–8, 60
    outsider smells and, 58–61
    perfume culture and, 146
    scenting of bodies in, 35–41, 72, 175
    scenting of living spaces in, 35–6
    scenting of space in, 180
    scenting of time and space in, 41–50
Duburquois, Alexandre, 109
dudou (chest cover), 47–8
Dukes, Edwin, 71, 74, 80, 84, 87
Dupée, Jeffrey, 74

Edwards, Louise, 54
Ellis, Havelock, 190, 215–17
Engels, Friedrich, 69

'Fandui dang bagu' (Oppose Stereotyped Party Writing) (Mao Zedong), 232
Fang Yexian, 166
femininity, 50–8, 61
fen (muck), 40, 153, 223, 228
Feng Futian, 161
fengshui, 116
fentu (dung, muck), 220, 234
'five scents' (*wuxiu*) theory, 20
Florida water, 149, 152, 159n56, 163, 167n80, 172, 175n110, 180
food smell, 74–9
    otherness of, 75–9
    racial stereoptying and, 76–9
The Foul and the Fragrant (Le Miasme et la Jonquille) (Corbin), 2, 14
'Fox Stench and Sweet Aroma', 252
fragrance. *See also* perfume culture
    culture of, 23
    pictographic symbol for, 5
fragrances, synthetic, 170–5
fragrant blossoms (*xianghua*), 235–40

fragrant breezes (*xiangfeng*), 235–40
Frank, Robert, 78
Freud, Sigmund, 81, 190
Fryer, John, 171

'Gaochou zichan jieji de geren zhuyi' (Make
    Bourgeois Individualism Stink), 233
garlic, 76–8
Geaney, Jane, 20
Gordon, Charles, 84
Gordon-Cumming, Constance, 66
Goubert, Jean-Pierre, 126
Gray, Richard, 51
Great China-France Drugstore, 167
great divide theory, 16
Great Five Continents Drugstore, 167
Great Stink, the, 15, 70, 125
Guo Moruo, 192, 196–7
Guoyu (Warring States collection), 23

H. Fogg & Co., 147
Haishang hua liezhuan (The Sing-song Girls
    of Shanghai) (Han Bangqing), 192
Halle, Jean-Noël, 2–3
Han Bangqing, 192
Han wudi (Emperor Wu), 23
hanjin (cummberbund), 47
hanxiang (chilly fragrance), 56–7, 176
Hazeline Snow, 150–1, 156
hebao (perfume sachet), 36, 47
Hengbang Creek (Hengbanghe), 136
'Hong meigui yu bai meigui' (Red Rose,
    White Rose) (Eileen Chang), 196
Hong (Rainbow) (Mao Dun), 208
Hongdeng ji (The Legend of the Red
    Lantern), 240
Hongkou, 109, 113–17, 135
Household Industries, 166, 178
Howes, David, 14, 16–17, 191
Hsu, Hsuan, 102
Hu Feng, 224
Hu Feng Clique, 223
Hu Feng Incident, 225
Hu Shih (Hu Shi), 192, 232
'Huanmie' (Disillusionment) (Mao Dun),
    210–14
huchou (fox stench), 252
Hundred Days' Reform, 95
Hundred Flowers Campaign, 224–6, 229
Hunter, William C., 78
hygiene, 218. *See also* perfume culture;
    scenting:of bodies

hygienic modernity, 69, 102, 181
Imperial Chemical Industries, 171
indeterminacy, 3, 13, 213, 248
    of scent, 201–7
Inglis, David, 106
intimacy, space of, 46–8

J. Llewellyn & Co., 145, 148
Jamieson, Alexander, 120, 249
Jenner, Mark, 18, 76
Ji Fengyuan, 222
jiao (smoky), 19, 49
Jin Ping Mei (The Plum in the Golden Vase)
    (Xiaoxiao sheng), 193
Jin Yucheng, 141
John Gosnell & Co., 147
Johnston, James, 171
Johnston, Reginald Fleming, 171
Jones, Andrew, 13

Kant, Immanuel, 61, 243
    disgust and, 92–3
Kazantzakis, Nikos, 87
Kiechle, Melanie, 66
King Lear (Shakespeare), 101, 104
kong (emptiness), 54
Kong Fengchun, 146
'Kuangren riji' (A Madman's Diary) (Lu
    Xun), 251
Kwong Sang Hong (KSH), 161–4, 169, 172

L'Essence de Fleurs, 50–8, 60
    in perfume advertising, 163
Lao miaoxiang shi, 146
Lao She, 132
Lean, Eugenia, 166
Lee, Haiyan, 3n10, 216
Lengxue, 250
Lévi-Strauss, Claude, 253–4
li (ritual principles), 21
Li Pingshu, 123
Li Tuo, 224
Li Weihan, 225
Li Yu, 40
Liang Qichao, 191
Liddell, Thomas, 71
Lin Daiyu, 32, 35, 39, 47–9, 52–7, 176, 178,
    190, 210
Lingling Incident, 225
Link, Perry, 225
Literary Revolution (1917), 192
Little, Alicia, 80

Little, Archibald, 67
Locke, John, 92
Lu Xun, 201–7, 251

MacMillan, Margaret, 85
'Mandarin Duck and Butterfly' school, 192
Mao Dun, 143, 208–14
Mao Zedong, 26, 133, 136, 143–4, 163
    fragrant blossoms rhetoric of, 235–40
    fragrant breezes rhetoric of, 235–40
    political use of smell, 219–43
    rhetoric of 'stinken' in, 231–5
    use of excremental metaphors, 228–31
Maospeak, 224, 228–9, 231, 233, 239
May Fourth China, 26, 96, 166, 198, 200,
    208–14, 252
    olfactophilia and, 190–5, 208–18
May Fourth Movement, 192
    European modernist literature and, 217
McLuhan, Marshall, 16
'Meiling zhi chun' (Spring on the Plum
    Mountain) (Zhang Ziping), 194–5
Menninghaus, Winfried, 93
Miao Cheng Shuyi, 183
miasma theory, 104–5, 123
Miller, William, 92, 101
Mingxing Chemical Company, 162
Morris, T. M., 68, 72
Morrison, George, 91
Morrison, Hedda, 76
Mudan ting (The Peony Pavilion) (Tang
    Xianzu), 195
Murray & Lanman Florida water, 152

Nahan (Call to Arms) (Lu Xun), 204
Nanjing Road, 128, 162, 164, 236–8
'Nanqian' (Moving to the South) (Yu
    Dafu), 200
National Products Movement, 163
neophobia, 78
neural network, of smell, 7, 137, 248. See also
    olfaction:brain activity and
neural plasticity, 10, 97, 137, 152, 172, 227,
    243, 252
neurasthenia, sexual, 216
New Book on Perfume (Xinzuan xiangpu)
    (Chen Jing), 46, 169
New Life Movement, 183
new sensationalism (Xin ganjue pai), 176
Nihongdeng xia de shaobing (Sentinals under
    the Neon Lights), 236–8

Ningbo Cemetery Riots, 116
Nongcun sanbuqu (Village Trilogy) (Mao
    Dun), 208

Odeuropa project, 15
olfaction
    animalistic heritage of, 5–6
    brain activity and, 5–8, 10–11
    Chinese vocabulary of, 19–24
    survival abilities of, 5, 10, 223
olfactophilia, 26, 190–5, 198–201, 208–18
olfactory revolution, 4, 32, 102, 104, 221
    advertising and, 152
    department stores and, 148
    growth of capitalism and, 150–61
    impacts of, 183–4
    of Mao, 221
    perfuming and, 144
    socialist, 136–7
    synthetic fragrances and, 170–5
olfactory studies, 14
'On the Correct Handling of
    Contradictions among the People'
    (Mao Zedong), 239
opium
    sensuality of, 82–3
    in travel writing, 79–83
Opium Wars, 79, 82
Orientalism, 65, 86
Orwell, George, 9, 221
otherness. See also stranger metaphor
    food smell and, 75–9
    garlic and, 76–8
Ouyang Yuqian, 239

Paladino, Carl, 242
Palmolive and Peet, 152
Patriotic Hygiene Movement (PHM),
    133–4, 231
Payne, Robert, 220
Perfume (Süskind), 31, 50–1
perfume culture, 36, 61
    bodies in time and space and, 175–83
    Chinese perfume industry and, 161–7
    commercial growth of, 147–61
    cult of the scented body and, 153–6
    department stores and, 148, 167
    European beauty industry and, 149–51
    golden age of Western cosmetics and, 158
    growth of capitalism and, 150–61
    impacts of, 183–4

Japanese cosmetics and, 159
moralistic criticisms of, 183
scenting of space and, 179–82
sinicization in advertising and, 164–6
synthetic fragrances and, 170–5
vocabulary of, 167–75
Western imports and, 145–6
perfume revolution, 23
perfuming. *See* scenting
pi (fart), 223, 228, 235
Pond's Extract Vanishing Cream, 151–2
Pratt, Mary, 70
Pro Viventibus, 60
Public Health Act (1848), 105, 110–11
purity
contamination and, 13, 25–6, 34, 50, 58,
60, 62, 89, 102, 116, 246
female, 50–2, 54
ideals of, 32
sexual, 56
Pye, Lucian, 222

'Qin Yuan Chun –Changsha' (Changsha, to
the melody of Qin Yuan Chun) (Mao
Zedong), 220
Qu Yuan, 72, 241

Red Inkstone (Zhiyanzhai), 53, 55–6
Redology, 32
*Report on the Sanitary Condition of the
Labouring Population of Great Britain*
(Chadwick), 69, 105
revererance, space of, 41–4
Rogaski, Ruth, 104, 111–12
Ross, Edward, 69
Russell, Bertrand, 87

Saich, Tony, 221, 228
Said, Edward, 65, 86
scented ornaments, 38
scenting
of bodies, 38–41
of living spaces, 35–6
of space, 41–50
of time, 48–9
Self, the Other and, 69–70, 72, 83
*Senses and Sensation: Critical and Primary
Sources* (Howes), 14
sensorial hierarchy, 17
sensory turn, the, 14–19
sensualism, 2, 92, 104, 200

sexual odour, 190, 193, 196, 201, 212, 214–18
Shakespeare, William, 101, 104
shan/sao (gamy), 19, 49
Shanghai
'Chinese deficiency' rhetoric and, 123
deodorizaton effects on social
stratification in, 129–30
destruction of city walls, 126–8
environmental pressures of urbanization
and, 123–4
modern sanitary degradation of, 123
modern sanitary ideology and, 124–5
pre-modern sanitary conditions of, 120–3
sanitary policing in, 125–6
Shanghai Land Regulations (SLR), 110–11
Shanghai Municipal Council (SMC),
111–16
Shangshu (Book of Documents), 22
Shao Yanxiang, 230
Shenbao, xiv, 94, 124, 152, 179, 182
shenqi (rare and unearthly), 21
Shi (Eclipse) (Mao Dun), 208
shi (shit), 20, 223, 228
Shishuo xinyu (A New Account of the Tales
of the World), 232
Shuowen jiezi (Explaining Graphs and
Analyzing Characters), 5
Simmel, Georg, 8–9, 144
Sincere Department Store, 167
smell
ambivalence and, 11–13
animalistic nature of, 5–6, 24, 191, 214–18
animalization of, 191
class distinctions and, 59
emotions and, 10
eroticism and, 197–8
excremental metaphors and, 228–31
femininity and, 50–8, 61
food, 74–9
grammar of, 10–11
methodological significance of, 65
political sense of, 223–8
polysemic nature of, 10
private language of, 8
racialization of, 72–4
scientific understanding of, 5–12
sensuality and, 198–201
sexology and, 215–17
sexual awakening and, 190–5, 210–14
social language of, 9–10
as stranger, 70, 221

Smell and History (Smith), 15
smellscapes
   changes in, 4, 18, 26, 63, 139, 149
   in *Dream of the Red Chamber*, 58
   ecological shifts and, 125
   globally homongenous, 181
   literary, 217
   modern, 107
   multi-layered, 141
   poetic vibe of, 86
   refined, 94
   re-ordering of, 103
   revolutionizing of, 103
   seasonal rhythm of, 38
   Shanghai, 109, 120
   taming of, 112
Smith, Arthur, 71
Snow, Edgar, 143
'Soap' (Feizao) (Lu Xun), 201–7, 218
'Sociology of the Senses' (Simmel), 8–9
solicitude, repressive, 218
Spence, Jonathan, 86
stagnant water trope, 103–7
stench
   allegorical meaning of, in Communism,
    133
   Chinese discourse of, 94–7
   as othering, 9, 69
   technology of, 67–9
   in travel writing, 67–70
stereotypes
   of Chinese cruelty, 91
   of body odour, 70–2
'stinken' (*douchou/pichou*), 231–5
Stoddart, D. Michael, 214
stranger metaphor, 3–14, 70, 90, 94, 207,
   221
Studies in the Psychology of Sex (Ellis), 215
Sun Baoxuan, 95
Sun Sun Department Store, 180
Süskind, Patrick, 31, 50–1
Suzhou Creek, 107, 119, 141
synaesthesia, 164, 202, 235
Synnott, Anthony, 17

Taiping Rebellion, 117
Talow Dispensary, 167
The Smell Culture Reader (Drobnick), 15
Thich Nhat Hanh, 246
Thomson, Andrew, 1–4, 245, 254
Thomson, Margaret, 1
Three Stars (*Sanxing*), 166

tianxiang (heavenly fragrance), 53
Tianxiang zhuan (On Heavenly Perfumes)
   (Ding Wei), 23, 46n65
transcorporeality, 11, 58, 144
travel writing, 64–6
   body odour stereotypes in, 70–2
   cult of the Chinese exotic in, 86–7
   depictions of stench in, 67–70
   disgust in, 92–3
   ethnography in, 87–9
   food smells and, 74–9
   hyperbole in, 84–5
   modes of representation in, 83–9
   neophobia in, 78
   opium in, 79–83
   poetic mode in, 86–7
   pseudoscientific racism, 90–2
   racialization of smell in, 72–4
   rationalization tactics in, 89–93
   rhetoric of difference in, 89–90
   satire in, 85–6
Treves, Frederick, 76
Tristes Tropiques (Lévi-Strauss), 253–4
Tsing, Anna, 1, 4
Two Girls (*Shuangmei*), 162–4, 167–8, 172

uncanny, the, 81
undecidables, 3, 12, 70, 246
urban organization, Confucian hierarchy
   of, 128
visual turn, the, 17
Voelkel & Schroeder Ltd., 148

Wang Shixiong, 104
Wang, David Der-wei, 208
Warm Factor School, 104
weisheng (hygiene), 95, 127, 171
Williams, Raymond, 221–2
Withey, Lynne, 64
Wöhler, Friedrich, 170
Wudi (Peerless), 166
   Florida water, 178
   orange juice, 178
   powder, 178
   talcum powder, 178
   toothpaste, 178
wuxing (Five Elements), 20
   seasonal cycle and, 49

xiang (fragrant), 5, 19, 40, 49, 127, 153, 167,
   183, 211
Xiang Detai, 115–16

Xiang sheng (Book of Perfume) (Zhou Jiazhou), 41
Xiangya (Perfuming Asia), 180
Ximen Qing, 193
xin (fragrant), 23
Xin qingnian (New Youth), 96
xing (rank), 19, 23, 49
Xingshi (History of Sex) (Zhang Jingsheng), 196
xiu (smell, stink), 5, 20, 49, 79
Xixiang ji (The Romance of the Western Chamber) (Wang Shifu), 53, 195
xun (smoky), 49
Xunzi, 21–2

Yang Er, 226
Yangjing Creek (Yangjingbang), 109, 117, 119, 125
Yangshupu (Yangpu), 113–14, 130
Yao Wenyuan, 239

Ye qiangwei (Wild Roses), 208
'Yinhuise de si' (Silver Death) (Yu Dafu), 198
youxiang (ethereal fragrance), 53, 55–7, 176, 178, 190, 210
Yu Dafu, 189–90, 198–201
Yu, Anthony, 51
'Yuanfenghuo' (Sealed Goods), 177
'Yuetanhe zhi shui' (The Water of the Jordan River) (Zhang Ziping), 193

Zhang Deyi, 72
Zhang Jingsheng, 196
Zhang Ziping, 192–5
Zhaojia Creek project, 138–41
Zheng Guanying, 94
Zhou Jiazhou, 41
Zhou Shoujuan, 192
Zhou Yang, 226
Zhuangzi, 21
Ziye (Midnight) (Mao Dun), 144, 208